Holy Smoke

HOLY SMOKE

G. Cabrera Infante

faber and faber

LONDON·BOSTON

First published in 1985
by Faber and Faber Limited
3 Queen Square London WC1N 3AU
This paperback edition first published in 1986

Typeset by Goodfellow & Egan, Cambridge
Printed in Great Britain by
Redwood Burn Limited, Trowbridge, Wiltshire

British Library Cataloguing in Publication Data

Cabrera Infante, G.
Holy Smoke.
I. Title
868'.6407   PQ7389.C233
ISBN 0–571–14594–9

To my father
who at age 84
doesn't smoke yet

LADY BRACKNELL: . . . Do you smoke?
ERNEST: Well, yes, I must admit I smoke.
LADY BRACKNELL: I am glad to hear it. A man should always
have an occupation of some kind.

Oscar Wilde
The Importance of Being Earnest

Lastly (and this is, perhaps, the golden rule), no woman
should marry a man who does not smoke.

Robert Louis Stevenson
Virginibus Puerisque (1881)

In the future all men will be able to smoke Havanas.

Herr Doktor Schutte
(an early Marxist)

Light me another Cuba.

Rudyard Kipling
Departmental Ditties

Here, have a cigar.
Light it up and be somebody!

Pete Kelly's Blues

In *Bride of Frankenstein* the infamous Dr Pretorius, a vicious but vivacious villain, is seen supping in a cavernous crypt deep in the churchyard of the Baron's domain. With a large, crisp and spotlessly white napkin tucked under his stand-up collar, the prim old scientist is using as a table an empty coffin – from which his minions have just evicted the beautiful corpse of the village virgin. 'Pretty little thing!' exclaimed the first gravedigger as if the dead girl were Ophelia. 'I hope her legs are firm,' said Dr Pretorius somewhat doubtfully. The doctor's dilemma came from looking at the girl's languid, livid limbs while thinking of dinner. You see, he had chicken in mind then. Dr Pretorius sighs her off and proceeds to have his gourmet supper by candlelight, the meal thoroughly washed down with a good Moselle, properly chilled.

It is only when he is calmly sipping his coffee (no milk, no sugar) that the aged necrophile notices the Monster intruding in his field of vision. The creature is coming fast towards him: a towering, stolid menace. Undaunted, Dr Pretorius offers the man-made wanderer a man-made wonder: 'Have a cigar.' He has, though, a pertinent confession to make: 'It's my only vice.' But the misshapen humanoid is no virgin either. His salutation to the Doctor was to call him Smoke, though he didn't know him yet. In spite of an atavic fear of fire the Monster had smoked his first cigar just recently. As a matter of fact everybody seems to be offering him cigars lately. Is it because he is a born-again creature? Be that as it may, he got the habit from a hermit earlier in the movie: the hermit played 'Ave Maria' on his violin, the Monster wept.

1

Later he became somebody by appreciating a fine cigar. The man that Frankenstein built puffed at his Havana in delight and in next to no time he was a connoisseur of some import: 'Good! *Good.*' That, even among corpses, is *savoir vivre*.

These two short sequences in a most felicitous film contain the entire history of the five-century-old relationship between the European gentleman and his smoke. It all started in the New World, where smoking was not for gentlemen but for sorcerers – and for the incumbent Indian chief: he who wore the feathers.

Like most things American, it began with Columbus. (He is our omnibus.) We can be precise about the discovery: 'At ten o'clock on the night of October 11th 1492 Christopher Columbus from the deck of the *Santa María* saw a light ahead.' It was America all right, though it was not America yet. As to cigars Columbus must be praised or blamed for it too. He accomplished such dubious achievement by simply landing on American soil that dawn of geography and morning of history of an afternoon. To be precise it all began with the Great Admiral's second best landing: trial came first, then error. (A trifle trying, I must admit.) It was on this occasion that he mistook Cuba for Cipango – or was it Cathay? This sailor who couldn't sail, couldn't tell either. In fact, he couldn't even *swim*! You see, he came only for the money. Or rather for the gold. Money makes the world go round (and can make you go around the world) but it tends to devalue sometimes and to decline from absolute to obsolete. Just like the Confederate dollar. Gold on the other hand is forever. Or so thought the Discoverer after reading Marco Polo's *Il Milione*.

But not many people know how much Columbus owes to two insignificant Spanish sailors named Rodrigo. (In medieval Spain every other man was named Rodrigo and every other woman was called Ximena.) It was Rodrigo de Triana who actually saw America first from the masthead of the *Santa María*. The Spanish flagship had been rechristened by Columbus in honour of the Virgin Mary. Before this the caravel was known as the *Marigalante* or *Bawdy Mary*, after a *mujer mala* or streetwalker who covered the waterfront in Puerto de Palos. Columbus reformed her. 'The lofty gaff on a lateen is unwieldy,' he claimed. 'It could cause dangerous gyps and even gossip.'

2

A discovery, seen from a ship, is very much like a shipwreck. There was thus some bewilderment on board the *Santa María* when Columbus discovered America. It was a very young Rodrigo de Triana who shouted from the top mast, 'Land oh!' Columbus chided him. 'It's Land ho! not Land oh!' 'Oh,' said Rodrigo, 'I mean, ho!' But before the echo of Ho! died, the echo of Oh! died. Then there was the noise, the alarm and the confusion on deck of the *Titanic* when Lt. Lightoller cried out, 'Abandon ship!' and the ship abandoned him. The *Santa María* reverted instantly to her *Marigalante* state and all hell broke loose what with the ship becoming very like a bawd at the waterfront. Pinzón, Columbus's jester pilot, even threw overboard the bowsprit, saying, 'There!' Columbus stared at him and glared. Pinzón didn't have a reason but he had a rhyme: 'The bowsprit got mixed with the rudder sometimes . . . This frequently happens in tropical climes.' The Grand Admiral seemed to cool off and asked calmly, 'Now, what would you do for an anchor?' From this acorn of a pun could come the mighty feud that grew between Columbus and the Pinzones like poison oak. At least it could explain why the other Pinzón brothers, Vicente and Martín Alonso, tried to beat Columbus on their way back to Spain bearing the good tidings, 'America has been discovered!' Pinzón's explanation was that Columbus suffered from some rush, probably gold, though he pronounced it rash.

Columbus wrote to King Ferdinand and Queen Isabella ten years after the event: 'In the carrying out of this enterprise of the Indies, neither reason nor mathematics nor maps were of any use to me: fully accomplished were the words of Isaiah.' Columbus meant Isaiah the prophet. This makes the skit seen above not only probable but also possible. Isaiah talks of an ensign of the peoples that the Gentiles shall seek. So much for those who believed that Columbus sailed by profession and discovered the New World with the help of the newly invented sextant and the eternal stars. Did Columbus discover tobacco by prophesy too? Smoking is never mentioned in the Scriptures. But once in America tobacco was the first discovery.

Rodrigo de Xeres (whose surname means that he came from Jerez, sherry country: he was therefore a born connoisseur) was sent inland by Columbus to prospect for gold.

De Xeres came back not with nuggets (comically known in Spanish as *pepitas*) but with some astonishing piece of news: he had found the land of the chimney-men. The *what*? Men who think they are chimneys: men who smoke. Columbus was disappointed in de Xeres. The man had not only been unable to find any gold, as Polo did, but he came back with this weird narrative. A likely story! What should he tell King Ferdinand? 'Sire, my scout became a boy scout.' Too much sun too soon. Or did he mean not chimney-men but chimeras? Too much Amontillado, that's what it was! But de Xeres explained soberly that these savages he saw *really* smoked like chimneys. Everywhere they went they carried about a brown tube burning on one end. They stuck the other end in their mouths for a while and seemed to drink from the tube. After they did so they smoked from mouth and nostrils. And they seemed to enjoy the experience! They used to light the tube with the help of a bummer carrying a firebrand. Most unusual, Sir. Your Excellency. I mean, Grand Admiral. Columbus said, 'That's what I like about islands. Here they call the bums, pariahs.'

But Columbus being an early Renaissance man and there-fore curious, decided to pay a visit to the land of the walking chimneys that de Xeres called To Bago. He reached instead an Indian village called by the natives Gibara. This is an Arawak name which root reappears in other Caribbean Islands and in South America: *jibaro*, *jibarito*, Jivaro Indians. Columbus proceeded to call it instead Puerto de Mares: Port of Surfs, or River of Seas for some scholars. The Admiral went ashore to see with his own eyes what de Xeres had witnessed with his before. What Columbus saw is best described by the candid friar Bartolomé de las Casas, to whom humanity owes woes galore according to Borges. To name only a few: the American Civil War, the assassination of Lincoln, *Uncle Tom's Cabin*, Nigger Jim on the raft with Huckleberry, Faulkner's novels, Black Power, Afro hairdos, Cuban music, the tango and all that jazz. The pious padre, horrified by the suffering of Indians, had recommended the king to let Africans suffer in their stead. As if by black magic the friar had created black slavery in America.

But that's in the future. Now, with the American past about to become historical present, Father las Casas was retelling the story of how Columbus discovered tobacco and didn't get the habit. Says las Casas in his *History of the Indies*, talking of those sweeping chimney-men: 'All the men were carrying a torch,' not for their women, obviously, but 'to take their inhalations very much like frankincense. Some of the herbs were dry and tucked in a dry leaf and rolled into something very much like those paper muskets made by boys during Easter, lit on one side. From the other end they sucked or drew or absorbed with each breath some sort of smoke, of which it is said that it drowses the flesh and almost makes you drunk in such a way that you never feel tired. These muskets or whatever the Indians call *tabacos*.'

La Casas was writing this account forty years after the act (*European Gentlemen See Men Smoke*, take one) and forty years then were more than a century in today's time, due to chronic inflation. But Alexander Esquemeling almost three centuries later described in his *Bucaniers of America* a similar scene: 'With uncut tobacco leaves the natives (in Cuba) make little bullets that the Spaniards call *gigarros*, and which are smoked without a pipe.' The muskets have become bullets. Improvement in the technology of firearms or better-made cigars? The fact is that Columbus saw this spontaneous Cuban combustion-cum-smoke as just one more attraction at the recently opened funfair that was America – or that wasn't America yet. For that we will be needing a man called Amerigo. But there were so many curiosities in the *Orbe Novo*! You could even make lists of oddities and specialties. Step outside, ladies and gentlemen! Step outside! See the side show!

First of all at the Discovery, that weird morning after 'they heard birds passing', all night long in the dark and wet, they saw mirages that looked like land. Perhaps Columbus remembered then St Lactantius, an early Christian doctor who saw the Phoenix – a bird that burst in flames once in a while – as a pagan forerunner of the Holy Ghost. Lactantius, a theologian, thought it foolish for any Christian to believe in the Antipodes. Men with their heads on the ground and their feet in the air? Grotesque! Incredible! But Columbus was later to say that he saw in America men with their heads on their chests. He also reported to King Ferdinand and Queen Isabella of men who stood on their heads forever – using a large foot as

5

a parasol. There were, besides, dogs that never barked. Nobody else ever heard of those mute mutts but even in the early twentieth century there were zoologists looking for that discreet canine all over the Caribbean. (Later, in the United States, there were many people keen after Bigfoot.) There were also trees whose shade made you sleep – the deadly night shade, a heady heath. Columbus also claimed he saw sirens but couldn't hear them sing. American mermaids, contrary to their Greek counterparts, were sweet and silent and never sang any polliwog to his wreck. And in Avan, or so they told him, people were born with a tail. Some, apparently, were born with a tale to tell.

Compared to the menagerie described above, a dumb man with a fat cigar, even if it was an ur-cigar, is only a vaudeville comedian who forgot his joke. Besides, there still was the pressing matter of gold, which was, as the alchemist thought, of the essence. By now, after three days ashore, Columbus was becoming obsessed with gold. Just like any prospector in a new Yukon, the admiral ate, drank and pissed gold. (Freud would say later that he defecated it.) The Grand Admiral was convinced that he was in the Orient (as in a cruel travesty, he actually was in Oriente Province, Cuba) and that the 'land where gold is born' was not far. Therefore these natives must know for sure. The Admiral of the Ocean Sea fanned away the heavy smoke to ask one of the fuming *brujos* if he knew where the Land of Gold was. Columbus, a hustler of genius (in Hollywood in the 1930s he would have been one of the Great Tycoons, the boss of Columbia Pictures perhaps), had brought with him his own interpreter. He was not going to rely on unreliable traducers from Kubla Khan, as the first Polos did. (Especially that Niccolo Polo whose name rhymed with solo.) One of Columbus's interpreters was called Luis de Torres, a Marrano who knew Hebrew, Arabic and according to Las Casas, even Chaldean! Probably this last language meant that Torres, a convert who accompanied de Xeres on his trek to discover tobacco, was a soothsayer with the gift of tongues. Or perhaps the Great Voyager was planning to do some time travel on the side.

Columbus was instantly mistrustful of the strange artifact with which the witchdoctor made clouds over the meeting. Could he make rain too? It was all a futility rite. Besides, the contraption really looked like a musket! The Admirable Admiral took de Xeres aside to ask concerned: 'Are you sure this thing is safe?' Was he afraid of being blown sky high? De Xeres was about to explain about the safety valve in the *brujos*'s mouth but all he did was to answer his superior almost with disrespect: 'An *exploding* cigar? Ridiculous!' Perhaps. But the Serene Sailor was nobody's fool and when the sorcerer opened his mouth and no smoke came out of it, he knew he was ready to tell about the gold. Columbus brushed his interpreter off to become his own translator. '*Cubanacan*,' said the chaman from behind his smokescreen and Columbus leapt like a lizard being smoked out. 'Ku Bana Kan! That's it! You heard him! Gentlemen,' he turned around to his men (a polite man, Columbus always called gentlemen the rabble of seven Spanish regions he brought along to America), 'gentlemen, we are in the land where the brothers Polo struck rich. In this very place gold was born!' – and gold sounded like God in his Italianate accent. Then he exited excitedly in a gold rush and never waited to find out that the *brujo* was actually speaking in Taino, an Arawak dialect, not Chinese. All the smoking old gentleman meant by *Cubanacan* was the 'centre of Cuba', an island as far from China then as it is from Russia now. This was the land that Firmanus Lactantius called in scorn the Antipodes.

Columbus never found gold on the island he called Juana, except for three or four *pepitas*. He was not to visit the fabled land where the yellow metal is born like a fruit of gold an evil. But his search for gold originated the legend of El Dorado and many men of fortune from Europe came to America on this quest for a city of gold on the banks of a lake of gold with golden tides on golden beaches. Columbus however had discovered (and disregarded) this vegetal brown gold called *tabaco*, *tabac*, *tabaka*: tobacco. Not many years after the Discovery untold riches would be made from rags of tobacco. In the New World as in the Old Continent (as in Asia) fortunes were spent on buying tobacco – just to see it go up in smoke.

There are also two by-products of tobacco, one indigenous and primitive, the other sophisticated but ludicrous – and both originated in America. One was a regional custom that stayed put and it is still practised in certain regions of

America, namely the Deep South. The other took Europe by storm in the eighteenth century and was once a European habit. After many years it died out: dust to dust. They were called by their practitioners, respectively, the plug and rappee – or chewing tobacco and snuff. This is another story, so I'll be brief. Snuff, as a dandified custom, had its heyday when the crowned heads of Europe all wore a wig under the crown. Though made with tobacco, the plug and snuff are not really tobacco. They are snuffed and chewed and their juice swallowed or spat out, but they never complete that fiery transformation from the plant whose dried and cured leaves are made into an object that burns to become ashes, like an everyday phoenix gone ashtray. In tobacco prepared to be chewed and used as snuff the weed, literally, is not for burning. This leaves out entirely the original Columbian astonishment and the mythic metaphor so evident in every man who smokes: he is, with a pipe, a cigarette or a cigar, while it lasts, a portable Prometheus, stealing fire from more permissive gods.

Or are they so permissive? Every smoker has in his packet of cigarettes and in his cigar box his own private Pandora.

Father las Casas gave his account of the first Europeans he saw smoke without suffering the well-known syndrome of human curiosity followed by rejection and violent, almost existential nausea. Fortunately, since Cuba, a most unfortunate island, does not bear the brunt of the blame for corrupting the world with a vice: those wayward Spaniards were seen by the good padre on the neighbouring island called by the misnomer of Haiti. The Indians called her Bohio but the Grand Admiral with his infallible ear heard them say, loud and clear, Haiti. Immediately after Columbus christened the island Hispaniola and forgot all about Haiti. He hated Haiti, you see. Las Casas wrote about those Spanish sailors on shore leave: 'I knew men from Spain on this island of Hispaniola who had got the habit (from the natives) . . . I do not know what pleasure or profit they see in it.' But we do, padre. We do.

That's tobacco being smoked on its native soil. But how did it get to Europe? There are several versions of how tobacco reached those European gentlemen for whom, like Dr Pretorius's *nicotphilia*, was to be their only vice. For some scholars the word tobacco comes from the Arabic *Tubbaq*. To add to the general confusion of *tabocas*, and *tobacos* and *tabacos*, Oviedo, the historian, in the early sixteenth century claimed that the *taboca* (or *tabaco*), the Y-shaped instrument, was not used for smoking but for *cohoba*, that is snuffing. But Oviedo called tobacco by the name of *cohoba*, 'which came to be accepted for a while in Europe as a native word for tobacco'. To lend obscurity to strangeness, Cuban Indians called the *cohoba*, *cohiba*. Confused? Please read on. But first a word from our impostors: *Tu boca* means in Spanish your mouth.

Another historian, the English Thacher, in his biography of Columbus, quoted from his son Diego's will a clause which began 'A Antonio, tobaco mercador' and translated it as 'To Antonio, tobacco merchant'. Another biographer of Columbus, Henri Harrisse, pointed out that *tabaco* and not *tobaco* would have been Spanish for tobacco and instead of *tobaco mercador* it should be, if it was to be Spanish at all, *mercador de tabaco*. The polemic that ensued was decided when in 1893 was published in Rome a *Raccolta di documenti* which revealed that the Columbian phrase began 'A Antonioto Baco, mercador'. Get it? Well, yes and no. *Mercador* is a very old Castilian word. The usual Spanish word for merchant then and now is *mercader* and Antonioto is a weird way of saying Antonio. One must remember that Diego Colón was no Christopher Columbus, an Italian with scanty Spanish. Baco, on the other hand, is Spanish for Bacchus and in those piously Christian centuries it was doubtful that a Catholic was called by a pagan name for the Roman god of drunks. Back to Baco then – or rather to tobacco. Here we see linguists shooting at each other with sharp lingos: *tabaco*, *taboca*, *tabococoa* – until they reach *An Impossible Etymology of Tobacco*: *Tob*-Bonus, *Ach*-FUMUS, *A*-EJUS, or 'Good is the smoke thereof'. (This bit of nonsense was published in *The Gentleman's Magazine*, January 1788.)

One Dr Ernst had a piece of etymological detection published in *The American Anthropologist* in 1889. Says Dr Ernst, when Rodrigo de Jerez and Luis de Torres saw a native smoking tobacco in Gibara, they asked him what was he doing and he answered with a phrase that in modern Arawak would be *dattukupa* or 'I'm smoking'. De Jerez couldn't care less, but de

Torres was a linguist of sorts. Be that as it may, the two discoverers transposed the syllables and heard instead of *dattukupa* something close to *dattupaku* – which sounds almost like 'that's tobacco'. Dr Ernst never mentioned how these two Spaniards straight from the Middle Ages could be speaking modern English. So much for the 'that's tobacco' theory.

One of the first botanical descriptions of the tobacco plant is found in *Gerard's Herball*, published in 1636.

> Tobacco, or henbane of Peru, hath very great stalks of the bigness of a child's arm, growing in fertile and well-dunged ground seven or eight feet high, dividing itself in sundry branches of great length, whereon are placed in most comely order very fair, long leaves, broad, smooth, and sharp-pointed; soft and of a light green colour; so fastened about the stalk that they seem to embrace and compass it about. The flowers grow at the top of the stalks, in shape like a bell-flower, somewhat long and cornered; hollow within, of a light carnation colour, tending the whiteness towards the brim. The seed is contained in long, sharp-pointed cods, or seed vessels, like unto the seed of yellow henbane, but somewhat smaller and browner of colour. The root is great, thick, and of a woody substance, with some thready strings annexed thereunto.

The very small seeds of the tobacco plant have a tremendous vitality. 'It's chief of many enemies,' says a herbal, 'is the hornworm, the caterpillar of the hawkmoth.' So Lewis Carroll was right all along: his smoking caterpillar is a worm addicted to the weed.

Now we know that tobacco was first found by European travellers in the New World, on the Caribbean, on an island called by the natives Cuba. But what about its name, so un-Arabic? Gonzalo Fernandez de Oviedo in his *General and Natural History of the Indies*, published in 1526, says with some moral indignation that won't be considered terribly out of fashion today:

> Among other evil practices, the Indians have one that is especially harmful: the inhaling of a certain kind of smoke

which they call tobacco, in order to produce a state of stupor. The *caciques* (Indian chiefs) employed a tube shaped like a Y, inserting the forked extremities in their nostrils and the tube itself (filled) with the lighted weed; in this way they would inhale the smoke until they became unconscious and lay sprawling on the ground like men in a drunken slumber. Those who could not procure the right sort of pipe took their smoke through a hollow reed; and this is what the Indians call *tabaco*, not the weed nor its effect, as some have supposed.

Oviedo contradicts himself on what exactly tobacco was, reed or weed, but finishes by saying something worthy of attention: 'They (the Indians) prize this herb very highly and plant it in their orchards or on their farms for the above-mentioned purpose.' Oviedo is the first European to give a record of tobacco being planted at all. Furthermore, he had seen Indians smoking not in Cuba but on Hispaniola. Others had seen them in Trinidad and on its smaller twin island we call Tobago today. Moreover Oviedo had noticed what Columbus failed to see: the value and price of tobacco. A true conquistador, Cortés, met pipe-smoking Mayas and snuff-taking Aztecs. Portuguese travellers and explorers found Indians smoking as far as Brazil and the Amazonian regions, though it is here that the tobacco trail becomes cold to finally disappear. In Columbia and Peru the Indians got their kicks from coca, in Uruguay and Argentine they drank maté the way the Chinese drink tea. Further down south there were the Patagon Indians in Tierra del Fuego: they had plenty of fire but not much smoke. But Jacques Cartier, the French navigator, saw Indians smoking in Canada around 1535. The pipes smoked by the Sioux, the Cheyennes and other tribes all over the present United States in the eighteenth and nineteenth centuries as a sign of peace are as well known now as the smoke signals from warring Apaches. We owed this knowledge to the movies, no doubt. But how did the habit of smoking for pleasure spread from America to Europe? By boat, of course.

British historian Hugh Thomas in his *Unfinished History of the World* says in connection with syphilis: 'That disease . . . was unknown in Europe before 1492, when it was brought back from Cuba by Columbus, along with tobacco.' Lord Thomas, a non-smoker, has accepted the view, reputed as false by many American historians, that syphilis, a venereal disease, was caught by the Spaniards from Cuban Indians. Thus two modern plagues, chancroid and lung cancer, are linked to the discovery of America. It is of course a vision of Paradise Found as hell. Thomas writes that those Indians imported by Columbus into Spain were 'the first syphilitics of Europe'. Presumably they were the first European smokers too. The pox and the box (of snuff) were the bane of the English dandy in the eighteenth and nineteenth centuries. Wolf's bane in fact and the after-effect of pleasure. But tobacco made its way to Europe and into gentlemen's mouths and pockets by many routes.

Furthermore, without tobacco we would know what love is for sure and perhaps even the meaning of the blues. But we wouldn't be able to tell herpes 1 from herpes 2. Herpes 1 is a virus. Herpes 2 is a virus too. But we wouldn't know what a virus is (considered as an agent for illness in human beings) if we hadn't first paid close attention to a spectacular growth on the tobacco leaf called mosaic. This amusing small malignancy was first spotted in the eighteenth century by tobacco planters in Virginia, but it was recognized as a virus only in 1892. (Virus, by the way, doesn't come from Virginia: it means a slimy, poisonous and 'leperous distilment'.) Until then we knew that the human body could be attacked by foreign organisms tinier than Alice or lice. We named them microbes and bacteria, malcontents all, but we couldn't see them, much less take body count of them. (These could be called biology form, as opposed to content.) I was ready to tell you all about mosaic, the beautiful and damning whose name is dedicated not to Moses but to the Muse. I prefer though to expand on the L Virus. Hermes and Aphrodite, so goes the myth, made love to beget the misbegotten, a handsome monster: the hermaphrodite. (I managed to see one already petrified on the staircase of the *Musée des Beaux Arts* in Brussels.) Now the mismatch is between monstrous Herpes and Aphrodite again. The continuing story of Love and her tiniest enemy will follow shortly. Before, a message from our sponsor, Venus Flytrap Jeans.

Talking of Xeres, which is the thing done before dinner,

Rodrigo caught the habit and was caught at it sooner than you can spell syphilis. Back in his native Ayamonte in Spain his wife surprised him smoking in his room: a sneaking vice. She, still in the vice of the Middle Ages, thought that Rodrigo had made a compact with the Devil and left the house in alarm and excursions to denounce her husband in the nearest Saintly Office of the Inquisition – a new and very virulent agency of God and goodness to fight Evil. Combustible de Xeres burnt at the stake and thus was made into a human cigar.

Count Corti, however, in his book *A History of Smoking* tells a different story about de Xeres's end among his fellow men. Rodrigo returned to Spain and gave a public demonstration of smoking free of charge and at high noon. It happened in Ayamonte a long time ago but Rodrigo's neighbours have not forgotten it. After seeing good de Xeres smoking through all his five orifices and not burning, they were convinced that the Devil had taken possession of his body. The parish priest denounced Rodrigo to the Inquisition and he was committed to prison in Seville for several years. When he came back to town he found that all his countrymen were smoking and not going to gaol for it! This of course is Rip Van Winkle without a wrinkle. On the other hand it could be a metaphor for men and fashions.

As to the other scout who discovered tobacco, Luis de Torres, the *Jewish Encyclopaedia* affirms that this translator and interpreter was not only the first tour guide in America (he took Columbus to see the smoking Indians) but the man who introduced tobacco into Europe, made the Europeans smoke the pipe, cigars, cigarillos, take snuff but not chew tobacco. He also taught them to roll their own, look at pretty girls swirling snowy sticks as if they were batons of a heavenly orchestra on clouds of smoke, gape at a bronco who reigns over and reins in the Marlboro country and accept that a camel as a Turkish animal is not as ludicrous as the turkey. Did only *one* Jew achieve all that? Not only that, he sculpted (or helped to sculpt) the first cigar-store Indian. I don't believe it! At least if de Xeres were also a Jew they could be Balaban and Katz. But a single Jew? I can't believe it! I cannot believe it! That's a stand-up comedian's material – or at least the stuff Gallagher and Sheal were made of. *Shean*. Yes, Sheen. That's what I said, Galahad and Shield.

13

Later, in France, where a more tolerant people lived in spite of being ruled by a cruel queen, Catherine de Medici, as ruthless a fanatic as an *auto da fé*, a Spanish Inquisition unto herself, tobacco however prospered. Catherine de Medici had a good man for an ambassador in Portugal, Jean Nicot, a linguist and the compiler of the best French dictionary of the age. Ambassador Nicot sent the Queen some seeds (*tabac de l'Amérique*) to be planted, cultivated and used as a medicine good for gargles, a potent powder and as an emetic. He recommended tobacco as particularly good for inhalations and as a dentifrice. Nicot called tobacco the Holy Plant. But in France it was called the Queen's Herb. In turn tobacco paid him off: Jean Nicot is known today not as a philologist of genius but as the man who gave its scientific name to the tobacco plant, *Nicotiana tabacum*, and to nicotine, the alkaloid that gives tobacco its value as a drug. It is also what smears your fingers and teeth when you smoke. Tobacco is in fact the only known dentifrice that bleaches the stains it produces!

As a last homage to Nicot in 1961 the *Confrèrie de Jean Nicot* was founded in France, a brotherhood called an *académie de fumeurs et d'amis du tabac*. This smokers' academy is composed of eight hundred friends of tobacco and it is divided in sixteen regional chapters. The irony of it all is that there is no proof that Nicot ever smoked, sniffed or chewed tobacco.

Every English schoolboy knows the story of Sir Walter Raleigh being found by yet another curious person in his household (in this case a manservant) smoking through mouth, nose and ears – or so it seemed. Believing that his master was on fire, the valet 'drenched him with beer'. This is a story fit for English scholars but it proves how different life was on this sceptic isle from that in Spain, even though both early smokers lived in the same age, so turbulent and dangerous – like any other age, for that matter. Raleigh, of course, ended like de Xeres on the scaffold but only years after the fact and for other reasons than just smoking in bed. He associated through poetry (and probably pederasty) with Christopher Marlowe, poet and playwright extraordinary. It is said that Sir Walter learned to smoke in Virginia, imported the habit to England and helped to spread the vice. Not even these 'facts' are true, for it has never been proven that

Raleigh was in the zone of America later to be known as Virginia. Apparently he smuggled his tobacco from Florida or even from South America. It doesn't really matter. What matters is that Raleigh smoked and wrote this poem:

> But a true smoke is a durable fire
> In the mouth ever burning

Robert Burton in his *Anatomy of Melancholy* criticized Raleigh for a double fault. According to him to run to Compostella was 'as prosperous a voyage as that of Guiana – for which Raleigh was ultimately executed. About Raleigh's import he claimed that 'there is much more need of hellebore than of tobacco'. The same Burton later called tobacco 'divine, rare, superexcellent tobacco, which goes far beyond all the panaceas, potable gold, and philosophers' stones, a sovereign remedy to all diseases'. After such praise, what a falling-off was there! Here is Burton again on tobacco 'as it is commonly abused by most men, which take it as tinkers do ale, 'tis a plague, a mischief, a violent purger of goods, lands, health; hellish, devilish, and damned tobacco . . .' He finally calls the weed 'the ruin and overthrow of body and soul'.

Raleigh gave the vice to Marlowe – Kit to him. Marlowe, now the first person to smoke in the theatre (during one of his own plays, probably *Dr Faustus*), concocted tobacco's best slogan: 'All they that love not tobacco and boys are fools.' Marlowe wrote *boies* instead of boys but every Elizabethan got the message and at least one man, his sponsor, was happie.

We know that Marlowe, who was described by a contemporary as 'intemperate and of a cruel heart', ended young in a bad way: stabbed in the chest, not cancerous of the lung. Spying not smoking was the indirect cause of his sudden demise. But I don't see any optician saying when he sells you a pair of spy-glasses that spying can be hazardous to your health. It's true, though, that the Surgeon General was called then by the more apt name of Witchfinder General. He took care indeed of the first poet of tobacco, who wrote, probably inspired by a smoking beauty:

> Oh thou art fairer than the evening's air,
> Clad in the beauty of a thousand stars.

15

Marlowe was not the only poet who sang to boys and tobacco. But today, as in Marlowe's times, you would be better off if you stick to boys. It's not by all means healthier, but at least you won't smoke when you go. It was a poet who loved both boys and girls, a romantic, who lived almost three hundred years after Marlowe died, who said precisely how the love for tobacco had to be qualified. 'Sublime tobacco,' began Byron by exalting the weed as divine in hookas, glorious in a pipe, to finish with the flourish:

> Yet they true lovers more admire by far
> Thy naked beauties – Give me a cigar!

Please notice the change from liking tobacco to adoring cigars. The metamorphosis occurred between the time legendary Raleigh brought the leaf to England from an invented or real Virginia. Past the rappee era (when snuff is enough), to the times when Byron was all: aristocrat, poet, lover, dandy and myth. During that lapse Europe learnt to smoke cigars taught by the Spanish from overseas who were no longer Spaniards and everybody was about to learn a new type of smoke, as different from the pipe as the cigar. This was to be called the cigarette.

Now for etymologies. Cigarette is French, and later English, for Spanish *cigarrillo*, while a cigarillo in English is a small cigar, almost a brown cigarette. Cigar comes from Spanish *cigarro*. According to the Dictionary of the Royal Spanish Academy *cigarro* comes from the Mayan *siqar*, without naming the name of the translation. As you can see even the spelling is suspect and there is some phonetical distance between *siqar* and *cigarro*. Most probably *cigarro* comes from *cigarra*, cicada in Spanish. Male cicadas are called *cigarros* in southern Spain. These insects are as big as cigars, with thick long wings and dark brown colouring. It is not difficult for the Andalusian animism to see a cicada in a primitive cigar. This, is, by the way, the etymology accepted by the *Oxford Dictionary of English Etymology*, which of course has a much better track record with words than any other etymological dictionary available.

Gonzalo Fernandez de Oviedo in his *General and Natural History of the Indies, Islands and Terra Ferma of the Ocean Sea* (full name) makes the first reference to the cigarette. It was seen by Captain Juan de Grijalva in Yucatan, Mexico, in 1518. Here Grijalva was received in a friendly fashion by a cacique (an Indian chief: this Arawak word, like tobacco, was first found by the Spaniards in Cuba) who offered him a small tube alight on one end. These tubes slowly consumed themselves without giving forth a flame. Their smoke was 'as fragrant as an incense stick from Valencia'. The chief indicated to Grijalva that he should inhale the smoke – which never could happen with a cigar. Therefore Grijalva was smoking the first cigarette offered to a European by an American. Or ur-American.

We owe to the cigarette as much smoke as urban mythology. We owe it the *femme fatale* with her long holder, black or white (which she played like a not-so upright piano), the Parisian gigolo, B movies where heroes and villains play at being smokers together, Bogart's philosophy (in *The Big Shot*, the acme of the gangster-on-the-run film, he virtually drew his last breath from a Camel and nobody, on or off the screen, thought then that a cigarette killed him and not the other way around: cigarettes were not yet the *bête noire* in white), the art of love by Bette Davis and her favourite prop for conquest epitomized in *Now Voyager*: Paul Henreid with an accent, Bette with a cigarette.

It is a moot point on the map of the New World whether cigarettes originated in Mexico or in Cuba. (It probably was in Spain.) But cigars were certainly smoked in Cuba before Columbus saw a cigar and decided that pure gold was better than a gold blend. There is no doubt that the plant was an American aboriginal. More so than the aborigines themselves, also called Redskins. Cigars were known once as brownskins and Havana is the name of the colour of a true Cuban leaf. What Jerome K. Brooks called 'The Mighty Leaf' in his book of that title is actually a delicate plant named in scientific Latin *Nicotiana tabacum* if cultivated. In fact *Nicotiana tabacum* has never been discovered in a wild state. Botanists once suspected *Nicotiana rustica* of being a henbane. It was as if the weed were under suspicion of being a murderous plant. Growing wild its name is *Nicotiana rustica*, which is the variety that both Raleigh and Nicot popularized with their respective, respected queens. Another variety of the plant is

17

known by the pretty name of *Nicotiana alata grandiflora*, or the weed with big winged flowers – jasmin tobacco. The latter, naturally, is an ornamental plant. All *Nicotianae* belong to the *Solanaceae* and tobacco is not only akin to peppers and petunias (whose names come from *Petun*, Tupi for tobacco) but also to plants as seemingly unrelated as the deadly nightshade and the poisonous datura, belladonna plus the eggplant, the potato and the tomato. And henbane, which Shakespeare made Claudius use to poison King Hamlet by pouring it into his ear while he slept: hebona the Bard called it.* Some of these plants can be crossbred unnaturally. You can have today for dinner a *pomato*, the cross of a tomato and a potato, a hybrid, a new breed. Due to the fact that they all are, like tobacco, *Solanaceae*, you'll soon be able to enjoy the *pobacco*. You could have a *pobacco* in its jacket and eat it – or have it with your smoking jacket on after coffee, in a pipe or hand-rolled. The choice must be a thrill to old Dr Pretorius, no doubt: 'It's my *new* vice, you know.'

It has always baffled historians and botanists (and some American explorers) to find no evidence at all of *Nicotiana rustica*, wild tobacco, in Cuba, while Cuban Indians smoked *Nicotiana tabacum* as a holy herb and as a pleasure plant. Where did this cultivated plant come from to be used by such uncultivated natives? The Indians on the biggest island in the Caribbean were very backward and some lived on wild fruits alone, while others fished with their bare hands! Even the Tainos, an Arawak tribe, were a primitive people who suffered syphilis gladly – or endemically, as the doctors say. The invading Caribbees had a warring motto, *'Ana Karina roto'*, which might sound like a sequel to a Russian novel but which meant 'Only we are people'. Accordingly the Caribbees treated the other Indians like cattle – and after killing them consumed their flesh as meat. Columbus, in his blind obsession for gold and with a bad ear to boot, misheard their Carib

As late as the early nineteenth century, when nicotine was already isolated, chemists in Florence sustained that a drop of the fifth essence or quintessence of tobacco introduced in any old wound could mean sudden death to the recipient. So Shakespeare was right after all: the cursed hebona killed Gustave Fougnies, whoever he was, poisoned by his brother-in-law, Count Bocarné.

name as cannibal and consequently deduced they were all the Khan's men. Shakespeare, who had an ear for English but not for Spanish (it happened after the Armada), made all cannibals into one Caliban, and the monicker prospered ever since to the cannibalized cars of today's Cuba: the Caribs no longer have a motor. But Columbus was still sailing from isle to isle on the Caribbean, doggedly after gold: he carried the day for his queen but he never could carry the Khan.

The Grand Admiral could have found tobacco being planted and harvested and even used for currency had he sailed as far as Brazil. Here, after being introduced to silent sirens in Cuba, he would have met the Amazons with two tits. But he didn't go that far, alas. There were other smoking Tainos in the smaller West Indies, though. They were more sophisticated than those found in Cuba, so they used a holder and even a pipe to smoke through their nose. Columbus was not amused with such antics by the Antipodeans. In fact he became the first European notable to hate tobacco, almost as much as Queen Victoria did later. He who discovered it, abhorred it. He was the first critic of Caribbean customs. Decidedly Christopher Columbus was not a vegetarian, for he also disliked corn.

The conundrum of corn (it can be called the maze of maize) is so similar to that of tobacco that it is small wonder that Columbus repulsed it too: as opposed to Van Gogh, he didn't have an ear for corn. Such similarity of origins has confused even the *Encyclopaedia Britannica*, so lucid and with so pellucid a style. *Britannica* has this to say about maize: 'The modern history of corn begins on 5 November, 1492, when two Spaniards, whom Christopher Columbus had delegated to explore the interior of *Cuba*, returned with "a sort of grain they called *maize* which was well tasted, bak'd, dry'd and made into flour".' That was Las Casas speaking Spanish, but from his quote to the tale of two sailors turned scouts, or rather prospectors, who brought weird tidings and a date – 4 November for corn, 5 November for tobacco – it all belongs to the history of tobacco and its fantasy fumes, not to the chronicle of staple food. If Britannia ruled the waves, *Britannica* read the facts as wrongly as Columbus disregarded them. The only vegetable that took the Admiral's fancy was a tree whose wood, when burnt, smelled like a familiar resin, mastic. Columbus pronounced the bark of the wrong tree to be the real thing and therefore 'a lucrative source of income for Our Sovereigns'. But in fact he didn't do anything about exploiting the mystic mastic, as for him every newly-found land had golden shores.

Before being banished back to Spain Columbus brought with him from the Canaries the banal banana. But the cultural contribution he made to folklore and fruit cocktails is enormous. Without the *Musa paradisiaca* (meaning literally the muse of Paradise) the banana republics in Central America would not have been possible, and the powerful United Fruit Company that elected their presidents for them, for life or for good, whichever came first, would never have existed – and of course there wouldn't be any Chiquita Banana today. Nor the banana split. Nor the Mafia *capo* Joe Bananas. And the glorious hat that Carmen Miranda imported and sported would have been just another corny cornucopia. Besides nobody could go bananas instead of being nuts, which is analytically a significant choice. What else? Ah yes! We wouldn't have that silly song, Wilder's medley, 'Yes, we have no bananas': the tiny tune that did to bananas what Lewis Carroll did with his *Alice* to the English tea party. From luncheon to lunacy.

Coming back to corn, the true mystery of maize is that Cuban Indians were able to cultivate it at all. As with tobacco they weren't supposed to know how. But they even knew how to unite the two to make one. They could roll up tobacco filler in dry corn leaves and enjoy a joint together: that's how the cigarette was born. According to Spanish historian Martín Fernández de Navarrete the encounter of Columbus with corn took place on the Venezuelan coast. Here the admiral found this other form of vegetal gold, more gold-like than gold itself, and he didn't do anything about it. Not even eat it. Had Columbus made maize into crispy layers he would have become rich for life: *Columbus's Corn Flakes*!

In any case the European gentlemen who discovered tobacco transformed the clumsy smoking artifact – 'paper muskets', my God! – into the work of art that's a cigar. The transformation took place in Cuba but it was done mostly by the Spanish. They took tobacco, *una sancta cosa*, a holy thing for the Indians, to Europe on their return trips and made it popular. But it was in Europe that people saw the cigar as an instrument

20

of pleasure for the gentleman's leisure, as it had been with pipe tobacco and snuff. In America (especially in Cuba but also in the United States) smoking was for everybody, thanks to the good old five-cent cigar, no doubt. But also due to the fact that Cuba was very close to the United States then and Havanas were cheaper there than anywhere else except, of course, Havana. Some twenty years ago the idea (come from England, no doubt) that cigars, like Loos's blondes, were for gentlemen only, was dispelled by the scraggly mien of Fidel Castro and Che Guevara's handsome head, both clad in US Army surplus fatigues, both enveloped in smoking beards and both sporting foul, fat cigars. These, gentlemen, were no gentlemen. It meant that even in the sierras in Cuba you could cultivate tobacco and smoke it. Moreover, you could even catch the smoking habit in those sylvan mountains. Before landing in Cuba as a guerrilla, Che Guevara was an asthmatic Argentine doctor who wouldn't touch a cigar with a ten-foot holder. As a matter of fact in his manual for a guerrilla fighter Guevara recommended the pipe as the ideal smoking artifact once upon a war: it was easy to carry, easy to smoke and easy to conceal and hard to detect by the enemy. Che Guevara began smoking cigars when he found out that in Cuba the pipe was considered so gringo that it was called a *cachimba*, the feminine form of *cachimbo* – a six-shooter in the Old West.

What de Xeres and the unknown Taino were to the discovery of tobacco, Demetrio Pela from the Canaries and Erio-Xil Panduca, a Cuban Indian, were to its cultivation. From a letter Pela wrote to his relatives in Tenerife (as with most historical documents, this was preserved for posterity more by chance than by intent) we know now how the cultivation of tobacco truly began in Cuba. This happened in the mid-seventeenth century as the Pela letter was dated 1641. Tobacco was becoming very productive when Panduca revealed his secret, the words of the tribe, to Pela, another islander. Thus the latter, says the letter, made the former his partner for life. They both shared the hard work and poor profits of labouring on the first *vega* of which we have any knowledge today. Barely fifty years later Havana was surrounded by similar *vegas*, all located on the margin of the main rivers in the province. The *vega*, by the way, is to tobacco what the vineyard is to wine. A *vega* in Spanish is any river bottom land, but in the particular Cuban idiom of tobacco it is a tobacco field of any length, what in the South is called a plantation. If planted with preferred tobacco the *vega* is called a *tabacal*. A group of *vegas* is a *veguerío* and the farmer-owner of a *vega* is a *veguero*. A kind of peasant cigar rolled privately by the planter himself is called a *veguero* too. For some choice smoker a *veguero* is always synonymous with a good smoke. Pela and Panduca were *vegueros* but they were far from producing *vegueros*. Havana was not yet a cigar.

But soon tobacco became the second most productive crop of the island, trailing not very far behind sugar. The tobacco road led to riches – and to hard work. There is an old saying in Cuba which says that you can plant anything on the island and sit and wait for it to grow. But tobacco, the saying goes, you just don't plant, tobacco you must marry. Sometimes the riches from tobacco even came even – and sometimes even first. *Nicotiana* became such a profitable crop that the *hacendados* (sugar-cane land barons) of the nineteenth and twentieth centuries in turn came second to tobacco planters in the seventeenth century. The *vegueros* were not rich in land but their land was rich with plenty. They were powerful enough to oppose the Spanish government on their *estanco* (official hoarding) of tobacco crops in the nineteenth century. The *vegueros* were rich, white and proud. They were also ostentatious. The first Cuban to drive his own coach across the recently cobbled streets of Havana was the Governor of the island, Don Lorenzo de Cabrera (no kin to the author), who bought his gilded carriage with the money he earned in some illegal, but not secret, operation involving a huge cargo of cured tobacco. The first title of nobility bestowed on a Cuban went to Don Laureano de Torres, as a reward for making easy a profitable sale of Cuban tobacco leaf on behalf of the Crown. Asked about this royal honour that seemed more like a windfall, Don Laureano could have said: 'The weed was the thing to catch the attentions of the King.'

Tobacco belongs to mankind, cigars only to the West. It is indeed difficult to imagine a maharajah with a Havana stuck somewhere between his beard and his turban or a Chinese warlord smoking a Manila while he sends invitations to a beheading, or a samurai having to do with any phallic symbol other than his short sword and his perfumed fan. But tobacco has been with us since the Renaissance. In fact the age started, as if by chance, with its discovery. In some ways the Middle Ages in England went up in smoke when Raleigh first set his pipe alight and not with the Great Fire that cleansed London as with a flaming sword of the medieval morass one hundred years later. Already under Queen Elizabeth 'in the churchyard outside, men about town patronized the shops which sold the fashionable new weed, tobacco', as Gamini Salgado says in the aptly called *The Elizabethan Underworld.* Here the accent of the historian is not only on the men about town, those who made history, or on the 'new weed', on which history was about to be made – but on what was fashionable: history in the making. For the Elizabethan age tobacco being sold by leaves in churchyards was as important as words being sold by the score in theatres: the world is a stage and the speech was garlanded with smoke every summer – especially in summer. Then the theatres were in bloom and men-about-town gathered to chat and smoke and once in a while overhear some poor player strutting and fretting for three or four hours on the stage: a madman who believed he was Macbeth, the one who left his head in the Highlands and then was heard no more. Dead tyrants tell no tales. Actors and smokers were then the skimmed-milk of humankind. But with summer came an unwanted visitor, the plague. Business as usual, it was death that did the skimming. Men and tobacco end equally in ashes.

Simon Forman, astrologer, physician and quack, a contemporary of Shakespeare and Queen Elizabeth, was such a keen smoker that he dreamt of tobacco. Says he in his *Case Books*: 'I dreamt of Stephen that he was come from the sea and brought more tobacco . . . They had sailed in the dark long and could get nothing.' Forman's commentator, A. L. Rowse, contemporary of Elizabeth II, affirms that 'when they came home Captain Watts sent to the ship for tobacco'. As usual they made light of the matter.

My First Cigar

I heard my father's smothered laugh,
    It seemed so strange and far;

23

I knew he knew, I knew he knew
I'd smoked my first cigar.

Burlington Hawkeye
Cope's Tobacco Plant

By one of those weird coincidences that made Michel de Nostredame a household name, Nostradamus, '*cum falsa damus*', in smoke signs that will never abolish chance, I was born in Gibara, that bay named by Columbus Port of Surfs: exactly the spot of soot where Rodrigo de Xeres, a man made of smoke, discovered smoking for Europe and the world – that is everybody except of course Columbus himself. But I didn't grow in tobacco country. Thanks to one of those freaks of geography that can eventually change history, Gibara was banana country, sugar cane country, a tourist resort in summer – everything but good land to grow tobacco. Meanwhile, a thousand miles to the west, in Pinar del Rio, you had Vuelta Abajo and all that name means. Nevertheless I grew up amid the tug-of-war of smoking and its detractors in my own family: father who disapproved, mother in vogue. Plus a great-grandfather who chain-smoked cigars, a great-grandmother who chewed tobacco leaves and their son and daughter who hated the weed intensely.

My great-grandfather was born in Almeria, Spain, and came to Cuba in the 1870s to fight against the *mambí* guerrillas during the first Cuban War of Independence. He stayed in Cuba with the Spanish army long enough to fight in the Little War and became an artillery lieutenant later. But he didn't wait in the army for the Guerra Grande, the Big War that led to the Spanish-American War, the American occupation of the island and Cuba's final independence from Spain. Between the two wars my great-grandfather met and married my great-grandmother, born in the Bayamo region in Oriente Province. They settled in Gibara, a walled city on the northern coast of the province.

My great-grandfather feared for his life when Spain lost the last war, but was truly moved when the first *mambí* column entered the city. The column was led by a guerrilla chief born in Gibara, General Sartorio, a man who had a Faulknerian name and who looked like Faulkner a lot: short,

24

lean, mustachioed and slightly crazy. My great-grandfather went to the door wearing his old Spanish uniform to watch the parade. He saluted his superior and General Sartorio raised his right hand in passing with solemn respect. This gesture made a Cuban for life of my great-grandfather. So much so that he adopted Cuban politics and ways of life. Adoption of the first involved proselitizing for General Menocal, his rival during the wars who later became president of the Republic; and of the second, wearing a perennial palm-leaf hat and smoking cigars. How he smoked cigars! Since getting up at five o'clock in the morning, until he went to bed at five o'clock in the afternoon, every day of the week. He used to smoke a third of each cigar leaving the butts strewn all over the house. 'For later.' Then he would smoke the cold dead cigars but he always seemed to have a fresh cigar in his mouth. His wife, my great-grandmother, chewed tobacco leaves and went about the house carrying a glass cuspidor as if it were an opaline jewel. My great-grandfather became stone deaf in the wars but was always blaspheming all over the house in a booming voice. My great-grandmother was a tiny, pious woman, who spent most of the night (she had the very queer habit for a town-dweller of going to bed at midnight and getting up at noon) whispering prayers in her very small but very private shrine to all saints and Mary and Jesus too. Both my great-grandfather and my great-grandmother got along famously during the short time of the day they saw each other and along the tremendous span of life each lived: my great-grandfather died at age 103, my great-grandmother lived to be 91. Only three years lived she without her blaspheming, smoking husband – but not without tobacco.

My grandmother's brother, my greatuncle Pepe Castro, grew up hating God, smoking in general and particularly cigars. He hated tobacco so much so that, when he heard or read somewhere that Hitler spurned smoking and smokers alike, he became a Nazi! He already was a vegetarian and a nudist and a mad genius: a small-time inventor who was always inventing things (like the propeller in the form of a screw for a two-keel boat) but created nothing because between his thinking and his actions always was a mental chasm. On the creative side of his mind was the building all by himself of a phonograph (he called it a gramophone) to hear his records, mostly opera, mostly by Caruso. But he ended, after admitting that Hitler could not be alive any more, by sleeping on the floor and eating only batata roots, raw. He died, though, at 87. My father was born on the Canary Islands because his father was a Canary (he wanted his last son to be born where he was) and a certifiable madman who later, shortly after coming back to Cuba, shot his wife dead and then killed himself, in some sort of Othello replay that went tragically wrong. My father disliked smoking and still does at 84. He is a teetotaller and a Communist and a widower now married to a woman thirty years younger. My mother, because she was a local fashionable beauty during the 1930s, used to smoke a Camel now and then for the same reasons that made her, together with my father, after being educated in the local convent, one of the founders of the Communist Party in Cuba: Moscow *à la mode*.

My most influential persons when I was a child, my father and my maternal greatuncle, were fanatically against smoking. So was my father's greatuncle, a local intellectual so stern that he adopted the pen-name Socrates. He did in fact out-Socrates the Greek: he died a confirmed bachelor. It was therefore in a challenge to all paternal guidance that I began to smoke when I was only a child. My first cigarette was a combination of a primitive *papelete* and an Indian *cohoba*: the dried leaves of the *chamizo* tree rolled up in a page of a notebook. It smelled and tasted and looked awful, I must say, but it was a successful experiment: it became a smoke. Or rather, all smoke. The smoke column I built in the profuse backyard was an Apache signal in reverse: I got caught and my father gave me forty whacks. My mother only gave me one: she was tolerant because she knew that smoking would become my only vice. I was eight at the time and already intimate with all the little girls in the street where I lived. If Mozart played at four, at eight I only played a little more.

But I had my first true smoke, better and worse than a girl, when I was about fourteen and we were already living in Havana. I had come back to Gibara on a summer holiday – remember that old resort of lore? I was too old then for a *papelete* made of *chamizo* under its shade and too young for a cigar, even if I already knew the exploits of Huckleberry

26

Finn. I couldn't follow in Huck's footsteps or fall into Finn's wake: you see, I didn't have a corncob. The done thing for my coming of age in Gibara was to smoke a local brand. I don't remember how I got hold of a cigar. Did I buy it? Did I borrow it? Did I steal it? It couldn't surely be one of great-grandfather's *dormidos*, the dormant stubs put down to sleep all over the old house. Be that as it may in July there I was, early in the evening, in the old Calixto Garcia *parque*, the mustachioed military man forever waiting for a message from the Americans to come his way. He had beside him another patriot for me, Donato Marmol, whose name means marble. For many years I thought Donato, his given name, was some white shade of marble, as when you say Carrara marble. Now there they were, Garcia and Marmol with all their marble, gleaming white in the centre of the green square, surrounded by the summer evening, all mauve and mist. I was going to add some smoke to the summer fire with my cheroot. Or so I thought when I lighted up my cigar to become somebody: to smoke a cigar and thus to be able to extricate myself from the mere boys. All I remember next was some sort of invisible, enormous hand that gripped me by the neck, making me puke the cigar as if it were a smoking snake I had eaten raw in a sudden nightmare. Then I was leaving the soft marble bench abruptly and falling to the lawn made of green hard coils to roll and rattle, a wretch being wrenched of tongue, talk-box and gullet: I was vomiting.

There is not, believe me, a worse hangover than that of a cigar: the after-effect simply comes together with the effect. Of course I didn't know then a basic rule of cigar-smoking, one that even Rodrigo de Xeres, right there behind me, beyond the square and the exotic laurel trees, must have learnt very quickly from the Indians that smoky afternoon in 1492 or suffered the seasickness he never had upon crossing the Ocean Seas with Columbus: you must *not* inhale. Under no circumstances, not ever, *never*. Otherwise the consequences might be dreadful, as if smoking the dry leaves of the black nightshade. (By the way, this plant, *Solanum nigrum*, is a near relative of tobacco.) That's what I did. It took me at least ten years to recover from my hangover and its lasting lesson. It is good for a boy to learn how to become a man: you either learn or you pass straight from boyhood into senescence. But there must be other writhes of passage.

Ten years must have lapsed because I was now 24 and in the next to last paragraph I was a mere 14, when I sat to watch television after having dinner, which I seldom did then. I mean watching television, of course. I remember I was smoking a Camel, which I did a lot then without being a chain-smoker. I had also smoked a pipe or several pipes seemingly chained together. But by then I had put aside this peace instrument to smoke cigarettes fiercely. I had taken the *cachimba* (its actual Cuban name) for an adolescent pipe dream and all I wanted then was to be a man. I had better hurry, I thought, if I didn't want to be, as it was customary at the time, a rebel without a cause – or worse still, a doctor without a case. Then the commercial came like snow in a tropical landscape. It was a crude advertisement for H. Upmann, with an old hammy actor playing the role of the oldest man in the world, the oddest man of the world: Santa Claus sitting in a rocking chair smoking a Havana in Havana. Santa came, Santa went but the smoke stayed forever. Now the actor, in the mellowest Cuban accent, portrayed an eternally happy man in black and white.

But Santa Claus, tricks that television played, resembled my great-grandfather, the oldest man I had ever seen until then – smoking a cigar. I was impressed not only by the resemblance but by the content the actor portrayed so cannily coming through white beard and white hair and of course white smoke, which is the smoke every good cigar must have. Poppycock! Too late. I was hooked forever. I welcomed the damned spot of nicotine, the thick smoke, the heavy odour of a cigar – and the poise, the peace and ponderousness it gave. Were not those the visible virtues of manhood? I buried my pipes and never lit a cigarette again. There and then I began to look for what every cigar-smoker looks for, sometimes forever: the perfect *fuma*, my own smoke, my *vitola*. When I found it it was for a fleeting moment, or rather spell, and it was called Por Larrañaga. I didn't know then that our meeting would be a brief encounter in smoke.

What Wilde said of music is also true of smoking: it always makes you remember a time that never was. Though that past

sometimes really existed. But it is not called music now, it is
called nostalgia. I was yesterday evening at La Antigua
Chiquita. Yesterday was sometime in 1957 and it was evening. It was evening at La Antigua Chiquita. It happened
more than a quarter of a century ago but it was just yesterday, for unlike music memory has no time. La Antigua
Chiquita was a noted restaurant in Havana. Its name means,
literally, the old little lady but it actually means that there
was a previous restaurant called La Chiquita and the present
establishment was a new version of the old famed haunt.

So there I was in La Antigua Chiquita at eleven-thirty at
night, but for me it still was my world in the evening. I came
here after watching a show or the opening of a movie and
getting ready to write a review during the wee hours and
into the morning perhaps. That's the way it was with me
then: the most dangerous man in Havana from 11.00 pm to
6.00 am: right between the eyes of the night. Or from the end
of a movie and the time the milkman came. I had even
concocted a brilliant Brillat-Savarinism: Having a heavy meal
at night makes you good in the morning and helps you stay
awake. Eating well was the best resource. So I ordered a filet
mignon, well done, fried green plantains, an avocado salad
and much milk but, as Bob Hope said, in a dirty glass. Now
I was ready to stay awake to write about the motion picture I
had just seen. Or perhaps not to write about it. Sometimes
I used all the tricks in my bag so as not to write my review,
avoiding writing the movie column: writing anything at all.
So I had to look first at the photos in *Pictorial History of the
Talkies*, then in *A Pictorial History of Silent Movies*. Then I
read books, useless books usually called *The Movies*, from
cover to cover, which wasn't difficult for they were mostly
pictures, stills. I even came to read the catalogue from the
Library of Congress with all the copyright entries for movies
made all over the world before 1929. Usually I did write my
review which was mainly about movies but for some weird
sleight of hand sometimes turned, for films, into a fifth
column.

It was at La Antigua Chiquita that I saw that one of my
shoes had fallen into disrepair. It was not easy to find suede
shoes in the tropics then. These boots of mine were bought
in New York some time before but now the shoes showed

alarming signs of desuetude. I was reflecting upon this need for new suede shoes when coffee came in the shape of a demitasse. '*Un puro de marca*,' I told the waiter before he left again, using this facetiae so usual in the habitué. *Puro* you and the waiter take for exotic, for in Havana a cigar is always *un tabaco*. *De marca* means of a brave brand. The whole phrase thus is, seen from behind my glasses, a tortoiselogy. Before I saw myself reflected in this golden pun, the waiter came with my usual marca: Por Larrañaga. This is a true *ci-devant* cigar. Or if you prefer, purely *ancien régime*. It was condemned to death by the Revolution and some prime Robespierre, on whose shoulders Saint Injuste had placed *la première pierre* of dogmatism, had banished the small, square, squat box. The cigar with no band on its Havanas disappeared into that long night: gently, noiselessly, in smoke. One mustn't forget that the contraption to cut the head of a cigar is also called a guillotine.

There I was then, a Cuban not yet thirty, sitting at La Antigua Chiquita, after a beef encounter, smoking a cigar and looking across the wide street, the old *calle* Carlos Tercero, that Charles III Avenue which was already an *avenida* when snuff was not yet popular in Europe in the eighteenth century. Right across the street, dark but friendly, was the Quinta de los Molinos, the Farm with Windmills, where later in the same century they used the windmills to rap tobacco leaves and make *rapé*, rappee, snuff. Now it belonged to the university of Havana and the visible dark bulk was the building of the School of Dental Surgery. I thought that not many people at the time knew even what snuff was. At least not anybody in my place. You see, there were not many people sitting in my chair at La Antigua Chiquita that night. If I was going to talk about snuff I could only rap to myself.

There I was then at La Antigua Chiquita smoking quietly and not thinking of snuff again. In the pursuit of the weed I had missed taking snuff and chewing tobacco. For me the plug was a plug-ugly and smoke was absent in both. I believe with Casanova that most of the pleasure in smoking is, of course, in the smoke. A cigarette is a dangling particule in your lips and the pipe is all clenched teeth and no fury. But a good cigar is like a passion: first it is set alight, then it burns red, then scarlet, scary, scarry – then it glows amber, grows ember and becomes ashes: a passion spent. Kipling was wrong. A cigar *is* a woman and a woman is a smoke. A passion made of that primeval leaf to burn in a slow flame and then smoulder avidly. A cigar is woman, to smoke divine! A good cigar is like a medley. I am thus back to square one: the muzak is all around.

I had just asked the waiter for a Larrañaga. He brought again the well-known box that needed no *cromos* or the painted paradise on earth. It said, in burnt lettering, *25 Aromas de Luxe. 1957 Crop/Hand-Made in Havana Cuba* and on top, on the sliding lid, *Marca Independiente* and the characteristic laurel wreath circling the proud name of the brand. The waiter had slid the lid now as usual and taken out the bunch bound by a yellow ribbon that once was silk and is now satin – or perhaps nylon, alas. Thus I chose my constant companion for an hour. They are thick but not fat cigars, neither long nor short and they all have the same *parejo* colour. This means that their shade of Havana is even all over because it was made from a choice leaf. This cigar is gone, the smoked as the unsmoked. They are visitors from another era: as far away and long ago as a distant planet we once visited. I know I won't smoke them again. Nobody will. But between me and that nobody is the past, which I can remember, which I did remember, which I remember now. Por Larrañaga means By Larrañaga but can also mean For Larrañaga, as in a toast in Spanish: a *brindis* to Larrañaga. Por Larrañaga! I give you Larrañaga!

These are my reminiscences on a cigar, Por Larrañaga. If instead of a Havana had I been speaking of the plug, even the plug-bubbly, then these would be my ruminiscences.

At La Antigua Chiquita a man was never alone when he had a cigar with him. I am asking the waiter again for a Por Larrañaga. I remember this now – time to come back, gang. Say good-bye, Time Traveller, said I, 'making spasmodic efforts to relight his cigar over the lamp'. A lume spent – say I'll be seeing you, Brick Bradford. *Dis au revoir, Marcel. Di adiós, tú. Adiós tú.*

Smoking my proleptic cigar I raise as many questions as I can answer but my cigar has already answered them all.

Were you able to drive on a road to the past (the past being 1955, take a year or two) in a Nash Rambler, and on leaving Havana were the time traveller to go across the province in a westerly direction, once you crossed the boundaries of Havana Province you'd go on to Pinar del Rio. By stepping on it, soon you would be on the tobacco road: go West, young eyes, go West. That hesperian route is called in Cuban-Spanish Vuelta Abajo. For any smoker, domestic or foreign, that's the land where gold grows. Nowhere else in Cuba is tobacco more lustily evident, even lush, than in Pinar del Rio. Most of the province is divided into *vegas*, some of them better known than the province itself, the way Bordeaux, a mere port, is better known than the Gironde Department. (The same goes of course for the names of Sauterne or St Emilion, all near the Garonne, a river of no returns.) San Juan y Martinez, whose funny name (it's like calling a town St John and Smith) is the memory of a distant duo of settlers, a Spaniard named San Juan and a Cuban named Martinez, his partner – Pela and Panduca again but in the eighteenth century. This is a *vega* in vogue. Writes Sydney Clark in *All the Best in Cuba*: 'In the tobacco village of San Juan y Martinez many of the humble-appearing inhabitants are very well-to-do and some are rich even by American standards.' (This was written in 1955.)

The other, even more famous place is Hoyo de Monterrey, which means what it is: a hole in the ground that belonged to some Monte Rey or other. In this hole and for some mysterious reasons (all is mist with cigars: must be the smoke: Pinar del Rio was the last Cuban province where tobacco was planted systematically) grows what is even today, after many a mistake, the tobacco leaf that wraps the best cigars in the world. Hoyo gives Havanas their good name – and all their pull.

Oscar Wilde poked fun at Southern hospitality by reporting to the English, upon coming back to London from America, that after praising the moon of Virginia his host sighed: 'Ah, but you should have seen it before the war, Mr Wilde!' This 'melancholy tendency' is also true of Cubans. Many exiles (and quite a few inmates on the island) are ready to swear that the sun was milder before the Revolution. This could be true of tobacco, the industry immersed today in one of its many crises – in which it grows sporadically: now the leaf thrives, then it founders, then there's a good harvest again. But by following that red-dust road through tobacco land you'd find many *vegas* where the weed blooms under the most exactingly controlled conditions.

Watching the Gauguin-like contrast of the almost pink soil and the lettuce-green tobacco leaves, suddenly you are hit by the unusual – with a surreal touch. Snowfields forever! Snow in the tropics? No, man-made snow whiteness: acres of Cuban land covered with white sheets, like immense beds for tired giants to sleep in the sun. What Christo did to Biscayne Bay in pink, Cuban tobacco planters did to Pinar del Rio in white many decades before, without fanfare and photographers and not for art's sake. At least they didn't call it art then. I do now. Some areas of the Pinar del Rio countryside are those times in the year when the sun is fiercest enveloped by these enormous *tapados*. They are fields covered with sheets made of cheesecloth that gives the landscape a ghostly appearance. It is as if the Flying Dutchman had landed in the middle of a tropical valley, that led far from his native North in his quest for a better cigar than the Schimmelpenninck they kept offering him in Holland every time he asked for a smoke.

Apparently the harsh, vertical light, filtered by the cheese-cloth pitched like a tall tent, makes the tobacco leaf lighter in colour. This leaf of a clearer complexion was used to make a pale cigar called with some imagination *rubio*, blond. Even Anita Loos knew that these blonds were preferred by American gentlemen. But such bleached blond Havanas were also much in demand in the Berlin of Bertolt Brecht and Herr Ishevood. Before the Second World War in Germany even cigars had to be Aryan. Though you couldn't hail Hitler with a cigar in your mouth. But I have news for Hitler the Havana-hater. The *tapado* technique, curiously, was invented by a Cuban Jew called Luis Marx, who was closer to Groucho than to Karl – both being Marxes together and cigar-smokers. Luis Marx called his invention 'my gentle butterfly net'. In Cuba it was commonly known as *mosquiteros* – mosquito nets. Sun tobacco for fillers, shade tobacco for wrappers. For some tobacco leaf the cheesecloth gives a shade worse than death: it becomes a paler hue of green. The leaf then looks like the end at the beginning: it is grey as ashes.

But Mad Marx, as he was called, was not exaggerating when he showed such concern for the weed. Tobacco must be planted yearly and from the moment it is planted out its care is a constant labour of love, not always won. An old Cuban tobacco planter's proverb says: 'He who spoils tobacco the most, gets the better of it.' To spoil here means to bring up tobacco 'complying with its desires'. Whatever the weed wants, the weed gets. Nicotiana is a spoilt brat of a plant. 'Tobacco is better here,' they used to say in Vuelta Abajo, 'because that's where it's more pampered.' Perhaps. At Vuelta Arriba, in the Remedios region, they knew how to take care of their tobacco too. In fact this was the second oldest tobacco land to be cultivated systematically and it yielded a leaf of high flavour and heavy body. However the Vuelta Arriba tobacco is only good for fillers, which is the *tripa* or the core of a cigar. Talking of the body of the cigar, the filler must have a lining to keep it in place. But the essential part of a Havana – of any cigar, in fact – what gives it its appearance, colour and true feel – its essence – is the wrapper. In Cuba the wrapper is aptly called *capa*, the cape, the cloak that lends a cigar its magic and its mystery – and its mask, because it can mislead you. It's not all brown gold that glitters. If one could smoke Greek words, *capa* then could mean charisma. The best Havana wrappers come from the leaf grown in Vuelta Abajo, either under the snowy sheets of Marx or in the eternally fierce Cuban sun.

Somewhere around New Year's Eve 1933 an American lady (young? old? – nobody knows now) named June Giddings received a postcard from Cuba. It was sent by a certain Ruth Linn (Miss? Mrs?) who lived at the time in Havana. It had been presumably written on Christmas Day and posted the next morning. Or was it afternoon? It arrived promptly no doubt, for those were the days when the postman rang much sooner than today. He also always rang twice. Miss Linn (I prefer to remember her as blonde and beautiful, an unmarried girl) in grammatically faulty Spanish wishes Miss Giddings (tall, young and a redhead, an outdoorsy type of woman: I can picture her playing tennis in the late California afternoon – it's all rather giddy around that Giddings girl) 'Felices Pascuas y Año Nuevo'. But Miss Linn takes some trouble about spelling correctly the Spanish word for year. That is, *año*.

34

Living in Cuba she knew that without the tilde the New Year could become an old-time obscenity.

The missive Miss Giddings received (or didn't she?) with the Spanish signs of good tidings in her house (13? 18? the postman, blue pencil in hand, hesitates in front of an address without a number: ah unnumerical Ruth Linn!) on East Colorado Street, Pasadena, California, is of much concern to us even today. If you turn around the postcard (as Miss Giddings would have done) you'll see the science-fiction landscape of a verdant vegetation growing mild on red soil under a sky that is never blue but white. It is not a northern clime but the tropics of course. Cuba in fact. It is an artificial ceiling made of cloth: a perennial dome of white sheets. The postcard (turned over again) explains why. It says in print: 'TOBACCO GROWN UNDER SHADE – By means of cheesecloth ceilings the tobacco leaf is given a light colour highly appreciated by some smokers.' Then the postcard-writer goes from folk to patriotic lore: 'Cuban tobacco is no doubt the best in the world. Its flavour has no equal.' Suddenly patriotism proves to be not the last refuge of the scoundrel but the actual abode of the absurd: 'Under the name Havana many millions of cigars are sold in the US and other countries (by fresh people).' I don't need, I think, to say *sic*. Then last but not lost to me there is an imitation English to compete with Miss Linn's spurious Spanish. But the English written by the postcard people runs a ring around the postcard that is, for me, an endearing flourish: 'Poor qualities bearing Spanish names are printed on the box, like a goose covered with peacock feathers.' That is called, I think, a tit for tat.

And all because Miss Linn sent that Christmas card.

Between the mask or the naked face of the wrapper and the entrails of the filler, the binder is the leaf that keeps the bowels in check. The peritoneum as it were. This vegetal sac contains the guts but it is as important as the outer skin, for it gives the cigar its flavour sometimes. Flavour is what a Havana cigar is all about and it resides, if you can pin it down, in the filler: that which burns the most. But it is the wrapper which guarantees that the cigar burns at all. Anything that happens to the wrapper (a cut, a pinhole made by an insect, carelessness in removing the band from the cigar) is a hole in the gentleman's cape that cannot be mended. Or the wound that won't heal. The cigar, like a defective chimney, simply won't draw and both smoke and breath (from the smoker) will leak out. English experts claim that a cigar 'with a broken wrapper can be smoked as long as the binder is intact'. Humbug! There's no way an ailing cigar can be fixed. I've seen stubborn smokers who instead of throwing away a defective cigar tried to stop up the leak with anything, from saliva to Sellotape – to no avail. The cigar was utterly plugged to death and no amount of mouth-to-tip respiration would resuscitate it. Death on delivery.

Perfect wrappers come from perfect leaves, naturally. The tip of the cigar, an inverted iceberg, is much less than a tenth of it and is usually called the head. The wrapper is rolled in a spiral around the body formed by filler and binder. A binder is always made of a single leaf but fillers can be made of cut tobacco or of long leaves folded together. This core is then known as a long-filler. Filler and binder are wrapped carefully so that the smooth side of the *capa* is always on the outside, like a wool cape you wear inside out: it is the crimson silk that others will see. The gold is on the lining.

Wrappers taken from the right side of the leaf are placed in such a way in this symmetrical universe of ours that the veins run down the cigar with a slow turn. When the veins run around the cigar to be on the right side of the smoker, you have a *derecho* or right-handed cigar. If the opposite is the case then the cigar is called *zurdo* or left-handed. The legend goes in the Cuban west, Vuelta Abajo, that left-handed cigars are quickest on the draw. If a cigar is wrongly wrapped, the veins on the leaf would wind around the cigar like a barber's pole! These cigars were teasingly called in the Havana of yesteryear Venetians. Some jokers insisted on putting them in a box the shape of a gondola. Obviously these clowns were working for *Punch* cigars.

Those luscious, lettuce-like leaves are picked by hand, one by one like the most delicate ripe fruit, and left to dry as dates or grapes are. But that's not enough. As all experts agree, tobacco leaves will have then little more odour or taste than any other dried leaf. *Nicotiana tabacum*, in spite of its prestigious name, will be like the autumn leaves that drift by the window or roll along the lawns in any garden of the West at closing time. It is the fermentation that gives the leaf its flavour and, from a weed, tobacco becomes the most valuable herb that has ever existed. Its green weight in gold is insignificant compared to its worth in diamonds after it has been treated – or cured. Curing is the drying of the sap of the recently harvested leaf. It can happen, partially, outdoors. The curing is done then by the sun, as in any solarium.

To further the process of fermentation, or ageing, the curing begins as soon as the *manojos* (or hands: eight make a bale) are stacked on the warehouse floor and left to ripen. The warehouse (more like a barn really) is called *casa de tabaco* – literally the house of tobacco. Curing really means a regulated form of drying in the curing barn. The natural process known as sweating varies with the packing and the seasonal changes in temperatures. It is then that the leaf undergoes a sea change. But the transformation takes a long time: longer than the neophyte (which by the way means newly planted) might think. Fermentation occurs in six to twelve months with some types of leaf. With other varieties it sometimes takes from eighteen months to three years!

Tobacco is a motherless child and indeed it requires a delicate balance to bring it up. Too short a stay in fermentation and the leaf loses its aroma or its taste. Or both. Too long a period of change and the tobacco is spoilt for good – and not in the loving sense of care. The analogy between a cigar and wine, made so many times in the past, is now not so far fetched. No wonder that they usually join each other for dinner.

The *casa de tabaco* in daytime is a hell house. Inside the temperature rises above human endurance and the tobacco fumes are overpowering: the leaf is silently sweating. At night, when the breeze cools off the roof, if you go into the house you'll feel like a stoker at work on the night shift. When the tobacco stench subsides (or rather when you get used to it) you can see the enormous dark shadows of the naked bales waiting for the next sunrise to cook in their own steam in an oven made of wood and tobacco leaves. Then you come out into the night and the open fields in Hoyo de Monterrey to see the moon and *l'altre stelle*. The tobacco fields are bathed in moonlight and the white sheets of cheesecloth are like the foam of a slow, silent surf, while the breeze plays gently among the few trees the weed allows to grow where she reigns supreme. Here nature's name is *Nicotiana*.

Next day the house tobacco built, with its walls painted oxblood red and a thatched roof of palm leaf, is melting again under the vertical sun of the tropics, where there are no shadows and sunstroke, as syphilis once was, is endemic. Sometimes beside the boiling *casa de tabaco* you see a spotlessly white lamb. The house and the little lamb and the cheesecloth *tapados*, a mask in the moonlight, is the landscape of the country where tobacco is born. All of it and the moonlight, after passing through the factory, will go into a small box of cedar wood embellished with some motley chromos and a brand and a name. To you it will be called a Havana. To those who know about cigars, as opposed to knowing about tobacco, this is the *vitola*. Catch that word.

What Karl Marx said of all merchandise (that it cannot go by itself to the market, therefore it must be taken there and the trip will be arranged by middlemen) applies to tobacco too: goods must be delivered. Tobacco is usually taken to Havana by truck. In the 1950s, the last time I saw Nicotiana alive, they were big Mack trucks. Later it came on Spanish Pegassus lorries. Now for all I know tobacco is carried by troikas in the Cuban snow. But it won't ever be transported by freight train. Don't ask me why. The leaf has its whims and I've been sworn to secrecy. After the smoke my lips are sealed by ecstasy.

Tobacco is in the factory now and the leaf is about to be rid of the stem by the *despalilladora*, the woman who does the stemming. Then the leaf is selected by the *escogedora*. This is a woman too, as is the *anilladora* who lovingly puts the band around the cigar. She also places each cigar in its box to rest – never in peace. They are, all of them, women whose working life revolves around the cigar. It will be difficult, though, to find a Cuban Carmen among them. These women have a keen eye for the shades of the skin: they are able to distinguish (and segregate accordingly) no less than *sixty-eight* different tones in the shading of the leaf! The eyes of the *escogedora* are as precious as those of a diamond cutter – and she wears no loupe. No *escogedora* can afford, like Carmen, to have said of her that she has the evil eye.

But back to tobacco sitting pretty in the factory. Here it will change again. Now it begins, *per ardua*, the last leg of the trek to smoke. This is a true metamorphosis that ends when a man wakes to find himself dreaming in a mist and saying with the poet: 'Give me the splendid cigar!' But first the cigar must be made, never in silence, by experts. The German General Heinz Guderian said once that all technicians were liars, which can be true of Krupt tank designers but cigar-makers are magicians: they lie to charm. The *torcedor* is our man in Havanas. He is not a bogus bullfighter. That's the *toreador* invented by Bizet when he needed a longer word for two bars of music in a march. The *torcedor* is a cigar roller: from *torcer*, to twist. He is a hard-working man. 'At seven a.m. he has entered the factory,' says García Gallo, a former cigar-roller become cigar-historian. 'Two minutes after seven he has taken off his coat and necktie and rolled his sleeves up before beginning to roll cigars.' He then puts his apron on and sits on his *taburete* or leather stool – and brings out his tools. The main instrument of his trade he brought along with him: his skilled hands. Now, from under the *tabla* or flat board he pulls out his *chaveta* or Cuban roller's knife, which is short and has no handle: almost like Lichtenberg's favourite *Messer*. It serves to cut out the leaf and mould the cigar and it is the least offensive of knives, with the possible exception of the fish knife. He then selects his *gavilla* or bunch of leaves composed of twenty-five wrapper leaves and enough filler tobacco for the day. He also tastes the consistency, smell and flavour of the glue, in case it has gone sour during the night. Then he puts in place the wooden mould to be used after the *entubado*. Finally there is on the table a contraption with a frightening name, the guillotine. This is also a gauge to measure the length of each cigar. The guillotine is used to decapitate the cigar after it has been rolled. All heads must be cut clean. Now the *torcedor* is raring to go.

This is Henry James on group work therapy:

> The best things come, as a general thing, from the talents that are members of a group; every man works better when he has companions working in the same line, and yielding the stimulus suggestion, comparison, emulation. Great things of course have been done by solitary workers; but they have usually been done with double the pains

they would have cost if they had been produced in more genial circumstances.

Hawthorne

Of all labourers I prefer cigar-rollers. Bricklayers are hardly ever on the level, carpenters are terribly superstitious – they keep knocking on wood; butchers insist on talking chop. Only cigar-rollers are happily smoking cigars while they roll their own – and ours. Bakers on the other hand cannot live by bread alone and brewers won't hold their bier when they die. As to gravediggers, I find them diggers tonight but grave tomorrow: very much like the rich drunkard in *City Lights*. Cobblers, it is true, stick to their last – but for how long? Finally, if you don't believe me, listen to what H. L. Mencken has to say on the subject: 'If authors could work in large, well ventilated factories, like cigarmakers . . . their labour would be immensely lighter.' (*The Author at Work*)

I'll ruminate over it with a bottle of Bacardi, the Cuban rum that with exile was forced to become universal.

Cigar-Making in Havana

The best workmen are employed on the very finest kinds. The rough and cheap kinds are very much more easy to make, and a good workman can turn out over two hundred cigars in eight hours. White men, negroes and coolies are employed in cigar-making; but white labour is found to be by far the most intelligent, and coolie labour the least so. Indeed the coolies are mostly employed in opening the bundles and separating the fillings from the wrappers, and very few of them are allowed to roll cigars.

The cigar-makers – at least, the white ones – are a thriftless, lazy set. A folder will work until he has enough money for his immediate wants, and then he will at once leave his work until he is driven back penniless. One young, good-looking folder, engaged in making the best kind of cigar, was pointed out by the proprietor as a curious example of his want of application. He works during five days of the week, making a tidy sum of money. Every Saturday night he visits a ready-made clothes shop,

buys a new suit, and early on Sunday goes either to the
sea-shore or to the river, strips, bathes and on coming out
puts on a new suit. Leaving the old one bought the
previous week on the bank, he goes on the 'spree' which
lasts until his money is all spent, when he returns to work.

Women are also employed in sorting tobacco, but they
are in a separate building, as it was found that the co-
education of the sexes does not work so well in a Cuban
cigar factory as in the aesthetic atmosphere of a New
England college. They are of all colours, ranging from a
pure white through every variety of cream and chocolate,
up to shining black that leaves Day and Martin's best
efforts in the shade. They all smoke, generally the very
strongest cigars. Unlike the clerk in the candy store, who is
allowed to gorge himself at first, and who never cares for
the sweet treasures again, men and women in tobacco
factories do not lose their taste for smoking . . . These
cigars are made by boys who are only beginning, and
whose productions are not good enough for market.

The New York Sun, 1880

Is cigar rolling a Cuban art? I have reasons to doubt it.
Cigars can be rolled almost anywhere by almost anybody.
Canarians do it, Javanese do it, Filipinos do it. It's the
islander's art then. Are you joking? Even machines do it! Let
me enlighten you. I once visited the big cigar factory (they
called it great those days) La Corona. The enormous building
was placed in front of the presidential palace and from its
arcades you could see the august façade and the famous
political balcony. I visited the factory not long after the
suicide raid against the palace in March 1957, so I asked the
manager when I came in (and out of nonsense) if they had
been frightened by the attack, what with all the shooting
going on across the street? 'Not really,' he said. 'You see, we
never thought it was firearms.' 'Firecrackers?' I cracked. 'Oh
no, exploding cigars.' A wisecrack indeed. I headed straight
for my business and asked the manager who his best rolling
man was and he pointed at a small black fellow wearing
glasses who looked like Mahatma Gandhi with a Churchill in
his mouth. 'Quite a Cuban *torcedor*, eh?' I said in flattering

41

tones. 'As a matter of fact,' said the manager, 'he's Jamaican.' 'I see,' I said. 'His name is Humphrey Bogart but, just to avoid confusions, we call him "Bogūs".' The manager shook with mirth as he grabbed me by the hand in a farewell gesture: guffaws wouldn't let him say good-bye properly. As I left La Corona in a hurry billows of smoke and laughter led me to the door. I looked back in time to see Bogūs rolling relentlessly over the factory floor. It was then that I knew what a great roller he was. Is cigar-rolling humour a Cuban form of art?

The cigar-roller is a skilled, highly specialized worker. It takes a long time to learn the trade and the *aprendiz*, in his four-year training, sometimes feels like a true sorcerer's apprentice. To make a cigar is a devil of a skill, but to roll so many in a day's work is sheer sorcery. Consider that *un largo* (a high-speed *operario* or fully-fledged worker) can turn out hundreds of cigars a day. But all is not speed with the roller. Each cigar must be perfected to a degree that not only implies length and form and colour, with the *perilla* or tip perfectly rounded, cut and sealed with *goma*, the mucilage specially made for cigars. This must be completely flavourless and odourless and ready to vanish without trace when the cigar tip is glued. If the *torcedor* is rolling *perfectos*, the cigar that tapers in opposite directions, then the roller must have the hands of a virtuoso: this is a cigar that, like the libertine's candle, burns at both ends. Finally the cigar, together with twenty-four identically-made *fumas*, is ready to be smoked, to become a smoke. One must always remember that this smoke was once a man. All that and the *vitola* too.

What's with the *vitola* then? What the hobby-horse that 'uncle Toby always rode upon' in *Tristram Shandy* was to the ordinary horse, and even to Rocinante, is the *vitola* to the bouquet of any wine – and to the cigar itself. *Vitola*, as a word, is 'well worth giving a description of', says ornate Ortiz. 'If it is only upon the score of its great singularity.' *Vitola* comes, of all languages, from Anglo-Saxon *wittol* which meant a knowledgeable person, though not exactly a sage or wise man. It is related to the Old Norse *vit* and therefore to wit. But *wittol* in obsolete English is a 'man who tolerates his wife's indiscretions'. Leopold Bloom in *Ulysses* was then the wittol as an urban Jew. Home is the cuckold, home from the street.

But it was Bloom who sentenced, 'Cigar has a cooling effect.' To pay the weed then a greater compliment in his *fin de siècle* manner or rather *esprit*: 'Narcotic'. Later in *Ulysses* when Bloom refuses a drink (to refuse means taking refuge in refuse), the Irish retaliation comes to the Jew, 'Hello, Bloom, what will you have? Bloom saying he wouldn't and couldn't . . . said well he'd just take a cigar', as a Bloomerang: 'Give us one of your prime stinkers.' Stinkers, stinkos. Blah blah Bloom! No wonder they call the book *Jewlysses*.

According to Raymond Jahn in his *Tobacco Dictionary* a *vitola* is the 'frontmark or shape of a Cuban cigar'. That's his first definition. His second one is that a *vitola* (which he always capitalizes) 'is also the mould or model of the shape and size of the cigar'. Too many opposite definitions already, I think. But then he goes on to say: 'In one collection of *vitolas* in a Havana factory there are nine hundred and ninety-six different types' – and then there's none! Obviously the *vitola* is an elusive concept that has nevertheless form and figure, like the shape of the newly born superman according to Chesterton: the creature was so singular that it created its own canon. That's the *vitola*! What complicates matters more is the fact that the *vitola*, originally, had only to do with the visible shape of a cigar. With the years this concept was left behind and now the *vitola*'s relationship with a cigar is what metaphysics had to do with physics before Aristotle.

One word or two about *vitolas* before they go. As Don Fernando Ortiz writes in his singular biography of a dichotomy *Cuban Counterpoint of Sugar and Tobacco*, which can be reduced to a close harmony of sugar and sigar: 'Tobacco is born to be a gentleman . . . it wins titles [according to its merits] until it reaches the aristocratic individuality of the *vitola*.' Then comes the brand and then the band. 'Every Havana cigar wants to have good manners, good breeding, distinction, *abolengo* (lineage), purity of race, nobility and pride of ancestry.' After this paraphernalia of blue-blood qualities the great anthropologist states bluntly that a cigar's vitola is its *figura*. 'This is not the expression of size and shape but of form,' says Don Fernando, using the term form as they use it aesthetically after Plato. '*Vitola* is the form of the cigar but only when the cigar-smoker chooses it for himself: the smoker looks in it for his own posture', meaning also his composure. 'A cigar's *vitola*,' he insists, 'is part and parcel of the smoker's own *vitola*.' The *vitola* is a form more tangible than the smoking man but less real than smoke: the measure of immortality of the *vitola* is like a veil painted with invisible ink: less than life and more than living. He could have illustrated this concept with Churchill smoking a Churchill. The *vitola* is not a trade mark like the Victrola but it sings and soothes and swoons like all good music – His Master's Vice.

Later Ortiz asserts: '*Vitola* means character.' In his book Dr Ortiz proves that the whole concept of tobacco, from the leaf to the finished product and hence to the smoker, is akin to a tauromachy, and its terminology is indeed close to the glossary of bullfighting and therefore impossible to translate. Not even Hemingway dared to find an American equivalent to *cogida* or *cojones*, not to mention the *querencia* in a bull. The whole concept of the *vitola* eludes not only translation but also definition and in a sense is like jazz being defined by Louis Armstrong. 'A cigar therefore, and every human being as well,' says old man Ortiz, meaning the smoking man, 'have their respective *vitolas* and each other's *vitola* looks for its own *semblable*.' Or equal but in the sense a Platonic Baudelaire would say it. 'Tell me the *vitola* you smoke and I will tell you who you are.'

Cigars must be the exact size of their *vitola*. Precisely. But one of the contradictions of every living body (and cigars are all alive even when they seem dead: they are only dormant) is that they are not always what they seem. Take the walking stick, also known as stick insect or living leaf. Or the death's head moth with a human skull marked on its thorax. Or the praying mantis which can never be found in church. Or the marine colonial coelentarate called coral, which can be harder than stucco when it dies but alive it is closely related to the hydra, the jellyfish and the sea anemone! Likewise, cigars uneven in length only show that they have been actually made by hand – and then again they might be just attaining the full perfection of their *vitola*. But some clever cheaters manufacture their machine-made cigars at an uneven pace by means of a switch or they change gauges constantly or they alter the peace – *pace*, pace – in their contraptions, slackening the rhythm of production, or by simulating the laxitude at the end of the working day or the erratic hand of tired rollers or the sloppiness of sick men who refuse to take leave of absence out of loyalty to the weed. Thus by shuffling cigars like cards the sharpies create a mix-up unthinkable in soulless machines which could be easily misconstrued as the work of all too human hands, expert yet fallible. Ah chic chicanes!

Today in Spain they call the cigar-band *vitola*. They have even coined the term *vitolfilia* for collecting cigar-bands, which is as popular over there as collecting postage stamps everywhere. Such neologism is a gross mistake according to Fernando Ortiz. 'The *vitola*,' he claims, 'is the figure of the cigar. The band is like a school necktie.' By which he means the concept of college colours as originated in England. The bands of course are something else and so exclusive to cigars that they cannot be related either to school ties or to stamps. The cigar-band has its own mythology. As the true story of the cigar-band is less poetic than the legend, one must hesitate between history and myth.

Here's the legend. English dandies were the first cigar-smokers in Europe. The legend forgets that Spain and Portugal are also in Europe, so do many Europeans. Then one day (or rather one night) the dandies noticed that their spotless primrose-coloured gloves became stained by nicotine from their cigars. So they asked their valets to place a ring of silk around each cigar and do it close to the end so as to protect the leaks of tinting fluids. Here's fact. Havana was terribly far away from London then for those damned dandies to order every Cuban cigar manufacturer to comply with their whims. Besides, silk was more expensive than it is now. On the other gloved hand, dandies everywhere affected to hate pipe-smoking, for they condemned it as too bourgeois and adopted the habit of taking snuff – which, contrary to cigars, really could stain gloves and nostrils.

And now for a famous female band. According to Sydney Clark, an old Havana hand, in his book *All the Best in Cuba*, 'Cigar bands have a curiously feminine origin, for they were first made – in Havana – not for ornaments or for purpose of identification but to enable high-born Spanish ladies to smoke cigars without bringing their dainty white fingers into contact with the weed.' Well, well. The Sydney Clark band now plays a coda: 'Very gradually the band lost its early significance and became almost a form of heraldry.'

History tells that a European manufacturer established in Havana, Gustave Antoine Bock, wanted to make his cigars look different even when taken out of the box. As he couldn't change the shape or length of his product he devised the band, which should be attached around each cigar. This happened *circa* 1830 (roughly the year the decline of the dandy began) and by 1884 the Union of Cigar Manufacturers in Cuba adopted the band as some sort of order of the garter. Since then all cigars, Cuban or not, wear a band. Bock by the way suffered from lambdacism and could not pronounce the 'r' in cigar. His three best *vitolas* he called 'My holy twinity'. His twibute to the twybe was to invent the cigawy wing. As he could not pronounce it properly he called the ring band, risking all kinds of puns and pains.

Now for another misnomer. Tony Randall (or was it Jack Lemmon: gentile or gentle comedian?) once said to a waiter: 'A Corona Corona, please.' Such a thing does not exist – and yet it's very possible for the scene to happen this side of the screen. Corona is the brand name of a Havana not made in Havana now. But Corona is not a type or a particular *vitola*. A corona is only a large cigar cut squarely off at the tuck end. The name originally came from the plant and meant the leaves taken from the corona or crown: the top leaves of the *Nicotiana* plant. Later a manufacturer appropriated the regal name. Cigar-makers have always been prone to sycophancy, as the Churchill cigar testified. Much later the cigar became very popular in the United States and was synonymous with a light Havana. When a layman wanted to appear knowledgeable, a somebody, and at the same time to sound sophisticated, he always asked for a corona. Like Lemmon – or was it Randall? Sometimes this green smoker became fresh and asked, 'Bring me a Corona *corona*' – or a '*corona* Corona.' The phrase has the same incantatory ring of popular perfection as when James Bond orders, 'Waiter, Dom Perignon' to project further authority and *savoir faire* than if he had said, 'Champagne, please.' But champagne is only a wine, like moselle, and not all champagnes are Dom Perignon – though cigars can be that too. It is as if by asking for this French brand you were ordering a magnum bottle of a light sparkling white wine of a certain vintage. But the wine being served could be just a *vino spumante* from Italy and even from Spain! With cigars you must be even more careful when you order one. That is, if you're planning to smoke them. Remember that there are many kinds of cigars – even exploding cheroots.

Leaving aside the metaphysics of the *vitola*, one must always consider a cigar by its length and size: what can be called its calibre. The corona we already know, though I didn't say it, is round and tight. It was once very popular in the United States as a cigar made with clear Havana leaf. *Perfecto* is usually a large cigar and it tapers from the centre towards each end. For a time it was considered the perfect shape for a Havana, hence its name. *Panatella* (in Spanish *panetela*: a piece of cake) means a somewhat long straight cigar, always proportionate to its diameter. It is open at the tuck end. With certain writers and film-makers the panatella has become a substitute for the corona: the epitome of a cigar. *Parejo* (it means even in Cuban) is a cigar with the same thickness from tip to tip, with both ends open. *Lonsdale* is a cigar that is round and tight, straight and thinner than the corona but fatter than the panatella. *Cetro* means sceptre but some authorities believe it is a corruption of *cedro*, cedar wood. This is a cigar sometimes known as torpedo and favoured by shady characters during the Prohibition: smoking was allowed in speakeasies but not encouraged. The *petit cetro* (or small sceptre in bastard French, a forked tongue sometimes preferred by cigar manufacturers) is a small *cetro*. *Demitasse* is a small corona. Dr Pretorius, that delicate fiend, was smoking one when he was so uncivilly interrupted by Frankenstein's most magnificent monster. Pretorius should have offered the Creature a Churchill but those had not been created yet. The Churchill, by the way, is a fat and heavy *Lonsdale*, while its opposite, the *Margarita* is a very small cigar indeed. It is as tiny as a cigarillo but it always retains its *vitola* gracefully. The Punchito is a *gracioso*, the clown consort to the *Margarita*.

Cigar-makers also classify cigars according to their colour and texture. *Oscuro* (it means dark) is a swarthy cigar, almost black. *Maduro* (it means ripe) is a shade of cigar between brown and dark. *Maduro Colorado* (which means ripe red) is dark brown. *Colorado claro* (*claro* means light) is a light-brown cigar. Exiled cigar-makers call the *colorado* (red) *rosado*, pink: a whiter shade of *rojo*. *Claro* is the Havana the colour of a Havana. *Doble claro* is a cigar that looks like a lizard: it's green! Once it was the cigar chosen by Americans as 'our cigar' – green goes the gringo. It must not be confused with a 'green' cigar, which is the cigar that has just left the factory. Sometimes these are called 'fresh'. Though not in Europe, where a fresh cigar is called anathema: the *excommunicado*.

Now you know, or should know, about the metaphysics of a cigar and all about the physical smoke. Take your pick. After selecting the cigar of your choice, here's what you must do to smoke it *comme il faut*. But first, a message from your friendly cigar-smoker. Most of the advice that will follow in a minute has been made obsolete by one single absolute: the cellophane wrapper introduced during the 1940s as, indeed, preservative of Havana cigars.

This is how Raymond Chandler wraps it all up in *The High Window*:

> I looked back at Breeze . . . He had one of his cellophane-wrapped cigars between his thick fingers and he was slitting the cellophane with a penknife. I watched him get the wrapping off and trim the cigar end with the blade and put the knife away, first wiping the blade carefully on his pants. I watched him strike a wooden match and light the cigar carefully, turning it around in the flame, then hold the match away from the cigar, still burning, and draw on the cigar until he decided it was properly lighted. Then he shook the match out and laid it down beside the crumpled cellophane on the glass top of the cocktail table . . . Every motion had been exactly as it had been when he lit a cigar in Hench's apartment, and exactly as it always would be whenever he lit a cigar. He was that kind of man, and that made him dangerous.

Yeah, such cellophane men are dangerous. So are their cigars. All highly flammable. Cellophane usually is. That's why the Surgeon General advises sternly that cigars mustn't be lighted up without first removing the wrapper. The cellophane wrapper.

Nevertheless never ape Louis Jourdan and have your

young sweet thing choose your cigar for you at Maxim's. Even if her art belongs to her sugar daddy. Try and avoid that she does the little number Leslie Caron did in *Gigi*. Forget all about the cute act even if it happened in *fin-de-siècle* Paris. I mean when she picked up a cigar from the box (it was an *etui* in motley mahogany: yes, I remember it well) to hold it to her lovely earlobe and rolled it between French finger and thin thumb to listen better to – to *what* for heaven's sake? Tobacco termites working nights Chez Maxim? The sound of a cigar being gently crushed to pieces by a feminine hand? (In the trade this is called 'listening to the band'. Bravo!) Miss Caron, a gorgeous Gigi, looks silly here only because she was being dutiful. Colette's instructions to her in the novel were: 'Let me try to teach you how to choose your man's cigar.' (Though Madame Sidonie said *songer*, to dream, instead of to try: French is a metaphoric language.) Colette was indeed a delicate writer but nobody, not even a fictive *femme fatale*, can tell what a cigar is going to be like as a smoke *before* being smoked. You can select your cigar by sight (colour), by touch (smooth skin) and by smell (aroma), but that's all you can do – and that's all you will be able to do before putting it between your lips to light it. Hold it! There's something else you can do to a cigar before letting Gigi light it. You can pierce the cigar – or rather its tip.

A Confucian proverb asserts that where there's smoke there's fire and where there's fire there will always be a Chinese. In Cuba the saying goes 'Where there's a good smoke there's a cigar smoker'. Tobacco is the opiate of the gentleman, the religion of the rich. But in Cuba once a Havana was everyman's frankincense. 'How did savages all over the world,' asks Cyril Connolly in *The Unquiet Grave*, 'in every climate, discover in frozen tundras or remote jungles the only plant, indistinguishable from so many others of the same species, which could, by the most elaborate process, bring them fantasies, intoxication and freedom from care?' Then he answers himself: 'How unless by help from the plant itself?' Connolly speaks of the poppy but this is probably how it happened with tobacco. The weed was asking to have its leaves picked like brains, then dried and made into a roll, then a bigger leaf wrapped around the roll to be lighted and finally smoked. We don't know how it really happened, we have only smoke and conjectures. But we know how the European gentleman discovered not the weed or its leaves, but a cigar already rolled up, 'like a musket', and lighted and being smoked by the *behique* (sorcerer), the cacique and a few Indian braves. The whole duration of the process from tobacco being discovered to cigars being smoked must have taken hundreds, thousands of years. For the European visitors (excepting Columbus) this was just a most unusual present. You see, nobody ever smoked in the Old World before the Spaniards discovered tobacco in America – except of course chimneys.

No cigars were ever made 'on the thighs of beautiful negresses/that rolled them up as if amid caresses'. If you care to remember, in the New York *Sun* article of 1880 there was not a single word of sweet negresses rolling cigars on their thighs (a sigh!) but there is a curious item from this thorough American correspondent in Havana: 'The cigar-maker takes from his hip of fillings enough tobacco to make a cigar . . . Many cigar-makers give the end a twist in their mouths, and this is especially the case with the negroes engaged in this . . .'

Actually the first woman to work in a cigar factory in Havana did so in 1878 and not as a cigar roller. She was white to boot. So much for yet another tobacco legend. Perhaps this one was concocted by an early Freudian after knowing that cigars were rolled by the hairy hands of burly men in macho country. Those dark, phallic objects were made to be introduced in most masculine mouths: a misfortune in other men's eyes. Prosper Mérimée's *canard* with naked legs was repeated by every writer who longed for the tropics and wanted to spend some quiet days in Cliché. But in *Carmen*, when Don José ventured inside the cigar factory and looked in, this is what he saw: all the cigar-rolling women were in their underwear, for they were gypsies. In Seville as in all Spain the reins stayed tight only in high places. It was then that Don José saw Carmen plain: the beautiful beast in a vest. Bad (or merely naughty) readers of the short story did the rest. I read 'Carmen', the abridged edition, when I was twelve – and I've been peeping through windows of Cuban cigar factories ever since. All I saw was ugly men sweating in their undershirts and hairy chests all in a row. So much for the smoke of myth.

The really astounding sight in Havana cigar factories was to find not even alluring *mulatas*, not to say negresses, rolling panatellas on their legs, but to see a group of some two, three, five hundred men working in total silence in the sultry air, while at the front of the enormous room, perched on a platform, with firm and resounding voice, a man read aloud from a book. This man was the *lector de tabaquería* – lector for short.

The factory is always a large shed or hangar with high open windows, the plant is peopled by columns and furnished with innumerable tables. Sitting at the tables are, let's say, five hundred *torcedores*. At one end of the *fabrica de tabacos* there is a man standing in front of a lectern or sitting at a table. He is the *lector*. His job is to read aloud while the cigar-rollers roll on. Before the advent of the PA system the reader was much sought after for his vocal strength. If he could reach the far end of the room with his performing voice, he had the job. For a moment it was thought that the radio might make the lector obsolete. But reading at cigar factories had a tradition longer in time than wireless waves.

Reading from books to cigar-rollers with a booming voice was not an original idea of Mr Bock or Herr Upmann. (Herr Upmann with a Baedeker – 'Where is Cuba?' – Mr Bock with a cigar band.) It all started in fact in a Havana prison, where an illustrated warden reduced the inmates into submission to the sounds of Hugo's bell *sans merci* in *Notre-Dame de Paris* read in Spanish. Readings usually included the ten volumes of *Les Misérables*, the continuing saga of an elusive convict and his shadow. Sometimes in that cultured Cuban prison instead of siesta they had Sue. But then we must remember that even Marx had read the novels by the author of *Le Juif errand* and praised him highly. (Obviously one more *mystère du peuple*.) The vogue for soul-searing Sue was copied by an enterprising cigar manufacturer, Jaime Partagas and from then on it was all read, rattle and roll. But it was not a man named Sue (Eugène) who profited by the move but Victor Hugo, *hélas*! His *Notre Dame* is an all-time favourite with romantic rollers. The unrequited love of the hunchback for the gypsy girl still throbs in Havana cigar factories like a bell in a cathedral, but nobody cares for the author of *Les Mystères de Paris*. When asked, cigar-rollers have been seen to shrug and say: 'We haven't got a Sue.'

Now for a fictive retelling of the above.

Says Garcia Gallo, a former cigar-roller, in his *Biography of a Cigar*:

The factory is silent. Only the unison of hundreds of knives can be heard as they hit the hard top of the tables. Right after the President of the Reading Committee rang the bell agitatedly all conversations stopped. A professional reader has climbed on the lectern placed in the middle of the workshop. From his place and with a voice more or less sonorous he reads from newspapers . . . In the morning periods, which last about three-quarters of an hour, he only reads from the morning press . . . In the afternoon there are two more reading periods . . . Most of the time during the first and second reading periods is employed in reading literary works . . . which go from erotic novels [a Freuday afternoon, no doubt], like those by the Daring Cavalier [pseudonym of one José María Carretero], Pedro Mata or Eduardo Zamacois . . . novels of customs and manners, adventure novels, scientific tracts, philosophical treatises and the like: from Jules Verne and H. G. Wells to Miguel de Unamuno and Gorki, from *The Time Machine* to *Thus Spake Zarathustra*: everything goes into that literary *olla podrida*. But it is the men in the workshop, not the reader, who determine the books to be read. In the choosing the President of the Reading Committee goes from table to table taking note of the books proposed by every roller, leaf chooser or stripper. He reads his list aloud and picks a first title making the rounds again at every table. The two books with the greater number of votes are tendered in yet another election, and the final winner becomes the book to be read.'

Writes on Garcia Gallo:

What the reader earns will be paid by the workshop, after the small sum that the President collects every Saturday . . . One of the best known readers of his era, Leopoldo Tejedor, became an actor on the legitimate stage . . . Another reader was Víctor Muñoz, the famed journalist who established Mother's Day among us. The origins of this curious institution go as far back as mid-nineteenth century. [Reading to rollers, not Mother's Day.] It was first established in the galleys for cigar-making prisoners at the Havana Arsenal. Back there, when work-time was over, the inmates gathered to hear a reader they paid from their salary as cigar rollers . . . The first tobacco workshop in which there was a paid reader was *El Figaro*, where in December 1865 they reached an agreement for one of their own to be a reader paid by a collection. A few weeks later Don Jaime Partagas followed suit.

This was the first big manufacturer to do so. He even gave his rollers a lectern as a gift. It was at Partagas that the American Secretary of State, F. W. Seard, then on a visit to Cuba, knew of the method, saw it in practice and was delighted. By the end of 1866 all the cigar factories in Havana had adopted the system.

Later came the innovations. The first galena-spark radio set installed in Cuba in 1923 was owned by the Cabañas cigar factory. Nowadays the reader uses a microphone and loud-speakers. Gone are the bellowers seen and heard by an enthusiastic visitor, Sydney Clark, as told in his *All the Best in Cuba*:

By all odds the most interesting feature of the cigar circuit to the average tourist is the spectacle of the paid reader who entertains the workers by reading aloud to them by means of his own wonderful 'bellows'. He reads them three hours a day and he 'had better be good', for the workers themselves pay him . . . In the rooms where men predominate the reader gives surprisingly solid fare including news bulletins . . . and even the classics of Spain and Cuba, not omitting *poetry*, a thing which would be unimaginable in an American factory but is entirely natural in Cuba. The girl workers, especially the strippers (who strip not themselves but the tobacco leaves – of their undesired central stems) prefer romantic novels, usually of the stickiest sort.

It all actually began in a Havana prison in mid-nineteenth century with a prisoner reading to his cellmates from *Don*

Quixote: books were scarce then, prisoners plenty. Later the readings were copied by Partagas, the enterprising Catalan cigar manufacturer. In the beginning the reader, as in jail, sat at the same level as the workers, but later Partagas had the idea of making the lector climb on a podium. The reader usually read the morning newspapers first thing and books in the afternoon, mostly what were considered then literary masterpieces, like the novels of Galdós and later Zola. Special favourites read over and over were Victor Hugo's *Notre-Dame of Paris* and *The Count of Montecristo* – hence the famous brand of cigar which proved to be a bigger treasure trove than the one Edmond Dantés found. Dumas and Zola smoked cigars and would have been delighted to know that their writings, albeit in translation, inspired many cigar-rollers to make an elaborate masterpiece destined, perhaps, to become poetic spirals of smoke in their mouths. Zola might have thought this revelation better than *les cuisses de négresses nues*. Dumas was utterly pleased that his *Fabrique de romans* served a *fabrique de cigares*. When Hugo knew that his novels were read aloud to workers at a cigar factory in Havana, he sent a letter of thanksgiving to Partagas. This was read aloud to the *torcedores* and in turn created a circular relationship. When the First War of Cuban Independence was raging in the late 1870s a group of Cuban mothers in exile wrote a letter to Hugo, begging him to intercede with the Spanish authorities 'to put an end to the carnage', the pen as mighty as the sword. Hugo, who knew what exile and civil strife meant, wrote a moving political plaidoyer in the form of a 'Letter to Cuban Mothers', which circulated among Cuban exiles until the end of the century.

Now this political letter is forgotten, but not Hugo's novels. Like radio, the Revolution came and went and the *torcedores* remained. After 1959 the Castro regime used the lectors as a source of what they thought would be subliminal propaganda. Perhaps Castro calculated that the cigars might smoke up into hammers and sickles in a capitalist club. But the workers rolled on, became listless, disinterested on hearing the same Communist slogans that were heard now everywhere in Cuba, over and over and never out. Worse still, they had to listen to Soviet novels about five-year-plan plots with enemy ploys of capitalist villains being smashed by the same positive hero, novel after novel. Finally, triumphant Hugo came back in the shape of crookback Quasimodo, but not with *Les Misérables* where the ubiquitous policeman Javert haunts forever the former peasant Valjean in a continuing story of penury and revolt. These were perhaps too exemplary pages to be read aloud to *torcedores*, the most alert and well-read (no pun intended) of Cuban workers. Those who in Tampa Jose Marti hailed in the 1890s as the 'intellectuals who work with their hands'. Those were the cigar-rollers of Ibor City, exiles all.

The best example of a European *lector de tabaquería* can be seen in *I Remember Mama*. Here an Englishman, Cedric Hardwicke, not yet a knight, entertains a poor Scandinavian family, settled in San Francisco at the turn of the century, who cannot afford any form of entertainment other than being read to from a book. The pedantic Sir Cedric (an impeccable, implacable reader) keeps his small captive audience spellbound with his readings from a sure-fire tear-jerker, *A Tale of Two Cities*. As it happens *Historia de dos ciudades* was a favourite read with the toughest cigar-workers until Fidel Castro banned its being read to 'real revolutionary rollers'. Sydney Carton was, as you certainly remember, a counter-revolutionary and a martyr. Who can ask for a worse hero within a revolution?

Gone are the days. Now the reader at the microphone reads – the *Complete Works of Fidel Castro*. They are mostly speeches heard over and over on the radio, on television, at mass rallies: everywhere in Cuba. I witnessed this last avatar of the lector in a 1984 programme on Thames Television shot in Havana earlier in the year. At the end of the speech (or of the reader's breath) there was a queer, weird sound like a surf of steel waves coming from inside the factory. It was the rollers hitting the tabletops with their *chavetas*. It all looked and sounded like the time and tide of the knives. It was, yes, a fascist sound coming from among the loving leaves: fascism in the place of pleasure. Gone are the days indeed!

Before being for sale and sold and bought most cigars are put in a convenient container. More often than not this is a simple box not at all like a coffin and yet not very unlike the box where Jack lives sometimes. Such boxes are always embellished with lively lithographs called *cromos*. The *cromo* is one of the two art forms native to Cuba – the other is Afro-Cuban music. This visual art originated during the nineteenth century when many European artists visited the exotic island that had an obscene connotation in a French nurture rhyme, 'A Cuba il n'y a pas de cacao'. They, together with local craftsmen, made possible a quiet revolution in the art of commercial lithography. Says Samuel Feijoo, a peasant turned poet, talking of cromos: 'Nobody knows that the cigar has created a style in lithography, a true new art expression.'

The cigar-box is always made of cedar wood, though today you can have a nasty encounter, a Jack-in-the-box surprise, with a cardboard box that looks like the real thing until you have it in your hand. Once upon a time the cedar of the box was Cuban, now it probably comes from cedar forests deep in Honduras: twice a tautology. When the cedar box is ready for the artwork, in comes a specialist to dress the container. He is called a *fileteador* and his activity resembles more the paper-hanging that is done in a doll's house. In the cigar world, though, his job is more like a craft than merely hanging paper: the *fileteador* must do his work inside a tiny box. The *cromos* are glued on the sides and on the lid but also in the interior of the cigar-box. The lithograph on the reverse of the cover, called *vista* (a view but also a show-off), is matched by a *cromo* that hangs from a side of the box, some sort of inner lid. This last leaf mustn't be printed on high relief, as are all the other chromos on the outside of the box and even the *vista* lithograph. The interdiction is mandatory. Otherwise if the design had any embossed pattern it could be printed in low relief on the wrapper (so delicate and sensitive a leaf this is) of the first row of cigars lying in the box, when the lid is finally nailed to close the box and its contents are committed to the deepest pockets. If this is not done you could end up by having a cigar with a view.

The band, though placed around a cigar the last, must always come off first, no matter what bogus connoisseurs might tell you. Douglas Sutherland, the U-historian, says in his pretentious little book *The English Gentleman* that 'most gentlemen smoke cigars but it is a practice which has its pitfalls'. Then he warms up that old chestnut about cigar-bands. They were originally 'put around the cigar by the manufacturer to protect the white gloves worn by gentlemen from nicotine stains'. Mr Sutherland goes on to say that 'now only the most traditionally minded and gentlemanly gentlemen and ostentatious bookmakers do not remove the band'. On the other hand (the cigar hand, I suppose) 'those who like to get their money's worth smoke the thing to the very end'. Balderdash to rhyme with ash! This statement is as prejudiced as one of Mr Sutherland's epigraphs he seems to cherish churlishly: 'Black men start at Calais.' This was said by an English gentleman on a rainy day.

A dark man born west of Calais, I'll try and explain to you why cigar-bands must never be confused with other bands, including brass bands. Whether the cigar band was created by a dandy, a trendsetter or by a cigar-maker is debatable. But the true moot point now is what to do with the band before smoking the cigar. None other than Stephane Mallarmé, a pedantic, precise poet if there ever was one, has written on the debate: 'What *volupté*', he used this very Baudelairian word, 'when I had lunch with my father *chez* Bignion or *chez* Paillard and at the end of the meal they brought over the boxes of sparkling cigars.' Here Mallarmé gives the cigar the quality of champagne (and Farquhar said of champagne: 'See how it puns and quibbles in the glass!'), even when it is still in the box: *'Clay, Upmann, Valle** and in those boxes I was able to evoke the future ballets of beautiful female dancers just by stripping their cigar bands off first – for that's how it is done.' *Bague ta littérature!*

Ginger Rogers dancing with Fred Astaire was Beauty and the Best. But Ginger on her own made Pygmalions of us all: she was indeed an animated statue. In *Vivacious Lady* sweet and sassy Ginger sings and dances in a sequence in sequins with which she could move a cigar-store Indian to tears. The title of the song is 'You'll Be Reminded of Me'. The tune is forgettable but the lyrics are forever:

---

* *Cigars used to have names then! La Flor de Murias, La Carolina, Aguila de Oro, La intimidad, Flor del Fumar, la Flor de Cuba, La Rosa de Santiago, La Flor de Naves and, above all, La Luna de Cuba, that Moon of Cuba. All of them sold the* flor fina, *that fine flower that was, together with the* regalia, *the mark of the* vitola.

You kissed my trembling hand
and on my finger you slipped
an eighteen-carat cigar band!

You must have a heart of cold ashes not to be reminded of Ginger every time you remove the band from your cigar. Le Bon Bock could never have imagined that he was creating a precious wedding ring when he invented a band to marry every smoker to his cigar – and to Ginger Rogers in his dreams. Could this be the beginning of a beautiful partnership, Ginger and Freud?

The dandy of French poets, Baudelaire, didn't pronounce on cigar bands because they were not in use in his time. Pity. Beau Brummel didn't write at all and Oscar Wilde, at the other end of the dandy century, preferred to smoke cigarettes even on stage: expensive gold-tipped Fatimas that he smoked only when he couldn't afford them – or sparkling words to that effect. (Oscar had even said: 'The cigarette is the perfect pleasure: it stimulates but does not satisfy.') What is the done thing then, when there are no longer any gloved dandies to show us? Of course you can leave the band if you want to advertise what you smoke, preferably an expensive brand, even when the cigar is no longer any good – as happens now with Partagas, which are mostly machine-made cigars but tough and primitive and virtually unsmokeable: *infumables*. On the other hand, if you don't want to appear too *nouveau riche*, you can strike off the band – and throw it away. But the best way, the golden rule, is to become a *vitolphile* and keep the band forever, after removing it from the cigar. Or the other way around: keep the band and throw the cigar into the nearest ashtray. In the past, bands used to wear (to tear off later) the *vera effigies* of that smoker in excelsis, King Edward VII, or as the Prince of Wales, a tyro. Or a tyrant or two, from Bismarck to Kaiser Wilhelm, archaic both. Ah, those were the days when the cigar band played on!

The Invisible Man had a problem with cigars. It was a common problem. He was an unrepentant *aficionado*, though together with rain and snow smoking could be bad for him: he became somewhat visible in the mist of a cigar. But he used to call smoking 'a blessed gift' and always demanded a cigar after a heavy meal. It was then that he committed the worst possible crime: 'He bit the end savagely,' writes Wells so well, 'before Kemp could find a knife', which was very wrong of Kemp too. It was on such occasions that the Invisible Man 'cursed when the outer leaf loosened'. Of course, though invisible he could see that the cigar had been ruined. Other men, very visible, had done the same – and what is worse, they will go on doing it, like a clumsy Don Juan ruining virgin after virgin. In the art of smoking there is no harder trick to learn than cutting the tip of a cigar. For most men, if we judge by what they can do to a cigar before lighting it, as happened to the Invisible Man, it is indeed a miracle to see them smoking at all. If we tell those smokers what is wrong with them we are liable to get, as Kemp did, a rebuff from the Invisible Smoker: 'For God's sake, let me smoke in peace!'

The physical principle that enables us to smoke a cigar is a very simple one – once it is known. As with many physical problems, it's not so easy to find a solution unless you give it as much thought as, say, Newton gave to gravitation – and even Newton needed a windfall. A cigar is lighted, kept burning and puffed on by the same principle as a chimney. Rodrigo de Xeres was not so wrong when he told Columbus of the chimney-men. With the chimney the puffing is done by nature: wind in the form of a draught. With a cigar, a man (or a woman: see George Sand) must take the place of Eolus – and puff. Like a chimney a cigar must be built (in this case, rolled) with the idea in mind that the tube (or shaft) must be made in one piece and tight enough to avoid any leaks or perforations. The chimney-pot is the tip of the cigar. Any holes made in the cylinder will mean not only a loss of smoke but the inability of the smoker to puff at it at all. Once lit, a cigar shouldn't be let out: that's all you need to be (or at least to feel like) somebody.

Pat O'Brien, an undercover policeman in a Chicago speak-easy in *Some Like It Hot*, uses his badge to pierce his cigar. He bores a hole in it with its pin, lights it up – and instead of smoke he blows his cover.

Where they call the wind Maria they call a cigar Polyphemus, on account of the single eye. But to get into your cigar – long or short, fat or lean – you must make a cut in one of its ends, preferably the blind one: Polyphemus unbound. This will allow your Havana (or whatever) to become a horizontal chimney, as de Xeres described the smoking column to Columbus. To declare your cigar open you can either slice its head off cleanly, cut a notch or make a hole. If you open a hole too big most of the cigar, rich or poor, would spill out. Not only the filler but part of the binder and even the wrapper will become loose. Catastrophe! If the hole is too small, as if made with a pin (see O'Brien), the smoke would be forced through a narrow gate, something worse than a Camel going through the eye of a needle. Soon you will find the bitter taste of nicotine on your lips and in your mouth. It means that the aperture is simply too small for the cigar, which is practically being squeezed like an orange by the considerable force of each inhalation. Have you ever tasted bitter oranges? They are bile.

Of course you can always bite the end off impatiently and spit it out and away, just like Edward G. Robinson did when he played snarling gangsters. Or Paul Newman as Judge Roy Bean, who just spits them ôut on to the prairie to roll along like so much tumbleweed; like burning tumbleweed in fact. Nails Hardener, the manicurist, reports that Princess Margaret has other ways and means and uses her lacquered fingernails to do the job. But he hasn't reported yet whether she smokes cigars or cigarillos – or even if she smokes anything other than chained cigarettes.

Now for other types of cigar-cutters less exclusive than royal fingernails. Perhaps their edges are sharper but on the other hand you can buy them in any cigar-shop. There is the plunger, which can take a neat plug out of your expensive cigar. There is also the razor-blade guillotine (disliked by most smoking Capets) and the swift Swiss scissors that can take a chunk off your cigar good enough for a plug. And, naturally, you also have your usual V-cutter, so called because it practises on the head of your cigar an incision shaped like a V. (This, by the way, was Churchill's favourite cut during the War.) Finally, there is the piercing drill which is usually made of gold or silver, when any small sharp sliver of wood would do. But you can buy it just for the cigar that has everything.

Never chew your cigar's head off to spit it out of frame, like Murray Hamilton did in *The Graduate*, where he played Mr Robinson, a man disgraced by Dustin Hoffman and his own ways with a cigar. If you do what Hamilton did you are bound to end up not only as an unhappy cuckold but also as the very, very worried mayor of Amity in *Jaws*, with a big white shark eating his job away the way he did with the tip of his Havana. Cigars can be a metaphor, you know.

Or so thought S. J. Perelman in his *The Last Laugh* of Groucho Marx's Havana: 'With the deliberation of a diamond cutter, Groucho bit the end off his cigar, and applying a match, exhaled a jet of smoke. "It stinks," he said and arose.' Groucho, let me tell you, was not talking of the quality of his cigar but of Perelman's script for *Monkey Business*, which Groucho used to call *Donkeys' Business*. Groucho, according to producer Herman Mankiewicz, was 'an old Hebe with a cigar'. A Hebe is, disparagingly, a Jew. Groucho was one, of course. But so was Mankiewicz. And so was Perelman. They are simply trying to make Gentiles of us all.

In *Prisoner of Devil's Island* James Stephenson, military governor of the infamous penal colony, perfunctorily cuts off the head of his cigar with – what else? – a toy guillotine. More in haste than in hate Herbert Lom (whose real name is Angelo Kucacevich ze Schluderpacheru), as Chief Inspector Dreyfus, Clouseau's suffering superior, used to employ a guillotine to cut the head off his Havanas. Once he missed his cigar – and his thumb too. The movie is called, unerringly, *A Shot in the Dark*.

Now for a folk fact – old Cubans used to stick a toothpick into the tip of their cigar, as if harpooning a dark, dead whale. (This habit perhaps originated the *brissage*, a long and slender cigar with a straw mouthpiece and a straw through the centre.) Some others, perhaps to soothe the pain in their catch, would immerse the tip of the cigar in a *demitasse*, actually to make their smoke sweeter and give their coffee a taste of tobacco. These Havana sybarites of old are as forgotten today as Nantucket whalers. But some smokers were more drastic than others. Isa Whitney, for instance, in 'The Man With the Twisted Lip', used to drench his tobacco with laudanum. According to Dr Watson that was how he first got the opium habit – Whitney not Watson.

It was not far from Baker Street that I found the perfect cigar-piercer in spite of the dearth of salesmen to satisfy my needs for a cutter. 'A cigar-cutter is the best tool to cut the head off a cigar,' claimed a vendor at the Dunhill branch in Burlington Arcade. Underneath the arch manners of his dictum was an offer one should always repel. I sauntered away, I always do. But the real find occurred in a smallish shop around the corner of the arcade. Embellishing the establishment was a beautiful poster of Romeo y Julieta cigars that must have been printed in Havana *circa* 1930. Half a century of looks, stares and praises has barely diminished its motley splendour: Renaissance play, Art Nouveau display.

I asked the salesman to let me see the small contraption hidden in the window. Speaking with a strong Hungarian accent redolent of garlic (was he expecting the Prince of Darkness at noon, day for night, the arcade a man-made Borgo Pass?) the gentleman's salesman didn't know how valuable this tiny *tirebouchon* could be. He couldn't even guess what it was for: the smallest bottle of wine ever? to clean fingernails? a toothpick perhaps? When I told him that it was currently used to bore a hole in a cigar he bored us all as he exclaimed: 'How chinchineous!' To extricate the piercer from the salesman's hand I had to use the corkscrew of money: it cost me £16, including VAT, obviously a Hungarian invention. I had seen a similar piercer in Barcelona only last summer and the Spanish shopowner wanted *solamente* £35 for it, obviously to make a hole in my pocket not in my cigar. Now, leaving the London shop almost surreptitiously, with that black-market feeling given only by true bargains, legalized theft, I stole to a nearby jeweller's to attach the genuine silver piercer to the chain of my watch and make the perfect fob for a fop. In my coat pocket now they are pendant to each other: the cigar borer, the bearer of time.

Then, before you smoke your cigar you must do something terribly important: you must light it. There are more ways than one to do anything, as the Japanese show you when serving tea according to Zen. To light a cigar you will always need that 'Promethean fire'. Nowadays you can have Prometheus at your finger tip, literally. You can light a cigar with a candle, a match or a lighter. Twenty-five years ago the lighter would have been taboo. Then they used gasoline for fuel and the smell of refined oil burning always impregnated the cigar. Today most *flaminaires* use odourless gas and are as sleek and elegant as the French word suggests. But for me nothing beats a match, not even a head-wind. As a matter of fact it was the habit of smoking that created the match, Prometheus in reverse.

Alfred G. Dunhill in *The Gentle Art of Smoking* gives you a brief history of the match, from the early tinderboxes to the self-lighting cigar: this Brunhilde panatella always commits immolation. The tinderboxes (some small enough to resemble a snuff box) originated the word match – from the French *mèche*, which means wick. But it was the Germans who invented the ur-match, no match for the *Wehrmacht* that created the flame-thrower. Later phosphorous was discovered accidentally in 1670 – the only precise date in the history of smoking since the discovery of tobacco on 4 November 1492. Phosphorous gave way to the so-called 'Instantaneous Lights' and from France, as some kind of *son et lumière*, came the *luminaires*. You could keep these in your pocket to light your pipe or cigar and sometimes even to set yourself on fire, as happened to Angelus Bulnes, a Cuban poet and chain-smoker, *circa* 1950. (Bulnes became a burning bonzo as the result of his habit of keeping his cigarette ashes in his match box.) Then came the 'Instantaneous Lightbox', in which the matches were tipped with chlorate of potash and beet sugar to match perhaps the sugar content in tobacco leaves to our content. There were other more or less experimental matches more or less perfected during the nineteenth century. A visual example of the pocket torch's progress can be seen in the demonstration Ray Milland gives John Wayne in *Reap the Wild Wind*, both men ardently trying to light a match with the striking Paulette Goddard, under the God-like supervision of Cecil B. de Mille, the producer with the divine spark.

By this time the Germans had invented the *Dobereiner Lamp* or ur-lighter, while the English stubbornly stuck to their gun of the match that must be struck. Later came in rapid-fire succession the friction match, then a copy-cat with a great name, Lucifers ('*Ex fumo dare lucem*,' said a lesser devil) and the phosphoric friction match called Congreve, which was as volatile as the playwright's dialogue. The Fuzee was designed 'specially for lighting a pipe and even a cigar', and later the smouldering Vesuvius erupted to light up your cigar and make a somebody out of every smoker. This, like the metaphysical Lucifer, promised brimstone and fire on earth. Nobody knows the troubles lighting a fire gave to man living as we are in the age of electronics and quartz. Finally came the Vestas, ordinary matches except for the fact that they seemed to be the gentleman's own private hell in his domestic heaven. J. M. Barrie, the smallest of all great English writers this century, in his *My Lady Nicotine* (the most splendid title of all books on smoking) says that a gentleman must always use a Vesta to light his cigar: 'Here, have a Vesta. Strike a light and be a gentleman.' Stuff and nonsense! Of course any match will do. To light up your cigar you have only to intone, 'Matchmaker, make me a match' – and have your cigar ready. Cigarette in hand, Burt Lancaster in *Sweet Smell of Success* said even less. He looked Tony Curtis in the eye and muttered softly: 'Match me.' Thomas Dekker qualified this with prescience in the sixteenth century: 'Match me in London,' he said. The most fiery match on the screen was struck by Lauren Bacall in *To Have and Have Not*, her first film. It was set alight when she said, 'Anybody got a match?' She found, of course, that Humphrey Bogart did.

Saki, that genial (both in the English and Spanish sense of the word), gentle story-teller died in the trenches of the First World War. His last recorded words were, 'Put that bloody cigarette out!' England expects (and with her the whole world) that the bloody cigarette was lighted, together with the other two Players, with the same match. Or so claims the superstitious. Of course for such belief (the killing match) to be born there must first be a cigarette, then a match. They were not always available, you know. Not until the nineteenth century in any case. That's why they say the superstition originated in the trenches of the First World War. But it isn't true. The phrase, the fatal third cigarette and the metaphysical concept of the solitary, deadly match was invented by one Ivar Kreuger, long before the Great War. Kreuger was never in that war or in any other war for that matter. He was born in a European country that remained neutral in the two World Wars, even when the first one had only Europe for its theatre. Kreuger was the Swedish match king and he just invented the superstition to sell matches. So much for beliefs. Saki, shot through the head 'while resting in a shallow shell crater', probably didn't even say his famous last phrase. Most probably he didn't utter a word. He died not for his country but for a commercial.

Ten years after Saki died so suddenly Von Sternberg could show in *The Docks of New York*, helped by his three actors (from Clyde Cook to George Bancroft to Betty Compson: a double play) and the single match trick, how neatly he realized his idea of the waterfront conceived as a battlefront. Even that poor gypsy moth Betty, about to lose her one-night-stand husband Bancroft, when she sees the fatal offer of the one light for three comrades, blows it off to plead to Cook: 'Do you want to bring me even more rotten luck?' This is, in a feminine way, a desperate reaction against fate as soldierly as Saki's famous last phrase.

But even twenty years after Saki was killed came the film *Three on a Match*, the story of three girls who meet again for the first time since childhood to have lunch in the trench of a cafeteria: on the counter. After coffee (those were the days when people didn't smoke between courses) they provoked fate by lighting three cigarettes on one match – and then of course pandemonium broke loose. Zwang! Bang! POW! Battle station! Dive! Dive! Dive into the social whirlpool. The movie means war by other means. The single match is seen as a mismatch.

> O, fellow with a will who will take no, watch
> out for these three cigarettes on the same, single match

> Kenneth Fearing

The latest in matches is now available on the smoker's market. It is a sulphur-free cedarwood match 'specially made for cigars'. There have been attempts in the past to perfect the self-lighting cigar. As it were, an exploding cigar but without the joke. In total seriousness Dunhill, the creators of the fuel lighter, report that even today these 'efforts continue – somewhat unsuccessfully, it seems'. The ignitable cigar, just like a match, 'combusts when it is struck on the side of the packet'. This must therefore be a cross between a cigar-box and a book of matches. It's either striking a match or doing what that most illuminating Marx, Harpo, did in *Duck Soup* to light Ambassador Trentino's cigar. He used a blow-torch. At Robert Lewis, tobacconists, you can have free of charge a box of matches, allegedly from H. Upmann. They are long and tinted brown. Each box wears a legend ('We have designed these matches especially for cigar lovers') and the well-known signature by Herr H. However they are not made in Cuba but in neighbouring India!

Meanwhile, back at the ranch, other smoking gentlemen preferred that reliable regular, the Strike Anywhere Match. These smokers are called Gary Cooper, John Wayne, Randolph Scott, James Stewart and, lastingly last, Clint Eastwood. All of them were capable of striking a match virtually anywhere: on a thumb, on the dumb villain's pate, on the forward chorus-girl's derrière, and egalitarians that they were, on the shiny seat of their own Levi's as well. Thus, with the least effort and the most effrontery, they were able to light up their cheap cheroots at high noon in Rio Bravo – and elsewhere. The only hitch in the yarn is that this type of match was not invented until 1890, long after the West was won.

If, as gunfighters in a Western, our mismatched heroes were ready to draw, so are you now. But one more thing before you go and light up your expensive cigar. (Nowadays everything is frightfully expensive: what this country needs is a good five-dollar cigar.) Never do, please, as Gigi does. That is, don't hold your match or your odourless lighter under the open end of your cigar and roast it until it is, like a chimney-sweep, all black and sooty. That's a good procedure to burn your cigar, obviously a de Xeres at the stake, not to light it. If you want your expensive cigar ruined, go ahead and do a Gigi on it.

That French *demi-mondaine* is a Circe of cigars. But if what you want is a smoke, light your cigar as a cigarette, only longer. You just sustain the flame underneath the head and draw until you see red on your cigar's farthest end. Is that all? That is all. Then your cigar will glow and be ready to become, as Othello put it so naively nicely, the instrument of your pleasure. Why Othello so often? He is the only Shakespearian character who would smoke a cigar if he knew how.

In *Pursued*, young Robert Mitchum sees Dean Jagger with an unlit cigar in his mouth and hurries over to offer him a light: one must always respect one's elders. Right! No, wrong. You see, Jagger bears a grudge against Mitchum and his kind

and though his name is Dean he behaves like a cad. Wrong?
No, right this time. A man shouldn't offer a light to another
man trying to light up a cigar. Even if, as in the case of
Mitchum versus Jagger, one man is the other man's junior.
No man is another man's elder when it comes to lighting a
cigar. (In fact all cigar-smokers are middle aged – or look it.)
To light up a cigar is a highly personal affair and nobody has
the right to intrude with his light and sweetness. Courtesy
might advise the opposite but when it comes to cigars every
smoker should be an Island intire of itselfe. None of that
mutual arrangement of cigarette lighters: if you scratch my
back, I'll scratch yours. (In this instance, if you light my
cheroot, I'll light your panatella.) Cigarettes are a sometime
thing but cigars are for keeps. He who keeps an unlit cigar in
his mouth could be not his brother's keeper but he certainly
is a keeper of the flame.

A most pressing question at this moment is: when, even if
you may, can you smoke? As with most crucial questions
there is more than one answer. First of all I must point out
that, although they all smoke and are smoked, cigars are
neither cigarettes nor pipes and certainly not cigarillos. You
can smoke, at your own risk, three packs of Camels a day,
even if by sunset you feel as if your mouth is as dry as the
desert and all the water you can drink is not an oasis enough
for you. But you'll never manage to smoke one box of cigars a
day, let alone two. There are of course smokers like Churchill
or Fidel Castro who chain-smoke cigars. Churchill was the
sole smoker capable of smoking himself: he only smoked
Churchills. He was, in fact, like Chateaubriand, who ate the
steak that bears his name: an onomastic cannibal, no doubt.
But according to reliable witnesses Churchill smoked half a
cigar, the Church part, and left all the ills for the next day.

I was once with Castro on an impromptu visit to a cattle
ranch on an island off the eastern coast of Cuba. When night
fell I watched a Western on television. Castro came into the
room to watch the show and immediately he asked: 'Who
has a cigar?' I had four Havanas in my shirt pocket, very
visible in the moonlight of the prairie. So I said I had. I *had*
to. I also had to give him a cigar. As he got involved in the

yarn of singing cowboys and wagons and their masters, Castro asked for a second cigar. Then for a third. Fortunately I knew that *Wagonmaster* was Ford's shortest Western, barely ninety minutes long. It was soon over. Castro stood up, all uniformed and pistoled six feet of him, and commented: 'Too many songs and not enough Indians.' We all agreed. Our Prime Minister was our first film critic too. He was also the sole talker, as usual: he made us turn the room into a Cuban chorus. Fortunately he was tired that night and soon went to bed, followed by his bodyguards. But before leaving he turned to me and said: 'I see we have one Indian left.' He was pointing at my pocket and not at my head: he meant my last cigar. He referred to it as if it were one more Apache. 'Do you mind if I borrow it?' What could I say? Don't mind if you do, *Comandante*? I surrendered my last cigar. When he left with that borrowed Por Larrañaga that he never paid me back, I turned to the TV set. It was off but around it on the floor were the other three *tabacos*, dead soldiers all but barely smoked. Obviously prime ministers make lousy smokers.

When can you smoke then? Don't do as Pancho Villa did. He always woke up with a fat cigar in his fat lips and ordered his men to do the same. On the double! The Mexican who felt nauseated was immediately declared a casualty and put, like a lame horse, out of his misery. But according to John Reed in *Insurgent Mexico*, 'Villa never drinks nor smokes'. Reed reeked with smoke and cigars though: 'The menfolk squatted before little corn-husk fires, bundled in their faded serapes, smoking their *hojas* as they watched the women work. At this moment arrived the husband and upbraided [the woman] for her lack of hospitality. "My house is at your orders," he said magnificently and begged a cigarette. Arrive now various uncles, cousins, wondering casually if we dragged any *cigarros*.' Then he sensed some sort of Columbian astonishment: 'At her husband's command the woman brought a live coal in her fingers.' In *each* finger? Was she by any chance a Mexican fakiress? Never you mind human pain: those were guerrilleros. 'We smoke.' With their fingers probably. Earlier on a 'peddler from Parral came into town with a mule-load of *macuche*.' What's *macuche*? 'You smoke *macuche* when you can't get tobacco.' But what's *macuche*, amigo? 'Somebody bought a little *macuche*, the rest of us borrowed from him, and we sent a boy for some corn shuck. Everybody lit up.' Ah, that's *macuche*! A primitive cigarette very much like the one the conquistadors found in Yucatan. Or was it *marihuana* to smoke? Reed, reefer in hand, squatted with his cuates to smoke 'three deep'. Not deep enough for marihuana. In any case, being so close to Villa to watch him squat to eat, sleep and defecate the *general* had no excretes for Reed: Pancho Villa definitely didn't smoke. There goes another Mexican myth three deep. No cigars before breakfast – or after meals for that matter. Lawful, awful truth.

In the movie *Viva Villa*, Pancho Villa is seen handing cigars to his *dorados*. It is not a festive occasion though. Those are explosive cigars: they serve to light the fuse of home-made bombs. Villa apparently is still a teetotaller: he lighted up his bomb but not his cigar. Remember that in 'La cucaracha', Villa's theme-song, the cockroach cannot walk because she lacks, because she has not got

marihuana que fumar.

I can safely advise you then: never in the morning. If you cannot feel at ease unless you smoke after breakfast and, like me, you hate cigarettes (I cannot stand the smell of burning paper: it reminds me of *Fahrenheit 451*, a bad movie, and the book pyre, a bad dream) then try to light a very small cigar, a Margarita, for instance. Or better still a cigarillo, preferred by the late Leo Carrillo. There are now nice Spanish cigarillos, like the Guajiros with their Señoritas. (A British cigarillo company announced their product as 'Señoritas from Havana', but when the next Cuban Ambassador came to London the envoy proved to be a woman and single. Then the slogan became a catch phrase. Needless to say, the original 'Señorita from Havana' was not Cuban but an English girl who was tall, dark and beautiful: everything that the lady ambassador was not! So much for clichés and smoke.) Finally and to paraphrase Bernard Shaw, a non-smoker: 'Cigars after dinner are delightful, smoking before breakfast is unnatural.'

There is a Brazilian king-size *tabaquillo* called Suerdieck – that is probably made in Holland. The Spanish novelist Juan Benet, a good but indiscriminate smoker, discovered in Manhattan, when he was lecturing at Columbia University last year, a cigarillo called Nobel. He might have been thinking of the Swedish literary prize when he bought his first box like a lottery ticket. Unfortunately the cigarillos were Danish. But this was a good buy anyway. Bingo! Nobel makes them but they are expensive not exploding. The Nobels are one hundred per cent tobacco – at least that's how they are advertised. They taste like a cigarette with a fine leaf for a wrapper. You can smoke the like of these if they help you shorten your long mornings. But please bear in mind what the Cuban doctor ordered the astronaut at Cape Canaveral: 'Remember, Commander, no cigars before launch.'

After lunch you can light a light cigar, even if the luncheon was a bit heavy. Though of course no midday meal should be heavy nowadays. We are no longer Edwardians, you know – and all the late Victorians are dead. Among the light cigars you can choose a *claro* or a *colorado claro*. There are certain *brevas* (the name means more than brief*) made with the expressed purpose of being smoked *après le repas*. One of the best after-lunch cigars is manufactured by Sosa, a Cuban exile based in Miami who makes his cigars in the Dominican Republic rolled with Cameroon wrappers: quite a Cuban combustion! I favour his panatellas or even better his *superfinos* as post-prandial *puros*. There are other hand-made Dominicans that look like friars but are as sweet as a nun. Or if you want propinquity you can buy a Tampa-made cigar with Cuban-seed leaf. Down there they have more than one hundred years of experience in making Havanas away from Havana.

Smoking in the afternoon is not always advisable – at least smoking cigars. Somerset Maugham, who knew about cigars more than any other British contemporary (he wrote: 'There are few things better than a good Havana'), had enough

* Breva, *in Spanish, is the early fruit of the fig tree, a black fig very esteemed in Malaga, where the word originated. In Cuba it used to mean a tobacco leaf treated for chewing now called* andullo. *Later it meant a dark, depressed cigar that brooded. Now it means a smoke in the sense given to the word by Kipling: as in 'a woman is only a woman but a* breva *is a smoke'. But then in slang the phrase* 'Es una breva' *means it's a cinch – and even worse, a pushover, chickenfeed. So much for male chauvinist Pig Latin or Latin Pig.*

money to buy them by the *rueda* (in tobacco parlance, one hundred cigars) and smoke them as he pleased, vowed: 'When I was young and very poor . . . I determined that if I ever had money I would smoke a cigar – every day after luncheon and after dinner.' Another English writer, Evelyn Waugh, also a connoisseur, said that he only wished to have money enough in his lifetime to drink a bottle of good wine every day and smoke a Havana – that is, *one* Havana. These two men knew what they talked about even when they were not on speaking terms. But their message was clear: don't smoke in the afternoon. If you work afternoons, don't smoke. If you don't work, do as the Spaniards do: take a siesta. Even Lyndon Johnson did it: John Kennedy taught him how. But if you are like the late faun and feel horny and ready to make love in the afternoon to a nymph you would want to perpetuate, go ahead and do it, by all means – but don't smoke after. Don't spoil both nymph and cigar.

'For those who taste the "naked beauties" of sweet Havana' is an old legend that seems to be penned by Byron. In any case it shows how much and for how long men have put together Havana cigars and sex. Talking of legends, Lord Byron has gone down in history, even in the history of literature, as a great cigar man. 'Give me a cigar!' and all that chat. The fact is that he could have equally been a great tobacco chewer. 'Give me the cud!' said the cad. Byron took 'to smoking cigars as he had formerly chewed tobacco', writes Leslie A. Marchand, Lord Byron's biographer, 'to prevent the gnawing pangs of hunger when he abstained from food in order to keep down his weight.' So much for Romanticism and the leaf. 'Sublime tobacco!' intoned Byron and perhaps at the time he meant a nauseous, black ball of nicotine, dry leaves and saliva in the lordly mouth.

> Then he spits on his spats
> The poet's brown sputum,
> All bravado and brass
> When he cries, 'Give me a spittoon!'

Here comes the evening: this is the hour of the cigar. After dinner, even if you don't drink wine (Count Dracula never did – or rather, never *does*) or coffee or a liqueur you should,

71

you *must* smoke a cigar. It's the compliment of a good dinner or supper. As Dr Pretorius explained to the hefty, heavy gentleman with the weird scars on his forehead and the funny screws and bolts protruding from his neck like a bad case of acne: it is the *only* vice. Zino Davidoff sings in Swiss: 'The *soirée* – the moment of great cigars, of a pleasure enjoyed with plenitude – approaches', sometimes with stealth. In the evenings you always smoke a full-time cigar: a heavy Havana or a Canary corona and even a domestic smoke is advisable – nay unavoidable. This cigar (a Montecruz Lonsdale, for instance) should last about an hour, smoked at a leisurely pace while talking or while remembering things past in translation – including the recent dinner. Or conversing with a woman who loves the smell of a cigar but won't ever dare confess it, not even to her husband. Davidoff, a cigar-merchant, advises the smoking gentleman to follow his cigar with yet another cigar 'which should be stronger than the precedent'. I don't agree, neither do Maugham or Waugh, gentlemen with a cigar in hand. A good large one or a fat but really good cigar should suffice. It will bring you happiness enough – and a bitter sweetness to follow. Says Maugham, the *bon vivant*: '. . . when you have taken the last pull and put down the shapeless stump and watched the final cloud of smoke dwindle blue in the surrounding air it is impossible, if you have a sensitive nature, not to feel a certain melancholy.'

That's what the *tristes tropiques* are all about. A second cigar followed by a second shapeless stump and a twice-disappearing cloud of smoke will spoil the feeling and the melancholy will become some sort of nausea. Maugham was thinking in fact of 'all the labour, the care and the pains, the thought, the trouble, the complicated organization that have been required to provide you with half an hour's delight'. That's why Jean Paul Sartre said in Havana, while he smoked a cigar: 'Every time I smoke a cigar *je dépasse la Maison Upmann.*' Sartre said in pedantic French exactly what Maugham meant in his careful English. Funny, though, that the flippant, fastidious English gentleman and the abstruse French philo-sopher should meet in a cigar just like that, as in a London club.

A cigar is not a club, of course. But a cigar is not for work or play either: a cigar means business. A good smoker, like a good lover, always takes his time with a cigar. So, smoke indoors always, never take your cigar with you outdoors. Not even on a stroll or to walk your dog to the nearest lamp-post. Cigars are like cats: fit for indoors, in a comfortable armchair next to a cosy fire in winter, near an open window in summer. But avoid both the radiator and the air conditioning – and of course don't watch television: they might be showing a skit of an unfunny funny man with a stogey. Besides, a cigar creates its own images and the pictures from a film or the new show interfere with its broadcast. You just watch your own visions: contemplate your cigar gently smoking as if the smoky spire, a spiral, a wise Solomonic column of smoke made clouds over your head: a vaporous canopy. Or, if you are lucky, a most magnificent firmament. But watch for the burning head as the live cigar becomes a dearly departed, all ash and memories.

Even after death you must respect your cigar – if it was good, for a good cigar is hard to find. About the ashes some smokers have had a *bon mot* or two in turn before they went away. 'Ashes to ushers', recommended Lew Grade, once the English Charleston champion, who lingered long enough to become Lord Grade, a movie mogul – a hideous Havana chain-smoker, with a firebrand always stuck in a corner of his mouth. Sacha Guitry, the famous French actor, a fragrance of a man, deceased, advised you to keep your cigar ashes in the palm of your hand before committing them, cold by now, to the cut-glass deep. He pronounced the experience *délicieuse*, a word he uttered with Gallic fervour. Baron Riccardo di Portanova, one of the richest men in the world, built himself a bungalow in Acapulco in which 1,500 artisans were employed to make everything by hand. His palatial cottage is called 'Arabesque'. Says photographer Norman Parkinson, an exceptional witness: 'The baron is a chain-smoker of his own brand of Havana cigars.' To add: 'He does not use an ashtray.' Obviously the Baron's domain is his ashtray.

Here is another cigar smoker with no ashtrays:

'There is nothing more agreeable than having a place where one can throw on the floor as many cigar butts as one pleases without the subconscious fear of a maid

who is waiting like a sentinel to place an ashtray where
the ashes are going to fall.'

Fidel Castro
in *Letters from Gaol*

Some experts believe that the quality of a cigar can be told
merely by looking at its ashes: the paler the ashes the
better the cigar. A mediocre cigar is supposed to have dark
ashes, a bad cigar black ones. Only the best cigars produce
white ashes. This theory, like most theories, has never been
proven. Otherwise it wouldn't be a theory but a fact. Or just
the opposite, cinisomancia, a superstitious belief that Sherlock
Holmes made into a science.

Holmes was such an expert on the subject that he wrote 'a
little monography on the ashes of cigars', and he boasted, in
his own stiff-upper-lip fashion, that he could distinguish, at
a glance, the ashes of any brand of cigar known to man – and
perhaps to woman. His pioneering treatise was titled 'Upon
the Distinction Between the Ashes of the Various Tobaccos'.
He deduced, at a glance, in 'The Boscome Valley Mystery',
that the killer of Charles McCarthy was not his master Ed
Bergen or too much Candy, but a man who smoked Indian
cigars – which he previously cut with a blunt penknife and
then used a cigar-holder. No gentleman he, but an atrocious
creature with insomnia.

Like all cigar-smokers Holmes was wary of visitors who
smoked, whom he saw as prospective kleptomaniacs. So he
kept his cigars in the coal scuttle. Neither Dr Watson nor Mrs
Hudson approved, naturally. In the same 'Mystery' in which
Holmes found truth through ashes, he created a minor mystery
of his own when he announced: 'And now here is my pocket
Petrarch!' This phrase has excited innumerable wonderings
in Holmesian scholars. They have been ever since in hot
pursuit of the 'two middle-aged gentlemen flying westward
at fifty miles an hour', as Holmes described himself travelling
in his private compartment with his constant companion.
Faster trains this century have never even approached them!
'I only quote this,' as the Great Detective said, 'as a trivial
example.' But perhaps Sherlock Holmes said something more
apposite when he expostulated (Holmes always expostulated)

firmly: 'Light a cigar and let me expound.' Elementary, he was talking to Watson.

To those who, like Holmes, are always worried that a visitor might be partial to the weed, I recommend a better hiding place than the coal scuttle, if you could find a scuttle today. I won't advise on a humidor. Too fancy and expensive. An obvious place, as in 'The Purloined Letter', is the best camouflage. Faithfully committed to my cigar, my lips are still sealed, but I can confide in you that I keep my cigars in their original box – in my refrigerator, that upright morgue for cannibals. I hide them not far from the daily bread and close to the fresh vegetables. That's where cigars belong: among the herbs. No hunting party would dare to look in the icebox for cigar-boxes. What about the smell then? Well, tobacco is a nice fragrance, better than garlic or French cheese, anyway. Besides, it was my wife's own idea. Being Cuban she believes in the virtues of the aboriginal seed.

In a recent interview Plácido Domingo, our Caruso, talked about Arthur Rubinstein's smoking habits. 'He smoked the longest cigars!' said Domingo. 'He took about *three* hours to smoke *one* cigar – and we had to wait until he finished.' That was not the longest cigar, that was a Montecristo *número 2* or perhaps the *A*, the fattest of fat Havanas. The shortest Havana, by the way, is the Montecristo *petit cetro*. At four-and-a-half inches this Montecristo is the shortest cigar to hold its *vitola*. It is so small that when it wears its brown band it looks just like a neat stub. The *cetro* is so petit that it is ill-equipped: the butt of all cigar jokes. The longest smokeable cigar is not a Havana but a Jamaica: the Colosal made by Caribe. When lit, a Colosal really looks like a horizontal chimney: the vindication of de Xeres.

What's interesting about Rubinstein, besides his piano playing when he was not smoking, is that he owned a *vega* in Vuelta Abajo – until the Revolution came as abruptly as a dissonance in a Chopin nocturne. The Cuban Government tried at the beginning to avoid a collision with the formidable five-foot Pole, a man not easily scared by revolutions, musical or otherwise. But his *vega de sol*, a pianist's pun, was finally turned into a *Sovega*, a Russian joke. Another formidable small smoker of big cigars, Darryl Zanuck, owned a Vuelta *vega* too and was able, like Rubinstein, to smoke Havanas he could claim his own from the roots of the plant to the tip of his cigar. Zanuck did smoke the longest cigars, especially during the shooting of *The Longest Day*, when his Lonsdale off the set competed with the Allied artillery on the set. His cigar band sported a zesty Z. The mark of Zanuck?

The smoking time of a few major cigars, according to Walter Kahn of Joseph Samuel & Sons, London, is: 'A Montecristo "A" takes about three hours.' That is, longer than it took the Abbé Faria to find Edmond Dantés. 'A Corona lasts around seventy minutes and a Petit Corona some forty minutes.' Kahn added some extracensor perceptions: 'Cigar smoking should be sipping, not gulping.' But he said something I don't agree with: 'The fatter the cigar, the better the smoke.' It sounds as if Kahn had an axiom to grind. The calibre of a cigar is measured with a ring gauge. The fattest cigar is a three ring gauge beast. Obviously good enough for a circus but not for a club or a dining-room worth its salt.

What do *I* think about the right time to spend on a cigar? I hold the same opinion Bergson had about Time: the knack of it is in the duration, *la durée réelle*. A good cigar should last for ever – or a few seconds: it's all on the lips of the holder: *matière et mémoire*. Good cigars need good smokers, of course. A lighted cigar is *une chose qui dure*, a thing that continues rather than goes on: a cigar is matter and memory connected by smoke. The *élan vital* can be found in a cigar as it is smoked. This is what the *vitola* is all about: the *élan vitola*. What happens if the cigar goes out? It shouldn't but if it does there's only one thing left to do: light it again. Zino Davidoff, a tobacconist, suggests that you light a *fresh* cigar – which means having to buy one for just that. Alfred Dunhill, being an Englishman, says: both are bad form. 'A cigar in good condition,' teaches Dunhill, having in mind a fine cigar, 'should not go out during smoking.' But what if it does? Then Dunhill advises to rub off calmly 'the charred end with a match (unlit) until it is level', then to strike the match and relight the dead cigar. But what if the cigar goes out again? If it is a good cigar then you are no smoker, you are a schmuck.

Though many gentlemen don't smoke, every cigar-smoker should aspire to the condition of a gentleman. According to Sir Thomas Browne, a gentleman is only a man who gives the least trouble. The smoking gentleman should make the least smoke, from matches to ashes. He must know not only how to light a cigar but also how to put it out with the least fuss. A piece of advice: make sure that the cigar is really dead and never kill a cigar as if it were a cigarette. Don't crush it either by rubbing it against the ashtray: that's not the done thing. Don't throw it on the floor! That's ungentlemanly – and a fire hazard to boot: good cigars die hard. As to the dying cigar simply leave the cigar in the ashtray as gently as possible and let it die its slow death. Some immortal cigars should be put on a pedestal instead. Those are legendary cigars, Phoenixes that burn to live again in memory: I remember *all* my Larrañagas: recreating matter born to burn. Other cigars must be put down in the ashtray as quickly as possible to be dealt with as incurably lame horses: those should be destroyed humanely. They blow up funny cigars, don't they?

Cigars come as we all must go – in a box. A good cigar, after being lit and smoked for a while, if left to itself unattended, unsmoked, will remain lit for a considerable time, even if in all appearances it looks like a dead cigar. It is this quality (and not the silly business of how long can the ash-tip be maintained before it falls off) that is the only valid proof of a good cigar. As to the longest-living ash-tip, it's all balderdash – ash said the echo.

Echo is one of the names for a feminine form of Narcissus, a myth. In *Cheyenne Autumn* there is the encounter of myth with myth: Wyatt Earp and his cigar. James Stewart plays quiet Wyatt at his gambling Sunday best: he is attired in a white linen suit. Earp is called out in the middle of a poker game to have a showdown with the Clanton clan. In order to make himself sure that nobody is going to disturb his winning hand, he leaves his cigar resting on the cards. The slim panatella, its ash-tip already more than an inch long, is protruding from the edge of the table and hanging on miraculously. The whole point of this exercise in myth-making by John Ford is that a true Havana can be left burning on its own and its ash-tip won't fall – provided you don't mess with the cigar. Wyatt Earp of course was no gentleman marshal as depicted in the movie: he was known to have shot an opponent or two in the back. That's in the history of the West, but how long a cigar can hold its ash-tip is a matter of conjecture: it has nothing to do with the quality of the cigar.

This bit of business with myth is as entertaining a fiction as Sherlock Holmes being able to tell the murderer just by examining the ashes of a dead cigar next to the victim, which could belong to the culprit – or to an innocent passer-by.

On the uses of cigar ashes: 'Cigar ashes mingled with camphorated chalk make an excellent tooth-powder; or, ground with poppy oil, will afford for the use of the painter a varied series of greys. Old Isaac Ostade so utilised the ashes of his pipe, but had he been aware of Havanas he would have given us pictures even more pearly in tone than those which he has left for the astonishment and delight of mankind' (*Gossip for Smokers*). Imagine then Gauguin, the cheat, with an Upmann up his sleeve!

'I've put some ashes in my sweet Papa's bed' – W. C. Handy sang the St Louis blues. But that's what the composer's father got for having an incurable smoker for a son.

Ashes in bed, blues to the blues.

ASH is the favourite acronym of all smoke-haters in Britain. Ash today, dust tomorrow. 'Ash is the dust of fire,' according to Gaston Bachelard. 'Smoke is then the antithesis of mud.' Mud, it must be said, combines the elements of earth and water, 'whereas smoke corresponds to air and fire'. Geber the Alchemist claims that 'smoke symbolizes the soul leaving the body'.

Never flick off the ash nervously. Cigars are not cigarettes. Don't be concerned with the ash of your cigar. Let it be, let it fall naturally. Or as a dead body falls, according to Dante:

> *Di qua, di la, di giu, di su li mena.*

Cash, dash, ash – the way of all smoke. Dusk to dust, ashes to ashtrays.

Never give cigars to a friend, that's my motto. Giving cigars away is a curious custom and as American as Santa Claus. It must come from another country, as Santa did, but it has been adopted by all Americans as wholeheartedly as apple pie. This absurd habit goes as far as to give cigars to anybody, friend or foe, whenever a child is born. According to Jung it is a phallic ritual. If so, why give cigars as a present when a baby girl is born? According to Jungians it is the father's phallus that's being wielded not the child's. Apparently

Freud told Jung: 'But a cigar can surely be just a cigar after all, you know.' Jung was as adamant as Adam: Father is phallic. What about Mother then? What about her? She never gives cigars away after labour, does she? That's why I kept my cigars with my wife in the fridge. After what happened to me with the lord who came to dinner I thought they were safer with her. Until one day . . .

Along came a Cuban friend of mine merrily married to an English girl. They lived in Middlesex but he stormed our flat one morning announcing stentorianly that he had just become a father, the baby son and the mother were alive and well in a Chelsea clinic. He was louder and merrier than usual and I wouldn't rule out the possibility that he was a bit tipsy or *bien borracho*. Abruptly my wife became as agitated as if she were a sudden victim of cerebral palsy, moved jerkily about and went straight to the refrigerator – to get a glass of water perhaps? Fat chance. She opened the refrigerator and took out – my cigar box! Mindlessly she lifted the lid and as a token of friendship said: 'Here, Tony, have a Havana.' Had I been an exploding cigar I would have blown up there and then! Was I fuming! She was offering this visitor with a baby one of my prized Montecristos! The same box of cigars from which I gave one to the lord that failed me as badly as Lord Jim did to the human cargo in his care. (See below.) My Cuban friend, an old smoker, rushed to meet the box and my cigars. My fear (it was certainly a lot more than concern by now) was that he might take more than one cigar, perhaps even two. Being fresher than his baby I knew my friend was capable of such a dastardly act. Fortunately he picked just one cigar and, bearded as he was, as if he were the Abbé Faria, exclaimed: *'Montecristo!'* Then he put the cigar in a safe place, just as Dantés did with his old cellmate. 'For later!' he announced and dashed off. (In search of more cigars perhaps). Since that fateful day I have never trusted my faithful wife with anything that's brown, cylindrical and to be smoked. I gained full custody of my cigars.

Never give cigars to strangers either, that's my motto too. Some years ago I was on the best of terms with an English lord and he came to dinner once. After coffee and perhaps brandy I opened a box of Montecristos given me by a Mexican friend, a film producer who had land in Yucatan. He was a wealthy man from the Caribbean who knew about cigars and what's more important, he knew of my passion for a good cigar, as driving a feeling as Fortunato's eagerness for Amontillado. Though I'd never declare a cigar, be it my own *vitola*, better than a woman as Kipling did with more biting sarcasm than smoking wit. They say that Kipling married an American lady because he couldn't be any more intimate with his American friend, her brother. Apparently he could never be as intimate with his wife as he had been with the cigars he smoked with his wife's brother, his former friend. That's another story, of course. Mine now is about cigars as a Greek present to people for whom all cigars are Greek.

After coffee or brandy I kept my box of Montecristos open time enough to tell you now that I never buy Cuban cigars: that's my policy. It would be as if a German Jew, in 1933, bought sauerkraut from Hitler. That's why my Mexican friend, who knew my predicament, brought me a box of Montecristos in the first place. In the second place I found myself in my place as in an alcoholic daze offering my English friend a cigar. But all of a sudden I was out of my mist and he became a stranger. Englishmen are among the best cigar-smokers and are moreover a gracious race. I was not then at all surprised when my English friend accepted the cigar graciously. I offered him a light in the form of a spill of cedar wood that I keep for occasions like this since my diplomatic days. He was delighted, he lighted his cigar – a Montecristo Número Uno. I still can see the distinctive dark brown band becoming almost purple under the light and on the cigar, as the taper flickered and I gave him light. He lit it up. That's all he did in the evening, I swear. He didn't even take a drag, I mean a draw at the cigar that was never his. I could see the Montecristo in his hand smoking all by itself, until it didn't smoke any longer: it smouldered. Then it grew visibly silent, became ashen and died. A few moments later my friend, a lord, a member of the House of Lords, an English gentleman, left the cigar, *almost* intact, in the ashtray, reclining it to make it repose in a pitiful way. In my eyes, he couldn't care less.

Writes Compton Mackenzie: 'I did not discover the perfect ashtray for a pipe-smoker until . . . I was in Rattray's famous shop in Perth . . . One of the problems of the pipe-smoker is knocking out the ashes. Once upon a time Mr Rattray saw a pipe-smoking guest at a dinner take a champagne cork, put it in the middle of a plate and knock out his pipe on it. So he devised a deep circular wooden tray in the middle of which is a squat wooden pillar topped with cork.' Perhaps Mr Mackenzie could have been interested in the cigar ashtray I discovered but was devised by Dunhill's. It is a long piece of thick glass, probably fire-resistant, with a heavy top and a sunk tray. From one side of the top to the tray runs a groove deep and wide enough to hold a cigar. If you rest your cigar in the duct (why a duct?) with the lighted tip facing inwards the ashes will fall naturally in the tray. The ashtray is a heavy contraption which can be placed on top of a table, on the arm of an armchair and of course on the floor, where all ashes go eventually.

Nothing new has been invented about smoking since its discovery. As in nature all is evolution with cigars. American Indians smoked cigars, crude and clumsy, in Cuba and on the big islands on the Caribbean. Further south they inhaled a primitive form of snuff, using a wooden tube to introduce tobacco powder in their nostrils. Aztecs, Mayans and the tribes of North America smoked the pipe in peace as in war.

In Mexico and not in North America it was that Europeans first encountered men smoking pipes. The Aztecs smoked 'reed tubes filled with tobacco and the fragrant resin of liquidambar' – that delicious deciduous tree with star-shaped leaves and exuding a yellow aromatic balsam. Other travellers found tobacco being smoked in North America and Canada. Cartier, the man who would be a gas lighter, met the Iroquois, who like the Tainos Columbus encountered on the beach in Cuba, spoke of a land not of milk and honey but full of jewels. Cartier's eyes, like his watches, glittered. He never saw the riches, though. But he witnessed the smoking of pipes, then a marvel to behold: men mouthing mist – and not in winter. Men who actually smoke! A contemporary of Shakespeare, John Florio, translated Cartier as he had done before with Montaigne's *Essays* to feed Shakespeare his canon fodder. Here's Cartier, here's Florio: the man who didn't invent the pipe but did the next best thing: he invented the word pipe.

There groweth also a certain kind of herb, whereof in Summer they make great provision for all the year, making great account of it, and *only* men use of it. [Feminists please note.] . . . first they cause it to be dried in the sun, then wear it about their neck wrapped in a little beast's skin made like a little bag, with a hollow piece of stone or wood like a pipe: then when they please they make powder of it, and then put it in one of the ends of the said cornet or pipe, and laying a coal of fire upon it, at the other end suck so long that they fill their bodies full of smoke, till that cometh out of their mouth and nostrils, even as out of the tunnel of a chimney.

There you are: the chimney-men de Xeres was so excited about.

Some other Indian tribes chewed tobacco and drank the brown juice to the bitter end. Even our modern cigarette that made the Surgeon General become so determined comes from the Indian custom of rolling tobacco in corn shuck. Already in 1518 the Spanish explorer Juan de Grijalva smoked in Mexico some rudimentary cigarettes. These were made of pressed tobacco cylinders rolled up in maize leaves. They were introduced in Spain some time later but not by Grijalva, who was killed in Mexico, providing the original ground base to the slogan 'Cigarettes can kill you'. In Spain Mexican maize was unavailable and smokers eventually substituted them with more hideous stuff: some even tried velvet! Finally a wrapper made with white paper was adopted. That's why the first true cigarettes were called *papeletes* or *papeletas*, from *papel*, Spanish for paper.

An old Catalan saw is sawdust in Cuba:

> *Qui te duros, fuma puros*
> *I qui no te, fuma paper*

A translation could say:

> He who has money smokes cigars
> But who has no money smokes paper.

This is an old adage still sage, for cigars can be very expensive in Spain and elsewhere. Everywhere cigarettes are made more of paper than pure tobacco.

A cigarette is what the narrator gives the gypsy girl in 'Carmen'. Prosper Mérimée calls them, correctly, *papelitos*. It's Carmen, after mentioning that she loves the smell of tobacco, who lets the narrator know that she would like 'one of those'. *Par bonheur*, luckily, he carried plenty of those early cigarettes with him and offers Carmen one, as he offered a cigar to the outlaw Don José before. (By the way, on that occasion the narrator and Don José smoked two cigars, one after the other, as if they were in fact cigarettes.) Carmen finds her *papelete bien doux*, a mild blend already.

All this happens in Córdoba, where gypsy girls took their collective bath in the river after sunset, dusky beauties all. But it is near the big cigar factory in Seville where the reader finds Carmen again. Mérimée says that there were five hundred women rolling cigars in the factory. The building is in fact an immense *zenana* where no man can enter because in there the cigar-makers *'se mettent a leur aise'* – above all the young ones when it is too hot. You see, the cigar-makers of Seville were almost naked when they worked. This description by Mérimée plus the opera by Bizet have given birth to a few French notions that are all wrong. First, Carmen in the short story was not the cigarette-maker she is in the opera. She rolled cigars, cigarettes were for her an unfamiliar luxury. 'She smoked,' says the narrator, 'when she found *papelitos*.' Secondly, the story was used later by a Parisian journalist eager for exotic copy to write that cigars were actually rolled 'on the thighs of beautiful negresses' in Havana. Thighs, nigh sighs! At the time 'Carmen', the short story and *Carmen*, the opera, were written women – black, brown or beige – were not allowed to roll cigars in Cuban factories, partly for religious reasons, partly for union rules. It's true though that some *escogedoras* still today half lift their skirts when they work and have a habit of placing the stemless leaves on their naked thighs. But *escogedoras* never work in the *fábricas*. Here all resemblance between fact and fiction in a cigar factory ends. Obviously with tobacco, smoke gets in every eye. That's fact. Here's fiction. Don Mateo, the Sevillian lover of Pierre Louys' *The Woman and the Puppet* (all, woman and puppets, come in fact from 'Carmen') used to drink 'icy syrups' only, but he was a heavy smoker. He is also a cuckold of the first fresh water. 'You must tell me,' he proposes his

newest rival, 'what you think of the smoke of the Havana
cigar mixed with fresh sugar.' I hope he does not, as old
Havanans did, dip his cigar in 'icy syrup', whatever that was.
The good Dr Watson might tell us that that, like cough syrup,
is addictive.

Soon 'Don Mateo's forced gaiety was extinguished in the
smoke of his cigar'. He is going to tell his guest (and us) why
is he, a Sevillian, so black and blue. 'One afternoon, out of
sheer idleness, I entered *la Fábrica*.' (He means the great and
grand cigar factory in Seville, so vile according to Don Mateo.)
'This immense harem of four thousand eight hundred women
as free in speech as in words . . . On this day, which, as I
said, was torrid.' He didn't say that before! 'They showed no
reserve in profiting by the tolerance which permits them
undress as much as they like in the insupportable atmosphere
they live in from June to September. Such a rule is pure
humanity, for the temperature of these long rooms is like the
Sahara and it is charitable to give these girls the same license
as given the stokers on the steamers. But the result is not less
interesting.' (He didn't pause here, neither did Louys but I
do now.) 'Those who were the best dressed had only their
chemises around their bodies (they were prudes).' This is
Don Mateo's own interpolation. 'Almost all worked stark
naked to the waist, with a simple Linen.' (I had an aunt who
always called Lenin Linen: the last line is a homage to her
malapropism that now allows me to wash my dirty Lenin in
public.) 'Simple linen petticoat unfastened around it and
sometimes turned up as far as the middle of the thighs.'
(There you are. That's where Mérimée and Mallarmé got
their naughty notions about Havanas being rolled on the
thighs of beautiful negresses. But the show must go on . . .)
'And they presented an extraordinary mixture . . . There was
everything in this naked crowd, virgins excepted, probably.'
(Another interpolation by Don Mateo.) 'And many of them
were beautiful . . . I regarded them curiously and their nudity
could not be conciliated with the idea of so painful a labour . . .
This contrast is singular between the poverty of their Lenin,
linen, and the extreme care they habitually take in the arrangement of their hair. Many of them use curling tongs like those
of great ladies when they are being dressed for a ball, and
they are powdered to the tips of their breasts even over holy

medals. Not one of them who has not in her handkerchief a little mirror and a white powder-puff. You might take them for actresses in the costume of mendicants . . . Almost deafened and rather weary, I was about to leave the third room, when in the midst of the cries and the sound of the deep voices, I heard near me a little sly voice which said to me: "*Caballero*, if you give me *una perra chica* I will sing you a little song." With utter stupefaction I recognised Concha!' Some time before Don Mateo had asked, apparently rhetorically, but truly haughtily: 'Who can be flattered in having the last word with a *cigarrera*?' Well, he just had.

Cigarettes are the perverse opposite of cigars: cigars are long, cigarettes are short, cigars are dark, cigarettes are white, cigars are thick, cigarettes are slim, cigars smell strongly, cigarettes are perfumed, cigarettes are for the lips while cigars are for both mouth and teeth, cigarettes never go out but burn up quickly, while cigars seem to last forever, cigars are big brutes, cigarettes are as feminine as jewels. Cigarettes are for chain-smoking, cigars must be smoked one at a time, peaceably, with all the leisure in the world. Cigarettes are of the instant, cigars are for eternity.

The European smoker, a sucker for fiction, prefers his cigars hard and dry in real life. This is of course like taking a liking to smoked salmon or salted cod. It's not a question of habit but of habitat. It is a historic, or rather geographic, necessity. In the past, Havanas took weeks to reach Europe and when they did the cigars (though properly packed in their boxes) had lost their natural humidity in passage. A soft, slightly damp cigar was the original, aboriginal Havana that took off for overseas. A soft, slightly damp cigar is still the ideal thing. That's what made an American invent the Humidor: to keep Havanas, coming from a tropical island, in a man-made climate. Though he has by now accepted the refrigerator, the European smoker still prefers, like Gigi, his cigar to crack under pressure: he has ways to make it smoke. By the way, Clint Eastwood's Man With No Name, a card-board American in Europe, always smoked Italian cigars in those spaghetti Westerns. They are *toscani*, the hardest cigar in the Italian West. That's why skinflint Clint seems to be lighting them up forever to become somebody with a name. Sometimes he just doesn't seem to bother and keeps chewing it between his clenched teeth. This proves that Clint is a full-time foreigner. Had Eastwood been Italian, like the rest of the roaring cast (dubbed), he would have cut his *toscano* in two with his penknife and then, only then, proceeded to light it. This is Compton Mackenzie, the tough Scottish writer, speaking: 'The Toscano is not very plump in the middle and tapering at either end. It is usual to cut a Toscano in half, though if one does not find a Toscano that draws easily [here comes Mr Eastwood: 'Hopalong, prairie mooncalf'] it is better smoked whole.' Or I'll fill you with smoky holes, mister!

But many people, not all of them American, have a cigar and don't smoke it: they simply hold it in their mouth like a brown dummy, the way the late Wallace Ford did on the screen. The wierdest non-smoker with a cigar I've known is Max Lesnick, a magazine editor in Miami who simply chews his cigar. He doesn't really chew it but chomps it, practically eating the cigar away. He bites it and reduces any cigar, from a twofer to a Macanudo, to a pitiful butt without ever lighting it – and yet the cigar is never made into a plug. Carlos Franqui, a Cuban revolutionary writer living in exile in Florence, can spend hours with a single cigarillo between his fingers without lighting it. At the end of the day he discards the intact cigarillo, takes another from the box and repeats the treatment. He has always been a non-smoker.

Now for something opposite. How many cigars can you hold in your mouth and puff at at the same time? The present record-holder, Simon Argevitch, is a cigar chain-smoker who does it all at once: he is capable of smoking *seventeen* cigars – or at least of holding them all in his seemingly elastic mouth, lighting them up and being somebody, according to the *Guinness Book of Records*. After all the cigars are lit and smoking, Simple Simon can whistle a tune. The last time I saw him on the David Frost television programme called *A Touch of Frost*, he whistled 'Smoke Gets in Your Eyes' slightly out of tune but all his cigars were in smoke. Unfortunately none of his smoking sticks was an exploding cigar.

Robert Stephens almost catches up with Argevitch in *The Private Life of Sherlock Holmes*, where Stephens smokes six cigarettes, three cigars and two pipes at the same time. As Holmes he is doing the smoking – but a bellows does the puffing. It is all part of his experiments with cold tobacco ashes considered as a hot trail. Watson explains to Mrs Hudson, 'Holmes is reading his ashes.' While she exits unconcerned Watson goes on: 'He already can tell the difference between a Macedonian cigarette, for example, and a Jamaican cigar.'

There is always something very dangerous in a cigar. Perhaps it is because, as to Columbus once, every cigar seems about to explode. That's at the origin of the exploding cigar, as old as dynamite. Putting it all at the service of guerrilla warfare that aspires to the condition of melodrama, a mediocre motion picture was advertised not long ago by a very well designed poster that was more memorable than the movie. In it you could see the familiar face of Sean Connery working hard at his usual mockingly menacing mood by wearing a moustache. His companion now was the askew but alluring actress Brooke Adams. Both actors however were merely part of the art work on a colour lithograph. This made up the cover of a bogus box of cigars. They were advertised as 'Genuine Havana' and between the heads of the players and the slogan there was the title of the movie, *Cuba*, as big as an island. The box contained several visible fat cigars, but among them were three red sticks of dynamite – tied together, their short fuses lit and burning in a TNT trio. Curiouser and curiouser, the fake cigars looked more menacing than the real dynamite. Perhaps it is because we know that all the sticks of dynamite can do is explode – but what about the cigars?

Now hear this:

> Suddenly, while the Privy-Councillor lay back in his chair pulling thoughtfully at his cigar, there was a bright, blood-red flash, a dull report, and a man's short agonized cry. Startled, I leaned around the corner of the deck-house, when, to my abject horror, I saw under the electric rays the Czar's Privy-Councillor lying sideways in his chair with part of his face blown away. Then the hideous truth in an instant became apparent. The cigar which Oberg had pressed upon him down in the saloon had exploded, and the small missile concealed inside the diabolical contrivance had passed upwards into his brain.

William Le Queux
The Czar's Spy

There are other ways of making an exploding cigar – or of making a cigar explode. Here is Ogden Nash, the man who invented the Nash Rambler:

> There was a young man of Herne Bay
> who was making some fireworks one day:
> > but he dropped his cigar
> > in the gunpowder jar.
> There *was* a young man of Herne Bay.

But not only cigars can be made explosive. Cigarettes too end more than in the whimper of coughs sometimes. The London *Evening Standard* printed this item some time ago: 'A Russian defector from the KGB brought with him a soft pack of cigarettes that fired bullets.' Live bullets or just blanks? Some cigarettes are more dangerous to your health than others.

Santiago, the Cuban fisherman, didn't smoke. But another hero of Hemingway, Robert Jordan, did. There is this comic scene in *For Whom the Bell Tolls*:

'What do you carry?' Pablo said.

'My things,' Robert Jordan said and he set the two packs down a little way apart where the cave opened out on the side away from the table.

'Are they not well outside?' Pablo asked.

'Some one might trip over them in the dark,' Robert Jordan said and walked over to the table and laid the box of cigarettes on it.

'I do not like having dynamite here in the cave,' Pablo said.' [This was the first time I ever heard of truly exploding cigarettes but Jordan explains my concern, and Pablo's, away – or does he?]

'It is far from the fire,' Robert Jordan said. 'Take some cigarettes.' He ran his thumbnail along the side of the paper box with the big colored figure of a warship on the cover and pushed the box toward Pablo.

Anselmo brought him a rawhide-covered stool and he sat down at the table. Pablo looked at him as though he were going to speak again, then reached for the cigarettes.

Robert Jordan pushed them toward the others. He was not looking at them yet. But he noted one man took cigarettes and two did not.

To smoke a cigarette used to be a foppish fashion. Next to snuff, cigarettes were considered as a sign of effeminacy in Europe during most of the nineteenth century. Oscar Wilde and his vicious circle smoked cigarettes only, in private and in public. It was precisely the theatre and later the cinema that legitimized cigarettes for men. (Today the only place you can smoke in a theatre is the stage.) But in silent movies only effete heroes smoked cigarettes, obviously to show their clitoris envy. In the early talkies he-men started smoking the delicate white things with the toughness of cigars. Humphrey Bogart in *Petrified Forest* probably was the first gangster who smoked cigarettes and stayed tough. From then on tough guys smoked cigarettes until they became fags.

John Cromwell, the film director, who died recently at age 93, knew all about female delinquents and cigarettes. In *Caged* beautiful, bashful Eleanor Parker goes from being a shy, modest prisoner to a corrupt inmate. She becomes a prostitute behind bars. When she leaves jail she demonstrates her availability by showing off her long legs and flicking away a prison-made cigarette. In *The Company She Keeps* Jane Greer, tall and dark, keeps her wayward ways after being paroled by making her own cigarettes with the help of a machine. Lisabeth Scott, a parole officer, objects strongly. 'Something wrong with rolling my own?' asks Greer, a vexed beauty. Counters Lisabeth Scott, precise to a point: 'It's a prison habit. I wouldn't do it if I were you.' Greer grows wiser but more resentful. Eventually she will earn back her civil liberties and learn to buy her cigarettes in the nearest drug-store. In *Remember My Name* none other than Geraldine Chaplin, who used to live in Spain, remains very plain but is seen constantly smoking a cigarette: at home, in bed, in her car, even at her job in some local Woolworth's and in all those nondescript streets in an upstate New York town. Or wherever. A new trend? Not at all. The film is actually a 1980 reproduction of one of those Joan Crawford melodramas of the 1940s in which she served in the name of American womanhood. Chaplin has more than a nasty habit: before putting out a cigarette, she beheads it, crushing the still burning tip with her fingers. Crawford, though a self-hater too, would never have stooped to that masochistic mess.

A languid cigarette at the end of a limp wrist was to Marlene Dietrich what the tough stub between forefinger and thumb was to Humphrey Bogart: an extension of the persona, not a prop. In *Shanghai Express* Marlene inhales and exhales so much that she creates an ambient of solid smoke in her compartment. Not to mention the steam and smoke of her passionate intensity: her nostrils really flare in the Oriental night. She sighs a little, smokes a lot and says things like 'It took more than one man to change my name to Shanghai Lily.' It should have been changed to Shanghai Chimney! At a given moment Marlene, enveloped in her gaseous aura, starts to cough so badly that the spectator is concerned that she might be struck with a sudden form of emphysema. She walks in beauty all right but she moves in smoke too, like the train.

The apotheosis of Misty Marlene occurs in *The Devil is a Woman*, where she plays a Spanish moth. She is none other than Conchita Pérez (remember her from the novel?), a vacuous vamp, who behaves like an enterprising temptress. As she did in *Scarlet Empress*, in which she was just crimson royalty, Conchita Marlene exuding mortal coyness, fatal to every man who approaches her and is struck by her eyelashes or her fan, whichever blows first. She is both Nemesis and Nepenthe. When the film begins she works in a cigarette factory in Seville: more blonde Venus than bloody Carmen. Many lovers later the movie ends with Marlene asking at her final train station in life for one more for the railroad. The station-master knows best: he gives her a cigarette. Marlene looks at it to ponder: 'You know, I worked in a cigarette factory once.' In spite of her garments, all silk and old lace, he believes her. Just by the way she caresses her last cigarette he can see that she really saw it first. The devil is a cigarette, according to Von Sternberg and Pierre Louys: the gospel *a gogo*.

In *The Band Wagon* the big brute in Times Square who steps on Oscar Levant's toe and squashes it, for Levant to howl in pain, was noiselessly smoking a five-cent stinko. Fred

Astaire is here an avid cigarette-smoker (so is Jack Buchanan) but Cyd Charisse is not. 'Of course. You're a dancer,' explains Astaire as if Cyd, who never looked lovelier, were a chimney-sweep. Like Paul Henreid in *Now Voyager*, Fred keeps inducing Cyd to smoke cigarettes. She is reluctant but he is relentless. She becomes firm: Adamant Eve. 'Oh, I beg your pardon,' exclaims Fred in mock tones of early reckoning. 'Dancers don't smoke. Do you mind if I do?' Later he forces a cigarette into a very distressed Charisse, worried to death about her oncoming appearance on stage. She is, to boot, literally groggy with exhaustion. Astaire even pushes the cigarette between her lovely lips: he definitely had become a pusher! All cigar-haters end in a bad way. Many critics found *The Band Wagon* anti-literary and anti-culture. I found it anti-cigar.

To top it all off Minnelli, in his next-to-last movie, *On a Clear Day You Can See Forever* (and by opposing it, end them: his very last is titled *A Matter of Time*) has a heroine (Barbra Streisand at her looniest) who chain-smoked to everybody's disgust and her own revulsion. A distressed and stressed Streisand is saved on the last reel by Yves Montand, her hip hypnotist who sings a hymnopaedia, shouting his love for her from the rooftops – all apparently smoke-free. Come to think of it, Minnelli does hate smoking. In his first movie, *Cabin in the Sky*, the devil's den was some sort of nightclub at night – which is a lot better than Buñuel's idea of Satan's site: a nightclub in daytime. (As depicted in *Simón del desierto* where Silvia Pinal is the devil's avocado: boobs as a bogey.) Smoke gets in everybody's eyes, ears and mouth.

Heard in *An American in Paris*: 'You'll need a radar to find your way through the smog' – and that is said of your average Paris nightclub not more smoky than the hang-out Tyrone Power and Gene Tierney patronized in *The Razor's Edge* six years earlier.

In the same *An American in Paris* a very confused Oscar Levant hears that both Gene Kelly and Georges Guetary are in love (inexplicably) with the same girl, Leslie Caron. As Levant listens to what for him is impending imbroglio, he asks the *garçon* (he is a French waiter) for coffee, cognac, another coffee. Levant is already smoking a cigarette, then lights up a fresh one. Now he smokes two cigarettes at a time, tries to drink coffee (or was it cognac?) and all his cigarettes end up in his cup of cognac or coffee – from which he fishes them out while revoltingly trying to smoke the hideous mess.

In *The Shop Around the Corner* lovable, eternally old Felix Bressart (the man who was Shylock before Hitler for three glorious minutes in *To Be or Not to Be*) must cut on his Hungarian cigars to save a wife. Part of the plot revolves, literally, around a cigarette-box that is also a music-box that plays 'Ochi Chornya' forever. The movie belongs to what we can call the Goulash Archipelago and was directed by Ernest Lubitsch, an eager lover who chain-smoked cigars. (He died in bed with a blonde on top and a cigar still burning in the nearest ashtray. A heart attack, no doubt. But how can you ask a man like that to give up smoking?)

'Cigarettes and music,' says Margaret Sullavan with her smoky voice, commenting on the music-box. 'It reminds me of the moonlight.' There was a remake with music and in colour that cut the cigarettes to none. Its title was *In the Good Old Summertime*. It should have been called *Chop Around Corners*.

One of the most hideous things in East Germany is their cigarettes. This is heretic gospel according to would-be defector Lila Kedrova. 'See this cigarette?' she is asking Julie Andrews and Paul Newman on the lam in East Berlin, in *Torn Curtain*, as she shows them a *Zigaretten*. 'Half tobacco, half cardboard. Disgusting!' That was just before her great escape attempt ended in pathetic fiasco. 'I am not communistic,' she explains to her sudden friends. 'I vant to go to Amerrika!' But the state police in communist countries are notoriously more nimble of feet than their ballet dancers. As they say in German, Gotcha! It is Iron Curtains for the smoking defector.

Why so many old movies, old boy? Simply because those who forget the movies of the past are condemned to see remakes. By the same token, or ticket, if one does not enjoy the movies of our time one will never be able to enjoy the movies of the past. Movies are not better than ever but those we have are for sure better than those we have not. Why, then, not enjoy them before it is too late? See to it.

In Maupassant's *Bel Ami* only the lowly concierges, almost all male then, seem to smoke cigarettes. At Forestier's bourgeois household the servants whisper in the guest's ear like discreet sommeliers the label of wines: Corton? Chateau-Laroze? *Du blanc?* After the copious dinner they don't offer Georges Duroy, upstart extraordinary, any cigars from Off David's. Our hero is not even disappointed.

It is only later, upon visiting Madame Forestier again, that Duroy is amazed at seeing her taking a cigarette to her mouth and lighting it. Even more amazing is what she says next about smoking: 'I cannot work if I don't smoke.' That this is being said in the 1880s (and by a woman) makes her modern and Maupassant's novel daring. Mme Forestier, a career woman, could easily walk down Fifth Avenue today (and of course up les Champs Elysées) without raising an eyebrow. One cannot say as much for Georges Duroy, soldier, gigolo and man about town but always the Norman provincial.

As the Burma maid said in Kipling, 'An' I seed her first a smokin' of a whackin' white cheroot.' Perhaps it is not a well-known fact that the Burmese speak in verse – or worse, they all alliterate.

'Do you care for a kiss?' Dustin Hoffman proposes suddenly to Vanessa Redgrave. 'No, thank you.' She is very strict. 'A cigarette?' 'Mr Stanton, how *dare* you!' Vanessa is shocked now. This exchange happened in *Agatha*, a near-murder mystery movie based on the facts and fictions of Agatha Christie's most famous disappearing act. The movie is actually about shocks, electric or otherwise. The sexual jolt young Agatha suffered at being offered an intimate cigarette by a stranger is true to type. In 1926, when the story happened (or didn't happen), skirts were indecently short and the Charleston was all the rage. But for Victorian ladies like Dame Agatha dresses were still ankle-long and women's tempers could be as short as the bit of skirt of those girls fluttering about on the dance floor, all flapping arms and naked legs. They were called, justly, flappers. American women (and their English counterparts), had to wait until after the Wall Street crash, when the stock market came tumbling down at the sound of jazz trumpets, to smoke in private and they did in fact wait for another World War to be able to smoke cigarettes in public. For well-bred (and therefore decent) women cigarettes were just another kind of sex then, love without a partner. These tiny paper dildoes for white women over twenty-one were an aid to masturbation. Sex-starved Vanessa Redgrave was so shocked she blushed at the offering. Dustin Hoffman, as a Jewish American, was inviting her to share, well, some sort of sex. The effrontery of the man! But these are the tell-tales of Hoffman and he leered and called it all mere chutzpah. 'Agatha, what about a murder then?'

There is always complicity in a cigarette that goes from one hand to another and then from lips to lips. Sometimes there is a hint of crime, of murder even. Glenn Anders, as sweaty shyster George Grisby, grabs Rita Hayworth's immaculate cigarette. She wants a light. It is Mike O'Hara (that is to say Orson Welles, masking his voice and intentions behind an Irish brogue) who lights the cigarette for Grisby. The latter in turn passes it on to Rita like some social disease. She is seen from above, flattened by flattery and the camera: she is sprawled on the deck of her husband's luxury yacht, wearing only a black bikini and a cigarette. Smoke gets in Orson's big eyes as she sings a sultry song. Meanwhile Rita's husband, Arthur Bannister (played admirably by popeyed, beaknosed Everett Sloane, who makes us believe that polio is either an honourable wound or moral mischief), the famous criminal barrister, watches everybody and her body. He sees every-thing from his invalid's chair, wheeling and dealing and popping his eyes like poison soda. All the plot is there on that cigarette travelling on board a cruiser. It is the snare in which Orson O'Hara will catch the little conscience that is left to king and queen, murderous both.

The title of the movie is *The Lady from Shanghai*, and it begins with Welles's voice-over, as faked as Barry Fitzgerald's: 'When I start out to make a fool of myself, there's little enough that can stop me.' Then he asks ash-blonde (also a fake), beautiful Rita for a cigarette – as she travels on a hansom through Central Park, New York. She doesn't smoke (or so she claimed then), consequently he offers her a start-lingly white but not innocent cigarette – which she carefully wraps in a handkerchief and puts in her handbag. (For later?) Here the story of murders and cruisings and double-crossings starts with a jolt, to unfold as if on deadly wheels. Yes, a cigarette can be very telling. Especially when it goes from hand to mouth and back again. Then a cigarette, more than a hazard, can be some sort of fate.

Fr. Rolfe (Fr. is for Frederick or for Father?) a.k.a. George Arthur Rose and, last but no less, Baron Corvo or Baron Raven, was even more striking than the O'Haras' priest. He was a padre that smoked like a *compadre* and also the once and future pope Hadrian the Seventh. 'I visited him every Saturday,' writes an acquaintance. I used to bring him twelve packages of different tobacco, named by him, which he would blend for his cigarettes.' The good father rolled his own *sancta cosa*. He had however a powerful reason: 'He liked, he said, twelve emotions of taste in his smoking.' There is another witness' testimony yet: 'Rolfe always rolled his own cigarettes and when in funds had his own "Corvo mixture", made up at a little tobacco shop in Oxford. It had a heavy full flavour evidently due to Latakia.' One John Holden, an early acquaintance, gives the final verdict: 'He was a great smoker.' When Alec McCowen gave his version of Rolfe's life and fantasies in the Haymarket Theatre in 1968 he smoked incessantly. At a given moment the stage was literally littered with cigar ends. The whole performance was a hazard to the spectator's health. But no Government's Warning was given.

Tom Stoppard is a chain-smoker who, after Wilde, goes on stage, when a friend or two have shouted from the audience 'Author!' once or twice, smoking a cigarette or two. But every time he signs himself with just his initials, as in a prologue, I say to myself: 'There's Eliot being coy again.' Here's Stoppard being Wilde again. Bennet and Henry Carr and not Stoppard are now on stage. Bennet is your traditional English servant: courteous, etc. Carr is your traditional English civil servant: courteous, etc.

BENNET: . . . I have put the newspapers and telegrams on
    the sideboard, sir.
CARR: Is there anything of interest?
BENNET: There is a revolution in Russia, sir.
CARR: Really? What sort of revolution?
BENNET: A social revolution, sir.
CARR: A *social* revolution? Unaccompanied women smoking
    at the Opera, that sort of thing?

Tom Stoppard
Travesties

Since their invention cigarettes were lusted as a woman's thing. Freudians might contend that if the cigar is just a surrogate phallus, a cigarette is only a clitoris misplaced: it is now between the lips, not immediately above them. *'Le malade fume des cigarettes. Freud fume des cigars – voila tout!'* said Alain Robbe-Grillet in conversation.

This is a commercial for

The Cigarette to Happiness
(A story from the *Sunday Times*)

In one police precinct in south-east Los Angeles the police go heavily armed. As well as their .38 service revolvers and their steel batons, most carry a fiendish device known as a *Taser*: at the touch of a button the taser spits out a pair of thin copper wires with small fish hooks on the end; these stick into the suspect's skin, and allow the policemen to touch the button again and fell the man with 50,000 volts of DC electricity. 'Works every time,' said Sergeant Howard Yamamoto. 'It fells a guy like a ninepin. But they're safe. They've even tested them on guys with pacemakers, I've heard, and they just get up and walk away.'

Tasers are used principally to help policemen deal with men who have had a bad trip on PCP – the vogue drug in Watts, made in backroom stills using, as Sgt Yamamoto explained, 'magnesium chips, ether and dog tranquillizer.' The drug, which is soaked into long cigarettes called Shermans, is smoked, and produces an instant and often very violent high. 'You get these guys who suddenly have the strength of five men. They snap handcuffs, bend metal – all sorts of crazy things. I've seen guys so high you need to zap them five or six times with the Taser before they're really down. It's frightening stuff. But it seems to make them happy.'

Obviously, Sergeant Yamamoto, a compatriot and colleague of another Japanese policeman, Mr Moto, can be called Mr Control Remoto. But he is the rarest of men, a policeman who believes in happiness.

'Mr Saidy, who owned the (cigar) store . . . was an inventor. He had patented a pipe for feminine smokers that held cigarettes in a vertical position.' Anything for a morally upright smoke, folks.

Chris Mullen does some mulling of his own in *Cigarette Pack Art* over spies and the nail in the coffin. 'It is no accident that no real-life spy scandal is complete without the unassuming but vital pack', and he does not mean Camel. Any cigarette brand will do. 'In the Martelli spy case in Britain a soft pack of Philip Morris concealing a tiny book of codes became a vital piece of evidence for the prosecution when it turned out to be a pack that could only have been bought in Switzerland.' Mr Mullen thus does his job at discloseting skeletons:

> For instance, in Britain in the early 1970s a skeleton was found bricked up behind a fireplace. In a shred of jacket a piece of a Crack Shot was found, which John Palmer, head of British-American Tobacco's Trademark Division, and an internationally known expert on packaging, was able to date to the early 1920s, a period when the building was a pawnbroker's. The skeleton was probably that of a burglar who became trapped when he climbed down the chimney to rob the shop and found the fireplace walled up.

Had Mr Palmer ever heard of 'The Cask of Amontillado'?

This is the Camel story according to Chris Mullen:

> In 1913 the American public were teased in newspapers and on billboards with the bare slogan, 'The Camels are Coming! The Camels are Coming!' Appetites were further whetted by the legend, 'Camels! Tomorrow there will be more Camels in this town than in all Asia and Africa combined'. The mystery was revealed when R. J. Reynolds' tobacco company unveiled their Camel cigarette . . . Camel appeared in a blaze of publicity [which is the only way for a cigarette to appear in public]. For a quarter of a million dollars the brand launch was undertaken by one of the leading advertising agencies of the day . . . Sales in 1914 reached 425 million cigarettes, and such was the national appeal that, by 1921, this figure had reached 30 billion annually. The pack, which has hardly changed since 1913,

has both proved extremely successful in visual impact . . . and also become synonymous with American smoking for generations of people outside the United States . . . Over the years, the Camel pack has acquired a mystique of its own . . . The design was so much a part of people's lives that, in 1958, when the company decided to tidy up the pack by shifting the pyramid that underpinned the camel's rump to the far distance, 'several tons of angry mail' protested at this radical interference in the nation's inheritance. The firm capitulated.

But the legend on the back of the pack remained unchanged: 'Don't look for premiums or coupons as the cost of the tobaccos blended in CAMEL cigarettes prohibits the use of them.' In other words, don't look for the golden tip. But Camels are still going as sure-footed as their old slogan 'I'd walk a mile for a Camel'. One small step for a camel but a Turkish trek for Camel. Where it said before 'Turkish and Domestic Blend', it now says 'Turkish and American blend'. A sense of national pride or defining domestic as something more exotic for foreign smokers?

In *The Treasure of the Sierra Madre* a cigarette is all Bogart's nemesis wants of him: *'Tiene un cigarro, hombre?'* He is Gold Hat, the brutal *bandolero*, Bogart is an amateur prospector who has just hit the jackpot. They meet in the middle of nowhere in Mexico. Gold Hat (wonderfully played by *el Indio* Bedoya) is accompanied by two cruel cronies. Bogart has only a pack of burros as constant companions. Polite as any old Mexican bandit should be Bedoya immediately translates his request into more-or-less good English: 'Have you got a cigarette?' But all Bogart has left is the bottom of his pouch. 'No, I haven't,' he admits, 'but I've got a few pinches of tobacco if that will do.' Gold Hat, a finicky *fumeur*, asks in turn: 'Any paper to roll it in?' It's here that Bogart really goes too far socially. 'I've got a bit of newspaper.' That's simply too much for Gold Hat. Vexed at having to make his own cigarette with a crumpled newspaper (old news not fit to roll), Bedoya borrows the burros from Bogart and the matching machete too. Before he leaves he has time to vent his smoker's anger on Bogart with two savage blows of the beheading long knife. Thus the cool winning Bogart of *The Maltese*

Falcon (to each his own roll) becomes a loser to death south of the border. The feeling lingers, though, that had Bogart been a cigar-smoker Bedoya would have been just too happy with a cheap cheroot.

Cigarettes were such a novelty *circa* 1875 that in de Mille's *The Plainsman*, hardly a plenonasm, a cigar-smoking Gary Cooper, playing a virile but doomed Wild Bill Hickok, is astonished to see his first cigarette. Cooper is in fact fascinated by Porter Hall (quite a name!), an effete fellow-passenger on a Mississippi paddle steamer, who is ostentatiously smoking something that looks like a pale cigarillo.

'Hey, mister,' calls out uncouth Cooper, 'your toothpick is on fire!' Porter is undaunted. 'That's no toothpick,' explains Hall fastidiously, 'that's a *cigareet*. It's the latest fashion way down East.'

That was the beginning of an awful acquaintance. At the end of the movie the point is bluntly made with ultimate finality (that's a plain pleonasm) when Hall shoots Cooper in the back. Obviously cigarettes can be hazardous to your lungs. Even somebody else's cigarette.

If Hickok could be deadly with his guns (except of course when his back was turned), even more accurate could be his girlfriend, Calamity Jane, with the plug. She was also a very vehement spectator. She was once watching a play and, disturbed by a female character, 'suddenly stood up in the audience and let fly a stream of tobacco juice', the cursing hebona, at the offending performer. 'The juice splattered the actress's long pink dress,' writes Carl Sifakis in *American Eccentrics*, 'and the stage and the audience were in turmoil.' Not only that: 'The actress screamed and the lights went up.' Calamity, still enraged, 'flipped a gold piece on the stage'. Addressing the actress verbally now she shouted: 'That's for your damn dandy dress!'

There are many billboards, huge, colourful displays, alongside the highway to London's Heathrow Airport. Most of them advertise cigarettes. You can see the moustachioed cowboy, ten-gallon hatted, lasso in hand, inviting you to Marlboro country: tough, rough, cough. Though the road to Heathrow is not strewn with rolling tumbleweed but with rolled weed. There is Winston, though no Churchill ever smoked it. A sheet of raw silk torn but not with violence to advertise

Silk Cut cigarettes. Green and gold for Dunhill menthol cigarettes, in which none other than Alfred Dunhill croons: 'The richness of the world's finest tobaccos cooled with a touch of natural menthol.' No cough here but cufflinks. There is also a billboard from Benson & Hedges – but not for cigarettes. 'ROLL GOLD/Roll over, all other roll-ups/Virginia hand rolling tobacco.' Then the masterpiece: 'HAVANA CIGARS AT REVOLUTIONARY PRICES/It's enough to make you *leave* the country!' After that one only the final solution is appropriate: 'LUCOZADE/AIDS RECOVERY.' Exeunt all except *Hamlet*. (*See* television.) Of course these smoke signals will never abolish that great coup of prescience by the *Rules for the Calcutta Subscription Dances of 1792*:

> *Hookers* be not admitted to the ball-room during any part of the night. But *hookers* might be admitted to the upper rooms, to the card-rooms, to the boxes in the theatre and to each side of the assembly room, between the large pillars and the wall.

Neck plus ultra
I saw the black hole of a doorless lift shaft and next to it a sign:

> NO SMOKING
> BEYOND
> THIS POINT

The girl on the billboard travelling in the London Underground looks a lot like Helen Walker, she with the lovely face, smart eyes and stunning body. But this girl is just plain Silly Jane saying of a nondescript guy gawking at her: 'My! Just look at those gleaming white teeth! At last a man who doesn't smoke!' I hate women who use more than one exclamation mark in a row, don't you? The man beside her says into another promiscuous balloon: 'Humm! – and for a moment I thought I was looking at a very clever advert for H. Upmann.' But it was only coy copy from a brand of toothpaste that isn't exactly truth pasta: it promises white pearly teeth to all smokers who dare use it. Clark Gable had a better remedy: 'Carole,' he crooned at Lombard, 'get me my new set of dentures.'

From *The Children and Young Persons Act*:
It is an offence to sell tobacco products to anyone under 16 years of age.

Heard at a London tobacconist in Soho: 'Sorry, sir, you can't smoke in here.'

The tobacconist's name was, I'm sure, Miss Anthropy.

Come to Lady Marlboro Country

Who would have thought that behind the billboard for Marlboro and its macho slogan ('Come to where the flavour is. Come to Marlboro Country') there is a lady's cigarette trying to come out of the pack? The cigarettes were even called Marlboro Beauty Tips and had their end coloured *red* 'to conceal those tell-tale lipstick traces'!

Navy Cut

Says *Cigarette Pack Art* about the term Navy Cut: 'During the nineteenth century, and our own, sailors in the Royal Navy were allowed to buy the whole tobacco leaves which they compressed into rolls of tobacco with tight windings of rope. Shredded tobacco, usually for smoking in a pipe, could be got by slicing the end of the roll thinly.'

On Alice Catering to Caterpillars

Lucky Strike had a burning cigarette that spoke in its smoke: 'I am your Lucky Strike. I am your best friend. Try me. I'll never let you down.'

The First King-Size Cigarette

Was Pall Mall and it happened in 1939.

And the last cigarette for Oedipus the King:

In *The Janitor* Christopher Plummer, looking rather more like a stray from the Trapp Family singers than Oedipus, makes evil of a good cause (smuggling Jews out of Russia) for the sake of a messy melodrama. After many a murder dies the felon. Unmasked Plummer is asked by the police to freeze. If you please, sir. But Plummer delves instead a hand in his coat pocket for just one cigarette before curtains. He makes his last gesture a trifle too sudden and Plummer instantly becomes plumbeous. That is full of lead. A lieutenant, after searching the body's pockets and holes in vain, explains the unexplainable with a smoking cliché: 'I thought he'd gone for a gun.'

Please don't involve me in your suicide
by Alexander Walker

Stapled into my passport is a document that has raised the eyebrows of many an official at the world's airports.

It is not a health certificate stating I'm protected against this or that. But I regard it as more essential to my well-being than anything medicine can give me.

It's headed 'The Heathrow Airport London Bye-Laws, 1972', and circled in red by me is the one that reads: 'No person shall smoke . . . in any place where any such act is prohibited by notice.'

It's a sign of the times when more than half of all adults in Britain don't smoke and more are quitting, that today I rarely have to rely on this document, as I used to, to get the zones set apart for non-smokers at Heathrow legally observed by those who use them.

Most people now observe the non-smoking signs and I'm sure that even people who still smoke welcome their dissuasive value. The same applies to more parts of the public transport we use in London.

There is a persistent, vigorous and continuing move among the general public in favour of no-smoking in the interest of us all, smokers or not.

Taxi cabs display notices that say 'Thank you in advance for not smoking'. One-deck buses are now non-smoking. A majority of Underground carriages are for non-smokers.*

The truth is that people's right to smoke ends where our noses begin. We need constant reminders of this.

What I will and do resist, however, is their right to involve me in their suicide.

Evening Standard

* *Now, smoking is forbidden on all London Underground trains.*

Later, in *Vogue*, Walker interviews Bette Davis: 'Throughout tea, despite her operation, she smoked continuously but only "vegetable cigarettes", made to sate a need, not incur a risk.' Walker took it all not with discreet coughing but with silent phlegm. He never explains by the way what a *vegetable* cigarette is. Are Camels animal?

Chinks in the Wall

Today the Chinese are among the world's most prodigious smokers. About 1 in 4 of China's 1 billion people are regular cigarette-users, most of them men. The state-owned tobacco industry produced 911 billion cigarettes last year, or approximately 3,600 for every smoker (neither cigars or pipes are widely used). The country's 140 cigarette factories turn out 1,000 brands, some of which sell for as little as 4 cents a pack and others for as much as 50 cents, or about half the average worker's daily wage. Unlike some other nations, China does not require cigarette packaging to carry any warning about health hazards. Total revenues from cigarette sales amount to about $5 billion a year. The figure would be higher were it not for the many peasants who grow their own tobacco and roll their own cigarettes.

Time Magazine

Ban on Smoking 'Unfair'

A proposal by London Transport's passenger committee to ban smoking completely on the capital's buses and Underground would be 'unfair, undemocratic and unpopular,' a smokers' defence group said today.

No further restrictions on facilities for smokers on public transport should be made without first ascertaining the wishes of passengers.

FOREST, the freedom to choose campaign, is putting its criticism to the committee, which recently asked the GLC to prohibit smoking on all Underground trains, buses and stations.

Evening Standard

The Time Traveller (courtesy of H. G. Wells) must be

quoted now. Excitedly he said: 'I have seen the future but my name is not Lincoln Steffens. It's Partagas.' He sighed heavily: 'It stinks!', he exclaimed. 'Or rather, it just doesn't.'

'How's that?'

'No smoke. No smoke *any*where. It's a smokeless world out there. Simply ghastly!' and he shivered badly, as if with fever.

Cigar sales, which recovered in 1983 after three years of decline, have taken another tumble in the past year. Manufacturers are also forecasting a further decline in 1985.

The Times

Humidor-Room Closing Ends Cigar Era

New York – Housekeepers, messengers, chauffeurs and all manner of hired help are bounding up the plush carpeted staircase at Dunhill's on Fifth Avenue these days, dispatched forthwith to fetch their employers' cigars.

The Dunhill Humidor Room, where monarchs, presidents, captains of industry and the merely rich have stored their finest cigars for decades, is closing. One does not wish to speak of such indelicate matters as financial affairs, but Alfred Dunhill of London can simply no longer afford to pay the soaring Fifth Avenue rents to store more than 400,000 of its clients' cigars.

In the Humidor Room, the private, climate-controlled cedar lockers – or 'keeps', as they are called – bear such names as President John F. Kennedy, Sir Winston S. Churchill, Alfred Hitchcock and Milton Berle.

Trouble is, a lot of the clients are dead.

William E. Geist
International Herald

Writes Wilkie Collins, the author of *The Woman in White*, in his famous Declaration of Dependence (he was an opiumite), that women will take pleasure in fumes derived from animal emanations, clarified fats and rarified spirits. He means perfume, of course, such as Chanel Number 5 and Diorissimo: smells from a trip in time. But then Collins affirms that they, women, illogically abhor the 'clean, dry, vegetable smell of tobacco'. Well, Wilk, read below. I know you are going to reply that woman is a sometime thing. Keep on reading, old boy. When it comes to smoking, if you roll your tobacco in paper, preferably white, and then add a little bit of tar (all roll-ups are half-caste), women will forget their favourite perfume to follow the scent of a cigarette. You see, they are holding it in their hand and next to their watch. It is so near to their heart that it ticks.

By the year 2002 men won't smoke cigars, all the best brands being priced out of the market in Europe and in the United States. The custom gone with customs, the country won't be needing any more a five-cent cigar as a democratic vista. But I'm not so sure about cigarettes. 'In women we trust,' could say the cigarette manufacturers in 2002 and after. Later, much later, in *We*, the Russian novel of 1922, by Yevgeny Zamyatin, the hero in a distant future country knows nothing of cigars but the heroine, called E–330, is a dishy number who knows all about the art of seduction and cigarettes, both absolutely prohibited by then. Says Zamyatin:

'I turned about. She was in a saffron-yellow dress of ancient cut. This was a thousandfold more wicked than if she had absolutely nothing on. Two sharp points, glowing roseately through the thin tissue: two embers smouldering among ashes.' Two cigarettes in the light perhaps? Two nipples? Two belly-buttons? No, no, no! – 'two tenderly rounded knees.' But wait: 'She was seated in a rather squat armchair; on a small square table before her stood a flagon of some poisonously green stuff and two diminutive stemmed glasses. In the corner of her mouth was the slenderest of paper tubes, sending up the smoke of that combustible substance the ancients used. (I have forgotten now what they called it.)' Let me help you. A cigar? No. A pipe? No, no! A holder? Warmer. A cigarette? That's it! Meanwhile 'she kept on sending up the smoke, glancing at me calmly from time to time, and negligently flicked the ashes from the tube on my pink coupon.' She will pay for that forbidden pleasure, you'll see. 'Listen,' I said, 'you surely must know that The One State is merciless to all who poison themselves with nicotine.'

William Powell is the triumph of style over content and of content over chagrin. He was an ugly, balding and perpetually middle-aged actor and yet his elegance, as natural as true elegance always is, his deft delivery and exact timing and the way he could wear a tuxedo and even white tie and tails and patent leather shoes to show them off and not seem to do so were not very usual at the time, roughly the Thirties – that decadent decade of the Depression and wars. He is not here because he was an *artifex elegantiarum* but because in *Jewel Robbery* he invented marihuana. He is a silk glove thief who administers his prospective victims with a cigarette that renders them so happy, helpless and sassy that they become carefree. Then, among smiles, giggles and loud laughter he proceeds to rob them clean. Now, if those slim white wands of instant happiness are not joints, what are they – livid nightsticks?

Auto da feu

Is it slang, right, as usual, when it calls a cigarette a nail in the coffin?

In *The Wild Angels* Bruce Dern, a dying motorbike rider who has been on grass all his adult life, has an urgent last request: 'Anybody got a straight?' – meaning of course a cigarette.

No smoking aloud

The ultimate dramatic use of a cigarette occurs in *Merry Christmas, Mr Lawrence*, in which David Bowie goes, literally, through the motions of smoking a cigarette while he is detained in solitary confinement in a Japanese concentration camp during the Second World War. Bowie in fact smokes a cigarette that isn't there: he lights it, he draws, he enjoys the smoke, throws the fag-end on the floor, and crushes it with his shoe, or rather boot. Though the cigarette is imaginary, therefore invisible, the enjoyment is as real as anything else on the screen, including Bowie. In terms of cigarette-smoking, who can ask for anything else?

Not Only The One State of the future but also the present state of things is against us smokers. In the end, in Zamyatin's novel, lovely, daring and carefree E–330, whatever her real name was, paid for her recklessness: she was apprehended, put in prison and executed. She was placed in a huge glass bell and burned to a puff. Smoke to smoke.

From midnight last night they banned smoking in Red Square too. A 'vast public ashtray' according to puritan Muscovites.

Evening Standard

So Zamyatin was right after all.

Smokers will be the last underground movement, smoke coming out of the grillework, gratings, vents, holes and man-holes – every city in the world aping New York in winter.

Cigarettes are for women – and can they be dangerous! But tough guys smoke them too. Some hard-boiled heroes roll their own cigarettes to look even more rugged. No Camels with soft bumps for me, sweetie. Mr Hardboiled Hero himself, Humphrey Bogart as Sam Spade, is seen rolling his own at the beginning of *The Maltese Falcon*. At least he is trying to roll his first cigarette of the day, an operation that requires him to be cool, calm and collected after hard-boiled eggs and dangerous black coffee. Rolling while drums roll on is Bogie when faithful Miss Perine comes in. She is his secretary. She is also honest Effie, the girl who calls Spade, Sam. She has come to announce that there is another girl outside who wants to call Sam, Spade. She's a knockout, she opines, a verdict that sounds queer in a woman, unless she is a referee. The knockout woman means business apparently. She is fateful Brigid O'Shaughnessy hidden under a spreading alias. 'Shoe her in, darling,' says Sam. *Shoe* her in? 'They shoe horses, don't they?' lisps Bogart still busy with his first roll-up of the day: the hard art of mugging.

The knack for rolling your cigarette, very much in vogue

during the Depression, out of necessity, became a true art in the 1960s. It was then, out of curiosity, that the young (and the not so young) were suddenly attracted, fascinated even, by some leaves of grass, marihuana, and its Oriental variety hashish, called hash by the initiated and the snob. They all dwelled in Cannabis Row and were known as Flower People when they should be known as scurvy grass. The hand-made marihuana cigarette came to be called a joint. In the 1930s this was known as reefer and was considered taboo. It was a scandal in fact to know that during a riff a reefer was found on jazzman Gene Krupa. They were as long as drumsticks, they say.

In *Sweet Smell of Success* Tony Curtis, as Sidney Falco ('A cookie full of arsenic' calls him Burt Lancaster, a sadist Satan for whom Curtis is a merry Mephistopheles), tries to smear the reputation of Martin Miller, who plays a jazzman of the cool school, by slipping in his coat pocket 'some shit', as marihuana was sometimes called. Luckier than Krupa, Miller goes to gaol but only briefly, his reputation as *intacta* as the *virgo* of Lancaster's sister, Miller's girlfriend and the apple of discord in the Big Apple, full of incestuous worms and righteous caterpillars of society.

But in the 1960s everybody was joining in on the act, even if all they knew how to play was possum on a stick. Some joints made then however were masterpieces of handicraft: the slimmest of slim cigarettes. Others were hideous *tayuyos* or tamal-like joints, a retrograde motion: back to Columbus. These were in fact crude white cigars. It is from these outlaw years, when smoking drugs made every house into a speak-easy, that several brands of rolling paper became even more popular than the best legit cigarettes. Such was Rizla, packed in bright red wrapping: the rice paper that the best heads preferred to roll, glue and pass around. In the 1970s smoking grass was substituted by sniffing coke and the best fingers became obsolete, superseded by a Lilliputian silver spoon and nostrils as sensitive as a Midtown tunnel. Today the art of cigarette-rolling is thriving again, probably because fashion is a vivacious, vicious circle. The paper snowtigers (as the joint used to be known under more Maoist mores) are back in town. Roll over, Spade.

The new rollers are among us not to sing and sin with

drugs but simply to increase their savings: thrift is a virtue again. The Boys from Chicago means now Friedman's men and not *mafiosi*. Cut tobacco can help you if not to kick the habit at least to cut the cost of smoking. Or perhaps the dandy in you would like to bring individuality back to your cigarette. Or you'll be able to smoke less. Consider this: when you are rolling up your own you are not smoking. Be that as it may, there are big billboards all over London, once a foggy town, advertising clear-cut tobacco for cigarettes with a catchy phrase. 'For a Real Roll-Up', says the sailory slogan for Old Holborn Blended Virginia. This is not by all means the only cut tobacco being advertised these days. (See a cut above.) Sam Spade would have been embarrassed not by Brigid's stunning body but by the choice of skin. He simply would not know how to start his day, caught among cuts. Tom also rolls his own – with a flick of the paw. But it is Jerry who must do the lickin', gluin' and lightin' up. Is he a man or – a mouse?

The first advertiser of the weed was that counterfeit intro-ducer of the tobacco plant in England, Sir Walter Raleigh. That honour (for some a dubious achievement) truly belongs to Sir John Hawkins, though Aubrey in his *Brief Lives* says: 'Sir Walter was the first that brought Tobacco into England and into fashion.' But Sir John was not a poet nor a friend of poets as Sir Walter was. Here is what Raleigh wrote in his 'Ode to Tobacco', an early jingle:

> But a true smoke is a durable fire,
> In the mouth ever burning.
> Never thick, never old, never dead.
> From myself away never turning!

Not a bad verse for a man who went in life from bad to worse. If Raleigh was not the first man to smoke in England, he was at least, with Spenser, the first to see the close connection between words written and the weed smoked. It was Raleigh by the way who lent solid currency in England to the American dream of El Dorado, first dreamt by Columbus after he read *Marco's Million*, many years before the Discovery.

All was not sweet leaf and light about the weed in England then. The man who gave us the Bible, King James himself, expectorated against smoking in his 'Counterblaste to Tobacco'. Though published anonymously it is a well-known fact that King James, who at least knew how to read, wrote it by rote. He begins by questioning the alleged medicinal value of the plant – and he was right. Tobacco is good for nothing except smoking. But then the king jumps like a knight from medicine to morals. This inkwell of virtue castigates in royal writing the habit of smoking for producing laziness – when it is just the opposite.

Aubrey tells a few tall tales about Raleigh, but one of them has some basis on fact. 'When Sir Walter was carried prisoner from the West to London, he lay at Salisbury, where by his great Skill in Chemistry, he made himself like a Leper.' If life were a mystery tale by Poe (who wrote of him) Raleigh would be made into a leopard. But one must remember that Shakespeare in *Hamlet* called the poison that killed King Hamlet a 'leperous distilment'. This is none other than the 'juice of cursed hebona' that Shakespeare took from Marlowe, who wrote instead 'hebon'. That is, henbane. But hebon is also ebony, the wood of night. According to Shakespeare the School of Night was the circle of magicians and nigromancers captained by Sir Walter himself. We've now come full circle. For Raleigh's contemporaries, a vicious one.

Raleigh was more ingenious than just disguising himself as a leper. He could weigh vapours, for instance. He in fiction even wagered with none other than Queen Elizabeth that he could actually weigh smoke. He then weighed some 'tobacco before he smoked it in this pipe, and then weighed the ashes'. He claimed that the difference was the 'weight of smoke'. According to lore the Virgin Queen paid up. But not before wittily 'remarking that she had known alchemists who could turn gold into smoke but Raleigh was the first to reverse the process'. Sir Walter never could achieve, though, an easier experiment with the weed: to turn tobacco into gold. That's what a pipe tobacco company did in our time. The name of that brand is, curiously, Raleigh.

Writes Andrew Sinclair in his brief biography: 'He ate a large breakfast and smoked a last pipe . . . He would be splendid at his final curtain.' That's Raleigh raked up.

Tobacco is always smoked at the smoker's leisure, not at the weed's pace. It's only with the introduction of the cigarette in Europe two centuries later that men (and women) were able to work and smoke. The pipe and cigars must be enjoyed in peace and quiet, and chewing tobacco needs space and a spittoon. Snuff is off.

But King James was a civilized man compared to the monarchs of the Orient. In Russia smoking was regarded as a moral crime: because it induced torpor and turpitude. What is this sin they called loaf? Vagrancy of course. The diligent Czar therefore imposed corporal punishment for the crime of puffing at a pipe. Twenty lashes was the best cure for all sinners. The unreformed had their unbending upper lips slit by law, inducing hare-lip in all staunch smokers. Others, with lips uncut, were sent to the Czar's first resort, Siberia. To the clandestine smoker the *samizdat* password was, Watch the Steppes. However today there are more smokers of *papirosha* (Russian for archaic *papelete*) in the Soviet Union than communists. Is this because both Marx and Stalin were heavy smokers? Dream cigars the former, pipe dreams the latter.

In Turkey an Ottoman ruler whimsically called Murad the Cruel, a true Turkish delight, left all Czars behind when he declared smoking a violation of the precepts of the Koran. He didn't number them but during the last five years of the reign of this sadistic Sultan twenty-five thousand Turks, turbaned or not, were smote for smoking. This is the same country that invented Turkish blend, which made possible all the Camels in America. Turkey in fact has originated more varieties of *Nicotiana* than any other country with the possible exception of Cuba. Obviously some of the heads the Sultan cut off were only empty turbans. Tobacco was introduced early in China by Spanish sailors from the Philippines and by Portuguese merchants operating from Macao. Smoking soon became as Chinese a habit as drinking tea. The Chinese are not cigar lovers but are as addicted to cigarettes as if they had invented them: where there's smoke there is a Chinese smoking a cigarette. The last ruler of the Ming dynasty attempted in 1641 to prohibit smoking, a ban that was not effective even in the Forbidden City. The Chinese gave the habit, together with art and ideograms, to Koreans and Japanese. Today China produces (and consumes) more tobacco than any other country in the world with the exception of the United States. Mao's chain-smoking gave the habit an imprimatur written in smoke on the Heavenly Gate. Tobacco is now the opiate of the Chinese.

Where the herb was greener, but more forbidden, was in Abyssinia. The Abyssinian Church sustained that the Fall occurred because Adam was tempted not by a serpent and a fruit coinciding in an orchard but by designing Eve herself. She had the knack of lighting Adam's tobacco and making him smoke and dream. That was not Paradise but *Parodyso*. Abyssinia is no more. There is Utopia, the best possible land ever. There is Dystopia, also called The Pits. And there is Ethiopia, the Holy Land of the Rastafarians, marihuana smokers all and the ballroom where Megistu dances his blood waltz. Abyssinia in all the old familiar phrases.

One of the first literary detractors of smoking in English was the author of a book very appositely titled *Work for Chimney Sweepers*. ('What did I tell you?' could ask de Xeres of Columbus.) Published in 1601 (the king's 'Counterblaste' was printed in 1604) it was signed with a pseudonym, Philaretes. It is widely accepted that it was written in fact by one Bishop Hall. Here, once more, tobacco becomes an *inventio diabolis* or the devil's design. Another English *tabakaphobe*, John Taylor, claimed that none other than Satan ordered his minions to propagate tobacco and smoking. Was Dr Pretorius the evil emissary or was the kind, musical Hermit the demon with a cigar? It is not a coincidence that this counterblast against tobacco was directed at the work of Catholic devils. Columbus was an Italian and a Catholic. So was Rodrigo de Xeres, so were the Spaniards, Portuguese and French who propagated the weed all over Europe. Even Sir Walter Raleigh was suspect, what with his Schoole of Night, his friendship with that man Marlowe, an atheist, and their slogan to Raleigh around the flagstaff, boys.

Taylor quoted an old saw, probably medieval, that warned 'Drink and the devil shall do the rest', to actualize it as 'Smoke and the devil shall do the rest'. Demonology, as *Malleus Maleficarum* proves, is an early Church doctrine. But it was precisely in England where tobacco clubs proliferated not long after the bishop's gambit. Compared to a Spanish writer like Francisco de Quevedo, a tobacco-hater in Madrid and in Toledo, Bishop Hall and John Taylor were very poor witchfinders. Thus Sam Slick, a contemporary held in contempt, was able to say: 'The moment a man takes a tobacco pipe he becomes a Philosopher.' In 1614 Doctor William Barclay published his *Nepenthes or the Virtues of Tobacco* and dedicated it to 'My Lord Bishop Murray'. Later one Dr Cheynell had the courage to defend tobacco-smoking against the opinion of his King James when the British monarch visited Oxford. All of this happened when Sir Walter Raleigh was still alive, though imprisoned in the Tower.

In 1642 Pope Urban VIII promulgated a raging Bull threatening with excommunication all churchgoers who smoked during the service 'the herb commonly called tobacco'. What happened then to those who had some Latin and called the weed Nicotiana? Or those who smoked grass? But the Pope was not joking about removing 'so scandalous an abuse from the temple of God'. He interdicted and forbade all 'persons of either sex, seculars, ecclesiastics and every religious order to take tobacco in the porches or interiors of the church, whether by chewing, smoking or inhaling it in the form of powder. In short, to use it in any shape or form whatsoever.' Which only shows that tobacco was a herb of a catholic persuasion.

A few years later back came the Plague again, accompanied as usual by the Distinguished Thing, and the new cure for it was – tobacco and smoking! The remedy became a vogue and the fashion was called Cuban Ebolition. Nobody knows what in hell (or heaven) this was – except that Ben Jonson wrote about it. In his play *Every Man out of His Humour* Jonson also speaks of Euripus and Whiffe, not two English comic characters but other forms of abolition. According to the erudite scholar Jerome Brooks, this 'suggests an agitated exhalation of the smoke' just like the retention of breath and then the sudden gulp and then again the whiff. The rest, of course, is a great tobaccanalia! (The term is not of my invention, alas, but true to the spirit of the seventeenth century.)

Whether the Bard smoked or not is a moot point, but that his audience did was a soot point. Edmond Malone in his *History of the Stage* (1780), drawing his dates from Ben Jonson and Beaumont and Fletcher, describes a Shakespearian audience *before* the beginning of the play, 'for as there were no reserved seats'. First come, first seated – or sated: 'while some part of the audience entertained themselves with reading or playing at cards, others were employed in less refined occupations: in drinking ale, or *smoking tobacco* . . . furnished by male attendants . . .' That was at the beginning of the seventeenth century. By 1660 'women smoked tobacco in the playhouses, as well as men'. Oh temperate mores!

Pepys has this to say of the weed and the plague (the entry is of 7 June 1665): 'The hottest day that I ever felt in my life. This day, much against my will, I did in Drury Lane see two or three houses marked with a red cross upon the doors, and *Lord have mercy upon us*! writ there which was a sad sight to me, being the first of the kind, that to my remembrance, I ever saw. It put me into an ill conception of myself and my smell, so that I was forced to buy some roll tobacco to smell and chew, which took away my apprehension.'

According to *Tobacco Talk*, 'It was popularly reported that no tobacconists or their households were afflicted by the plague.' Furthermore, 'physicians who visited the sick took (tobacco) very freely. The men who went round with dead carts had their pipes continually alight.' Naturally, 'this gave tobacco a new popularity, and it again took the high medical position accorded to it by the physicians of the French Court'.

The pendulum swings back from the pits in Spain and everywhere in Europe, even in Germany, where Luther in spite of the Diet of Worms (or perhaps because of it) didn't say anything of tobacco smoking. Though he had words for other worldly pleasures in a tone that comes very close to Marlowe as an elegiac poet: 'He remains a fool all his life who loves not women, wine and song,' said Martin Luther. This is the priest who threw an inkwell to the devil but not his pen. In France, another writer who loved wine and women and song as all too human, proclaimed tobacco divine. Said Moliere, *'Le tabac est divin: il n'est rien qui l'égale!'* Nothing equals it! This according to some historians, was the end of the Capet dynasty. That's probably going too far. I'd rather say that this was the beginning of the Gaulois Dynasty. Later came the Caporal.

Cigars always go up in smoke but they can become solid riches and even a sound investment. The scions of the wealthiest families in Britain take their treasure troves to deposit them in cedarwood cabinets in the cellars of Dunhill as if in the vaults of the Bank of England. Recently Sir

Maxwell Joseph died and left an estate of over £28 million – plus his stock of cigars. At the reading of his will his heirs eagerly wanted to know who got the Havanas. Who said cigars are a smoke?

What can be worse than tobacco then? Why, a tobacconist of course! Of those England had, according to Robert Burton in *The Anatomy* (take two), more than her fair share. Or in any case as many as 'Germany hath drunkards, France dancers, Holland mariners . . . and Italy alone hath jealous husbands'. But surely Burton must have heard of jealous Arabs manufacturing eunuchs and beheading interlopers in harems and seraglios? He must have read of one Moroccan mercenary in the service of the Venetian State who 'loved not wisely but too well'? But then again the 'honorary murderer' claimed that he was 'not easily jealous'. Burton the melancholy declared that 'there is much more need of hellebore than of tobacco'. What did he mean by that? He called all men 'misaffected, melancholy, mad, giddy-headed'. But why berate tobacco and praise hellebore, a plant with showy flowers but poisonous parts? To hell a bore!

Some old cigar smokers in Havana used to talk of a legendary Don Gil 'who knew all about cigars'. As a boy I thought he might be some Spanish gentleman living in Old Castile. But when I was old enough to ask, they told me that the famed Don Gil was a Londoner. '*Don Gil de Londres*,' the elders said. I failed to make the connection. Only after many a moon, when I first came to London, I heard of Dunhill: this was the Don Gil Cuban smokers were so much in awe of! I discovered then that Don Gil or Dunhill of London was in turn in awe of Cubans – not of the people but of the cigars. The original Alfred Dunhill opened a modest shop near Piccadilly in 1907. His shop still exists there but it's far from modest. It is now at 30 Duke Street, St James, as if advertising its nearness to the Court of St James. They will never do it blatantly, of course. It is the merest hint of their connection with royalty, which began with Edward VII, a lover of Cuban cigars and of English women – perhaps in that order.

Dunhill's is still an elegant place but they are rather nostalgic and melancholy in their publicity. 'About life's sadly declining pleasures', they state in a brochure that Robert Burton would have signed, 'of refinement and elegance the delight of smoking a fine cigar – with its subtle aroma and agreeable sense of satisfaction still reigns supreme.' The tone induces one to say 'Perhaps' and then to ask rhetorically: But for how long? One day cigars too will be the smoke of yesteryear. In the meantime let's enjoy the pleasure that was once only for priests, then of princes and has now been priced at what is an outrage for most mortals and certainly a reason for railing Thomas Marshall: there will never again be a good five-cent cigar.

Besides its famous shop, which stores cigars 'in individually-named Cedar Wood Cabinets' – against future needs or till death calls it a life. Dunhill's have fine cigars in stock and there's even a Havana cigar, Don Alfredo, 'hand-made exclusively' for the House of Dunhill, named after Alfred Dunhill, the founder. It is a pity though that they didn't call this superb cigar Don Gil.

Dunhill was followed by Zino Davidoff. Davidoff's name, as the aristocratic-looking English lady says in the potato chips commercial, is 'with two effs' – and just for being a snob and a phoney she is banished from the Captain's table forever. Monocled Captain ffoliot might be a potato chip addict but he is also a stickler for rules on board. No gate-crashers in the Captain's Party! The dinner is off. With two effs. Like the last Czar. But Davidoff doesn't have a Don Zino named after him in his chain of stores for chain-smokers of cigars in Switzerland, Paris, Spain and even London – on St James Street precisely, the street with old gentlemen's clubs that virtually surround the shop on the corner. It is Davidoff's lot that his establishment is a bit too garish for the street where he dwells – or at least where his cigars do. In his windows Davidoff displays not a cigar named after him but a whole artillery of Havanas especially rolled for him. They bear his name as a brand: Davidoff is now what old Bock used to be, almost what H. Upmann once was.

Zino Davidoff has a cigar factory in Havana where and with official approval – even with blessings from Castro – they make cigars that wear Davidoff's name on each band and on each box and even on the lids. One almost expects, as with Zanuck, the mark of Z on each cigar – or a Havana that writes in smoke a clear sign of Zino. The boxes have Davidoff's name burnt into costly genuine cedar wood and there are no *cromos* or any other embellishments, except for an imitation-silk ribbon that ties the cigars in a bunch. Davidoff's cigars ape sedulously the dramatic *mise-en-scène* of the Por Larrañaga of old, down pat to the dimensions of the box squat but proud – like a dwarf who knows he has just been promoted to midget. Davidoff doesn't print on the box the crop year, as Por Larrañaga always did, but everything else in this *nouveau riche* cigar brand comes from Larrañaga, even the sliding lid and the ribbon.

Davidoff's pretensions of transmuting cigars into wines remind me of Des Esseintes in *A rebours* claiming that his mouth was a pedal organ and how wine played 'silent melodies' with his palate – more cleft than clever or deft. Such transfers from one sense to another are always dangerous in art. (Beethoven's *Pastoral Symphony* is more a miss than a mass.) But to transmogrify cigars into keepers of smoke as a palatable spirit, is making them into some sort of jinny in the bottle. This won't do. A cigar is not a bottle of wine but yesterday's leaves that come in a box to haunt us: spectres, memories.

But Davidoff has made a major mistake. A man who undoubtedly knows about cigars (he lived in Cuba when he was young, worked in a *vega* and has been in the cigar business for nearly fifty years), Zino Davidoff enjoys his Goldoni reversal: he is now a master where he once was a servant. He has accomplished the fabulous feat of having workers in a communist country working full-time for a full-fledged capitalist in an all-profit venture. Now comes the blunder, now comes high hubris. Zino Davidoff named his cigars after French wines! Together with his proud name so full of effs, a guarantee caption (no seal but Zino's zeal) says 'Hand Made in Havana Cuba', in English and on each *boîte*, almost as big as his signature in calligraphy, the name of what Davidoff calls his *châteaux* in French: *Château Margaux*, *Château Latour*, *Château Yquem*, until we have the whole map of *vins de France* posing as cigars – or Cuban cigars posing as French wines.

Davidoff claims that he had this astonishing idea (bulb!) in 1947. He has been addressing his cigars as wines since then.

Rather presumptuously, Davidoff claims that his name has become synonymous with Havana, when he ought to say Havana cigars. He wanted to associate, as he says, *grand cru* cigars with *grand cru* French wines. (Gulp!) No wonder then that a Cuban ambassador in Paris diplomatically told Davidoff that 'the idea was impossible to realize' – at the time, added Davidoff. The design of the *mise en bouteille – pardon, mise en boîte* – is entirely Davidoff's, as he proudly presents it. But did it ever occur to Monsieur Davidoff, a shrewd businessman living in Geneva, that this *gaucherie* (to name Cuban cigars after French wines in neutral Switzerland) could be lucrative but ludicrous?

Talking of *nouveau riche* the Davidoff No 1 (there is no way to tell it from a Montecristo *Número Uno*) is the most expensive cigar in the world. It costs in Madrid, without the taxes you must pay in England, around 1,500 pesetas (around ten dollars *each*: Thomas Ryley Marshall would have turned in his grave!) and it is prohibitive in the USA: on Havanas considered as Cuban caviar to the general. This cigar is called, predictably, Dom Perignon (wham!). Actually the most expensive cigar today is a Havana Havana, the Montecristo A, which costs in England £11 (almost $17 per unit*). It is a nine-inch-long cigar, but the Dom Perignon is even more expensive at £9.90 (around $15) and only seven inches long: inch by inch the *Dom Perignon* is the most expensive cigar ever. The dawn they discovered cigars they also invented champagne.

Almost five hundred years after the Discovery Havanas are the best cigars in the world by far. Though the different

All quotations of course are from the time the pound was sound. Here are some other figures from Yesterday's Shopping of 1907. Por Larrañagas at 8/11d per sample, the very expensive Aguilas Imperiales; Partagas at 5/1d the Coronas and the cheapest Princeses Finas at 1/3d; H. Upmann Coronas at 5/5d and the most expensive cigar then, Villar y Villar at 10/11d the Villares! The catalogue is decent enough to inform its members that 'the Society has secured a large stock of the 1904 and 1905 Crops'. To add the caution: 'This is considered important in view of the partial failure and poor quality of the 1906 growth'. For Davidoff all Cuban crops, even if crap, are splendid.

brands that are still extant in Cuba are only names: they all are made in three unified factories to eliminate capitalist competitiveness and, supposedly, greed. 'At the beginning,' says a Dunhill salesman blowing rings of U-phoria out of the slim panatella of his body wrapped in brown, 'they wanted to make *all* the cigars in *one* factory and put *all* their cigars in one big box with no label on the lid.' He closed his eyes and then opened them again. 'That wouldn't do, of course,' he went on, 'so we persuaded them to do otherwise. That is, as before. Now we have all the old brands with those mottled, sorry motley, colours for the labels where they print their medals won at the exhibition of 1800 or whenever.' He breathed the dry air of Dunhill's as if it were men's cologne to add, inviting me into a secluded cedar wood cabinet with no name on the door: 'Do come in to peruse.' I looked at him, tall and wan as he was and told him: 'You should invite me to Cuba not to Peru.' 'I beg your pardon!' He didn't quite follow me, but when I followed him he let me know that he didn't appreciate my pun. The English, you see, have no sense of humour. He lifted his retroussé upper lip to show all his buck teeth without bothering to grin and exclaimed in a mock-Oxford tone but with genuine non-U finality: 'Oh, *that's* what you meant.' End of visit.

But there are other cigar-shops in London. There always were. Though old cigar-shops were sometimes more like curiosity shops. Take for instance Mr Salas's Cigar-Shop. 'There used some years ago to be a little tobacconist's shop somewhere between Pall Mall and Duncannon-street, by the sign of the Morro Castle. It was such a little shop, and it smelt so strongly of cedar and of the Indian weed, that itself was not unlike a cigar box . . . The Morro Castle . . . did a very modest but, I believe, remunerative business in cigars at from threepence to sixpence each. Well do I remember courtly old Mr Alcachofado, the proprietor of the Morrow . . .'

I'm sorry but I must say that Salas, he who has a palindrome for a name, is a fibber or perhaps a fib himself. The Morrow Castle is *el Castillo del Morro*, a fortress at the entrance of Havana harbour, which the British seized (castle, bay and city) in 1762. But the shop like a box is an invention. Its proprietor, Mr Alcachofado, gave the tale away. To call a man thus in Spanish is like calling him Mr Arty Choke. I know, I know, both Lana Turner and Ava Gardner had a husband with a similar name. But he was called Artie Shaw. Shop. There are other shops though that are more like enchanted cottages.

John Croley, a cigar-merchant in London, reveals the strange transformation suffered by H. Upmann, a true *Verwandlung* out of Kafka: 'The cigar manufacturer H. Upmann used to be a banker in the City of London with a branch in Havana. One day their manager down there, this is maybe one hundred years ago, had some cigars wrapped with the bank's name on the box and shipped it to London. Those cigars proved to be so popular that H. Upmann eventually gave up banking and went full-time into cigars.' That is the tallest story ever told!

Croley owns Robert Lewis, a concern in St James' Street, a shop which should be known as a cigar magic box. 'Kings have walked here,' says the man from *You*. 'Puffed here too,' interpolates an interloper. 'The walls are wood-panelled and lined with cigar-boxes. The cheap stuff is nearer the front door, a smoker's hand-me-down.' Really? 'The goodies are in back of me,' says the shop with a breath of fresh cigars. Some eighteen different brands that range between 350 and 400 different shapes and sizes. 'My, this is serious stuff!' claims a wooden voice. It is a shelf in search of a shoal of cigars or the self after the soul of the cigar – whichever arrives first. Shh! 'Here, people must speak in measured tones,' begs Robert Lewis in a disembodied voice. Some of them even speak in half-tones. Those are musicians, like Sibelius who liked to smoke between bars. Schoenberg, an infidel, smoked either in twelve tones or in no tone at all. He was atonal, do you hear. As to Cage I prefer a bird in the hand. 'If the salesman feels you are truly worthy,' says you, 'you might be invited downstairs to the basement.' They also have an attic upstairs, but that is only for exploding cigars.

'In the basement John Croley has established what might be the nation's only attempt at a cigar museum.' List!

Cigars are no longer a pastime reserved for the wealthy, says *You*. 'Such an expensive tick of smelly brown leaves!' That's a good definition of a cigar if I ever heard one. It must be Carroll's. But why not Lewis? 'King Victor Emmanuel used to come in to the shop himself.' That was the King of Hearts, no doubt. 'But most of the present royals are non-smokers,' said

Mr Croley. Most of the present royals are non-royals. Swiss! Switzerland is a republic, you know. 'In one glass showcase there is a mahogany cigar-box bearing the simple inscription, "The Fort". This was Edward III's personal humidor.' There are also humidors and a glass box of Havanas made for the Great Exhibition of 1851. 'I'm afraid they are unsmokable now.' You wanna bet? Send them all to New York for an auction and claim they are true Flor de Farach. *Farach?* Never heard of it. Neither have I.

Ledger books dating back to the mid-nineteenth century: 'I'm sorry to say,' a very old book says, 'that all our earlier ledgers have been lost.' One ledger opens to point at a handwritten account: 'August 9, 1900: 50 small Havana cigars at a cost of £4, plus 100 Turkish cigarettes for 11 shillings.' Those were sold to one Mr Winston Churchill. The man who was a Havana? Yes! I didn't know Churchill smoked cigarettes. 'Sir Winston didn't smoke good cigars until late in life.' Why is that? 'He didn't have any money then. Somewhere around the middle of the war the Cubans gave him a gift of 10,000 top quality cigars . . . My father was summoned to Number 10 to vet them.' But why? 'Just in case someone had adulterated them.' I have a better reason. What is it? Churchill was afraid that a Cuban had made one of his Havanas into an exploding cigar.

Robert Lewis sells spills, apparently from Cuban cedarwood. They might be so but what is undeniable is Croley's contention that London is the cigar capital of the world. One more truthful assertion of mine I am sure Mr Croley won't dispute: Robert Lewis is the most beautiful cigar-shop, barring none – in London or elsewhere. From the floor to the ceiling the display of cigar boxes, old and new, with or without *cromos*, is not only striking, it is most agreeable to the sight. The odour of Havanas is overpowering to the heathen but myrrh and mirth to the initiated. If I had to live in a shop I would dwell in Robert Lewis forever. The prices are, as in every cigar shop in London, forbidding. Forget therefore about the pound and the sound of silver and concentrate on the sight of so many cigars and the smell: the smell is like inhabiting the Odorama – and then there is the prospect of the smoke. They sell spills, yes, but they also sell spells.

I said good-bye to the shop but it didn't answer back. Shops never do. Old Man Proudhon was right: property is deaf.

Non-vintage Havanas

There is a new commercial line called *Non-Vintage Havana*. The vinaceous hands of M. Davidoff, he who smokes wines, must not be very far from this habit of calling any cigar a Havana. But off Davidoff they too cultivate the new vine. Some other cigar merchants in London advertise what looks in the bag like a category. 'Available in this country for the first time ever, these new exciting ranges of machine-made Havanas now offer a truly competitively priced cigar within the high standards of the world famous Havana brands.' This long sentence in the Queen's English is more or less saying that these are not hand-made Havanas but cheaper cigars made, like cigarettes, by machines in Havana. They offer the British smoking gentleman several brand names: La Flor del Caney, Flor de Cano, Troya and the bogus Quintero. Puros are for purists, therefore I don't see any heresy in smoking machine-made cigars, be they Havana or Manila. What is regrettable is the price of these cigars, definitely out of price if we compare them with a Dominican Ma Haya or a Hondura-made Don Ramos, all cigars rolled by Cuban hands in exile. Flor de Cano is a good machine-made cigar but it is not a cheap cigar at all. The Selectos of Flor de Cano are sold in England at £51.70 the box of 25 cigars. Ma Haya's box of coronas costs £61.00 in London, the nearest European cigar market from New York. While twenty Honduran Don Ramos cost £48.90 the Magnums, £47.20 the Gran Coronas, and £59.00 the Churchills. All these are very good cigars indeed and the Honduran Churchills are for deep-seat smoking.

With Cuban cigars nowadays you cannot simply rely on well-known brands of famous *marcas* any more. *Marcas* have become *maracas*: you must play them by ear. As William Tell said once discussing apples, 'It's all a question of trial and arrow. Tell Willie Boy I'm here.'

Says *The Guide to the Architecture of London*: 'Burlington Arcade, 1815–19, between Piccadilly and Burlington Gardens, W1, by Samuel Ware. This arcade built on a narrow strip in the garden of Burlington House in the years after Waterloo, is the archetype of London's arcades, and one of the few to have remained fashionable over the years.' It was Urban Grandeur, the well-known Edwardian architect, who built

the club in front of the arcade. Across the street again, a little
bit further down, almost at the corner, there, right there,
don't move, it won't take a moment. That's it! It's only for a
cigar and some matches at Fox Cigar Merchants, one of the
best tobacconists in London. They do Bolivar, Rey del Mundo,
Hoyo de Monterrey, Montecristo, Partagas, Romeo y Julieta,
Punch and H. Upmann – you name it. But, alas, they call the
old Larrañagas by the name of *Larranga*: a spurious name for
a fake cigar. Larrañagas, as we knew them, are no longer
extant. To call them Larranga makes me recall that old Tyrone
Power movie, *Captain from Castile*, in which the prototype for
Don Juan, the legendary Sevillian Don Miguel de Mañara, is
consistently being called *Maraña*, which in Spanish means
thicket. As soon as that tyro Power arrives in America the
plot thickets.

But at Fox's they have the courage of their confections.
They were the only English tobacco merchants to import,
display and sell Sosa cigars, made in Miami by that inde-
fatigable captain from the Canaries, Arturo Sosa, formerly of
Remedios, Cuba, who died in his Miami house, still fighting
after several exiles, still making cigars and still talking,
breathing and dreaming of the possible perfect Havana out
of Havana: the perfect *perfecto* Perfecto.

No matter what it says on the Cuban cigar-labels or bands
you now have only light Havanas, dark Havanas, short
Havanas, thick Havanas and slim Havanas – plus mild and
strong Havanas. The rest is propaganda. You don't buy a
Montecristo any more, but a full-flavoured cigar that can
have that particular brand or wear the Romeo y Julieta
colours in chromo. No matter which it will be made in
Consolidado Numéro 1 or of *Fabrica de Tabacos 3*. Nevertheless
at Dunhill's their Don Alfredos, their Don Candidos and
their Flor de Puntos still look as specially made for them and
as alluring as the fake Por Larrañaga they now make in
Havana – elegant, in spite of the brass catch on a fair
imitation of their old *boîte nature*: Por Larrañaga's nature box
of *ci-devant* cigars. 'They keep changing boxes,' said the man
from Dunhill in Havanas. 'But the cigars are the same.' Are
they really?

Hunters & Frankau, the English cigar importers who have
been doing business with Cuba for the past 130 years, didn't

agree with Dunhill on the number of factories that are making cigars in Havana now. 'It doesn't matter if there are three or five,' said Hunters or perhaps a frank Frankau over the telephone. He was non-committal enough to give the impression that merely talking shop with a Cuban exile might suddenly imperil their business deals with Cuba. He summed up all his courage to add: 'Anyway the whole point is futile as all the cigar factories in Havana are now closed.' Why was that? 'Lack of leaf.' He meant not to describe Eve before the Fall but not having enough tobacco in Cuba to roll one cigar. This is some sort of culmination.

The 1979–80 crop was terrible because of the great damage caused to the weed by the blue mould. The 1980–81 crop was disastrous because of hurricane Alberto (formerly Alberta: even hurricanes can change sex in mid-course now) which destroyed whole plantations in Vuelta Abajo, all of them declared disaster areas. 1981–82 was good again: the weed is strong. The Cuban chart adopted by Davidoff and published by him claims that it was 'Exceptionnelle', with Gallic flavour – or is it favour? The truth is that if in 1980 the Government was forced for the first time in Cuban history to import tobacco leaf from abroad, 1981 was too soon for such a miraculous recovery. Apparently the 1981–82 crop was only fair. Then there was a partial recovery when suddenly earlier this year heavy rainstorms virtually destroyed all the crops in large zones of Vuelta Abajo, affecting the Hoyo de Monterrey zone. The charges against the CIA, made by the Cuban Government, of poisoning not a cigar but obliterating whole plantations, became more ludicrous than fantastic.

And yet, 'the luxury, the elegance, the snobbishness of smoking a cigar, and therefore its aesthetics,' writes the anthropologist Bronislaw Malinowski, 'are certainly forever associated with three syllables: Havana'. But what of the Havana far from Havana then? Not only cigars but whole factories were exported from Cuba to the United States since the last century.

In 1831 a chinchal was established on Key West. A chinchal (literally a room full of bugs: chinche, a bedbug, is another name for a cheap cigar) is less than a cheruta, the smallest of factories (from cheroot, a home-made hand-made cigar), but there were no more than fifteen cigar-rollers working full time. It was from these humble beginnings that the cigar city of Ibor (the Borough of Ibor City) made Tampa famous in the smoking world at the turn of the century. Much of the money to fight for Cuban independence from Spain was collected by José Martí and other Cuban patriots canvassing for bullets not ballots. The Havanas made in Tampa became thus true exploding cigars. According to some historians it was one of their dynamite sticks that blew the battleship *Maine* in Havana harbour, the ship that launched a war and an empire.

When I visited Camacho in Miami on a Sunday morning there were *torcedores* at their job. Curiously one of them was a woman – or rather a girl. After talking to a man busy with some cigar-boxes, he went inside to return with a tall, dark man. He was Camacho all right. He was reserved too, almost mistrustful. He had reasons to be. The Camacho family left Cuba when Fidel Castro, after seizing power, seized their thriving factory in Havana. They didn't leave in a Dudgeon, as reported, but on a Douglas DC10. The Camachos fled to Nicaragua of all places. There they prospered again. When the Sandinista Government threatened them with Nicaraguaing (Camacho's own words) their factory or else, they didn't have to wonder what else would be. Nationalization, as in Cuba, was then a consolation devoutly to be wished: or so they thought. They offered Camcho *fils* to become the official head of their cigar factory in Managua. That's what Fidel Castro did with Camacho *père* in Havana twenty years before. Young Camacho knew what that resistible offer actually meant: to become an officially appointed manager in his own business: some sort of surrogate for the boss but on the Government's payroll. He said *no* in Spanish twice in a decade. Penniless he left Nicaragua and came to Miami FLA. This land, as it had been for Ponce de Leon, had to be a land of riches or land enough for a grave. Six feet of Florida was all that Ponce got, but Camacho was a winner. When I told him that I was an author in search of cigars he seemed to be skeptical. When I said that I was looking for the Holy Grail of smokes, he opened the inner door of his factory and opened up. What he had to say was not particularly interesting, though. I wanted a myth, he offered me figures instead. Camacho's sole concern is his concern.

His Miami factory is dealing with tall orders from all over

the United States and his agents, of all people, are Savinelli Pipes, from Decatur, Indiana. Camacho manufactures more than 150,000 cigars a day, most of them made in El Sagües, Cuban Spanish for Miami's South West, in spite of the publicity which claims that all Camacho cigars are made in Honduras. Contrary to May Rosa the Camacho cigars are presented in an attractive way, professionally and even nostalgically correct: their *cromo* is exactly like the one Camacho used to wear in Cuba. They manufacture an outstanding variety of *vitolas*: from El Cesar, one of the biggest cigars ever, to their stubby Monarcas and the Elegantes, slim and mild panatellas. They also make a Conchita that is like a *media panetela* or half a panatella: a piece of a tart. All the cigars are available in Natural, Maduro and Claro which is like the *claro pajizo* (literally the colour of light straw) of lore: a paler shade of Havana.

The cigar from the Canary Islands (what Bertolt Brecht called *die Zigarren von des Kanarischen*) is nowadays the only true *puro*, the Cinderella of cigars. The smoker who meets a Condal, for instance, can look for the glass slipper, now made of cedarwood instead of crystal, and see how just before midnight the cigar becomes fragrance, then smoke, then myth, then ashes, then memory, then nothing. In yet another quest the Spanish go looking for the Holy Grail of smoke. Last year it was the Cohiba from Cuba, now it is the Condal from the Canaries, especially its Number 6, which cannot be found just anywhere. From Saragossa to Seville and from Bilbao to Barcelona, Condales are hardest to find. This is the most expensive Canarian cigar ever and if you are after it, like I was, perhaps you'll get lucky and find it – in old Madrid.

After chasing after it all over Spain I found it in Santander of all places. Santander is a city on the northern coast of Spain, at the bottom of the Bay of Biscay. Therefore it is a huge humidor made by a smoking God who knows all about cigars. It was there that I smoked my first Condal *Numéro 6*, a longish panatella with a longing: she wants to live in luxury. She is therefore expensive. As with many famous professional beauties my first encounter with the panatella was a disappointment. Some cigars taste of ashes even before they are lit. The Condal panatella didn't taste of ashes: it tasted of the weed all right, but it also tasted of the straw. It was a faint odour of hay, I admit, but there it was: a whiff of dry grass that aspires to the condition of leaf. It was straw, dried straw, at last, at least, but a straw strong enough to break a camel's pack. Or a pack of Camels.

But on the Canaries you can smoke a cigar which is the opposite of a Condal: cheaper and sometimes better. It is the cigar of Breña Alta. Writes Enrique Calduch, a Spanish connoisseur:

> The people of the small town of Breña Alta, on the Island of La Palma (Canary Islands) claim proudly to be the world's most discerning tobacco smokers. Theirs is no idle boast, for the greater part of townsfolk earn a living from the production of cigars though not in factories or in organized industry, but rather individually in their own homes, hand-rolling and constantly on the lookout for those qualities in a cigar which most satisfy their many clients.

These cigar-makers from the Canaries are known as *chinchaleros*, from the Cuban *chinchal*. There are many Cuban words, mostly Havanan, that made the trip back to the Canaries: from island to island. One is *guagua*, Cuban for bus, another is *chinchal*, the smallest concern that makes cigars. 'These cigar artisans,' claims Calduch, 'go round personally selling their bundles of cigars in bars and shops: indeed such has been their success that they now head the domestic market on the Canaries . . .' The cigar-makers, many of whom have worked previously in Cuba, buy tobacco from the Cameroon, Mexico, Indonesia, wherever, storing them in their own homes – where they also have their factories: a *chinchal*. According to Calduch 'all the bars on the Canary Islands always have stock of these enjoyable, inexpensive and perfectly finished craftsmen-rolled cigars. There cannot be many towns in the world like Breña Alta where the locals proudly – and even a little pompously – confer upon themselves the title of *Professors of Cigars*.'

There you are. On the Canaries you can find the cheapest and one of the most expensive cigars made in Europe. Wherever.

Is there something worse than bad verse? Yes, a bad cigar.

And worse than that? A cigar that goes dead on you. Let's say you are smoking contentedly and you are suddenly distracted. Or that the worse has to do with you and the night and the music. Or even more catastrophic, that you are smoking and the girl is willing. You forget all about the cigar and even about yourself and you let yourself (and your cigar) go. Then, some time later, when you come to, you remember the cigar and see it is still in mint condition. Which is more than you can say about the night and the music. And even the girl, whom you have utterly forgotten by then. You now take it all back and put your cigar in your mouth and you drag and you pull and you puff – and you know what? You have a stiff, buddy, in your hand. The damned smoke won't smoke. It's dead!

Now you'll feel the most godawful taste in your mouth: the taste of ashes: a feedback. Ugh! But let's say that you loved that cigar as you've never loved another cigar on earth. What is to be done? Well, you can bury it in the nearest ashtray. But what would I do then? Try an epitaph? Is that a new brand, Epitafios from Hoyo de Monterrey? No, just try to say something sass about the dead cigar. *De mortuis*, you know. Let me think. 'It was too soon that it was done for/I wonder why it was begun at all.' Is that all right? That will do. Or you can forget about it and light a new cigar. Cigars, as life, must go on.

9 December 1983 was a momentous day for American cigar smokers. An unusual full-page advertisement in *Variety* announced 'The First Auction of Its Kind – A Vintage Collection of CUBAN CIGARS'. What was unheard of was not the sale of Cuban cigars in the United States but for *Variety* to announce it. This confirms once more the association from time immemorial between the cigar and show business.

The auction was of 200,000 cigars to be 'divided into varying amounts'. This could attract the attention of 'individual smokers, gift givers and cigar dealers alike'. The auction took place at the Seventh Regiment Armory, on New York's Park Avenue. The catalogue alone cost $5. The event lasted from 10 a.m. until 6 p.m. – and it was a riot!

New York magazine announced, though did not advertise, the sale. But its copy was better than any ad: 'Havana Cigars

Evade the Embargo', said a title and the story claimed: 'For the first time since the United States embargoed Cuba, in 1960, New Yorkers can legally lay hands on a supply of Cuban cigars for Christmas.' *New York* also clarified the smoke: 'The cigars are a pre-Castro product, but we had to get government permission to import them,' explained Arlan Ettinger, president of Guernsey's, an East Side firm that will auction the cigars. 'The cigars were being shipped to Spain when Castro took over. They sat in a Spanish warehouse because the importer died and his heirs spent fifteen years bickering about the will.' The story ended like the silver lining on a golden cloud of cigar smoke: 'The bidding is expected to go as high as $300 a box.' But it was the *New York Times* that gave the event a seal of approval with just one front-page headline: 'CUBAN CIGAR DISCOVERY LURES BUYERS'. Then, after the fact, they had a story on the front page next day with a photo showing the auction hall with standing room only. A few gentlemen buyers were seen sporting big cigars already. As the photo was taken early in the morning, it only shows that those cigar-chomping New Yorkers could be prospective buyers of very expensive cigars but, of course, they were loud and lousy smokers. Says the title underneath the photograph: 'Sold: Cigar Boxes of Legal Cuban Treasures'. Then the copy ran and ranted, grandly: 'This,' said one George Warner, standing before a six-foot high altar of golden cigar boxes containing what he considered ambrosia of the gods, 'is a religious experience.'

Well put – and better sold. Soon all the cigars were gone (with the smoke?). 'Price estimates in the catalogue,' said the *New York Times*, 'showed that the auction house expected to get $2 to $12 for each cigar.' Wow! 'But Arlam Ettinger had a wide grin as a bidder who identified himself as Al Goldstein', a true gold nugget of a smoker, publisher of *Cigar* and, what else?, *Screw Magazine*, outbid a standing-room-only crowd of several hundred people for the first lot of 25 cigars. His bid was $2,100 or $84 a cigar. The rest was not silence but shaking of hands, rattling of money and rolling of eyes.

Cigars sold so expensively need some explaining. It was done by Lew Rothman, president of the J. R. Tobacco Corporation and – 'discoverer of the Cuban cigars'. Practically, if not another Columbus, at least a second Rodrigo de Xeres.

Our present-day de Xeres, as his ancestor de Torre, spoke of his find. He guaranteed their freshness, elaborating that 'they had been kept in a climate-controlled warehouse in Spain since their shipment from Havana in 1958 . . . He had refreshed them for six months in a humidor and had test-smoked a few himself.' Mr Rothman didn't explain that cigars so sold can never be 'refreshed' – whatever that is. Cigars are actually highly perishable. Besides, they are all practically unfit for smoking after ten-year storage. You see, no matter what Davidoff tells you, cigars are not wine, in spite of the brand name. Talking of names, all the auctioned cigars were made by Flor de Farach, a lesser manufacturer in old Havana. But Mr Rothman had a gracious turn of phrase to end the auction, bearing in mind (and word) everything that has been said above: 'I guess no more than 10 per cent of these cigars will ever be smoked,' he said. (He never explained: he could not complain.) 'It's like the rarest bottle of wine. There's no occasion good enough to drink it.' The band in the room played, very fittingly, 'Smoke Gets in Your Eyes'. It could have played a Twain variation: 'All Crowds Have a Silver Lining'. Riley was right. What his country needs is an $84 cigar.

At exhaustion point: 'Young man, don't you ever dare put a cigar on a pedestrian.'

Connoisseur, the American magazine with a French name, published recently an article on cigars written by a journalist called Alan Schwartz. This cigar scholar tried the impossible twice: to find the 'best cigar' in the world other than in Cuba and to demythify the Havana. The magazine displayed the article fully and gave it the cover, in which nine cigars appeared to be 'The World's Best Cigars'. (One must assume that the tenth little Indian is a hidden Havana.) One of the nine is a brand already famous from its Cuban days, Hoyo de Monterrey, which is of course the name of a valley in Vuelta Abajo, Cuba. Some of the other eight have a familiar ring to them (Santa Clara or Vuelta Arriba, Cuba) but the rest sport such names as Mocha and Fundadores. Come on, fellas! Even Davidoff could do better than that. But between the ranks of Don Pepe and Mocambo (the last named in honour of John Ford, I suppose) is the name of the cigar which for Schwartz is *the* best in the world – or close to it. It is called Excalibur. If only King Arthur smoked at the Round Table! Obviously he could have made his sword into a cigar. That's an easy trick for any old magician. Cigars do burn, but to transform a cigar into a flaming sword? Obi Wan Kenobi shook his head. Merlyn said: 'This, sir, is, in two words, *in* possible.'

Schwartz begins his cover story with a statement about the Cigar Rush suffered recently by New York smokers. Ludicrous! he says after handling as evidence what looks like a pile of decrepit boxes of Farach cigars. 'The only thing that matters about the cigars shown here,' he states, 'is that they were made in Cuba.' But that's exactly what Havanas are: cigars made in Cuba. As the song sings it: 'There's no Havana cigars without Havana'. Then there is a witness for the prosecution with more evidence. 'I'd say Hoyo de Monterrey Excaliburs from Honduras,' attests one Mr Wagner of the Cigar Warehouse in Los Angeles, 'is the closest to the finest Cubans.' Schwartz then embarks on a visit to all the best cigar-makers in the Western Hemisphere (excluding the Philippines), who turn out to be Cubans all.

It goes without saying that I could agree with Schwartz (*) about the excellence of Honduran, Dominican and Tampan cigars. But I cannot concur at all with one bit of historical fact that is actually false. 'The Dominican Republic,' says Schwartz to support the claim to excellence by Dominican cigars, 'is where Roderigo de Xeres, who travelled with Columbus, is alleged to have smoked the first cigar in the New World on October 28, 1492.' This is more than a blunder, this is a howler. Rodrigo de Jerez (modern spelling) first saw and smoked tobacco in what is today Gibara, formerly an Indian village in Oriente Province, Cuba. Columbus (and this is a historical fact) discovered Cuba exactly on 28 October 1492. Although the Admiral of the Ocean Sea could work miracles with geography, he would have needed more than magic to be on the *same* date discovering the Dominican Republic *and*

I'll do more than that: I'll surrender to evidence. After being smoked, Excalibur cigars manufactured by Hoyo de Monterrey in Honduras proved to be a great cigar indeed. Especially Excalibur Number VI (why the Roman numerals, so confusing, so uncigar-like?), which is one of the best cigars I've ever tasted, a true panatella flute. What melody is makes!

Cuba. As a matter of fact what Columbus discovered at a later date was the island of Haiti, which he proceeded to call Hispaniola. Both modern Haiti and the Dominican Republic share today that tiny island. The first cigar (or its rough sketch) was smoked by de Jerez on, appropriately, Sunday. That is probably why, being a profound Catholic, Columbus refused to share a smoke on a Sabbath.

All the cigars named above by Mr Schwartz are placebos for pleasure. Just like the Spanish cava wine. It comes in a champagne bottle, it bubbles like champagne, it even tastes of champagne – but of course it is not champagne. All is not lost however. If the quest is over, the spirit of a smoke is felt like the spirit of love in this story. Asked Dan Blumental, appropriately talking of cigars, 'Who is the girl of your dreams?' Schwartz had to answer, 'She had a Cuban name.' Then he went to compare her 'to the inaccessible prom queen'. Ah yes, *hermano* Schwartz! Right you are! I knew her once too. But never well enough, alas.

The best tobacco in the world is theoretically still grown in Cuba and the best cigars are allegedly still made in Havana, but one of the best Cuban cigars out of Cuba is made in Manhattan, that city of cheap cigars and fat smokers – or is it fat cigars and cheap smokers? What Thomas Riley Marshall, Vice-President of the United States under Woodrow Wilson said ('What this country needs is a really good five-cent cigar') is probably still true. But what America has, now costs more than five cents (not even an exploding cigar costs five cents anymore!) but it is certainly more than a good cigar: it is an excellent cigar. It is called May Rosa and is made in the middle of Manhattan, off Union Square, where Martí held so many meetings in the 1880s. Don't expect if you go there a posh establishment with splendid windows, like those of Dunhill's and *chez* Zino. You won't even find the little black boy at the door used to advertise cigar-stores in Europe as wooden Indians did with good old US of A. By the by, this iron black boy originated the nursery rhyme 'Ten Little Niggers' that in turn inspired Agatha Christie's novel. Why Hollywood changed the original title to *Ten Little Indians* remains a mystery within a mystery. (A clue: it had nothing to do with cigar-stores.)

May Rosa cannot compete with Davidoff or with Dunhill

in their glossy displays and dressed windows but they stock eight or more *vitolas* (Churchill, Senadores, Imperiales, Cetros, Presidentes, Ambassadores, Queens and Panetelas) and they are all winners: the smoker takes all. For Cuban *fumadores* in exile in New York they are cigars fresh enough to be compared with a Havana smoked in Havana, a feat possible only in winter dreams – that can become nightmares so suddenly in summer. For some American and English smokers these cigars might be pronounced green. In England, for instance, they let a cigar that is fresh and soft and smells of the tropics rest until it 'matures'. This could take a year sometimes. Why the difference between a Cuban cigar in Havana and another one in London? The answer is simple. In Cuba all cigars are fresh. Today there's no reason why a faraway smoker shouldn't have his cigar as fresh as in Havana – except of course for what travels slowly and Tevye sings in praise: tradition.

May Rosas are made (and this is only my guess) from Jamaican or Dominican filler and a wrapper from Cameroon. That's how another good Cuban cigar in exile, Sosa, is made. Though Sosas are rolled in the Dominican Republic, with banding, boxing and sales done in Miami. As are other Cuban-American cigars like Benedit, Caballero and Moro. José Padron, the biggest Cuban cigar-maker in the USA (he claims to be selling close to 3 million cigars a year – and thatsa lotsa cigars!), recently suffered the misfortune (or the miscalculation) of going back to Havana with a commission of exiles on a nostalgic bender. Down the Cuban way he distinguished himself by offering one of his Cuban cigars made in exile but non-poisonous to Fidel Castro himself – near a photographer as bold as Señor Padron to capture the burning offering. Upon his return to Miami Padron saw his best cigar store blown sky high late one night. It was not, of course, an exploding cigar *ex tempore* but an opportune counter-revolutionary Cuban time-bomb – the only punctual thing with exiles.

The colour of May Rosa cigars is dark Havana and they wear no band. But they are no Por Larrañaga: unfortunately they come individually wrapped in cellophane. This is a drag for the smoker who knows better than to sniff at his cigar. (It is something worse than what gorgeous Gigi did to Gaston's Havana by placing it next to her jewelled earlobe to wait for the cigar to crack above the din of dim Maxim's and the thunder of the rocks in her ear-ring: a brass band.) For us faithful smokers it is the sight and the skin of a cigar that counts: good cigars are notorious soft touches, both generous in fragrance and smoke. All May Rosas come in odd, large boxes of some light wood that is definitely not cedar but that could be called, as in cheap coffins, pitch pinewood. The box is poorly made and the lid is crudely closed with some sort of pallid masking tape. To top it all off the cigars are wrapped collectively in hideous polythene. They look in fact like the casualties of exile wrapped in a plastic bag. But the brown body of the cigar, like a beauty in shabby clothes, is what counts. Naked, a May Rosa is like a single thigh of the negresses that made Mérimée dream of Cuban caresses: May Rosa is perhaps the best Cuban cigar made in the USA today. It is, indeed, a most exotic American product: a cigar made on Broadway. Had T. R. been a producer and not a *politico*, he could have said that what this city needs now is a good five-cent peepshow. May Rosas have what you can call a draw-back though. They must be smoked fresh, for with age they tend to become strawy. This is true of most cigars, I suppose. But before the memory of May Rosas fades, May Rosas fade.

The cigars I've been talking about come only from the western hemisphere. I want to comment briefly on the excellent cigars produced in the antipodes: the Philippines.

Filipino cigars were exceptional from the very beginning. Spanish sailors took the first Cuban tobacco seed to the Philippines at the end of the sixteenth century. Spanish planters profited from the rich Filipino soil and the climate of the Asian islands so similar to Cuba's. Early Spanish traders formed a tobacco monopoly that was abolished only in 1881, long after the royal trade *estanco* was suppressed in Cuba. Today the Philippines produce quite a few cigars of good quality, like the constant cheroot Ben Gazzara smoked in *Saint-Jack*, which the crooked Bogdanovich (it rhymes with rich) found so distasteful. He lured Gazzara into his trap with genuine Havanas: cigars as black pieces in a power chess game. To my knowledge Manilas are worth being bribed with, especially those from La Flor de la Isabela, with their box with the name branded by fire and all the legends in Spanish. Once the official language of the Philippines,

134

Spanish is now like Greek in Egypt: the verbal memory of a past nobody remembers any more and it's only perpetuated on the name of an island and a box of cigars. Manilas were the cigars poetess Amy Lowell preferred. She was so addicted to the Filipino weed that when she saw the First World War coming from afar she bought 10,000 'of those'. Filipinos were cheap cigars those days but not *that* cheap.

After the War and 10,000 Manilas, Amy Lowell was still going strong. Here is how Robert McAlmon saw her seeing the War:

> Before I had come [to Paris] it had entered my mind that Amy Lowell and Gertrude Stein were much the same type . . . That is not an experience I had had personally with her, but the source is authentic. So also is the source for the story of Amy being caught in London in 1914 when war was declared. She was late for an appointment because of the crowds massed in the streets, and she was indignant that the police had done nothing to help her make her way to the hotel. 'Don't they know I'm Amy Lowell?' she shouted and lit herself a long cigar and strode up and down the hotel room. 'And it's in such a moment that my book of poems is going to come out here!' . . . But one thing was certain, Amy did weigh a good deal more than Gertrude.

I don't know if McAlmon in *Being Geniuses Together* means literary or physical weight, what I know is that he describes Amy Lowell as an inveterate cigar-smoker. She was also a hardy lesbian. But Gertrude Stein, who was a lesbian too, didn't smoke. On the other hand, though George Sand was no lesbian she smoked cigars. McAlmon, quite simply, was a gossip. But so was Scott Fitzgerald and so was Hemingway, who in his letters is always begging to be sent over the 'latest dirt'. This was no lost generation, this was Lot's Generation, always looking back in the general direction of Sodom and telling it like it was. This is in fact the Get Lost Generation. Gertrude Stein with a Baedeker, Amy Lowell with a cigar. 'Drop, drop the dirt / O'er the thin wrapper of my Manila at large.'

Bonnie Parker smoked cigars and wrote poetry, just like

Amy Lowell. Does this make Parker with a cigar a Lowell with a gun? Who is best remembered? Who wrote this, Amy or Bonnie?

> As the flowers are made sweeter
> By the sunshine and the dew,
> So this world is made much brighter
> By the likes of folks like you

That was of course Amy Lowell. Yes? Definitely! Wrong. It was Bonnie Parker writing on the run. Poetry of the running board, one might call it. Laments on the lam.
    And this? Bonnie or Amy? Or both?

> But I won't die. You'll see.
> I'll find some way o' livin'.
> Even if they bury me, I'll live.
> You can't kill me. I ain't th' kind to kill.
> Ef there's a Devil to help me do it!

The gay desperada or Amy the orotunda? Amy Lowell of course.
    Nellie Melba, the Australian coloratura who invented the Peach Melba, was no lesbian. Sopranos seldom are. (Men sopranos were called castrati even before Castro.) They can be bald, like Ionesco's, or bold, as Enesco's, but never belong entirely to the tribe of tribades. Madame Melba was actually named Mrs Armstrong, née Mitchell. She took her stage name from Melbourne and her vocal strength from smoking cigars: she had a Havana before every performance. She loved to blow smoke rings, a childish thing, really. But she never sang in *The Ring*. Dame Melba knew that *L'Africaine* was an opera by Meyerbeer but also that La Africana was a cigar factory in Havana. Its owner always sent Dame Melba his choice *torcidos* everywhere she went to do a Melba. By the way, it was at La Africana where the first Cuban woman rolled a cigar in 1878. She was neither a slave negress nor a freed *mulata* but a white woman. Shades of Mérimée. She was no lesbian either. Shame of Pierre Louys.
    A notorious cigar-smoking lady early in the century was the English benefactress (of James Joyce, the Sitwells and

later Dylan Thomas), Bryher Ellerman. She was married to (coincidence?) Robert McAlmon, and the American poetess H. D. (initials only please) was her lover for life. H. D., in turn, called her constant companion Fido. Typically, Fido's mistress didn't like smoking and, among other American eccentricities, during the London blitz she refused adamantly to eat chicken for fear that it might be cat. She was, in psychiatrist Havelock Ellis's curiously physical description, 'a shy sinous figure, so slender and so tall that she seemed frail, yet lithe, one divined, of firm and solid texture'. Freud, another consulting detective, was more to the point and divined more accurately: he told her that she was bisexual – but, mind you, 'a classic example of bi-sexuality'. Did the master analyst ever guess that she suffered from cigar envy?

The greatest cigar-smoking woman on the screen was not Merle Oberon as George Sand in *A Song to Remember* (and a film to forget) with Cornell Wilde playing Chopin. In fact she didn't smoke at all in this romance *à clefs* of a weak Chopin and a strong Sand plus a pianoforte. Merle Oberon didn't even caress a panatella close to her ear the way silly Lilly Caron did in *Gigi*. Though the film's director, Charles Vidor (a Hungarian, therefore as devoted to cigars as Michael Curtiz and Alexander Korda were), constantly prodded the star to imitate George Sand – whose name Vidor insisted on pronouncing, God knows why, George Sanders. Miss Oberon was as adamant as a leading lady should be. 'Smoking is unladylike,' she would insist. 'I won't smoke!' And she didn't. But a true first lady did. Beulah Bondi, enacting Mrs Andrew Jackson already installed in the White House, smoked a yellow corncob in *The Gorgeous Hussy*.

Briefly about corncobs, a curious item appeared in *The New Yorker*:

(When President Truman relieved the General of his command in Korea in the spring of 1951, a corn-cob-pipe company in Washington, Missouri, where the manufacture of that device had begun, in 1872, and where a brisk-selling item was the Mac, received a slew of orders from numbers of ruffled adherents of the General who wanted to send him the pipes as evidence of their unwavering loyalty. People who had seen MacArthur off camera, though, had the strong impression that he preferred to smoke cigars.)

An iconoclast is a breaker of sacred images, according to *The Concise Oxford Dictionary*. 'Fig. One who attacks cherished beliefs!'

When Dickens went to Paris in 1885 he met Aurore Dupin, Baronne Dudevant, the woman Ernest Renan called '*la harpe eolienne de notre temps*'. (I hate to translate this as 'the Eolian harp of our time' – whatever that means.) This Frenchwoman was none other than George Sand. She was ahead of her time, according to Joyce Read, an Oxford specialist on French literature, 'leading a trousered life in Paris'. Trousered and cigared. In the movie Merle Oberon kept only the trousers. Both ladies were billed by Hollywood as 'exotic'. Neither by the way was the least erotic. But rhyme has its reason.

'Cuba was known for her cigars, made from a crop in a tiny stretch of western Cuba which produces tobacco as much respected internationally as the wine grown on the Cote d'Or in Burgundy,' says Lord Thomas of Swinnerton. The analogy between French wines and Havana cigars is, it seems, unavoidable. It is now indeed a long way from the time Panduca revealed the secret of the tribe to Pela, formerly from the Canary Islands. In fact a cigar is the culmination of the most sophisticated cultivating, harvesting and processing of a plant (in this case its leaves not the fruit) the world has ever seen since the monks in the Middle Ages revived the art of making wine from grape to glass. This was after the dark long jump from Horace's Falernian and hence to the invention of both cork and bottle. Not forgetting the discovery of the *pourriture noble* or art of letting the grape rot on the vine. The counterpoint between agriculture and culture that is wine is also present in cigars. It's true that the weed, actually a giant herb, doesn't have a Noah who 'planted a vineyard' in the Bible or a Theocritus to sing its praise in Greek or a Horace to show the layman in Latin that a Por Larrañaga, gone with the winds of history, was a cigar that deserved an ode. Havanas have a bard or two, it's true. But Byron is not enough. If only Marlowe had settled his bill instead of his accounts!

Once discovered and its only use known, it is not possible to imagine modern man (and woman too) without tobacco.

Ironically not even a clumsy reconstruction of civilized life can manage without it. This was true already in eighteenth century England. Such was the predicament of Robinson Crusoe after the wreck of his ship. Swept ashore as a castaway and all alone, he must find human society again or go mad. As he obviously can't meet other men on this isolated piece of land, a desert island, he recreates as many features of civilization as he can by using what materials he finds at hand or he dangerously rescues from the wreck.

No sooner had he begun a survey of the terrain than he 'found a great deal of tobacco, green and growing to a great and strong stalk'. The find is doubly surprising: to the castaway and to the reader. How could this city-dweller recognize so easily a herb he had only seen before as a dry brown leaf or as smoke? Not only that. He finds other plants which he had 'no notion of understanding about and might perhaps have virtues of their own – and consequently decides to forget all about them. Why, for all he knew they could have been potato plants or tomatoes or some other edible and nutritious vegetables!

Immediately after harvesting the weed, Robinson feels the mad desire to cook himself a stew. He confesses then: 'The second thing I would fain have had was a tobacco pipe.' Obviously the castaway wants to have a smoke: the man is a smoking gentleman and this is his only reconstructed vice. But it's impossible for him to smoke. You see, he needs a pipe. He could have re-invented the cigar there and then but he is an eighteenth-century Englishman and must smoke a pipe. As pearls to swine, history comes before nature.

An Englishman is an Englishman even on a desert island and Robinson's considerable ingenuity is employed in producing a very English contraption of everyday use: 'I spent a deal of time and pains to make me an umbrella.' He takes it on his promenades along the beach and the umbrella looks like a caricature of a London brolly. But it is useful both as a parasol and a *parapluie*. Crusoe refines his technology and is soon able to reproduce many utensils in clay. 'But I think,' he confesses, 'I never was more vain of my own performance than for my being able to make a tobacco pipe.' He declares himself 'exceedingly comforted with it'. No wonder. A pipe is a very difficult appliance to make, even to repair, as every pipe-smoker knows. But Robinson is more happy than proud: now he can indulge in his old dark habit and feel as if he had returned to the society of men. He enjoys his pleasure, even if it is a solitary one. I can understand why Crusoe was so proud of his pipe and so happy with his crop of *Nicotiana rustica*. But happiness is a sometime thing. The next sentiment he feels is a 'dreadful alarm on seeing footprints on the shore'. Every time I get to this part of the story I always think that Robinson Crusoe does not fear for his life but for dear tobacco. Has, perchance, a man from the Temperance League just arrived on this desert island for the Sabbath? But of course it's only Friday. Later, reversing the process begun with Rodrigo de Xeres, the European sailor teaches the noble savage to smoke – a pipe.

It is quite a jump from Crusoe's smoking utensil to 'The Perfect Pipe of 1984'.

When Sherlock Holmes smoked his pipe and brooded, a mystery unravelled. The relationship twixt pipe and man was elementary. Yet the choice of a good briar for today's pipe smoker (confirmed or novice) is almost criminally tangled. No wonder: Glossy bright finishes ringed with silver and gold dazzle the eye; pricey imports lure with promises of class and status; and images of tweeds, autumn woods, and hunting dogs either haunt the imagination or are consciously manipulated to sell that hunk of wood and the processed leaves you burn in it.

Which tobacco is best?

Basically, there are two types of pipe tobacco. There are mixtures based on Virginia or Burley tobacco plus a variety of condiment tobaccos such as Turkish (many varieties), Latika, and Perique. These are complex and rich in taste, like a good blended Scotch whisky. The other type, 'straight' tobacco, usually Virginia or Burley, tastes simpler and more direct, like bourbon. The much-abused term 'cavendish' generally applies – or should – to a straight tobacco that has been 'cased', or flavoured. These range in taste from relatively plain to candy-sweet. I don't think that one tobacco can be all things to all men; rather, the pipe-smoker should try to cultivate a taste for a good, subtle mixture for indoors, a vigorous straight Virginia or Burley for outdoors (especially in cool weather), and a mild, not-too-aromatic cavendish for after breakfast or a warm-day smoke.

Most new pipe smokers begin with the lighter cavendish tobaccos and work toward the heftier mixtures. It's important, though, not to confuse your tongue by constantly switching pipes for each smoke. A pipe broken in with a particular tobacco brings out its flavour better; it takes a while to adjust to a change. Give each new weed a chance, and try to keep one pipe for each type of tobacco.

Alan Schwartz (not again!)
Esquire Magazine

But remember, Friday or Crusoe, when you smoke a pipe you are not smoking only tobacco. With each pipe you smoke: anise, honey, bergamot, *boit de rose*, cascarilla, cassia, cinnamon, cardamon, gentian root, geranium, menthol, nutmeg, peppermint, rosemary, sandalwood, vanilla, valerian – and sage, which gives the smoker the allure of an old wise man. All of the above are added as perfumes and oils and blended with the tobacco. No wonder the smoke of a pipe smells like the rainbow.

With a pipe you can get away with murder, as it is the case with the avid smoker in *Ironweed*, by William Kennedy: 'Francis's father smoked roots of grass that died in the periodic droughts afflicting the cemetery. He stored the root essence in his pockets until it was brittle to the touch, then pulverized it between his fingers and packed his pipe.' The love of Francis's father for the weed (actually weeds) endured even death: 'Francis's father lit his pipe, smiled at his wife's discomfort, and looked out from his own bit of sod.'

Compton MacKenzie claims that 'to England belongs the credit for the spread of pipe-smoking through Europe; Spain can be praised for the cigar. Portugal, however, carried pipe and cigar around the world.' What about chewing and snuff, the dirty duo?

Snuff came and went as in a puff.
As to chew,
It was only done by the unhappy few.

The Portuguese introduced tobacco to Ceylon early in the sixteenth century as a cure for beri-beri. Pellagra of course was 'aggravation of the skin' and it was hardly smoked out but caused by a lack of proper nourishment. Though at the time people didn't smoke tobacco but preferred to drink it. In Ceylon, of all places, they call tobacco *biri* or *bidi*. Why not *biri-bidi*?

Here's some smoking stuff from MacKenzie's pipe-dream shop the House of Rattray in Perth, Scotland:

Charles Rattray, born in the late 1880s and bred in the Scottish tobacco industry, spent the first years of his working life in Fairweather's tobacco factory in Dundee. He, at the age of 23, decided to go into business and produce his own blends of fine quality pipe tobaccos.

After a long search he found a large shop with work-rooms in the High Street of Perth, known as Fair City and Scotland's ancient capital. In the street, horse-drawn trams passed slowly by. The shops were crowded with bustling people from the town and those who had made long journeys from the glens. Perth, full of life, is astride the River Tay, the salmon fisherman's Mecca and from where is drawn, by the distillers, the pure sparkling water to make Scotch whisky.

He acquired No. 158 High Street and transformed the premises into what was to become one of the most remark-able tobacco businesses of all time.

Six decades have passed, two world wars have come and gone and the way of life has changed for millions. But here, in the Fair City, things are much the same. Old Charles and his original staff are no longer there and have been replaced by new faces, but their dedication shows no relaxation.

A Bit of Perth Talk:

Observe a confirmed pipe smoker – he has an air of tranquillity with his pipe a'glow. Here is a man at peace with the world, himself and his favourite tobacco. What makes such a smoker? Some, from their first urge to smoke took to the pipe and seldom, if ever, bothered with any other form of smoking – these are the naturals. Others, finding no real satisfaction in cigarettes or cigars turned to the pipe, persevered and became confirmed PIPEMEN.

Now what of the smoker who has tried from time to time to settle with the pipe but never reached Utopia? It is more than likely that he, mainly through lack of good advice chose the wrong tobacco and an unsuitable pipe. Such a combination is not far short of disaster for a man who has spent good money with the best of intentions and finds himself with smoking equipment which he will never use again.

Sir Thomas More invented Utopia, a land ruled more by reason than by rhyme, so More was called 'a man for all reasons'. Though he himself was not very reasonable and, to King Henry, highly treasonable. He lost his head though not his reason. He never smoked, among other reasons, because tobacco had not been brought to England yet – and it never grew in Utopia.

Was Sir Isaac Newton really so distracted or was he a mysoginist? 'It is recorded of him,' attests *Tobacco Talk*, 'that on one occasion, in a fit of mental abstraction he used the finger of the lady he was courting as a tobacco stopper, as he sat and smoked in silence beside her.' I must remind all Newtonians (and old Etonians too) that Stan Laurel used a chubby finger from his fat friend, perennial Hardy, for the same purpose. But Stanley didn't need Ollie's finger to light his pipe: his own thumb became combustible. It happened once in *A Chump at Oxford*.

Cigars are always associated with Hollywood, not only with John Ford or Orson Welles but even with other directors like John Huston and Samuel Fuller. Said John Kobal, the film historian, talking of an interview with Joe Mankiewicz, who was digressing on William de Mille, Cecil B.'s older brother, and was surprised when Mankiewicz mentioned Olga Baclanova (the Volgan vamp turned freak in *Freaks*) as a beauty of the silent era. 'Here he was,' said Kobal, 'a man who looked like an old cigar, talking from the side of his mouth, words in the place of the cigar!' 'But John,' I interrupted Kobal, 'Mankiewicz was a pipe man. He never smoked a cigar in his life.' 'Are you sure?' 'Positive. Take a look at his old photographs and you'll see him always clenching a briar in his teeth.' 'Well, there he was,' Kobal went on undaunted, 'Mankiewicz of all people, his face twisted as if he were clutching an invisible pipe in his mouth, talking about Baclanova's beauty.' Kobal made the director of *All About Eve* sound as if he munched a baclava forever, all almonds and honey in the hell of a Lebanese restaurant in downtown Beirut. Enter a terrorist wearing a balaklava.

Cary Grant is the best pipe-holder in Hollywood's history and even he looks awkward, ill-at-ease and phony when he is holding a pipe. Sometimes he looks more like a plumber than a dream-boat. In *Every Girl Should be Married* Ole Cary goes about town pipe in hand and sometimes even pipe in mouth. He is doing his calls then. But he is so busy playing doctor that he doesn't have time to smoke his pipe. Or even to light it. Well, he lights it up once in the middle of the street and then forgets to suck and puff. That is the problem with pipes: they are so utterly phony that you don't simply have to smoke them to look at least funny. Besides, pipes do rumble in the middle of the night and make all kinds of funny noises. Those are called Raleigh's *borborigmi* or air in the piping.

In *People Will Talk* Cary Grant is a doctor (he once was a patrician pediatrician, he is a gynaecologist now) and he deserves favour. He doesn't get it but his director does. Joseph L. Mankiewicz is the notorious pipe holder who never graduated to lighting. (But his cameramen did.) Mankiewicz simply had no match. In the movies by Mankiewicz there is always a man smoking a pipe – and sometimes even a woman. (That is Beulah Bondi in *The Gorgeous Hussy*.) Mankiewicz was also the producer of a pet project: the film of a kid smoking a pipe and acting like a veteran river-boatman. That mere boy they sent on a crate down the Mighty Mississippi to do a man's job was Mickey Rooney as Huckleberry Finn. He smokes a corncob but in the movie every pipe is a dream downstream.

Granted nothing can be funnier than to watch Cary as a phony country squire (from New York) wearing riding breeches and tweeds in the Connecticut morning. He is standing at the entrance of his manor, his retriever (actually a hound no bigger than the one that haunted poor Baskerville) sitting by him and, just as naturally, a solid pipe stolidly clenched between his teeth – unlit. He is Mr Blindings posing in front of his dream-house. Obviously a pipe-dream house. It shouldn't come as a surprise to you that Cary's favourite expression in this movie is 'Holy Smoke!'

In *Mr Blandings Builds His Dream House* – that's the title – all the upper-class (bracket should be more apt here) characters, such as copywriter Grant, lawyer Melvyn Douglas and architect Reginald Denny, sport pipes. But in a reversal of roles, all the labourers smoke cigars, especially Nestor Paiva, who seems to be glued forever to the stogey in his mouth. He unsticks it just to say to Cary Grant as a parting sting: 'I'll send you the bill.'

The only pleasure Captain Ahab allowed himself, except to holding on to the hunt (and revenge) like grim death, was to smoke. 'Lighting the pipe at the binnacle lamp . . . he sat and smoked.' Ahab, his pipe alight, delighted on his ivory stool as if on a Norse throne: 'Some moments passed, during which the thick vapour came from his mouth in quick and constant puffs, which blew black again into his face.' Apparently Ahab is smoking tobacco of inferior quality: 'How now,' he soliloquized at last, withdrawing the tube, 'this smoking no longer soothes.' Then from soliloquizing he goes into a sea-chant!: 'Oh my pipe! hard must it go with me if thy charm be gone!' The good captain has not been smoking inferior tobacco or a poor pipe but being placed facing the wrong wind: 'ignorantly smoking to the windward all the while.' Hark, there's the rub! But the sinful sailor wants no truck with his pipe at all: 'What business have I with this pipe?' Ahab makes a vow on the bow: 'I'll smoke no more.' Then: 'He tossed the still lighted pipe into the sea.' Everything with Ahab was so powerful that his lighted pipe must have been more like a fiery furnace than a pipe: 'The fire hissed in the waves' and the ponderous pipe is gone: 'the same instant the ship shot by the bubbles the sinking pipe made' – which is a swooning sound and a silly sentence. Captain Ahab, as usual has the last stance: 'With slouched hat, he lurchingly paced the planks' – pegleg, pipeless Ahab.

What's a Kemble pipe? A Kemble *pipe*? I know a Fanny Kemble, niece of Mrs Siddons, an actress as memorable as a smoke. But a *Kemble* pipe? According to *Tobacco Talk* 'a poor

145

Roman Catholic priest named Kemble was hanged in 1679, in his eightieth year, he having been implicated in the plot of Titus Oates. He marched to his fate smoking a pipe of tobacco. The people of Herefordshire to this day call the last pipe they take at a sitting a Kemble pipe.' Ah, *that* Kemble pipe!

Everybody knows what a peace pipe is but only a few know what a pipe of tranquility was. A. W. Kinglake in his *Eothen* describes it thus:

> Methley began to rally very soon after we had reached Constantinople, but there seemed at first to be no chance of his regaining strength enough for travelling during the winter, and I determined to stay with my comrade until he had quite recovered; so I bought me a horse and a 'pipe of tranquility'*, and took a Turkish phrase-master.

Axel Munthe's greatest discovery was not made in the field of medicine nor on the rocks of Capri but in the corner of Anacapri called San Michele. He was helped by an Italian farmer: 'Old Pacciale who had been digging in my vineyard at Demecuta took me inside with an air of great mystery and importance. Having ascertained that nobody overheard us, he produced from his pocket a broken clay pipe black with smoke.

* *The 'pipe of tranquility' is a* tchibouque *too long to be conveniently carried on a journey. The possession of it therefore implies that its owner is stationary, or at all events that he is enjoying a long repose. (N. of the A.)*

One question or rather several questions that look like one still bug me. What is a tchibouque? *Is it a dakka or just a pet hookah? Or perhaps a narghile? Or a* chaloumeau *also known as a calumet? The calumet was the sacred pipe of the American Indians, those who roamed the prairie after the buffalo. One calumet with white feathers was a peace pipe, one with red feathers was a war pipe. Most Indian pipes were made not of wood but of pipestone, from a quarry near Pipestone, Minnesota. The quarry was known by the Indians as Fountain of Stone. Columbus was not that wrong after all. He only missed the right quarry – where gold was born.*

146

"*La pipa di Timberio,*" said Old Pacciale.'
Timberio is none other than Tiberius. Apparently Tiberius Claudius Nero Caesar Augustus had been the first Roman smoker!

But what about snuff? What about it? What do you think of it? Why, snuff is something not to be snubbed. Up to snuff!

'Snuff suits studious men,' said Flaubert – or was it brave Bouvard or perhaps poor Pecuchet? 'Tobacco,' to the suave Gustave, 'is the cause of all the diseases of the brain and spinal cord.' But the great-granddaddy of French letters later recapitulated (he loved long, lean words): 'The government brand [of cigarette tobacco] is not so good as that which is smuggled in.' All this occurred in his *Dictionnaire des idées reçues*, a dictionary of clichés from Clichy.

My snuffist friend is rather stuffy. Once he took a walk on the safe side of the West End in search of a tobacconist who could satisfy his craving for the brown stuff. He said that he was going to powder his nose: he is a joker, I'm afraid. You should be afraid too. But he was merely trying to hide the purpose of his trip abroad. As a leper cannot change his spots, he announced as breezily as a sneeze when he came back:

'Went to Courtauld Gallery and Tate too.'
I knew where he'd gone all right.
'Tate *two*?'
'Tate too!'
'That too?'
'Toot toot.'
The Duke of Wellington was an avid snuff-taker and a regular cigar-smoker – Napoleon was neither. That's why he lost at Waterloo: cognac courage is two o'clock in the morning courage, as Napoleon himself observed. Wellington didn't smoke a pipe but Napoleon in exile said that 'Wherever wood can swim, there I'm sure to find this flag of England'. Cigars can swim, pipes cannot. Obviously what Napoleon ere saw was not Elba but a cigar with a flag on top. (A Churchill maybe?) And yet, Napoleon was a writer at heart. All he planned for St Helena to stop time was to think of writing his memoirs. Wellington in turn cursed all writers: 'Publish and be damned!'

Sign seen at the Smokers Centre of 142 Knightsbridge:

SNUFFERS

THE EASIEST, CLEANEST, NEATEST
WAY OF PUTTING OUT CIGARETTES

SNUFF!

Snuff – le *vice anglais*:

> *The Snuff-Taker*
>
> . . . before I budge an inch
> I hail Aurora with a pinch;
> After three cups of morning tea
> A pinch most grateful is to me;
> If then by chance the post arrive,
> My fingers still the deeper dive.
>
> The Rev. W. King (1778)

Interviewing Saul Bellow for the London *Observer*, Martin Amis notices that 'His hair is white and peripheral' – and one must hold one's breath before going on: 'but the eyes are still the colour of expensive snuff.' Should this Bellowing remark be taken with a pinch of Saul?

The nose strikes back

After a summer advertising offensive by Britain's largest manufacturer, the British snuff industry is gathering itself for a campaign to convince the public that snuff-taking is no mere relic of the Victorian age.

Early analysis of its £20,000, five-month campaign has persuaded J. and H. Wilson of Sheffield that its efforts, aimed primarily at the young, seem to have been justified. 'The response,' says the company's general manager, Jerry Jones, 'proves without doubt that an immense interest is developing.' This initiative is reinforced by a more moderate sweep by the Snuff Grinders and Blenders Association, which hopes to revive the boom days of the late seventeenth to early nineteenth centuries when men and women of every age and caste enjoyed their snuffle.

148

LONDON (IHT). – In his pale blue shopkeeper's smock, Jeremy Palmer stands at the sales counter and talks snuff. He also talks cigars, cigarettes and pipes, or anything else to do with tobacco and smoking. It is what he has done for forty years.

His forum has been Fribourg & Treyer, one of the world's celebrated tobacco shops. For 258 years, it has been a sort of Mecca of the weed.*

Snuff is a powder made from a blend of choice tobaccos and perfumed with scented oils – carnation, jasmin, lemon, sandalwood, etc. F&T claims it sells an unequaled variety of snuffs (32 kinds), including Attar of Roses (200,000 roses are used in making one half-ounce), which retails at £26 per ounce. Snuff-takers consider an ounce a day a generous allowance.

Modern-day snuff enthusiasts, whose number the Society of Snuff Grinders, Blenders and Purveyors says is on the rise, still follow 'the true artistic method of taking a pinch' set forth by A. Steinmetz of London in 1857.

Mr Palmer says: 'Snuff made its first appearance on British soil in 1702 when Sir George Rooke, commanding the fleet, captured two huge cargoes of it – one Spanish and the other Cuban on its way to Spain. It was sold cheap in British ports, and its popularity grew steadily (and F&T with it) through the 18th century until the time of the Regency (1810–20) when the habit was almost universal.'

The so-called Age of Snuff received a stamp of social approval around 1800 when the Prince of Wales, later to be the Regent and George IV, announced his fondness for snuff, causing the highest ranks of British society to flock to the snuff room at F&T. When George IV died in 1830, so did snuff's popularity.

Not any more. The House of Snuff, 34 Haymarket, is sadly boarded up. After laughing like mad at some Congreve at the Haymarket Theatre Royal, the memory of the golden boards was almost obliterated by the blue planks all over Fribourg & Treyer. To think that Congreve's 'last and best play' lasts longer than the rappee actors and author took for granted. The way of the world indeed!

The Fall

Snuff's final fall came when the British aristocracy went away to the Crimean War in the mid-1850s and returned home with Turkish, Egyptian and Russian cigarettes in their mouths. Thereafter, to smoke those blends became a sign of status. F&T sold its first cigarette in 1852.

International Herald Tribune

In case all smoking is banned and snuff makes a come back, here's

But, before you reach for the snuff box, remember that every tobacco product carries some health dangers. The whole issue has recently been raised because an American company wants to import a type of 'wet' snuff called Skoal Bandits. The snuff is packaged in a tea-bag and eased between the bottom lip and gum. What worries David Simpson, director of the anti-smoking organization Ash, is that the marketing strategy in America suggests that Skoal Bandits carry few health risks.

Yet a report in America in 1981 suggested that among a group of white women from North Carolina there was a significant increase in mouth and throat cancers which could be directly linked with 'snuff dipping' – the use of these bags. In addition other researchers have linked bad breath, teeth and gum problems and a loss of sense of taste and smell with chronic use of smokeless tobacco.

The Times

How to take snuff according to Steinmetz

The true artistic method of 'taking a pinch' consists of twelve operations:

1. Take the snuff-box with your right hand.
2. Pass the snuff-box to your left hand.
3. Rap the snuff-box.
4. Open the snuff-box.
5. Present the box to the company.
6. Receive it after going the round.

7. Gather up the snuff in the box by striking the side with the middle and fore-finger.
8. Take a pinch with the right hand.
9. Keep the snuff a moment or two between the fingers and before carrying it to the nose.
10. Put the snuff to your nose.
11. Sniff it in with precision by both nostrils, and without any grimace.
12. Shut the snuff-box, sneeze, spit and wipe your nose.

Dickens and Wilde (who called America 'an enormous expectoration') would have objected to the sneeze-and-spit bit. Two hundred years earlier the Spanish writer, poet and wit Francisco de Quevedo called snuff-taking 'a black-snot abomination worse than the catarrh'. But folk wisdom at the time was all for the rappee:

> What introduces Whig or Tory
> And reconciles them in their story
> When each is boasting on his glory?
> A pinch of snuff!

No Englishman ever has had his name linked to tobacco as George Bryan Brummell, the celebrated Beau Brummell. Not even Churchill to his cigar was what Brummell was to snuff. The first and foremost dandy was an *arbiter elegantiae* to the aristocracy, a friend of royalty and the intimate of writers. Of him Lord Byron said that there were only three great men in Europe: Brummell, Bonaparte and Byron. Remember the Three Bs in music?

Carlyle praised him as 'the Clothes-wearing man, a man whose trade, office and existence consists in the wearing of Clothes. Every faculty of his soul, spirit, purse and person is heroically consecrated to this one object: the wearing of clothes wisely and well; so that as others dress to live, he lives to dress.' A wit (or wag) commented that Brummell was only 'clothes wearing a man'. Said Baudelaire, his disciple, 'Dandyism is not an exaggerated taste for fine clothes . . . It is primarily a desire to be original as a person . . . Dandyism is the last heroic gesture amid decadence. It is a setting sun, glorious but without warmth and full of melancholy.' The

151

sun of Brummell shone bright once. But the Beau's stratagem (or King's gambit) backfired and he died obscurely, forgotten and poor.

> Brummell [says his biographer Hubert Cole] was deeply addicted to snuff. There is a story, true or false, that he once went into Fribourg & Treyer's when hogshead of Martinique – his favourite – had just arrived and found that it had been taken up in advance by his friends. He asked to try and pronounced it abominable. The other purchasers cancelled their orders, whereupon Brummell asked the proprietors for three yards of it, assuring them that they would sell the rest as soon as it became known that he had bought. It sounds like a fiction made up by George himself for his own amusement and aggrandisement, but it is an indication of his standing as a connoisseur.

Brummell could never have imagined that the snuff of the London dandy, that rappee of Frenchified gentlemen about town, had its origins in Cuba, among the heathen. Actually it was a sacred ceremony that gave birth to the habit. Snuff was taken only by the *behique*, or witchdoctor, in the presence of the cacique or Indian chief. The *behique* used a tube, sometimes with a forked end, to inhale the powder of tobacco, called *cohoba*. For this he prepared himself during a week of fasting and resting. When he was ready for the ceremony, he fortified himself with coca leaves (then abundant on the island) and immediately after he sniffed the snuff and talked to the cacique in the most familiar terms. Two centuries later, in London, Brummell, after fortifying himself with spirits, asked a courtier who escorted the future King George IV, now the heir to the throne and once his patron in leisure: 'Who's your fat friend?' Then, calmly the dandy opened not his veins but his small bejewelled box and took snuff after the snub. The Cuban savage would have killed himself rather than insult his cacique. Even the slightest reference to fatness would have been considered a remark worthy only of a Carib thinking of dinner.

At the beginning of the nineteenth century, though, a very strong snuff called Penalver was exported almost exclusively to England. F. W. Fairholt, one of the first and probably best of the tobacco historians, wrote about snuff in his *Tobacco: Its History and Associations*: 'Perfumed snuff sometimes was the recipient of poison.' That's why it was sometimes called 'Jesuit's Rappee'. But it was not all mere metaphor. The Duc de Noailles, a snob, gave the French *dauphine* a box of Spanish snuff. There was poison in the stuff and the *dauphine*, poor girl, died five days later complaining of a terrible headache – an acute case of murder by snuff. Cigars can be dangerous too. Apart from the exploding cigar, it was alleged not so long ago that the CIA tried to assassinate Fidel Castro with a poisoned panatella. Unfortunately, the Cuban dictator stuck to his own brand first smoked by his cigar-taster and the conspiracy was aborted *in partibus Fidelium*.

Then only the pipe remains blameless? Yeah, put that in your pipe and smoke it. Haven't you heard of opium, dreameyes?

The rascal rappee survives in disguise today: 'In the simple type of pudding-faced boy pituitary extract is either injected or given in the form of snuff.' (*Pears Medical Encyclopedia*)

The conquistadors, just like royalty later, despised tobacco. 'It's a habit for savages, not Christians,' affirmed Hernán Cortés, who then ordered all cigars, like his ships from Cuba, to be set alight behind his back. But Cubans have always been cigar-smokers. (Given time they became cigarette-smokers too.) Since the inception of the Cuban nation and long before its independence as the aftermath of the Spanish-American War (which began when a cigar butt blew up the *Maine* in Havana: the noisiest exploding cigar ever) cigars had the strongest appeal for Cubans: it's the national vice, you see. Even though, already in the sixteenth century, there was a racist proverb that stated: 'Cigars are for negroes: brown goes with brown.' But a Cuban cartoon from 1858 shows a man and a boy, both white, both smoking black cigars. In the caption the man says to the boy: 'Smoke, kid. Smoking is what differentiates man from animals.' By making him a somebody, perhaps?

The quantity of tobacco smoked in Cuba amazed all visitors to the island since early 1800. Everybody smoked! Women smoked until they were long in the tooth and short of breath. Young ladies smoked after meals and, to the horror of the French, even between courses. Children smoked behind their parents' backs in the back alleys and lunatics smoked in the asylums – and set them on fire sometimes. Men smoked everywhere, literally. From Cuba then came not only the best cigars but also the best cigarettes (recently adopted and adapted by Spain) and pipe and chewing tobacco, the *andullo*, of prime quality (the famed Andouille): Cuba should have been named Tobacco and not Tobago. A myth wants that the snuff cargo that British sailors looted from a ship in mid-ocean and that allegedly started the snuff craze in England was in fact Cuban and not Spanish. At that time an unknown but enterprising Havanan invented the cigar-holder: this later became the cigarette-holder. It was not the photogenic device favoured during the 1930s by FDR and his Chinese counterpart, conniving Dragon Lady, or our American cousin, caddish Allison De Witt. But she could only draw an O. (Virginia Woolf favoured a cigarette-holder held like a pen.) There are holders made of ivory even – and uneven. Others are made of whalebone. Articulated holders for articulated late holders of holders, thus:

> The end-bone
> connected
> to the mid-bone
> connected
> to the jaw-bone
> connected
> like jointed poles, like anointed Poles.

But the Cuban contraption was made of gold or silver. This was some sort of tongs with which to have and to hold the cigar and a fixed small ring attachable to a finger, usually the forefinger. Some Cuban smokers considered this instrument of pleasure too *afeminado*, worse than effete, and sometime later it fell into desuetude. In fact the *tenacinas* uncannily resembled the roach-holders used by some chic addicts to marihuana in the 1960s, the kind Leigh Taylor-Young used in *I Love You, Alice B. Toklas* to lure Peter Sellers where the grass was burning green.

Cuba was also a strong cigar exporter very early in her history. By the mid-nineteenth century Havana cigars had already become masters of the smoking world. This was a man's world then, as seen in 'Carmen', for the *papeletes* favoured by women were not in vogue in Europe yet. Before President James Buchanan announced in 1857 that he would raise the import tariff for Cuban cigars, 360 million cigars were exported yearly from Cuba to the United States. One hundred years later, by 1950, the American cigar imports had dwindled to 50 million cigars a year, which still made an enormous deal of smoke – and many people stinkingly rich. Two years after Castro's takeover in 1959 the import figures plummeted to exactly nil, except of course for the few cigars smuggled into the United States from Canada and Mexico. They were called then Have-and-Have-Not Havanas. This does not include the official smuggling done by American diplomats abroad who kept President Kennedy so well provided with his favourite Montecristos. After he was assassinated nobody in the USA dared boast that they smoked Havanas, in private or in public. That's when Cuba became a four-letter word too. The reputation of the Cuban cigar, however, reached mythic proportions then. It actually was the forbidden leaf.

After her trip to Havana in 1840 the Comtesse de Merlin (1789–1852) published in Paris a book called, inevitably, *Voyage à la Havane*. The Countess, born in Cuba with an aristocratic name (Maria de las Mercedes Santa Cruz y Montalvo) became in France a French noblewoman by marriage and a Parisian from head to toe by make-like. She was thus able to look at Cuba with fond but foreign eyes, exactly like José María de Heredia, the French poet, would do fifty years later. In her book she gives an exotic and truthful view of a slave society, refined but remote, cruel and yet coarse. Once she made a comment that is valid even now: 'There are no people in Cuba: only slaves and masters.' She was very observant of customs and fashions and what she saw in Havana was a city where everybody smoked: masters and slaves were all slaves of the weed. Even in the Cuban countryside she noticed the extent of this habit not exactly foreign to her, but worthy of her attention as a passion. In the enormous colonial house of her relatives 'the men come and go smoking along the corridors to talk shop or seduce by candlelight'. She joined (and enjoyed) the evening promenade in the streets of Havana 'where nobody went on foot' – meaning of course the whites: those who are somebody. 'The men were gravely tucked in the back of their hansoms, smoking calmly: quietly having a taste of their *bonheur*.' But if the blacks must walk in the tropical sun 'the streets belonged to the negresses', already a French obsession. 'You could see them in numbers in the shade of the arcades, almost naked, with their soft, shiny shoulders – a cigar in their lips.'

The image of a woman smoking or rather of women smoking cigars struck Madame la Comtesse paying a visit to the Philistines as peculiar, even though she was a Cuban and came from Paris, where George Sand, her friend, was a trendsetter with a cigar and many trousers.

La Comtesse de Merlin has a narrative of an occurrence in Havana some time before she left for Paris again and for good. It goes like this:

Last night I had just written a letter to one of my friends, describing to him the way in which the subject of death is discussed in Havana, when one of my elderly relatives came into my room and wanted to know what news I was sending to Europe about the island.

'You are right,' he told me after he had read my letter to the Marquis of C . . . 'Here we don't know, or want to die. Tell me, do you know what a *velorio* is? A wake in Havana.'

'It's true that it can be quite fun,' I said ironically.

'Much more than you think.'

Well this personage, to whom I owe a lot, came to my house the day before yesterday, and said to me innocently:

'One of my relatives has died.'

Then lowering his voice, but with a merry and mysterious tone, added:

'You would have much fun. There will be a lot of good humoured people and a magnificent meal at the wake.'

It was nine in the evening, and I put on my mourning clothes, and went toward the *velorio*. I had hardly arrived when I heard a voice which rang out amongst the murmurings of the other people:

'Which *calzones* is the deceased wearing?'

'We don't know yet,' replied a trembling voice from inside.

'The *cutí color de rosa*, or the *paño de violeta*?'

At that moment an old lady went across the corridor, passing right in front of me, and lifted the black curtain.

'What do you mean *calzones*!' she exclaimed. 'Longjohns? He will wear a monk's robe.'

A few minutes later they showed us the dead man, and each one of the people present sprinkled him with holy water. And then I, too, opened the black curtain.

On a few steps laid out as an altar, you could see the livid cadaver surrounded by candles, whose red light shone sadly on the blue pleats of his monk's robes. It was a terrible spectacle. The *tumba* or coffin* was isolated; the dead man's face was uncovered; his eyes closed with hot wax looked as if he had tears on his eyelids and over the stiff and immobile body there was a theatrical and irresolute clarity.

This melancholy spectacle wasn't to the taste of Dr Saturio who came with me: thinking that it was his duty to present me to the widow and relatives of the deceased who occupied the house next door.

On my part I left the widow and went to another room. There the spectacle offered me was the least analogous to sadness and quiet than in the funeral ceremonies. There were nearly 40 people of both sexes who were forming lively groups; the younger ones were playing a game of forfeits; others were talking in loud tones, and alternated the conversation with bursts of laughter; others were surrounding this old lady which was the same one who had presided over the shroud of the dead man, and who was recounting the days of his youth, his virtues, his wealth and all the particulars of his illness.

One person who was louder and more whining than anyone on that place was Dr Saturio.

I went out for a moment to get some fresh air, and on going past the corridor I heard some whispering. Not far from the room where the deceased was, there were two young girls talking, one leaning on the shoulder of the other.

O delicious delusions of life! I was about to exclaim:

*The Countess erred here. A tumba is not a coffin but a tomb.

ardour of the creative passions, how you hide the horror of death from the eyes of the *criollas*.

I then saw Dr Saturio in the room where the deceased was laid out lighting a cigar with one of the candles on the coffin!

The Cuban Countess from Paris couldn't know that the nonchalant, gallant *habanero* was only following the deceased in his wake at his wake. She couldn't see that a *velorio* was very much like an Irish wake where cigars and not whiskey are the dominant passion.

Had she lived a little bit more the Countess would have witnessed how a Cuban could smoke cigars all his life – and even after death. In his very curious *American Eccentrics* Carl Sifakis tells the story of a Cuban family, a man, his wife and their daughter, all wealthy, who settled in a room of the America Hotel in Dream Street, New York. The man, Señor Romero, smoked Havanas in Manhattan. After many a winter Romero died and his widow and daughter dressed in black but never left the hotel again. Writes Sifakis:

Life, such as it was – as far as the outside world was concerned – continued on in the same way. A news dealer on the corner sent up a copy of the Spanish language newspaper, *La Prensa*. The bell captain carried up an expensive black cigar and three *table d'hôte* dinners to the suite.' Sifakis tried to explain the mystery away with everyday life probabilities: 'True, they ordered three meals. Was one of them for the departed Papá José? Or did they simply eat a lot? We do know that neither of them smoked the expensive black cigars. But the word from employees (of the hotel) in the Fifties was that even the cigar was not for Papa but rather for Mama Michaela's rheumatism. Acacia (the daughter) would soak it in water and poultice her mother's leg with it.

This is not explanation enough. Dr Saturio and I know that the cigar was *brevas para los muertos*. Eventually even Madame la Comtesse would admit this. Otherwise, why try to cure rheumatism not with any five-cent cigar (even a stogey would do) but with the expensive *Por Larrañagas* that Señor Romero enjoyed so much when he was alive?

Another early, dearly departed was Doña Gertrudis, a woman so ardent that she could make George Sand go to a nunnery. Like the Frenchwoman who was so avidly manly she was prolific too. Gertrudis Gómez de Avellaneda, also known as La Avellaneda but whom you guys can call just Gertie, was the greatest Cuban poetess of the nineteenth century – and there were quite a few poetesses in Cuba then, believe me. That Avellaneda woman devoured men and smoked cigar – and vice versa. She also blew smoke in people's faces. She was forced to leave Cuba in 1836 on account of her smoking habits and chose Madrid as her Paris, where George Sand roamed. Her senior sister Brigida (you girls can call her Brigid, or, perhaps better, Rigid) disapproved strongly of dark men and long cigars – or vice versa. She left for Spain, where both men and cigars were lighter but the days were shorter. (She arrived in winter.) She wrote a poem about it all or rather about the way she went away. It is called 'Departure', though it can be roughly translated as 'Parting Shouts'. It goes like this:

> Something, something, something and then
> some –
> 'I depart!
> From these parts!
> The ship decidedly lifts its prow!
> The manoeuveur's being helped out
> By a diligent crowd!'
> (Though the bowspirit got mixed with the ruddy
> sometimes.)

She left and left her heart in San Francisco de Paula, where Hemingway too lived. They were neighbours in space, though, not in time.

But this is what Jacinto Milanés, a strict colleague of Doña Gertrudis (1814–63), has to say on finding his mistress Petra, of all people, smoking! The poem is titled, of all titles, 'Tobacco'! But it could be called 'Infidelity':

> What is this?
> *You*, you – *smoking*!
> You, *la crème de la crème*,
> Venus of foam, goddess of love.
> Is it possible that you
> Would consume your lungs
> In such horrid, hideous sport?

Milanés is our contemporary, scientific even, in relating smoking and lung cancer. But Petra, unable to grasp the fact that all her fiancé objects to is that it is *she* who smokes (women who are dancers rarely get cancer), has only this to declare about customs and desires:

> I can never be at ease
> If I don't smoke cigars.
> When I sew and when I wash,
> Even going to bed at night
> I have to have it with me: I must!
> Though I really prefer, truly,
> Any old stub of mine
> To one of those fat cigars.
> So I always must hold fast
> To my old faithful *stumpen*.

A stumpen was 'a short cigar open at both ends' – very much like a cigar-butt. A preference that Petra in the poem shares with Brahms and Brecht and Chaplin in *Gold Rush*: everybody who is somebody must light up a stumpen.

But Milanés was right. When all is writ and read there's no denying that a cigar looks definitely masculine. This isn't sexism, for a lipstick in turn is always a feminine object. Yet both sticks are visibly ithyphallic – and if the phallus is not a male attribute you just tell me what is. It could be a club, of course. But remember, a member is only a limb.

Contrary to Freud's dictum a cigar *is* a sexual symbol in Cuba. Here is Beny Moré, the great Cuban singer of *sones*, in his hit of 1958. 'Se te cayó el tabaco' is its title and the Cuban way of saying that you have become impotent: the lyrics are in fact in ithyphallic meter.

You just dropped your cigar,
my brother.
You just dropped it!
You told me and told me
how good you were with women.
But you forgot to tell me
that you smoked your cigar
so much, my brother,
that it all fell off!
That it all just fell off!
Even its butt is out now
and for good!

In *Gigi*, tautological, illogical Gigi inveighs against indifferent Gaston Lachaille as she intones: 'An ugly black cigar is love!' But a cigar, contrary to Kipling's verse, is very like a woman in the Spanish gypsy song that claims that there are no ugly women:

But if you find any
just bring her over to me
and I'll find her beauty spot!

There are no ugly cigars. Not even the truculent Burma cheroot is ugly enough. Or the Rothschild called by Thompson of Tampa 'the magnificent imposter', though it looks more like the Neanderthal stout stick Alley Oops used to carry to tread softly in his strip. By the way, Thompson sells also the elegant Arabella and the slim Comtessa, whose names I like because it is difficult to find a cigar named after a woman. Thompson's *panetelas* (sic: he uses the Cuban spelling) are called Emeralds when he could call them, after Hugo, Esmeraldas: a quasar for queasy Quasimodo. *A propos* slim ladies, Thompson produces the thinnest cigar ever made. Why he calls it a Rembrandt is a mystery: is it after the painter or just after his brush? There are no ugly cigars. Not even the Yukon Jack, though looking mean enough, is not as ugly as its maker claims. It doesn't even look like an outlaw. But come to think of it, Don José, the Basque brigand Carmen made, didn't look like an outlaw to Mérimée. Did you know that

161

Carmen was such a temptress that she pronounced the narrator's name 'Marry me'?

There are no ugly cigars, only ugly smokers. H. L. Mencken, son of tobacco traders, an ugly man, was a handsome smoker in spite of his mug face, which Anita Loos adored.

> Recently, Mayor William Donald Shaefer turned out himself as a hair-parted-in-the-middle, cigar-chewing Mencken look-alike to award the $300 prize in a citywide Mencken Look-Alike contest, sponsored by publicity people of the Cigar Association of America.
>
> *International Herald Tribune*

Rip Torn, a passably handsome actor who dared sharing shots with David Bowie at his prettiest in *The Man Who Fell to Earth*, is an ugly cigar smoker. Sometimes he even looks hideous with his cigar stuck in his mouth. So does John Huston, who since *Treasure of the Sierra Madre* smokes and talks cigar in cheek. These two actors mistake the cigar for a plug. Edward G. Robinson could be both an ugly smoker and a beautiful man with a cigar. He is my favourite cigar-smoking American: this should be considered a trailer then. A tip to actors who are ugly smokers: stop sticking your cigar in your mouth to speak. That's obscene even if it is off scene.

One of my favourite live cigar-smokers is David Hockney: he smokes his cigar as if he bought it from a stub dealer. Another famous stub-smoker, Bertolt Brecht, smoked three-penny Opera cigars. He seemed to have always picked up his stubs straight from the gutter. Too bad that he proved not to be the genius I once thought. He was merely a Shakespeare from the stockyards: a dime-a-dozen smoker. That is why I took exception to what Joseph Losey, who knew him well, said to me: 'You're worse than Brecht.' Should I thank him? 'You smoke better cigars, though' – and I agreed. 'What about Pinter?' I asked him. 'What about him?' 'He smokes some seemingly seedy cigarillos rolled in *pectoral*'. 'What the hell is that?' '*Pectoral* is a cigarette paper made from cloth and stained brown with liquorice. It was much used in Cuba once.' 'Good God! Brown cigarettes is another of Harold's affectations, like his dark brown suits and pink shirt with brown ties. He smokes common-or-garden cigarettes, but he likes you to believe that he's smoking something more dangerous. Though for me plain cigarettes are enough danger already.' 'What brand are they?' 'Dunno. Does it matter?' 'Not with cigarettes, with cigars, yes. He could be smoking brown Tiparillos, you know.' 'Are those good or bad?' 'The gamut for cigarillos runs from bad to worse. Tiparillos are the worst.' 'Are those Cubans?' 'Oh no. They're as American as apple pie.' 'Then Harold smokes something else.' 'Being from the Mid-West and a Lutheran,' said I, 'you are as American as apple pious.' Losey smiled as if he knew. In fact his very name was very close to that *Lo sé*, Spanish for 'I know', said in *High Noon* by Gary Cooper, as American as apple pie in the sky.

There is always a feud of fumes going on between the long cigar and the stub. A very visible long-cigar smoker is Peter Bogdanovich, who follows Orson Welles closely. Brecht and Hockney seemingly smoke stubs only. The question is, where do you want to be aligned – with the show-offs or with the intimate lovers of the weed? You are always, in fact, in both camps. When you light up your cigar to be somebody, see Welles, you are well-endowed. But when you have smoked your cigar almost to the short and sweet end, you are cut-up cute: look at Bert and Dave, see how they grin. Only one man has never suffered from such dichotomy. He is (or rather was) a real person, as the newspapers love to say. His true name was Cigar Stubbs. There is no question about the authenticity of the name: an affidavit from the Florida State Bureau of Vital Statistics proves it. Stubbs is. But the question is, does he smoke?

Mark Twain who smoked cheap cheroots, many Manilas and all the Havanas he could afford late in life, said once: 'Man is the only animal that smokes – or needs to.' But I would trade all the famous smokers in the world for one who never boasted. His name is Marcel Duchamp and he played chess badly. He married the idea of Rose Selavy, an ideal, had his photo taken by Cartier Bresson and became famous. Like Brecht, he never cared if he was photographed smoking a stub. You can see that he enjoyed smoking as much as he enjoyed playing chess or riding his bicycle. In the photo, a jewel by Cartier, the worn-out bicycle has only one wheel left and it is almost a circle and radials: a study in geometry. But Duchamp holds his cigar aloft, just like the Statue of Liberty lifts her flame of iron and glass and neon lights. Duchamp, always aloof like his cigar, said once: 'I, who was born to do nothing must do everything at least once.' Obviously he used to smoke his cigar more than once.

That's how this book came to be written. William Shawn, of *The New Yorker*, made it possible in more ways than one. But my American publisher, editor and friend Cass Canfield Jnr, of Harper & Row, insisted more than once:

'You ought to write a book on cigars, you know,' he used to say to me, but I was as adamant as Adam.

'Cass,' I said as I made rings with the smoke, 'all I want from cigars is to enjoy them.'

Then I remembered Duchamp and made some more rings. Things are in smoke, art is in the rings. The wheel of a bicycle can be a ring too. The book, I thought, could be for Duchamp and the rings would then be considered Marcel waves, but he would remain aloof, aloft. Just like the rings. Hello, halo.

In *The Suicide Club* Prince Florizel, the hero, smokes a cheroot, but in the movie version, *Trouble for Two*, he is always in white tie and tails and smokes cigarettes. The actual president of the infamous club's mouth 'embraced a large cigar, he kept continually screwing round and round and from side to side'. He is the typical screwer smoker for whom to smoke is to turn an infinite screw. To enter the Suicide Club you must step into a smoking-room. 'Most of the party were smoking,' points out Robert Louis Stevenson.

What makes The Suicide Club members particularly anxious is that 'sometimes they smoked extraordinarily fast, sometimes they let their cigars out'. They are in fact smoking cigars as if they were cigarettes. They are obviously in hell.

Stevenson even knew those dark, secluded places where you could smoke in London (a city he called the Bagdad of the West) at your easiest. On the northern pavement of Leicester Square one character says to the other:

If you will allow me to guide you . . . I will offer you the best cigar in London.

And taking the arm of his companion, he led him in

silence and at a brisk pace to the door of a quiet establishment in Rupert Street, Soho. The entrance was adorned
with one of those gigantic Highlanders of wood which
have almost risen to the standing of antiquities; and
across the window-glass, which sheltered the usual display
of pipes, tobacco and cigars, there ran the gilded legend:
Bohemian Cigar Divan, by T. Godall. The interior of the
shop was small, but commodious and ornate; the salesman
grave, smiling and urbane; and the two young men, each
puffing a select regalia, had soon taken their places on a
sofa of mouse-coloured plush and proceeded to exchange
their stories.

Except for the mouse-coloured sofa (it was better to call it
tobacco- or Havana-coloured), Stevenson has given the best
description ever of a London Cigar Divan. Godall, by the
way, was a favourite surname with Stevenson. Any one for
frankincense?

Says Compton Mackenzie *à propos* of divans: 'It was presumably the opposition of the senior members of the London
clubs in Victorian days that led to the institution of the cigar-
divans and smoking-rooms . . . These were fitted up with
comfortable chairs and sofas in what was believed to be an
authentic Oriental style, and, to the accompaniment of Turkish
coffee, men frequented them to smoke cigars.'

There you are, two Scottish authors writing about a typically
Victorian London institution. Yet another writer, H. J. Nellar,
writes in 1832 of the divans, which he lists as follows: The
Oriental Divan, of Regent Street; the Private Subscription
Divan, Pall Mall; the Royal City Divan, St Paul's Churchyard;
the Royal Divan, King Street, Covent Garden; the Royal
Divan, Strand; and The Divan, Charing Cross.

Nellar probably had the last word on divans: 'The whole of
these divans are fitted up in a style of Asiatic splendour and
comfort, that produces to the uncultivated eye a very novel
and pleasing effect; while upon a closer examination, the
other senses are no less delighted.' What caused the decline
and fall of these divine divans? According to Mackenzie the
clientele: the young turks who adopted them used the divans
as springboards to 'go up west'. They smoked cigars no
longer but cigarettes. But even 'Turkish blend' cigarettes

could never fit up a divan. They are best for an ottoman – which the Oxford Dictionary calls a 'cushioned footstool'.

But Queen Victoria, closer to Gigi than to Carmen, thought cigars were nasty, un-British and long. She of all modern monarchs was the only one to disapprove of tobacco so intensely that she made Buckingham Palace, together with her German Prince Consort Albert, into *ein feste Burg* impregnable to smokers. She loathed and abhorred smoking so much that she forbade even her son, the Prince of Wales, to smoke on the premises. Therefore Victorian society decided to detest it too. In Victorian times English gentlemen could get away with murder (Jack the Ripper did) but not with smoking in front of a lady – Pretoria never dared to show in public her private vice. Accordingly a gentleman never smoked if there were ladies present. After dinner and coffee the English gentleman remained in the dining-room or went to another room to smoke, while the ladies retired to the drawing-room to chat the post-prandial time away. This custom is still observed in certain circles of London today. To some of my friends' chagrin I've always preferred the company of women to that of men. Women are beautiful (at least some of them can be just that some of the time, as the Singing Gypsy proved) and never, ever talk shop. Not an Englishman yet and being no gentleman, I sneaked out of the dining-room and into the drawing-room with the ladies one English evening and entered into a parlous situation as I set foot in the parlour: not only was my host angry but even my hostess was vexed. That's not the done thing! The Englishman's home could be his castle but certainly his parlour is his *zenana*. The cigar in fact seems like the white woman's burden sometimes. Some English women on going into a room full of men smoking at ease feel like a female Kurtz in *Heart of Darkness*.

But as things would have it, the Victorian male image was given by Edward Prince of Wales, a heavy smoker of Havanas in private and in public. Of course smoking was not permitted at all in the Palace which Bertie (the Prince's nickname) called the Forbidden Citadel. When Queen Victoria finally deigned to die at 80, after the funeral, Bertie, now King Edward VII, gathered his intimate friends in Buckingham Palace. They were led into a big drawing-room and then the

King entered smoking: 'Well, gentlemen,' he pronounced, 'you may proceed to smoke now – and that's a royal command!'

An American girl called Lorelei Lee wrote home about Bertie: the King too preferred blondes. 'Piggie,' she began, 'is always talking about a friend of his who was quite a famous King in London called King Edward.' Lorelei Loo went on: 'So Piggie', whose real name in the novel is Sir Francis Beekman, 'said he would never forget the jokes King Edward was always saying.' Explained Lorelei to a girlfriend back home as backward as she: 'He would never forget one time they were all on a yacht and they were sitting at table and King Edward got up and said, "I don't care what you gentlemen do but I'm going to smoke a cigar".' That killed Piggie and almost killed blonde Lorelei too, for she laughed like mad. Canned-laughter. Lorelei knew when to laugh at a royal joke: 'I mean you can always tell when to laugh because Piggie always laughs first.'

Some cigar-smokers always laugh last. With the Revolution as with many Cuban things, the tobacco industry was wrecked first because that's where capitalists were entrenched. Then the tobacco plantations were seized, though they were not the property of *latifundistas* or big land-owners. It is easy to nationalize a factory: even Groucho Marx's proverbial five-year-old child can do it and start a five-year plan. But it is very difficult to collectivize the *minifundios* in which each planter owned only two or three acres. Some *vegas* were given back to the original land-owners (most had already left Cuba by then) but the factories remained in the Government's hands. Though seemingly, as the Dunhill man said, most of the different traditional brands are still extant and others have been revived by the Cuban Government through *Cubatabaco*, this is actually swindle on the grand scale. But in spite of the dirty tricks with names, played on the European gentleman who can still afford a Havana, the *vitola* lingers on, like the melody of a cigar – which is smoke, which is a song.

The nationalization of all factories, including *chinchales* and *cherutas* that proliferated in the past, gave way to The War of the Brands. Curiously enough there was a precedent in the struggle to liberate the cigar from its band that is a bond. There had been cigars made in Cuba that had a quality of their own, distinctive and sometimes even unique (such was the *Por Larrañaga*) since the early nineteenth century. Like the Cuban dance that conquered all at every ballroom later in the century was called a habanera, the cigar made in Havana was known as a Havana. Havana was all of Cuba to the world then. But as Bizet composed the famous *habanera* for his opera *Carmen* on a borrowing close to theft from the then popular composer Sebastian Yradier, a Cuban-Spaniard, there were in Europe then sprouts of Havanas that had never seen the Cuban soil or sun. They were called Havanas nonetheless. Some sort of universal fair, the World Exhibition (where of course not all the countries on earth were represented) was created in that most enterprising age, the nineteenth century. Havana cigars won prizes in as many exhibitions – but so did other Havanas that came from such tropical isles as Liverpool and London.

The practice of calling everything that was cylindrical, brown and smoked (with the possible exception of a chimney) a Havana continued until 1907. Then an international court of law at The Hague (where no Havanas rolled) ruled that only cigars coming from Cuba could be called Havanas 'to protect this country (Cuba) from cheaper imitators'. (Nothing was said by the way of costlier imitators.) It is now 'an offence by British Law to use the term Havana for cigars that have not been made there'. Havana, the true colour of a cigar, must always be spelled with a small h. But there was a consolation ruling for foreign (that is native) manufacturers of cigars: 'Spanish terms for colour, shape and size are not objectionable.' You can copyright geography (as in the case of Champagne) but you cannot copyright the King's language, even if it is Spanish.

But you can register marks – internationally, that is. That's what the Bacardi family lawyers did so shrewdly years before Castro seized power. Now you have Bacardi rum made everywhere, from Spain to the Bahamas to Brazil – except Cuba, where the original Catalan family first distilled the potion Telly Savalas should try as a hair lotion. Some Cuban cigar manufacturers, like La Corona, imitated the Bacardis wisely and they roll their own abroad now. You could not perhaps smoke a Havana (though sometimes they are better than some Havanas) if it was not made in Cuba, like Hoyo de Monterrey, the cigar made in Honduras with the name of Excalibur: the sword in the evening. But a cigar, as Kipling ventured, is a smoke. Now cigar-smokers have quite a choice: Havanas that are not what they are called (a true Havana that is a fake Montecristo: more Dantesque than Dantés) and cigars that are what they claim they are but that are not Havanas. Obviously, as in *Finnegans Wake*, *c'est l'embarras du Joyce*.

Havanas will be awful (or *infumables*) for a while but the cigar, made of smoke, will always roll by like a cloud with a golden lining. After all, they have endured everything: Castro, communists and commissars plus plagues and pests and politicians in the past – but cigars, as if of rubber, always bounce back. Today not only the best Havanas come from Havana but The Best Cigar in the World is made in Cuba. As with Havanas always, this cigar has already become a myth. It is called Cohiba, one of the Indian names for tobacco. (The Incas had sixty-five names for the potato: this shows how important those two plants were for the natives.) The Cohibas come as coronas, panatellas and slim Margaritas very much like strong cigarillos. They are shiny *rosado* in texture, which is a rare colouring for a cigar, though there had been a precedent or two in Cuba before the Revolution. This of course implies a more rigorous selection of the wrapper to obtain red capes. Is this the communist cigar at last, the one Che Guevara wanted the New Man to smoke? I should say not. This is a cigar for millionaires.

The Cohiba panatella is exquisitely made, with a round straight shape, a clean-cut tuck end and the tip ending in a *perilla*: a tapering goatee-like volute that anticipates the smoke as spiritual spires. From the point of view of manufacture it is the acme of hand-made cigars. Everything spells perfection in this new Havana with an old name. Everything except its band and the box, both ornated with that kind of late 1950s pretentious bad taste called *hortera* (kitsch curl) in Spain. So *hortera* in fact that any Hollywood producer of yesteryear would have found it the ideal design for a garish poster in Cinemascope. Jerry Wald would approve, Saul Bass would frown for ever.

In the much-vaunted present independence of his island,

Fidel Castro has resumed an old Spanish custom: the best Havana in a crop was always sent first to the Bourbon king in Madrid, for him to taste. This colonial habit was broken for good when Cuba became independent in 1902. It is only eighty years later that a box of Cohibas (the 'first flower' as it is called in Havana: as the King (or Queen) of England has custody of all the swans in the realm, the King of Spain had and still has the privilege of cigar-upping. More than a census on cigars it is a consensus of one. In fact, a first flower is some sort of Royal Command smoke) is sent as a present by Castro to King Juan Carlos – who smokes them in the privacy of his Zarzuela Palace. A *zarzuela* is some sort of satyrical-lyrical-musical comedy but the smoke in Spain won't stay mainly in the reign. Another box (tobacco flower of the second kind, I suppose) goes to Prime Minister Felipe González, who, as a politician, smokes them in public and in office – but a Churchill he ain't, though. A third box is sent by express to the third man in Spain, Adolfo Suárez, once the prime minister and now a politician aspiring to the condition of statesman in retirement. He who smokes last.

One of those who smoked first was Jean Paul Sartre. Since his visit to Cuba in 1960 Sartre was presented with a regular box of Havanas: from the big tyrant to the tiny philosopher. Sartre was a keen smoker but one day, after 1968 and Castro's support of the Russian invasion of Czechoslovakia, he said no more cigars, thank you but no thank you. When novelist Alejo Carpentier, cultural attaché at the Cuban Embassy in Paris, tried to reach Sartre with yet another box of choice Havanas, the author of *Being and Nothingness* chose nothing and Carpentier didn't return to the embassy empty-handed: he came back with his boss's cigars. Cubans bearing gifts or straight from the Horse's mouth.

Politics in fact has always played games with tobacco in Cuba and sometimes Havanas have become explosive issues. Dr Fernando Ortiz in *Cuban Counterpoint* says pun in cheek: 'He who governs Cuba must rule over Havanas.' Fidel Castro was the first Cuban leader to smoke cigars in public. During the 1940s and 1950s President Prio smoked cigarettes but both Batista and Dr Grau were non-smokers. In his Nuremberg-like rallies Castro's cigar is a smoking counterpoise to the perennial pistol on his hip and the evergreen fatigues he wears. The cigar became for Castro one more offensive weapon to tote. Later it was revealed that the CIA really tried to transform Castro's corona into an exploding cigar. Or rather a poisonous panatella that could release lethal fumes. They forgot that there already was in Cuba a dangerous cigar called *horro*, so close to horror, which according to lore was poisonous by nature and exuded a venomous distilment ('the juice of cursed hebona', after Shakespeare) that instead of your ears sought your nostrils with 'an enmity with the blood of man' – and of woman sometimes. Golda Meir and Indira Gandhi did not smoke cigars and Mrs Thatcher is impervious to the weed.

It was Aldous Huxley, a non-smoker, who said that there were only three kinds of intelligence: human, animal and military. Now Huxley would have to recognize the existence of a vegetable intelligence. Such intelligence, in turn, originated a counter-intelligence, this time a native intelligence. Cuban officials in the past had accused the United States Government of trying to assassinate Castro. In 1981 the Cuban dictator claimed that the CIA was poisoning not only his cigars but his tobacco plantations as well! What juice could kill then the cursed hebona? *Quae mundi Plaga?* What pest? It was something borrowed and something new, something old and something blue – and with a beautiful name in Spanish to boot: *moho azul*. Blue mould, but why not blue *mole*, to give it the status of a spy burrowing in the garden? A blue snake in the grass or the *blue* bird in your own backyard?

I asked Arturo Sosa about this in his house in Miami where he kept a rare parrot and cigar boxes with his name as a brand. He had suffered the loss of one leg to circulatory problems and with his entourage he looked like a benevolent version of Long John Silver, though somewhat shortened. But he was the same kind old man I met in Havana in 1960, sleeping on the floor of some relative's flat. A man in flight, he had been given shelter there as if in sanctuary. He reminisced now out of the blue on the blue mould.

We had the same problem in the Remedios region in 1934. But Dad [it was endearing to hear a man of 80 call his dead father Dad] knew what it was. Of course he knew. He knew all about the leaf. I was afraid at first when I saw all the plants destroyed as if with wantonness. But Dad knew all right! 'It's a fungus that comes from Africa,' he told me. 'From *Africa*, Dad?' 'Yes, from Africa, son. Just like slavery. It crosses the Atlantic Ocean on high hot winds and lands on the first land it can find. Just like Columbus.' Dad was right for Columbus came from the Canaries. Dad also taught me how to get rid of it. You just work a safety path away from the fungus. A counterblast as it were. Then you destroy all the plants around the infection. All of them! You must, you know that? For the fungus, once it has landed cannot spread but from plant to plant. Sometimes this remedy is worse than the sickness. It cannot be applied because you destroy the plantation. You must wait then to see the mould ruin it, more slowly but much more effectively! You always kill a man with the fungus, the poor planter. He simply cannot be spared. That's all there is to it. The blue mould is just a bug that instead of smoking tobacco chews it and eats it too. But it can burn it up. Or char it like fire. Then that's man who's doing all the grass burning.'

Sosa, who died in 1983 in Miami, knew more about tobacco and cigars than any other Cuban I know. He was the typical tobacco plantation owner, of Canary stock but a true-blood Remedian. His father had been a Canarian planter in Cuba in the 1920s and his son became a tobacco manufacturer out of love for the leaf. He too was partial to the weed. He died longing for the sierras, complaining that the city was actually Miami, Flats.

Sosa entertained his friends frequently and they were quite a few, queer fellows mostly, old cigar men. Though Sosa himself never smoked he was a true connoisseur. Bernard Berenson never painted a painting nor Anthony Blunt organized a *tableau*. So Sosa was like such experts who know more about it than the artist. Or the critics who couldn't write a novel, like Leavis-Strauss. He was a scholar on cigars. There he was, reigning over his matter that was the stuff of which smoke is made: tobacco. He held court among the tropical vegetation in his drawing-room, presided over by the damned jungle bird, the grey parrot he brought all the way from Brazil, the Ultima Thule for cigars according to him. He

172

spoke of the lands *ultra mare*, across the seas, never reached by his travels but travelled well by his cigars. Europe, he claimed, smokes well but smells awfully. He had never been to Africa either but he was certain that tobacco did not grow well over there – and fungi thrived. He never forgot the blue mould of his blues. But he had a good word or two for the Cameroon before he went: the land of his wrappers. And he loved all African animals. Except the cheetah, which he believed to be just a leopard that cheats. As to Asia – better leave her as is.

Sosa was born, and lived until 1960, in Taguasco, in the Sierra del Escambray, central Cuba. Still tobacco country but known in the trade as Vuelta Arriba or Up Island, the land that produces the Remedios leaf, filler tobacco of high flavour and heavy of body. There he prospered and was well-known in the cigar market as a dedicated planter. He was esteemed all over the region as a fair employer and a kind man. After Castro's takeover, his plantation, including his farmhouse, was brutally expropriated and in a personal vendetta he was persecuted by the actual *comandante* that was once his foreman. Penniless, he emigrated to Florida. First to Key West and later to Miami, now the centre of cigar manufacturing in the USA. In Little Havana, South West Miami, he managed to build his own factory from scratch, which was rather taxing to an exile long past his prime. But he managed to earn a reputation as a producer of quality cigars at reasonable prices – which is considerably more than what Marshall dreamt as the good patriotic smoke. Sosa achieved quite a feat and before he died at age 83 he secured a foothold in England. He was one of the few Cuban exporters in exile who sold his cigars to the English gentleman, always a hard man to please when it comes to his true smoke. Sosa cigars, his own monument in brown, memory in smoke, are sold today in Fox's the exclusive Burlington Arcade shop off Piccadilly. Old man Sosa loved tobacco and, fortunately for me, was always willing to talk shop. I listened, he glistened: Pela and Panduca in reverse.

Pela and Panduca indeed! They sound like a vaudeville duo. At least like a Cuban version of vaudeville, the *teatro bufo*: Pela y Panduca *pioneros*. To those enterprising Cubans vaudeville owes more than one laugh and the exact timing of a comedic genius or two: W. C. Fields for ever, the ways of a Groucho. 'Writing about cigars?' asked Arturo Sosa speaking over the screeching noise of his pearly-grey parrot. 'My boy, you are going to have a field day!' I had, in fact, two field *years*.

Italo Calvino, a countryman of Italo Svevo, the author of *The Confessions of Zeno* (the man for whom giving up smoking was the parody of a paradox: before you give up smoking you must smoke, before you smoke you must light your cigarette, before you light your cigarette – and so on and so forth until the paradox became paralysis) was born in Cuba not far from tobacco land. Being younger than Svevo (né Schmidt) Calvino does not care for Freud but cares about Marx. Calvino claims that the cigar is what sets Groucho apart from 'all the great comedians of the screen'. Perhaps. But this doesn't set Groucho apart from all the lesser comedians of the small screen like George Burns and Ernie Kovacs. For Calvino a cigar means 'the eternal [sorry, *external*] attributes of prestige, success and *savoir faire*'. Even when it is done in a crypt. But Chaplin's tramp was the opposite of prestige and success and did he love cigars! Preferably in the form of a butt in the gutter. In *Gold Rush*, even after he struck rich and came back from the Yukon first class, another passenger threw away the stub of a cheap cigar on deck. Charlie saw it and right in front of journalists, photographers and admirers (the external attribute of success) he jumped, literally, after the stump, though he could now stomp at the Savoy and put in at the Ritz forever. He indeed could afford all the Havanas in Cuba, a small island then.

This is a trifle compared to the extremes Charlie is willing to go for a smoke in *City Lights*. In the later movie he is taught to smoke Havanas by – who else? – an eccentric millionaire he had met in Dire Street, where the tramp always lives. The rich man is very rich indeed. He is also by turns suicidal and very, very friendly when he is drunk – but haughtily forgetful the morning after. The tramp is thus alternately (and confusingly) pampered and rejected by the millionaire, a manic depressive of the first water. (As a matter of fact the former made the latter's acquaintance by saving him from drowning when he tried to kill himself in the nearest river earlier in the movie.) On learning how to smoke a real cigar Charlie sets a lady's evening gown on fire and plays havoc in a posh restaurant where he was the rich man's guest. But only for the night. It is a Jekyll and Hyde situation and Charlie must do the hiding.

Next morning, on leaving the millionaire's mansion (the night before he even gave Charlie his brand-new convertible as a present) the tramp feels like having a smoke. A pedestrian lights up a cigarette beside him to become more than an extra. Brother, can you spare a fag? But now a gentleman comes down the street smoking a cigar. What a pleasure to smoke is! think visibly both men. The smoking gentleman passes by and Charlie almost falls in his wake. But he has a better idea. He clambers in the shiny convertible and borrows it to follow the gentleman with the cigar. A few streets down the avenue, the smoking gentleman throws his butt away: it was burning too close for comfort. Charlie, in the background, stops the car and actually jumps from it to dive after the cigar – in close competition with another eager beggar. Charlie wins by a nose. He goes back to his costly convertible contentedly smoking the left-over, to the utter amazement of the second, unlucky tramp. The latter scratches his lousy head, dumbfounded at what he believes must be the latest trend in slumming.

All American comedians on stage, great or small, have either smoked or used a cigar as a prop. That's exactly what it was for Groucho, who confessed that he got the habit (or the practice) from an old vaudevillian on the road long before he learnt to smoke. That was so long indeed that at the time of the interview he had forgotten the name of the comedian who spoke loudly and carried a cigar as big as a stick – just for a shtick. But Groucho could still remember his *first* cigar. 'It was an Imperfecto Perfecto – and did it give me trouble. Boy! Even though I never lit it I got seasick. We were on a boat on the Mississippi at the time heading for Peoria. That's Spanish for the pits, nor far from Pittsburgh.'

Near Pittsburgh, in Philadelphia, one Claude Dukenfield was learning to juggle and smoke at the same time – he juggled five and ten cigar boxes. Sometime later he changed his name, which he found atrocious, to the slightly scatalogical W. C. Fields. This comedic artist can be hailed as a man who, admiring Dickens as he did, which was a hell of a lot, hated

175

Christmas even on Boxing Day. He couldn't be the cigar lover he was and also a practitioner of the art of exploiting cigars. Fields, much to his credit, made them an instrument of his pleasure. In one of his first films *It's the Old Army Game* he can be seen sweetly smoking. But that's only because somewhere on the prowl is that uncertain feline beauty Louise Brooks. She can become instantly into a *felix culpa*, as she reveals in her admirable *Lulu in Hollywood*. In the movie it's her fault, naturally, that that ever unhappy Fields sets a cigar-box (and its full contents) alight and the fire brigade must come to the rescue with their usual finesse when facing anything that smokes. Fields had to comply in a comedy called *Flaming Youths* and he did all the smoking there was about the flames. I almost forget how he smoked in *The Dentist* but I always forget all about dentists, including their drills and bills. In *International House* by way of proving how cosmopolitan he could be, Fields wore kimonos and cigars, manic Manilas mostly. All over *Tillie and Gus* Fields smoked, sometimes as the brave captain who sinks with his rowboat – wearing a fake yachting cap and a genuine Havana. When last seen W. C. Fields was not permitted to smoke and could only have a sniff of an unlit cigar.

Fields wrote an epitaph in aspic for Mae West when he called her 'a plumber's idea of Cleopatra'. He should have added, 'and an Anglo-Saxon plumber at that'. Or at least a WASP plumber. But he had previously incurred a day's ire of Miss West because of his drinking and smoking habits on the set. As told by Louise Brooks, the woman who was Lulu, Fields's 'bar was an open wardrobe trunk, fitted with shelves which was planted, as if it were an *objet d'art*, beside his chair'. What Fields would have called his accoutrement was attended by Shorty, a dwarf. He took care of his cigars as well as his drinks. While Fields literally powdered his nose, a bulbous burden, beautiful Brooks danced around him: a cigar in his mouth, a drink in his hand, drinking and smoking in his dressing room. Mae West was to disapprove strongly of 'such filthy vices'. I think she was right, but never proven. Alcohol diminished Fields's considerable talent and all his fans and admirers can only wonder now what could he have done in movies had he not drunk so much. But I still cherish the still of that memorable moment, apprehended by the camera *cine die*, in which that lisping Thespian, John Barrymore, his close friend in real life, offers a cigar (it had to be a Havana) to a bemused, amused W. C. Fields for ever.

I always wonder why Fields said that the best thing in the movies was the still. Now I know he didn't mean the photographs but his unmoveable trunk.

Even in his first short, *Pool Sharks*, Fields is seen smoking a cigar – that is later changed into a cigarette to comfortably ride on his right ear. Fields was pursued by the law for revealing the facts of life to an Indian. Could it be how to smoke a cigar?

W. C. Fields's love of cigars can go to extremes. In his best comedy, *It's a Gift*, he comes down to breakfast already smoking what looks like a cross between a cheroot and a stogey but it is only the comedian's version of a five-cent cigar at seven o'clock in the morning. On his way to the dining-room he steps, inadvertently, on an abandoned roller-skate (junior's naturally) and does a double somersault plus a double take. When he manages to sit at table he is wearing a carnation in his hand – which he is about to light up. Then he pins his cigar to his lapel. Can't you see that for this man a cigar is like a flower?

In the long association between the fat Southern gentleman with the fine tenor voice and the lean Limey with a squeaky Cockney accent contaminated by the American idiom, it is Oliver Hardy who smoked the best cigars (price: 5 cents each; value: staggering riches in laughs) and his associate Stan Laurel who always managed to wreck his smoking happiness somehow. Of all the hazards that smoking a cigar brings to Ollie's health the most memorable occurs in *Chickens Come Home*. Ollie is a politician and following his old motto, 'Be Nonchalant', he daintily smokes his first Havana of the day in the privacy of public office. Suddenly there is a knock on the door. Our once and future mayor, still smoking, goes to the door but Stanley opens it first to come in – and slams the door right on Ollie's Havana. Ollie looks at the camera, in misery, a round face with a dark star where his moustache was. He is *not* nonchalant. Believe me, nobody can be nonchalant with a squashed cigar on his face.

When it comes to cigars Laurel and Hardy are masters of give and take. No sooner have they given a cigar away than they take it back. They are, as Columbus showed us, Indian givers. In *Pack Up Your Troubles*, one of their few feature films, they use both cigars and sausages as props when they visit their bank. You know the way normal citizens exchange pleasantries. They give the bank manager a cigar that is actually a sausage and the elderly gentleman accepts it with what you can call banker's bonhomie. Laurel tries to light his sausage. He can't of course. So he eats his cigar instead. That is, his sausage. Oliver dabs and stabs his hat with his sausage and with a flourish of his cigar (or sausage) he asks the manager for a loan. 'Have you got any collateral?' asks the manager, naturally. They have never heard the word before. 'Collateral?' asks Hardy and what with all those sausages changing hands, Ollie really says: 'Colesterol?'

In *Below Zero* a florid Oliver Hardy calls the waiter: '*Garçon*, a *demitasse*.' 'Me too, Gaston,' says Stan Laurel. Is Ollie displeased with this copycat! 'Waiter, hold the *demitasse* and give me a *parfait* and a *perfecto*,' he orders. 'Perfect,' nods the waiter. 'Me too,' says Stan Laurel – and so he was, so he was! A perfecto.

In *Busy Bodies* Stan is Satan with a cigar. He and Hardy work in a saw mill near an enormous warning sign. NO – it begins. Stan gives his nearest colleague a cigar. His co-worker accepts. Stanley, almost overdoing it, even lights the cigar for his pal – just before calling the ferocious foreman's attention to both the sign that says 'NO SMOKING', in big, bold lettering and to the smoking transgressor, obviously as illiterate as he is a *bon fumeur*.

Silent comedy was a heaven for smokers – but also a hell. In a very primitive Harold Lloyd one-reeler, *Luke's Movie Muddle* (an inner-sanctum affair in which a very young Harold without his tortoiseshell glasses crudely imitates Chaplin, curly hair, moustache and all), early movie-goers go to the early movies too early – to be manhandled by the usher, a crashing boor. There is the usual gross display of violence in the dark at which silent comedies were so adept and so apt. The rough passage culminates with a late patron who arrives smoking a loud pipe. To get into the house of fun ('No smoking aloud!' shouts Lloyd the doorman) the patron must put his pipe in his pocket still alight. By trying to stop the customers from smoking, the management, or rather the old man, sets the house on fire. The short ends in panic and smoke, and nobody gets a chance to watch the movie they paid to see.

Nowadays British theatre managers are no less restrictive than Lloyd (or even Lloyd's) but are more intelligent, therefore more lenient. They let patrons who want to smoke 'sit on the right-hand side of the auditorium', to smoke through the show in peace. Fire hazard (and smoke) has thus been reduced by half.

Oliver Hardy and Stan Laurel smoke even in Switzerland – and their menacing monkey, the hairy ape on a hanging bridge over a Swiss chasm, sedulously does it too. It was from a chasing gorilla in fact that Lou Costello retrieved his last cigar. Minor American comedians do it too. Like Milton Berle (who smoked the fattest cigars in show business) for instance and Jackie Gleason on many instances. The only major American comedian besides Buster Keaton (but Keaton lived in another country: the past full of steam locomotives, steamboats and steaming Southern hospitality) who professes not to do it and not to like and even to hate cigars is Bob Hope – and he is British. In *My Favorite Brunette* he is offered a Havana by the villain and Hope says quickly, 'No thank you. I'm driving.' He is by the way the only one of the old-timers that is alive today. Coincidence? Perhaps. But when it comes to sticks Hope always sticks to golf.

An early, even remote example of the close relationship between the burning cigar or a dead one or a merely defused cheroot is that couple of swells, Mr Gallagher and Mr Shean, as seen: Shean with a Baedeker, Gallagher with a cigar. Or was it the other way round? It doesn't really matter. What matters now is that Al Shean, that prehistoric Jewish comedian, was Groucho Marx's uncle in real life – or whatever Groucho called that laughter barrier. Al Shean dutifully introduced Groucho to show business. The rest, as Hegel said, is hysterics. In *The Coconuts*, his movie debut, Groucho makes his first appearance on top of a staircase – and he is already smoking a cigar. Groucho is surrounded by a mob of dumb bellboys, but his cigar is alight. It is in fact the only thing alive in the number.

Groucho with his cigar did to comedy what the other Marx with his cheroot did to economy: revolutionize it and in so doing destroy order, hierarchy and rules. It's all there in *Das Kapital* and in *Duck Soup*, one of the Marxes' first pictures in constant motion, probably their best effort to release sheer anarchy loose upon the world. In his second (or fifth coming) Groucho on trying to save Freedonia for Freedom or for Mrs Teasdale (whichever came first) annihilated both (she came first) and the finale is called a Harpo End. Groucho accomplished all this with the support, financial or otherwise, of Margaret Dumont, who looked exactly like Engels minus the beard: Jewish, tall, well-bred, rich. Both capitalists helped with the Kaput all – and got Economo's Disease. That's also called dreaming, or rather sleeping, sickness.

Please bear in mind that in the movie *Duck Soup*, as in every picture by the Marx Bros, all Groucho truly loves is his cigar. At least he is kissing his *vitola* all the time, even when he is sleeping or slapping his adamant rival, Ambassador Trentino: an enemy envoy on a friendly mission. Curiously Trentino is slapped by Groucho not because he makes passes of peace to Margaret Dumont but because he inadvertently calls Groucho an upstart. By the way, as with Mrs Thatcher, one can never call Mrs Dumont, Maggie. Is that a first name?

One of the forms sabotage of law and order takes in this manic movie is in the shape of a cigar. When Trentino (Louis Calhern at his phoniest) interviews his so-called spies, Chico and Harpo (at his funniest), the so-called Chico cuts Trentino's costly corona (it might have been a Havana, for Christ's sake!) with a concealed weapon, some swish scissors. But not before trying to set the cigar and its owner alight with a blow-torch – actually an early version of the flame-thrower, a vertical Bunsen burner. (See gag lighter.) All Chico has to say (Harpo as usual has nothing to say) on seeing the Havana cut down to stumpen size is: 'Datsa good quarter cigar.' The third brother in the meantime is making love in his fashion (that is making puns not love) successively but not successfully to Mrs Dumont, a consummation he is devoted only to wish, and later to sultry, dusky Carmen Torres, his Mexican match. After using her to light up his cigar, Groucho, now a somebody, proceeds to stand her up – as he stood up the delectable blonde Thelma Todd in *Monkey Business*. In this earlier mayhem, adding smoke to mockery (that should give you smockery), Groucho, fully dressed and with squeaky shoes on, lay in bed with his cigar, while in a revealing glossy gown gorgeous Miss Todd paraded up and down the room talking of miching malecho. She fumed, he only smoked on – and on and on. Forever. Lonsdales can give you lone dallies.

This is how Perelman describes his first meeting with our Marx: 'Garbed in his time-honoured claw-hammer coat, his eyes shifting lickerishly behind his specs and an unlit perfecto in his teeth, Groucho irrupted.' Please observe the 'unlit perfecto' jab. Groucho might take exception to that. He did, apparently for there's a correction of sorts: 'His (Groucho's) outsize corona and eyeglasses were at variance with his nutical dress.' But that's my fault, folks. Whenever I see Groucho wearing anything nautical I always write nutical. From knots, really. Or rather nuts.

Long is the story of the association between this comedian and his cigar. 'I always smoked a cigar,' Groucho told Richard Anobile, a member of his school of biographers: serious, Gentile, non-smokers all. 'I was well known for smoking cigars. A lot of comedians smoked cigars, like George Burns.'

Thackeray, who called tobacco 'that kindly weed', has this to say about cigars and timing in his *Sketches and Travels in London*:

> Honest men with . . . cigars in their mouths, have great physical advantages in conversation. You may stop talking if you like – but the breaks of silence never seem disagreeable, being fueled up by the puffing of the smoke . . . the cigar harmonizes society, and soothes at once the speaker and the subject whereon he converses. I have no doubt that it is from the habit of smoking that . . . American Indians are such monstrous well-bred men.

'I don't smoke good cigars,' claims Burns in *Hello I Must Be Going*, a Marxian chronicle. 'They're too strong for me. I only smoke cigars that fit my holder.' A cigar with a holder! That's anathema, worse than an edema. 'I smoke these domestic cigars.' Did he say *dogmatic* cigars?

'I love them because they fit my holder.' Next Burns will be smoking cigars with a philter! 'I think that when you smoke a Havana cigar,' he goes on, 'you should get paid for doing it.

They're very strong. Like Milton's cigar.' (Burns means Berle not John Milton. Berle, together with Ernie Kovacs, was the television comedian who smoked the most aggressive, ostentatious and fattest Havanas – probably king-size Lonsdales.) 'You know, *two* dollars,' says Burns as he makes the v sign with an obscene reversal, 'if I spent two dollars on a cigar, first I'd go to bed with it.' (I have good and bad news for Mr Burns. First the good news: Groucho did just that while blonde Thelma Todd connived and contrived. Now for the bad news: today that cigar as dear as a hooker would cost Burns as much as a call girl. That's Riley Marshall's First Law of economics.)

In *A Night in Casablanca*, the brothers nightcap, Groucho is doing the rumba – hectically. (There's no other way for Groucho to do the rumba.) He is dancing and smoking – frantically. (There's no other way for Groucho to smoke.) As he dances in front of yet another blonde who's watching the dancers from a ringside seat, Groucho gives her his cigar: 'Here, hold it for me till I come back.' Only one more turn by the shrewd dancer and he announces to the lady with his cigar: 'Surprise! I'm back' – and deftly he retrieves his Havana. This reminds me of Fidel Castro in a big rally in Montevideo in 1959. Acclaimed by the Uruguayan crowd, he got up to speak – when he noticed his smoking Havana in his hand. On his way to the microphone he handed his lighted cigar to Conte Aguero, then his political adviser, and told him audibly: 'Hold it for me, will you Conte?' Marx and Marxists are all alike: crude conceits.

FOOTBALL REFEREE: What are you doing with that cigar in your mouth?

GROUCHO: Why, do you know another way to smoke it?

DEAN OF COLLEGE: It would please the faculty if you would throw your cigar away.

GROUCHO: Tell the faculty members there will be no diving for this cigar.

CHICO: What is it got a big black moustache, smokes a big cigar and is a big pain in the neck?

GROUCHO: Now, don't tell me. Has a big black moustache, smokes a big black cigar and is a big pain in the –

Those past (and present) exchanges led to the following correspondence. It could have ended with Groucho saying, 'My seconds, Chico and Harpo, will see you in the morning, sir!' Unfortunately it didn't. Even Groucho could be awed – or rather ohd.

Dear Groucho Marx:

   P.S. I like cigars too but there isn't any cigar in my portrait either.

Yours sincerely,
T. S. Eliot

Dear Mr Eliot:

   I read in the current *Time* magazine that you are ill. I just want you to know that I am rooting for your quick recovery. First because of your contributions to literature and, then, the fact that under the most trying conditions you never stopped smoking cigars.

Regards
Groucho Marx

Dear Groucho Marx,

   P.S.* Your portrait is framed in my office mantelpiece, but I have to point you out to my visitors as nobody recognizes you without the cigar and rolling eyes. I shall try to provide a cigar worthy of you.

Yours very sincerely,
T. S. Eliot

*If T.S. seems to be writing letters that are all a P.S., this is only due to my abridgement – As to Groucho's rolling eyes and cigar please see cover. GCI.

Dear Groucho,

Whether I can produce as good a cigar for you as the one in the portrait appears to be, I do not know. But I will do my best.

Gratefully,
Your admirer,
T.S.

Dear Gummo:

Last night Eden and I had dinner with my celebrated pen pal, T. S. Eliot. It was a memorable evening . . . Eliot asked if I remembered the courtroom scene in *Duck Soup*. Fortunately I'd forgotten every word. It was obviously the end of the Literary Evening, but very pleasant none the less. I discovered that Eliot and I had three things in common: (1) an affection for good cigars and (2) cats; and (3) a weakness for making puns – a weakness that for many years I have tried to over come. T. S., on the other hand, is an unashamed – even proud – punster.

Yours Tom Marx

If Groucho didn't have a *Punch* in his mouth he had a pun. So was Sigmund Freud. The Professor was a Jewish tragedian but he loved cigars. Freud used to smoke twenty cigars a day – and a few more at night. All his colleagues smoked cigars, the analyst's tool in those days. (c.f. Robbe-Grillet.) The evenings at 19 Bergasse, always on Wednesdays, were the occasion for *der Meister* and his disciples (Adler, Stekel, Ferenczi and Otto Rank) to smoke in friendship and to fume at enemies who labelled them as a pack of quacks. Vincent Brome, a biographer of Jung and Jones, writes: 'What the atmosphere must have been like with four, five or six other people all smoking cigars!' Not all, for Jung smoked a pipe.

Freud as a host: 'Sit on the couch.' Ouch! 'So sorry. I should have fixed that spring since summer.'

But he didn't mean it as a joke.

The most astonishing non-Marxist smokers of them all are 'the Negritos of Luzon, in the Philippines, who scarcely ever stop smoking cigars – but is the lighted end that they place in their mouths!' Zowie!

When he was a boy Groucho used to smoke rolled news-paper, very much like the paper muskets Father Las Casas saw the Indians smoke in Cuba. Groucho could do better than that – and he did. 'When I was young,' he told an interviewer, 'there was a cigar called La Preferencia and it promised "Thirty Minutes in Havana". It was a ten-cent cigar, so I bought one and went to my room, got into bed and lit it. I set the clock. After twenty minutes the cigar was out. So I went back to the cigar store and said: "You advertised thirty minutes in Havana and it only lasted twenty-five. I want another cigar." So they gave me another cigar.' How's that for literalness? Groucho got two more cigars this way but he never got to Havana. 'It wasn't Havana,' he admitted, 'it's tobacco that was made (*sic*) in Connecticut.' Groucho grew rich and famous and old but he didn't get any wiser. He should have known that Connecticut is tobacco-land too, second to none in the United States, planted with Havana leaf seed originally.

There's even a motion picture, *The Wedding Night*, set in the Connecticut tobacco belt. Gary Cooper is the leading man, a writer who believes that the block in writer's block has to do with the city. As his name is not Urban Clearway, he moves to the country, far from Manhattan but too close to Anna Sten, a Russian editor in exile who unblocked Cooper even though she was a writer's bane. He suffered from mental block just by trying to pronounce her real name. No wonder: she was called Anjuschka Stensky Sujakevich! Further South, in *Bright Leaf* (you don't have to guess by now which leaf this is), Cooper, always the gentleman, is a gentleman farmer who becomes a tobacco tycoon. Here smokes really gets in your eyes and makes you cry, above all on account of the patrician beauty that was that Neal woman, whom Cooper inherited in *The Fountainhead*, not an architectural monu-ment on film, as intended, but a paean to camp constructions with the motto 'My house, Wright or Wrong'.

But back to basics with Groucho. He explained to Anobile why the American funny-man always revolved around a cigar, as if it were a flagpole with a burning issue. 'A cigar gave you time to think,' he theorized after Thackeray. 'You could tell a joke and if the audience didn't laugh you could take some puffs on the cigar. So it had a kind of value.' Anobile asked what you and I are asking now: 'What if the joke wasn't funny?' Groucho answered quickly: 'Then you used a different cigar!'

For a different kind of cigar – Marx, Karl, said in *Das Kapital*: 'Nothing can have value without being an object of utility.' What about the utility of diamonds and cigars now that we have the laser beam and free sex? There's no utility at all in smoke, the butt of a cigar, except to herald a fire, and ashes, unlike diamonds, are not forever. Marx knew the value of pleasure there is in smoking as well as in music. But where does the pleasure of a cigar reside then, in smoke or in ashes? Sacha Guitry said in both. Strange this commodity produced to be consumed, not by digestion or by time but by fire. Marx conceded the spiritual value of cigars and yet it is a vice, a spiritual snare. Karl Marx was the man who wrote 'you have nothing to loose but your chains', but like Zeno he was unable to stop smoking. Though of course, when he talked of chains he wasn't alluding to chain-smokers.

This is Marx, seen in this guise by his friend and follower but non-smoker Wilhelm Liebknetch:

Marx was a keen, even a passionate smoker. As with everything he did, he was an unbridled smoker. As British tobacco was too expensive for him every time he could he bought cigars which he proceeded to chew half of them, to augment the pleasure or perhaps even to double it. However, as in England cigars were very expensive then he was always in search of cheap cigars. One can easily imagine the cigars he came to smoke! All of them of the 'cheap and nasty' variety, therefore the cigars Marx smoked were feared by all his friends. Five-penny dreadfuls ruined his sense of smell and taste. In spite of this he thought of himself as an extraordinary expert on cigars. Until the day we set a trap to get him.

Marx's passion for cigars was a spur to his economic genius, not theoretically but practically. During a long time he had smoked a certain brand of cigars stinkingly cheap for England. On a trip to Holborn one day he found another even cheaper brand. I believe that a box cost as little as a shilling and six pence. Here his economic genius met his saving sense. With each small box that he smoked he 'saved' exactly one shilling and six pence – therefore the more he smoked the more he 'saved'. Thusly when he managed to smoke a small box a day he was on the brink of living on his 'savings'. He gave himself so intensely to this 'saving system' that he had expounded about it to us many times. An evening his doctor intervened to forbid Marx, categorically, to become rich following his 'system'.

If Marx was right then there should be more class distinction in smoking than in drinking: a wino is just a drunk not a connoisseur. This is neatly expressed by that supreme haute-bourgeois Jew, Arthur Schnitzler, in his otherwise seemingly frivolous play *La Ronde*. Schnitzler, a physician, was very precise on writing his prescription for not smoking above your station. All the following stage directions are his. At the beginning of the play the lower-class Soldier draws on a 'Virginia cigar', while the Young Gentleman puffs at an unidentified cigar (probably Dutch) and reads a French novel. His cigars must be very expensive for the maid to steal one of them 'for later' the moment he leaves the room. So let's say that the Young Gentleman was smoking a Manila mauler or a jovial Java. But he eats *marrons glacés* and drinks cognac. His cigar then should be a Brazilian or a Macanudo. Later in the play the Husband smokes a Havana cigar. Accordingly he must be rich and generous, even somewhat extravagant. His *vitola* should be blonde but thick, as the Germans and some Austrians preferred them at the time. All the women in this daring play, from the Prostitute to the Maid and from the Lady to the Actress, are equal in bed. But the men's social differences are clearly seen in their smoke. Once a democracy, in Cuba these class barriers didn't mean a thing. You see, in Havana all men smoked Havanas.

To his audience crying out 'Author! Author!' Oscar Wilde responded by going on stage smoking a cigarette. Could you believe it? He created a scandal. Could you believe it! The Prince of Wales had been in the Royal Box watching the show. An insult to royalty, no doubt. Oscar had loyalty only for royalties. But he excused himself by saying that he didn't understand the outcry about his being smoking on stage. It

187

was the best cigarette he could afford for the occasion: gold-tipped, long and very, very expensive. This happened the night *The Importance of Being Earnest* opened at the St James's Theatre on 14 February 1895. From such acme came the downfall with a crash of symbols: Wilde smoked a slim Fatima, the Prince a fat Villar y Villar.

Bertolt Brecht, a cigar-smoker (he only smoked stubs and his favourite word was but) wanted his theatre to be re-christened the 'epic smoke-theatre' and he dreamed that his audience of the 'smokers' theatre' might be more willing to think as they watched 'if they were allowed to smoke at the same time'.

A propos Brecht's cigar says Jean Genet: 'When you smoke a cigar as a cigar smoker should, when you can be defined as a cigar smoker, when you listen to Mozart's *Requiem* and the act of smoking a cigar is more important than the *Requiem*, it has nothing to do with *Verfremdung*, it has to do with not having much sensitivity.' Genet of course is not after the cigar but after Brecht and his effect of alienation: the player with a theory, the playgoer with a cigar.

Brecht begged his audience to smoke. A request that was not necessary in England twenty-five years ago or in China today. The difference was that in Drury Lane they never used the cuspidor, a fixture as common at the Peking Opera as the fortune cookie in a Cantonese restaurant in New York. By sheer coincidence it was at a New York Cantonese restaurant that I opened my last fortune cookie, an unfortunate experience. The fine print on the celestial strip of paper said, 'A man cannot be too careful in the choice of his enemies.' Confucius? No. Madame Mao? No, no! Oscar Wilde. That fateful evening I lost all respect for Oriental wisdom. A man cannot be too careful in the choice of a Chinese restaurant in New York. It could be the shortest way to take a walk on the Wilde side.

When writers meet a cigar while escorting a beautiful woman anything can happen. Cesare Zavattini, the neorealist screenwriter from Italy, first visited Havana in the early 1950s, accompanied by a Silvana Mangano as slim as a cigarillo. He observed then a strange Cuban ritual – and it wasn't voodoo. In cafés or restaurants Cuban customers, young and old, usually called the waiter and said aloud, '*Ecce homo!*.' This biblical quote instead of creating a religious response in the *camarero*, as would happen in Italy, made him dash off – to come back immediately with a *cigar*! It happened more than once at different Havana cafés Zavattini visited with La Mangano. Every time a patron cried out *Ecce homo*! he was rewarded for his apparent piousness with a real Havana. *Corpo di Bacco!* All Cubans were either Pilates or co-Pilates: *Ecce homo* indeed! Later Zavattini found out that what the Havanans were actually asking for was an H. Upmann, the cigar brand name. Cubans pronounced it exactly like Italians pronounce *Ecce Homo*, aitch uomo. Zavattini was charmed by the confusing homophony no end. A non-believer as well as a non-smoker, Zavattini was given to ordering an *Ecce homo* after every meal and even after every cup of coffee, either espresso or *demitasse*. Silvana Mangano, herself a Catholic, lividly demurred.

Cyril Connolly says in *The Unquiet Grave* that 'of all the drugs the poppy has the noblest literature'. What Connolly says of opium (he elegantly avoids the word as a void) can be said of wine too. This is debatable of course but I could gather an anthology written with smoke from Kit Marlowe to Philip Marlowe and then some. (*See Separata.*) Moreover I can move over and state that of all the herbs tobacco has the best movies. There are many masterpieces made under the influence of cigars precisely, like all the movies directed by Samuel Fuller, some masterminded by John Ford and one masterpiece or two created by Orson Welles – a man who once said that he made movies to be able to smoke cigars for free. 'That's why I write so many cigar-smoking heroes and villains who chomp their cigars,' declared Welles. 'Cigars are my inspiration. The bigger the better then.'

Samuel Fuller is your constant cigar-smoking director. He smokes cigars on the set, away from the set and on camera, as he did in *Pierrot le Fou*, in which he acted to help Godard act out his fantasies. At the end of the film Jean Paul Belmondo blows himself up with a king-size chastizing belt made of dynamite: he is a truly exploding character. But Fuller is a chain-smoker, which is bad. He also has in his lips a phrase that is a parody of Kipling, which is worse: 'A woman is just a script but a cigar is a motion picture.' Then he smiles his New York Jewish smile, like a wise Norman Mailer whose Nile is the Hudson River. Now he opens an old humidor (to maintain your cigars fresh all you need is a sense of humidor) a crimson crypt, bringing out – an already-lit cigar! He handles the Havana with care, as if it were about to explode. He takes it to his mouth – the biggest Lonsdale ever. 'This is my only vice,' he mutters and looks like a mighty midget grinning behind his two-foot pole of a cigar. Nothing can touch him now – except of course his smoke.

Big cigars and small men go together, cigarettes are for tall men and the pipe is usually associated with the man in the middle: middle height, middle age and middle class. Bums and the rich favour cigars, gunsels and molls prefer cigarettes. The pipe is for mystery writers and for sleuths, except for Sam Spade, who rolled his own. Movie men sport the pipe but John Ford always had his handkerchief tucked in his mouth, to chew the fat and the linen. Barnum first presented General Tom Thumb in his circus act as 'The Smallest Man In the World!' – smoking an enormous Havana. Since then dwarfs aspiring to the condition of midgets and a show-business career have been partial to the smoking stick as a gauge for height. Today Michu, with the Ringling Bros and Barnum and Bailey, is the smallest man on stage at barely thirty-three inches tall – and a cigar-smoker. The aim of dwarfs in show business is not being perfect but being smaller: small is bountiful. Michu the Midget decreases his stature by smoking cigars that dwarf him even more. Some small movie men, like Zanuck and Robinson and Fuller, looked bigger with a cigar.

There are motion pictures galore about drunks but not necessarily about drunks on wine. Not even *Days of Wine and Roses*, a picture on whines and cyrrhoses, is about wine – and of course it is not about rosé. There's an old story of a lush gentleman who is trying to cut down on his drink and then he confides to his audience (he is actually a stand-up comedian) with wild hiccups: 'Last week I lost three days.' That's where the title *The Lost Weekend* must come from. In the movie Ray Milland goes to the opera but he forgets his precious pint in his raincoat, left in the cloakroom. The opera is *Traviata* and now comes the party-in-progress scene. Alfredo is proposing a toast to Violetta: '*Libbiamo, libbiamo!*' Suddenly all the party-goers on stage become in Milland's eyes and misfortune a chorus of dancing raincoats with champagne glasses in their sleeves! *Traviata* means the woman gone astray, but I haven't seen one single scene in a movie where a character had delirium tremens with songs by Verdi because he or she cannot smoke at the opera. Though in *Cold Turkey*, the most savage satire on cigarette-smoking ever, there was a woman gone to ashes – a female Phoenix?

In all those drink-and-be-drunk movies the name of the villain is booze, but cigars are for heroes. If cigarettes were Humphrey Bogart's demise, he was killed early in his career. After smoking in *The Maltese Falcon*, where his role forced him to roll his own, Bogart smoked securely in *Casablanca*. Here he is shown for the first time in the picture as a headless figure elegantly attired and playing chess. Then the hand that moved a chessman picks up a cigarette from an ashtray and both hand and the camera go up to reveal Bogart as the smoker's thinking man. In *The Big Shot* Bogart is killed not with a kiss on his lips but with a cigarette falling from his mouth to his hand to the floor, in a deadly triple play. A male nurse in the prison's hospital is then seen killing the butt by stamping his foot on it. Thus with a cigarette and not with a stogey ends Bogey's life as a big shot.

But cigars are something else. Resuscitated by the magic of the movies, Bogart is seen two or three movies later in Africa, no longer off colour but rather ruddy of complexion, courtesy of Natalie Kalmus's Technicolor. He is shabbily dressed almost like a tramp, and wearing a captain's cap that has seen better days and better travels and better cigars. He is in fact smoking a cigar butt now, probably a dead soldier from last night on the river. In any case it is a stogy. Bogey is about to enter the village church where a singing, spinsterish Katharine Hepburn is waiting for him or for God, whoever comes first to deliver her from boredom. But before he goes inside Bogart takes off his cap. He is on the threshold of disrespect when he remembers his Brechtian butt. No Groucho he, still alight, he throws it away and into a huddle of black men, all eager to pick a fight for the stump as if it were a fresh Montecristo: Parkinson's law of the jungle no doubt.

A measure of our present rate of inflation is that in *Double Indemnity* in 1945 that connoisseur of cigars that was, rather *is* (great movie actors never die: they just fade out – to fade in again) Edward G. Robinson always buys his from the cigar stand on the ground floor at *two* cigars for 15 cents! But for 2 cents that is exactly what Thomas Riley Marshall envisioned as the American panacea.

Now for a smoking shtick.

A middle-aged, stocky, well-dressed American gentleman of obvious Hungarian descent whom you can call Eddie Robinson, real name Emanuel Goldenbird, comes to a cigar-store seen in the foreground and asks for a panacea with panache.

'You mean a panatella, mister,' says the tobacconist.

'I mean what I said: a cure for all ills. That could be a panatella to you, my good man, but for me it's a panacea.'

The vendor is slightly flustered.

'What country – Dominican, the Philippines, Canary Islands?'

'That's the spirit, my friend. Give me a Florida. That's not an island yet, it's a peninsula.'

'Here you are, sir – and more power to you.'

'What are you selling, brother – exploding cigars?'

Of course Robinson's cigars were not Havanas but neither were they considered stogies at the time. As a matter of fact Edward G. Robinson smoked them in the movie all the time (a bad habit that, smoking cheap cigars) but he had problems with lighting them. As with his actor's art Robinson never could find a match. In *Double Indemnity* he was an insurance detective, in *The Woman in the Window* he was a university teacher. 'Assistant professor,' he confesses to the police as if it were a privilege and not a crime. After committing adultery and manslaughter Robinson is promoted to a full professorship and eventually to better cigars: the dean in December, *upmann*ship for Christmas.

Edward G. Robinson was always in character, cigar in hand – or rather in mouth. Even such an unkind man as director John Huston, himself a cigar chomper, has this to say of the acting ability of Robinson's cigar: 'I think *Key Largo* is best remembered by most people for the introductory scene, with Eddie in the bathtub, cigar in mouth. He looked like a crustacean with its shell off.' Eddie is Edward G., of course.

In 'The Crime of Lord Arthur Savile' (from *Flesh and Fantasy*) Edward G. Robinson is his affluent old smoking self and always puffs at a Havana. But his evil double, the wrong-doer from the criminal classes, smokes cigarettes. I have no doubt that it was Edward G. and not the director Julien Duvivier who dreamt this fantasy of fumes. 'To smoke is what matters,' he mutters. 'That's my only grime.'

I can see (and hear, above all to hear) Edward G. Robinson in a movie of my own in glorious black and white, made in a celluloid heaven, one finger stuck in his waistcoat as he takes his cigar out of his mouth, to qualify: 'Discigar my last remark.'

Bogart was the greatest cigarette smoker in moviedom – and were there giants smoking cigarettes on earth then! Bette Davis is the greatest puffer of them all though. Look at the way she takes one cigarette already lit from the two Paul Henreid is constantly offering her in *Now Voyager* as a passkey to life. See then cigarettes act. Hear how she tells him 'Why ask for the moon?' and makes our silent satellite sound like some old cigarette brand: menthol Moons. But Edward G. Robinson is the greatest cigar-smoker ever, any-where. He could use his cigar dead or alive, alight or gone out, in his mouth or in his hand, to affirm and to hold, to stab an opposite argument and to fend off an attack or to pinpoint a fact forever and make a point, and finally to smoke it with an obvious relish nobody else shows in the movies like him – with the exception of Orson Welles. It is curious that when both men coincided in *The Stranger* Welles did not smoke (he was a Nazi, don't you forget it) and Robinson smoked a pipe! Almost until the end of his career Robinson kept the use of his faculties to handle a cigar not as a prop but as a proposition that can be self-evident and inquisitive at the same time. In one of his late pictures, *Two Weeks in Another Town*, Robinson is still being Burbank and Blaustein in one: a Baedeker in his mind and in his hand a cigar.

Orson Welles is a connoisseur and *bon vivant* who has become our fat friend. But in *Citizen Kane* he introduced the theme of smoking as character. This is so brilliantly done that the spectator does not notice it until the screen is full of smoke. Kane smokes (a pipe), his closest friend Jed Leland smokes too (cigars), his faithful factotum Bernstein smokes as well but not too well (cigarettes) and it is in the midst of clouds of memory that the unknown journalist starts his quest for the famous last phrase now only one word, the password to Kane's shuttered public life: 'Rosebud'. The press room is as filled with smoke as the screen, a smokescreen. The tender button of a name is for the newsmen (and for the movie and for us too) the *madeleine* of a dead man. 'Rosebud' goes up in smoke, from word to phrase to catch-phrase to slogan to sleigh and into the enormous, vertical, final cigar of the chimney in Xanadu (shades of Xeres) to write a sign in smoke in the sky as the film finally fades out forever.

Citizen Kane is the apotheosis of the love story of a man courting his smoke like a bride and even the cigar-band is sometimes used as a wedding ring. The first words said by Leland (a youthful Joseph Cotten, if that is possible: Cotten was never young) are 'I'll just borrow a cigar'. Bernstein (the amanuensis who doesn't want his name to be pronounced Bern-stine) says 'From Cuba' meaning a cable he has in his hands but delivering the words as if saying 'Amen'. Kane, like a taller version of Stalin, watches the scene as he lights his pipe. When Leland, already an old man, is interviewed by the newsreel man he asks the journalist: 'You don't happen to have a good cigar, do you?' Like Riley, Leland is not only asking for a cigar but for a good one too. The interviewer, whom Evelyn Waugh would call 'a squalid American', does not have a cigar: you see he does not smoke. 'A good cigar?' Cotten insists. Then later in the interview he asks again: 'You're absolutely sure you haven't got a cigar?' At the end of the interview Leland-Cotten comes back once more to his only passion: 'Listen young feller, there's one thing you can do for me.' What is it? 'Stop at the cigar-store on your way out, will you, and get me a couple of good cigars.' Presumably the same cigars Edward G. Robinson used to buy in *Double Indemnity* and not the toofers Katherine Hepburn talked about impersonating a gangster's moll in *Bringing Up Baby*: 'Yeah, toofers,' she said, ever so lowly, lovely. 'Two for a nickel, see?'

Cotten's passion has become, like most passions, an obsession by now: 'You won't forget about those cigars, will you?' I can say for the interviewer, 'I won't.' Cotten gives the journalist final instructions: 'And have them wrapped up to look like toothpaste or something. Or they'll stop them at the desk. You know that young doctor I was telling you about? Well, he's got an idea he wants to keep me alive.' How is the young doctor going to keep Joseph Cotten alive then? 'He thinks I'm going to stop smoking.'

The cigar, fat or slim but always erect, could be a symbol of youth and in fact as a great honour the young Kane announces that Richard Harding Davies is doing all right: 'They just named a cigar after him.' To Leland this is not so hot and he says piqued: 'That's hardly what you'd call a cigar.' Kane has a Cainite remark as a parting shot: 'A man of very high standards, Mr Bernstein' – and we'll never know if Kane meant Davies honoured or Leland jealous. The cigar could be a phallic symbol in *Citizen Kane* – and then again it could not. Auden, who should know, called our attention to a distinct possibility: 'Clearly even Freud said that a cigar could be simply a cigar.'

But Cotten, who in *Citizen Kane* scrounged cheap cigars and couldn't get any and could get all the girls he wanted but didn't want any, suffers in his next picture, *Magnificent Ambersons*, a reversal to remember. He got cigars aplenty but would never get his woman, his grandest passion after cars. 'I don't suppose you ever gave up smoking?' asks none other than Major Amberson, magnificently played by Richard Bennett, a father of beauties in real life: Joan and Constance Bennett were his most famous daughters. 'No Sir!' answers an eager Cotten who anxiously wants to be his son-in-law. 'Well,' says Major Amberson, 'I've got here some Havanas' – and genuine Havanas they are. A moment later, when Cotten is puffing on his cigar with Ray Collins, the band strikes up some Joplin syncopations. The only American rhythm that in effect remembers Havana, in ragtime it always sounds a beat of the *habanera*.

In *Shadow of a Doubt* the same tall, suave, elegant Joseph Cotten (a gentleman caller for ever in *Ambersons*) is a manic-depressive with a cigar. He smokes avidly when he is manic, he just holds the cigar in his hand when he is depressed. A simple cigar (if a cigar can be simple) will tell the spectator how he feels. Right at the start of the movie Cotten is seen lying in bed, soft shoes on and fully dressed, an unlit, listless cigar between his slim fingers. You are right: he is not manic now, he is depressed. He is in fact Uncle Charlie, a murderer, about to meet a girl named Charlie. She is only his niece but she will be his Nemesis very soon. That's a Greek word and Greek words always come in two on the telephone. The other Greek word occurs during an unwittingly witty exchange between the nice niece and the amiable lady telegraphist at the post office. Charlie is about to send a telegram to tell her uncle to please come back. But instead of handing it out to the telegraphist she is handed a telegram from Uncle Charlie saying, no kidding, that he is coming on the next train. 'Mrs Henderson,' asks a radiantly beautiful Teresa Wright playing Charlie, 'do you believe in telepathy?' Mrs Henderson, who couldn't tell a Wright from an awfully wrong Cotten, dismisses her: 'I ought to. That's my business, you know.' But who could dismiss the young Teresa Wright from his memory? That's not your business, you would say. Your business is cigars. Of course it is! But that was just an interpolation. I love interpolations, don't you? They sort of give a new appearance to things. The verb is interpolate. Interpol is a noun and means something else altogether.

Now Cotten is a wealthy man and can afford his cigars. He has earned enough wages of sin as to open a bank account in tidy, tiny Santa Rosa: population $40,000 – and in 1943 you could call that money. Suddenly Cotten cannot smoke his elegant panatellas any more. They are Havanas, no doubt about that, but he has lost his zest for living. The police are after him in mufti. Or, as Samuel Goldwyn once put it, *pains*clothesmen. (That's really being sartorially touchy!) As he can't smoke, Cotten's constant headaches become migraines and his paranoia is activated further by the police. Though he of all people should know that the moment the police are on to you for real, paranoia should subside: persecution mania disappears when somebody *is* after you. In the end insane Cotten gets killed when he is rammed by a cylindrical, dark, smoking thing – a train coming in the opposite direction.

Joseph Cotten was terminally young then. In movies they usually forbid only the oldest actor in the cast to smoke. We've seen just that happen in *Citizen Kane* to the same Joseph Cotten whom they offered Havanas when young to deny him later in life a mere five-cent stogy.

In *It Started With Eve* an ailing Charles Laughton smokes in his deathbed and even under the shroud-like sheets. But his doctor finds him out and takes away his cigar. 'That's a two-dollar cigar!' complains Laughton, who had always had problems with smoking in movies. Now the doctor comes back to take with him his box of cigars too. It might have started

196

with Eve but in 1941, when the movie was made, inflation hadn't really hit cigars yet. Today the ghost of Laughton would dive back into his grave the minute he knows that the same cigar would cost him $20 – and it would not be a Havana.

In *Witness for the Prosecution* it is Laughton, ageing again, who is denied his instrument of pleasure. In *Sabrina* it is Walter Hampden, the father of Bogart the bridegroom. Cotten looks the poorest of the lot, reduced as he is to a wheelchair. Hampden sneaks into a wardrobe to puff at his Havana in hiding – and to choke in his own smoke. (Earlier in the movie Audrey Hepburn tried to commit suicide with carbon dioxide when she shut herself in the garage full of Rollses, their motors silently running. In a humbler garage Cotten tried to kill his niece Teresa Wright by asphyxia with carbon monoxide pouring from the family Ford's exhaust. Garages can be hazardous for women who smoke.) In *Witness*, Laughton, on the brink of witnessing a cardiac arrest by the police, smuggles into court Havanas that he had previously hidden in his hollowed cane: he is a rich criminal lawyer. His nurse, the ever-lovely Elsa Lanchester, still the bride (and the pride) of the Monster, a cigar-addict by now, uncovers the ploy. Laughton agrees to defend cigarette-smoking Tyrone Power (who died in the movie and in real life: in the latter of a heart attack) on a murder charge only when his barrister bribes Laughton with one of his crisp Havanas. Unfortunately for purists (the real smokers of *puros*), Laughton cannot find a match, literally, and lights the costly cigar with Power's gas lighter. A Dunhill no doubt: the movie is set in London.

Some old actors play doctor but are not yet ready to stop smoking. Thomas Mitchell in *Stagecoach*, is one of those. But there is always society butting into the amenities of life. In one of the most endearing scenes ever shot around a cigar, Mitchell is Doc Boone, a derelict physician unable to heal himself of alcoholism (he could claim that drinking is a necessity but cigars are his only vice), is sitting in the coach in front of the town's whore now banished by her elders: the destitute and the prostitute. But Boone is smiling cheerfully at Peacock, a small man in black carrying a black bag, who looms like a mortician but looks big in the doctor's eyes: it is his good fortune that Peacock be a whiskey drummer. Doc is thus contentedly smoking and holding Peacock's simple satchel on his lap, caressing it like a black baby. But there is trouble ahead – and I don't mean warring Apaches. Smoke signals drift from Thomas Mitchell's stogy. (Please note that the scene would have played the same if the good doctor had been smoking a Havana: the test of a cigar is always in the smoke.) Hatfield, another passenger, impersonates a Southern gentleman and is vexed by the smoke that is now annoying Lucy, a Southern belle. She is pregnant and on her way to becoming a war mother.

Dr Boone is absently puffing on his stogy and contentedly cradling Peacock's satchel. 'Put out that cigar!' snarls Hatfield, enacted by John Carradine with lugubrious undertones and grim overplaying. Now Doc looks at Hatfield while Lucy stifles a cough. 'You're annoying this lady!' says Hatfield as he grates his teeth. Doc Boone looks at Lucy, acknowledges the fact that she is pregnant and shows her his cigar, a bare butt. 'Excuse me, madam,' says the doctor and tosses the remains of the cheap cigar out of the window. 'Being so partial to the weed myself,' he explains politely, 'I forget it disagrees with others.' Lucy smiles wanly but Hatfield, who represents Victorian morality with Southern manners, says curtly: 'A gentleman doesn't smoke in the presence of a lady.' Doc Boone, or rather Thomas Mitchell, shows finally who is the gentleman on the stagecoach. 'Three weeks ago,' he recollects, 'I took a bullet out of a man who was shot by a gentleman.' He looks ahead benignly: 'The bullet was in his back.'

Charles Coburn, another old man under doctor's orders and nurse's surveillance, was not allowed to smoke Havanas in his sumptuous mansion, but the moment he moves to the poor house of his putative descendants he smokes freely the stogy he buys every evening at the only drug-store in town. The walk to the corner keeps him fit: a cigar is the best constitutional.

Coburn is my second best man with a cigar but in *Monkey Business* he does not do any smoking at all. He just stands there agape and with a dead cigar in his hand. I don't blame him, for his secretary is Marilyn Monroe in the tightest outfit. *Monkey Business* is actually Dr Jekyll and Mr Hyde as written by Feydeau, the author of *Mais ne te promène donc pas toute nue!* But Marilyn Monroe only has to take a walk around the office as she is and Charles Coburn becomes a sitting doc. Now he tells her, in front of Cary Grant, to give his latest letter later for a true typist to type. 'Oh, Dr Oxley,' pleads Marilyn, 'can I try again? You promised.' 'No, Miss Laurel,' says Coburn sternly making a moron of Monroe, 'you find somebody to type this one for you.' Grant is aghast the way only he can be: with a noiseless ghast. Charles Coburn must explain, though he didn't have to, really: 'Anybody can type.' To hold this line at age 75 while Coburn watches Marilyn Monroe walk away bringing up the rear is the highest point of the movie – and one of the first jokes made about the killing anatomy of a murderess. That's exactly what Marilyn Monroe was in her next movie, *Niagara*. By the way, Charles Coburn's next picture was *Has Anybody Seen My Gal?* (Look above.)

In *Idiot's Delight* Coburn is an affluent old man who can afford his cigars but not war. He has struck a friendship with Clark Gable, a song-and-dance man with a blonde he won't covet. He was once the sugar-daddy and teddy bear of the desirable, desired doll in *Gentlemen Prefer Blondes*, but there his treacle tart was, again, none other than Marilyn Monroe, the eponymous epitome. Now the blonde is Norma Shearer, a much maligned actress, wearing a wig and a fake Russian accent: it sounds more like Swedish to me. They are all stranded somewhere in East Europe on the brink of the Second World War. Earlier on the train Gable has lectured on frontier posts, before which he must produce passports for him and his gals: 'That's my analysis of what the problem is with Europe: too many borders. They keep waking you up.'

Later, cooped up in a summer resort in mid-winter and right in the middle of muddles and war, Gable saves for later what looks like a terribly mauled bit of chewing gum by putting it in a small pillbox. He explains to Charles Coburn, who is quietly sitting beside him and smoking his Havana, why he must save his spearmint gum, formerly from Wrigley's: 'That's a museum piece, period of Louis Quince', which he pronounces like the rosacea. 'You've got to hoard it when you come over here.' Old man Coburn, a twinkle in his eye and with barely the hint of a smile, says nothing but takes his cigar from his lips, fishes from an inner pocket a silver cigar-case, opens it, places inside the still burning Havana (a gentleman putting his cigar to sleep with the least fuss) and closes the case with some finality. Now he smiles with content but also with a bit of nostalgia: in peace as in wartime the Havana days are always over for the elderly.

When it comes to cigars Charles Coburn can go very far even when he is unmoved. Here is how far he can go. He offered a cigar to Don Ameche when the latter came to tell him that he had just invented the telephone. 'What in heavens is that, Mr Bell?' asks Coburn, Ameche's prospective father-in-law and a reluctant investor. The inventor explains: 'It's a device to send the human voice to far away places by means of a wire.' In other words, strictly for the birds to perch on. Coburn stares at Ameche, then invites him to have a seat and calm down. He then offers him a Havana: 'Here, Mr Bell, have a cigar.' Ameche is flustered: he was not a father. Not yet in any case. 'Go on, take it. You look rather excited.' Then Coburn plugs the weed hard, the hardest he ever did in fact. 'Cigars, Mr Bell, are the best things to settle the stomach.' He does not care to mention other organs, like the human ear for instance. Obviously Coburn believes more in smoke signals than in talking wires.

In a life of Don'ts Ameche finds his final nesting place in *Heaven Can Wait*. No wonder. His favourite father was his grandfather, none other than Charles Coburn at his jolliest: every now and then he exclaims boisterously, 'Holy smoke!' and puffs at his perennial Partagas. The best plug ever for this book.

Some signs seem to be a clear indictment of cigars: they are bad for your physical and moral health. But the Surgeon General's determined warning is directed against cigarettes: cigars are never mentioned in his caution, as if they were ambassadors in a truce mission from Middle Tar. In fact a corona has less to do with a coronary than a piece of buttered toast, not to mention the familiar gravy with everything till the grave us do part. A Corona corona could crown a dinner but is less rich in calories than the whole meal taken piece-meal: from salad to soup to the steak and French fries and the *bombe surprise* for dessert.

That's cigars and the heart. Now for the cigar and the arts. Since the beginning the movies have in fact been a great advertisement for cigars, from live Havanas to dead soldiers. Chaplin's little bugger of a beggar used to pick cigar butts straight from the gutter, as I've showed you, in a thousand words per frame per second.

Ever since cigars have been burning bright in the forest of bad jokes, either as great props or splendid property.

Cigars have also been some sort of symbol of wealth and power. They were indeed blatant signs of sinecure since the early talkies. In *Scarface*, Muni-Camonte offers a stogy to Osgood Perkins, his boss called Lovo and the first *capo* from Hollywood. Perkins sees immediately that it is a cheap cigar and tells his henchman, 'Here, have one of mine'. Muni lights it up to be the second to a somebody. But soon cigars and silk and the *capo*'s mistress (all this and a Thompson machine-gun too) are the end and means of power. In those prohibition days Scotch was taboo but Havanas were all the rage. *Da capo* in the movie Muni takes a cigar, smells it, guns his head to approve and admire: 'That's nice.' Then he looks at Boss and smiles: 'Expensive, eh?' Expensive for Muni-Capone here means class. Actually his struggle for power using any available means is class warfare – with Marx's approval.

In the *Blue Dahlia* the villainous Howard da Silva gives the crooked house detective Newall a vital piece of information as he leaves: 'You forgot your cigar.' Old man Newall is a grateful snoop: 'Why, thanks!' But da Silva has the last word: 'I guess it's gone out' and then he intones in tones that could be menacing to the smoking crook: 'A cigar goes out awful easy, don't it?' In the screenplay Harwood is even more forbidding when he adds: 'So does a man – sometimes.'

But cigars can be hazardous to the young too. In *Little Foxes* cretinous Dan Duryea, not yet twenty-five, is fascinated by cigars as the sign and symbol of wealth and he day-dreams of untold coronas. Just before his dream could come true Duryea's uncle, Charles Dingle, smashes his unlit cigar on Duryea's astonished albino face. This is the same Charles Dingle, still the villain but now genially, who in *My Favorite Brunette* offered Bob Hope a cigar in peace. Hope, funnily enough, was the first American stand-up comedian to reject the cigar as a prop. So did Jack Benny but he had his violin. So does Heynie Youngman and he still has Benny's Stavagarius.

The same Leslie Caron who chose and lit cigars so lovingly for Louis Jourdan sang sometime earlier (in the movie and in this book), 'An ugly black cigar is love!' I quote her twice because she did it twice. But one must forgive her: she was too young to know then. Though she learnt fast the facts of life.

In a moronic movie that must remain nameless a young tyro on board a boat docking at Havana Harbor asks a man about downtown before they disembark: 'Can you buy a panama hat in Havana?' 'No', says his elder putting him down, 'but you can buy a Havana.' In fact you could buy both in Havana. Skinose's constant rival for the affection of Dotty that took them everywhere, from Ethiopia to Utopia, sings in *Blue Skies*, Bing with no Hope but a low Kaye, what is a message to Caron on her ferry to *Maxim's*:

> Cuba,
> Where the girls
> who like their fellas
> always light their panatellas.

While King Cole Porter, who was born in Peru (Indiana) asks rhetorically:

> What's a cigar without Havana?

Walter Burns in *The Front Page* is always about to flare up, not because his cigar had a short fuse but because he always exploded to exploit the news better. Thirty years later, in 1954, a contemporary of his can still be seen travelling on the Twentieth Century in the same compartment but not together with several movie moguls. Out of modesty he hides behind the front page of *The New York Times*. The movie-men have been talking shop and shop is now a certain song-and-dance man called Tony Hunter, a washed-up hoofer they dismiss as only a bad case of box-office poison. He has been pronounced *curare* to the general.

As the train slows down into Grand Central the man who had been behind the screen of all the news in a fit to print, lowers his paper to expose his face and smile sourly at the producers. Look! It's – it's Tony Hunter! Or rather Tony hunted. Tony, an acting Acteon, gets up and on his way out offers each gentleman in agreement one of his genuine Havana cigars made to measure. 'Here,' he amiably suggests with a gang's grin, 'have an exploding cigar!'

Tony Hunter is played by Fred Astaire in *The Band Wagon*, but the character's reaction to his critics is based on T. S. Eliot's exploits. The author of *Murder in the Cathedral* used to hand out exploding cigars to all his ravaging reviewers.

Exploding cigars have saved, literally, the life of more than one comedian. It is always amusing to watch the sumptuous Havana (or whatever) go up not with the whimper of smoke but with a bang and then see instead of the perfect form of this instrument of pleasure, a charred cheroot: a black star on the face of the unwary smoker. The oldest exploding cigar on the screen that I remember is one being smoked by long-legged Lee Tracy playing a gangling, bungling reporter in *Dr X*, an *infumable* movie. He was rescued from his girl's family freak by a cigar given to him by a friendly policeman on his night beat. But the cop was just another practical joker on whom Tracy had used a hand-shake electric buzzer earlier in the evening. The cigar, you've guessed it, was an exploding twofer. As inevitably as fate, when he sat to have a quiet smoke at midnight in the garden, the house monster came out swiftly to smite him thus. But the cigar Lee lit exploded in the freak's face in the nick of time. Neat? No, clumsy. *Dr X* is as awful a mess of a movie as Lee Tracy is a comedian, but it is an early example of exploiting an exploding cigar on the screen. The latest in things that go bang in the night is a trick not yet perfected by comedian Richard Pryor. He didn't have an audience when he performed his act but he was heard the world over. What a combustion! One can only wonder what Pryor would do for an encore – smoke snuff?

Rocky, Jim Rockford's father, the son of Noah Beery and Wallace Beery's nephew, tries to console Cleavon Little, the first black private eye in *The Rockford Files*. He offers him – guess what? 'Here, have a cigar, a genuine Havana.' 'Really?' says a grateful but dumbfounded Little. (Or is it a Little dumbfounded?) He was the first Negro Sheriff in *Blazing Saddles* and the first black blind DJ in *Vanishing Point*, but he now cannot believe his black eyes: 'Gee, thanks Rocky! You're a pal.' But judging by the way James Garner looks at his putative father and his credulous gumshoe friend some-thing seems to be afoot, as always is with private detectives since Sherlock Holmes pitched tent. Can Rocky afford a Cuban cigar? Can he give Havanas away just like that – as if they were ripe bananas? Where the hell in California did he buy them? Today in the USA possession of a Havana can be an explosive issue. Or an exploding cigar.

Sursum Korda! Lift up your cigars, ladies and gentlemen. According to his nephew, Sir Alexander Korda always travelled with his brass-bound morocco travelling humidor, which had 'a dovetailed sliding lid and his initials, "AK", stamped in the fragrant leather'. That was a portable humidor and like Merle Oberon a dubious affair. (There is a new type of humidor in the market now which is battery-operated and works up a steam instead of using inert water. It seems to be very successful in Belgium. At least it is secretly made in Boom, near Brussels. It has had with Belgian smokers what I could call a *succés de* steam.)

Sir Alex was a bulky smoker. Michael Korda shows his famous uncle wearing three cigars in his breast pocket. No respectable smoker would do this, mind you. That's like smoking your cigar with the band on. Cigars must be carried, always, in an inner pocket preferably inside a cigar-case or *etui*, in case you have decided to become a Frenchman this year. In his 500-page family biography *Charmed Lives* Michael Korda talks at great length of his cigar-smoking uncle, but he never let his genius shine through the haze of smoke. Louis B. Mayer, a rival producer, with only one phrase is instantly carried aloft on to the *puro* pantheon. Talking of Ricardo Cortez, a famous silent actor who was, like the Korda brothers a Hungarian by birth, said Mayer: 'Cortez is the only man in Hollywood who ever named himself after a cigar.' Those were, you must remember, boon years for leading lads with Latin looks and Spanish surnames. Where did Jakob Kranz pick up his name? Why, from Don Cortez cigars, that's where!

In a very different success story David Niven, the man who loved to hate Errol Flynn, talks like winner tells all of Ernest Lubitsch, the great film director and even greater cigar smoker. 'Lubitsch was a tiny little man,' says Niven, who was a tall little man, 'with a heavy German accent.' Why all German accents have to be heavy escapes me. Kick dat Kraut Kliché! He who plays the heavy, Lubitsch had 'straight black hair slicked down', but never licked, 'twinkling black eyes and a cigar out of all proportions with the ensemble'. His working habits were as singular as his cigars were plural. 'Lubitsch perched himself atop a small step ladder.' Was he perhaps to direct his actors reaching for the stars when he already had the moon, which for Niven was only a balloon? The ladder was 'at the side of the camera', and Lubitsch had an 'inevitable howitzer-type cigar in his mouth'. 'All directors have their little idiosyncrasies,' muses Niven. 'Lubitsch had his cigar and his step ladder.' Finally he assesses the director: 'Lubitsch was a pixie.' A moving pixie perhaps? According to Niven's book, *Bring on the Empty Horses*, Ernst Lubitsch was a talking pixie.

'Holy schmuck! You should have been on top of the ladder by now and not on top of a woman,' said Ernst Lubitsch to himself, in German, when he was about to finish *That Lady in Ermine*, his last comedy. (A tragedy, really.) But he was not on such an unsteady position as he believed and as ever, when in doubt, he lit a cigar. He also lit one when he was steady as a camera. He always did, everywhere. But he was not your usual dwarf with a big cigar, despite what Niven wants you to believe. (Though he was only five foot three.) Actually one of the legendary cigar men of the cinema, Lubitsch died as he had lived: smoking in bed. He didn't die in bed precisely. He has just finished making love to an extra. (Every lovely lady in Hollywood then was an extra: so was the rose according to Sherlock Holmes. Listen to him, 'Ah but you see Watson, the rose is an extra!') By a happy coincidence this extra was called Rose too. Lubitsch lit up his *último* (the last one in Spanish) and getting up (or down: you never can tell with extras) he said in smoke: 'I'll take a shower now. Won't be a minute.' It was the equivalent of Saki saying, 'Put that bloody cigarette out!' Lubitsch left the bathroom as corpses do, two hours later, after the coroner of the Beverly Hills Office came to take a look at the bodies, one stiff, the other trembling like a petal. Verdict: death by misadventure. Or rather by a missed adventure. The adventure of course being the movies.

Thus passed away the man who made the innuendo into

an art by merely opening or closing a door and walking into a closet furnished with a skeleton that exits smiling. He also made Garbo laugh, no mean feat this. (Pity though that when Garbo talked Garbo garbled). Lubitsch directed every set up of every scene in every picture of his with a cigar in his mouth, silently running. 'Akshon!' he would cry out and the world stood still until he yelled 'Cut!' Then they took the stills. He was a genius who dwarfed them all. Lubitsch had the touch: the Lubitsch touch. Especially with the ladies. But a miss was his demise. His epitaph, considering his job and looking at the dumb blonde extra, Rose, still naked in bed waiting for Ernie to come back, should be 'It's a wrap!' Lubitsch, and the coroner, would have agreed. But of course we all know that Lubitsch never wrapped up *That Lady in Ermine*, which became his unfinished sin. Rose faded out guilty but unpunished.

Ah alibis!

Director Billy Wilder 'was in awe of Ernest Lubitsch and was to remain so until Lubitsch died', says his official biographer Maurice Zolotow. When he died, Lubitsch not Wilder, who is very much alive and complaining, he cried all the way to the cemetery. Wilder had worked, as a writer, in several pictures directed by Lubitsch, who was also a shrewd producer. They were together especially in *Ninotchka*, where Garbo loved and laughed (she pronounced the two words identically) among Russian emissaries and commissaries. After the burial Billy Wilder's almost letter-perfect namesake Willie Wyler ('It's like in painting,' countermanded Wilder when the Studio wanted to change his name. 'Manet, Monet – who cares about an A?') came over to him and whispered: 'No more Lubitsch!' A louder man, Wilder sighed: 'Worse than that – no more Lubitsch movies!' Ernest Lubitsch died with a cigar in his mouth. Wilder inherited the showmanship but not the cigar.

Billy Wilder is a heterosexual Oscar Wilde, only Wilder. Instead of gold-tipped cigarettes he buys when he cannot afford them, he wastes Havana cigars on people who cannot smoke them, like Fred Clark, the downhill producer in *Sunset Boulevard*: he that plays de Mille. Later he has the true C. D. to welcome Norma Desmond out of pity: a real de Mille gloriosus. Wilder, even at its milder, does not smoke cigars.

That's why he isn't Lubitsch. That and the fact that he does not need a ladder to paradise. He is already in hell. At least that's what he gives his players with fire – or is it *Players* on fire?

In *The Bitter Tea of General Yen* Walter Connolly, a gun-runner during the Civil War in China, points at a Chinese general with his 45 caliber cigar and shouts: 'Keep your shirt on!' A cigar can be so persuasive that the venerably bearded general abandons that round table and departs annoyed by this barb that sends him not to a nunnery but to a laundry: 'Keep your shirt on, General!'

General Yen, a tough Chinese warlord, doesn't adopt what you can call a humanitarian stance about motherless children, even if they are Chinese. When an American gentleman of the Methodist persuasion tries to make him help with the rescue of some trapped orphans he retorts: 'Orphans! What are they anyway? People without ancestors – nobodies!' The Preacher becomes speechless but remains in his missionary position.

Later Nils Asther, as General Yen, delivers a really tough fortune cookie. When scolded by Barbara Stanwyck, because he has killed with his car 'her ricksha boy', answers Ashter: 'In that case, Madam, he is very fortunate. Life, even at its best, is hardly endurable.' And that's the way the cookie crumbles. But the implacable general commits a fateful blunder. 'A cigarette?' he offers Barbara Stanwyck. 'I have both Turkish and Virginia.' Take your pick, Madam. Barbara takes exception instead: 'I've never heard something so cold-blooded in all my life!' 'But, but,' butts in the general. He does not understand her, he never could. Inscrutable Americans!

'Care for a smoke?' says amiably Leif Ericson as he offers Dick Powell a cigar in *The Tall Target* – while he holds a gun in his right hand. They are both dangerously perched between cars of a speeding train to Philadelphia. 'Grace *before* pressure?' seems to ask disdainfully Dick. 'It will keep your hands occupied,' adds truculently Ericson as he is about to pocket the cigar 'for later'. 'In that case, I'll take it,' says Powell, who in this movie is a dick: Hollywood loves tautology like the Pope loved mambo. 'It will be a pity to see good tobacco gone to waste.' But when Powell is about to light the cigar and be somebody in history, he throws the match at Ericson and both become engaged in the deadliest fight: it is the President's life that is in danger. The movie is in black and white (what with all those Southerners and their servants) and based on a real Confederate conspiracy to kill Abraham Lincoln, then the newly elected leader of the United States travelling incognito to Washington to become president. He is the tall target of the title. What makes this small picture some sort of prophecy is that Powell, the man who aborts the conspiracy, is called John Kennedy. Neat, isn't it? In case Joe Hind Sight wants to know, the movie was made in 1950 – ten years before the real John Kennedy was elected.

Coincidence? Perhaps. But Oscar Wilde would have been delighted with it anyway. 'Life always imitates art,' he said once or twice.

In *I Soliti Ignoti* (that Italian masterpiece of comedy of 1956 which Louis Malle remade into a mess in his *Crackers* of 1984) those unknown soldiers of crime Memmo Carotenuto and Vittorio Gassman *et al* achieve the ultimate in smoking: they smoke a bottle. Or rather they drink smoke from an empty wine bottle previously filled with the smoke of fag ends of other, more fortunate men. It all happened in a Roman prison and the story was set in a very poor Italy still in black and white. It was told by neorealist film-makers making nonsense of their creed. Today the *soliti ignoti* are well-known Mafia *capi* who smoke Havanas imported exclusively for them in gaol.

In *Scarface Two* (1959) Rod Steiger as Al Capone only sniffs that fateful first cigar and leaves it still unearned on the desk of Jimmy Torrio, the man he must kill to succeed. This is a Capone with a future: more gun power to him. Later in the movie Capone, now a cigar-toting *capo*, wants to bribe a certain captain of the Chicago police. What does he do? He sends newspaperman Martin Balsam, a.k.a. Messenger Boy, with a gift if not from the Greeks at least from the Italians. 'Captain,' asks Balsam as he offers the policeman a fat Havana, 'have you ever tried one of these?'

In *Elmer Gantry* doubtful, dutiful Artful Kennedy smokes cigarettes in a sly way, while ruseful, rueful Burt Lancaster savours a cigar whenever he has the chance. But us cigar-smokers know whom to trust: Lancaster is our man for a generous heart, a strong handshake and a lusty body: he is a travelling preacher. Kennedy begins his relationship with Lancaster by offering him – a cigar. And giving him a light. Hallelujah! It's the light fanatic.

In *House of Wax* the infamous arsonist Reggie Rymal sets fire to Vincent Price's *Original Waxworks* with a box of matches and a cigar. Thank God, he never lights up his cigar. All he was doing, really, was trying to be somebody by collecting insurance money from the house (of wax) on fire. Or perhaps he was just one of those crooks that let their cigars go out and grow cold before relighting. Fortunately this movie had the late Carolyn Jones exclaiming delectably at some banal wonder, 'Holy smoke!' That's enough to make me forget all about her bosom friend Phyllis Kirk, real name Kirkegaard. Ah that dreadful *Concept of Dread*!

In *The Cincinatti Kid* there are several cigar-smokers in a room full of cards, sharpies and punters. There are also some punsters. They all play poker but Edward G. Robinson as the old 'king of the five-card stud' uses his panatella as a club and out-cigars the rest of the cast. Steve McQueen, playing the lead, sticks to menthol cigarettes, the Koolest. Rip Torn, the millionaire player and bashful backer, licks his cigars as if every corona were a social disease. Jack Weston (called Pig in the movie for no other reason than that he looks like a pig) is a sore loser and a worse cigar-smoker. 'You'll pay for this, Lancey!' he yells at Robinson and he doesn't mean his half-chewed cigar but the two grands he lost to Lancey not very grandly. Cab Calloway, who claims to a natural sense of rhythm, wields cigarillos and Tiparillos and smiles like Leo Carrillo. In the room there are a few shady ladies. Melba, who looks like a peach, is played by Ann-Margret: she is the biggest bust west of Mae West. Good ole Joan Blondell, playing Lady Fingers, is the one with the poker eyes and card-dealing hands.

McQueen loses in the end to Professor Robinson, who outstares him, amidst the funniest voice-overs ever: 'He has the Queen of Spades!' 'No, he has the King of Diamonds!' 'He's going for the flush!' But Robinson gets up and says: 'I'm going to the lavatory.' Anyway, McQueen is the loser but gets a consolation prize: Tuesday Weld every other day. (My God, the names actors choose for themselves! Rip Torn, Tuesday Weld, Ward Bond. Stripteasers used to do better:

Gypsy Rose Lee, Ann Corio, Rita Cadillac. But that's all they had on – that and what Bach called the G-string.) McQueen of Hearts, a born-again loser, lost what the flyer calls 'the coveted title of *The Man*', but got his woman instead. Ah, if men played poker as women play strip-bridge!

Steve McQueen in *The Thomas Crown Affair* did for the slim panatella what Faye Dunaway did for gliders: sleek, beautiful and perfectly useless objects to soar in the sky. They came across almost as *objets trouvés*. But one mustn't forget Marcel Duchamp, the man who said 'I, who was born to do nothing, must play chess!' Duchamp's best find among his ready-made objects was something white, sleek and curvaceous but a very useful object: the toilet. Like Robinson he disregarded the flush.

In *Crisis*, a curious movie, Cary Grant is the American surgeon who on a visit to South America, must try to save the life of José Ferrer, a local tyrant with a brain disease. Sight unseen Grant doctorally warns Ferrer not to smoke the cigar he is about to light up. The diseased dictator throws away his *vitola* as if it were a viper. Two days later Ferrer, obviously better, is seen smoking a cigarette. He even offers one to Grant, who hardly registers. Moral of the movie: cigarettes can give you lung cancer but are the best cure for a brain tumour. Obviously those days a Camel had only one hump!

War is hell, I admit. But it's hell and a half for cigars. Cigars are chewed during wars not smoked. They cannot be as deleterious as the third cigarette with only one match, but in any war movie cigars are never lit. Cigar-smokers live longer in wartime but cigars suffer a lot. Take Major Darro in *Operation Petticoat*, for instance. From his jeep he complains to Commander Cary Grant and shows him his badly mauled cigar. It looks very dead: 'See this? It belongs to my captain. I stole it!' and he puts it back in his pocket as if the Filipino stump were Deborah Kerr cavorting on the beach with Burt Lancaster toward eternity. War does that to you, you know.

As a matter of fiction, in *Fog over Frisco*, when Douglas Dumbrille offers to light Henry O'Neil's cigar with a gas lighter, I instantly knew that Dumbrille was the elusive villain. Elementary, my dear Waugh.

In *Point Blank* and under extreme duress (a tough Lee Marvin is pointing a gun at him) chubby Carroll O'Connor suddenly reaches for – a cigar hidden in a drawer. That's bravery. Bravery is very unexpected from a Mafia boss in a movie, even if the *mafioso* is Irish. They're all Irish in this movie anyway: the *capo di tutti capi* is Keenan Wynn! Begorrah, not Camorra. But O'Connor, if not a good man, is at least a good cigar man. That's why I felt chagrined when they killed him at the end, double-crossed in Alcatraz.

Why should I feel pity for Carroll O'Connor? Because he could not light up that cigar he needed so badly. A bullet got him before he could reach for a match. No, that's not right. Fear got him first, then a bullet. He was a reckless but cowardly smoker, trying to light up a cigar before breakfast. A brave smoker would have died with his cigar on.

The best tobacco chewer in the movies was Percy Kilbride, a much better man with the dead plug in his mouth than Chill Wills, his runner-up and an actor who chewed tongue in cheek. Kilbride could ruminate in a folksy way (all tobacco-chewers in the movies are full of folk wisdom and they spit and speak), so slow that his chew was, chew, purty, chew, effective. You never saw the plug Kilbride kept in his mouth – simply because there wasn't any. You didn't even see his jowl swell, as he kept his cheek in check. Kilbride was the perfect movie ruminant: he who offers the illusion of chewing while he talks. He became famous for the Ma and Pa Kettle series but in *Keeper of the Flame* he was a sly, slow, small-town taxi driver and he drove around as he chewed: sputtering information in a leisurely, purring, drawling way. He copied his old Model T Ford to a T. But he didn't need any spittoon tricks. After all a cuspidor is only a pitcher of warm spit.

The best line I ever heard about chewing had to do with tobacco what chewing has with smoking. The mythical Belle Starr said to her suitor Cole Younger, 'Here, have a chew,' and handed him her black velvet belt. It was to have and to hold in his mouth while fighting to death in a duel with her husband, a half-caste (and now a better cast) Sam Starr. He had the other chew. Each man was wielding a sharp bowie knife, then a dangerous offensive weapon that now sounds, alas, more like a flashing step favoured by some rock star. The real Sam Starr was a six-feet-seven hunk who weighed almost three hundred pounds and sported a ferocious mien. In *The Long Riders*, where the scene takes place, David Carradine, playing Cole with his right hand, faces a very tall half-Indian hefty lefty – whom he proceeds to cut down to size. Meanwhile, Belle Starr, called here a whore more often than Mary Magdalene in the Bible, watches and chews her fingers between her 'cambered lips', whatever that is.

In *Pat Garrett and Billy the Kid*, a pseudo-Borgesian mess, James Coburn smokes more cigars than Charles, his older namesake, in his long career. But Coburn chomps cheroot after cheroot, all black and blacked out. He wears black too from head to toe, with friends and foes. Soon we know why. He is Mr Death. Death comes for the gunslinger in the shape of a man dressed in black who smokes cigars and packs a gun. But cigars are of no consequence here, really. The devil Alcohol is. Everybody must get stoned, muses Dylan (he is in the movie as an actor and as a singer on the soundtrack), and they do it with whiskey, aguardiente, tequila, mescal. You name it, they'll drink it. Smoke is for men, booze for desperadoes. Alcohol is not only the *modus operandi* in this movie, it is the *modus morendi* too. *Tragos para los muertos.*

In *My Fair Lady*, when Eliza's lessons on paper burn on the flame of her aspiring haitches, Rex Harrison doesn't look at lovely Audrey Hepburn with love but disapprovingly at Colonel Pickering, who is seen smoking a cigar, obviously from Higgins's humidor. It is clear that the professor is rich but rather raggy when it comes to Havanas. Later, in his triumphal return from the Embassy's Ball and to celebrate victory over 'that phoney Hungarian' he smokes one of his choicest, picked blindfolded from an ebony *étui* – at midnight! Even Enry Iggins should know that cigars are not for taps or for reveille, but for dinner and luncheon. He just couldn't wait.

That British roving robot also known as James Bond was once under the hefty, hirsute command of Sean Connery. Bond was then a heavy cigarette-smoker. He favoured, as his creator Ian Fleming, black Balkan Sobranies. But beautiful, blond Roger Moore, the incumbent 007, makes Bond into a cigar man. In *Live and Let Die* Bond (also called later in the sequence Mr B) shaves in his Guyana hotel bathtub while his enemies seek revenge by dropping the hint of a mamba down the ventilator shaft. Unknowingly Moore stops shaving to let into his suite a black waiter bearing champagne in a bucket and two tall tulip glasses. Is he expecting company? Bond I mean. After dismissing the waiter James lights up an extra-long Upmann and returns to the bathroom. It is while spraying himself with some aftershave that he sees the abmam in a mirror and thinking quickly he decides it is a mamba. Bond coolly (it must be the aftershave) turns around to make both spray can and cigar into an ad hoc flamethrower. Presto chango! The snake is transformed from moving mamba into charred coils. Suddenly someone comes in uninvited (thrills always happen in threes) wearing only a Saturday Night Special. 'This must be the speciality for Saturday night,' says Bond and thinks twice about the interloper. Then once more he uses his cigar to brand the brown armed arm. That the intruder turns out to be a black CIA girl only reveals how deftly Bond took advantage of his one-Upmannship.

Bond is outgunned by the villain in *Foxfire*, the television series. Here the cigar held by this updated dastard (he wears camouflage fatigues), becomes a killing dart-thrower – the deadliest blow-job ever.

It is in *The Scalphunters* where one can find, among the Indians, another cigar-smoking lady. In this Western we see Shelley Winters 'chomp on a stogy', as a lady reviewer put it. But I would surely have to declare Shelley Winters no contest. Shelley is in this movie her usual self: a sorry sight. You must be in possession of a flinty heart not to laugh at her even in her prime. In *A Double Life*, her first major movie, Shelley smokes cigarettes only and she gets killed not by cancer but by her ignorance of the classics. She was not conversant with Shakespeare, you see. Such knowledge is of the essence: the double life of the title is Ronald Colman's, an actor who is going mad after playing Othello for two years on Broadway. Colman usually does some slumming off Broadway after the show and that's how he and Shelley meet cute in a late-night eatery. Colman is the one with the moustache, Shelley is the waitress with the big boobs and the scanty menu. She is also dangerously forward: 'Do I know you from somewhere, mister?' she intones. But her vulgar beauty reaches Colman in waves of Dolores Haze – and smoke from an invisible cigar: a burning minister. He dismisses her: make coffee, not love. 'You'se so cute,' says Shelley. She probably meant acute but her pass comes to pass. Her next step proves fatal, though. She takes Colman (who is by now in his third year as a tragedian in blackface and getting battier all the time) to her room, the slut. She makes herself comfortable in bed and then tries to put Colman at ease. But she gives away the password: 'Come on, put out the light.' What she evokes in the deranged mind of the actor is not love but just the opposite: a terrible moment that happened once and long ago 'at a Sea Port on the Isle of Cyprus' and on a Cyprus of cardboard and make-believe every night now. He utters the faintest heart murmur: 'Put out the light and then – .' Dark Othello must murder in darkest night: ' – put out the light,' sentences Colman with the finality of a hangman. But why kill the strumpet? Was Miss Winters smoking in bed? Or was she terribly naked? Was Colman then a prude? Did he once see Shelley plain?

In *Kid Glove Killer* (why not call it *Kid Glove Kidder*?) Lee Bowman is the killer – and the holder of the title to the worst cigar-holder in the world. Who is he trying to kid? When we see the city elders comfortably puffing at their six-cent cheroots (all tobacco plants have roots, cheap cigars only cheroots), Lee Bowman, one of those kid brothers of Clark Gable, all velvety hair-pieces and pin-stripe moustaches, holds his Havana with awkward forefinger and thumb. The costly cigar was given him by the ruthless Mafia boss who intends to make Sin City into a Capo Town. But something is very wrong with the way Bowman smokes: he sustains his panatella between fingertips, just like a prim prima donna. 'Listen, kiddo,' Brod Crawford would say, 'sissies don't smoke no cigars.'

The entire movie is a battlefield of cigars versus cigarettes. There is a running and deadly gag by forensic expert Van Heflin who is incapable of smoking a cigarette – unless it is lighted up first by assistant Marsha Hunt. The fag end of both the picture and the battle comes when Hunt says yes to Heflin but only after he had uncovered his rival, dubious dude Bowman, and sent him to the hell of rotten smokers. As she takes the unlit cigarette from Heflin's male lips (or is it labia? Freud only knows), says suave and sassy she: 'Match me' – which he does docilely.

But Fred Zinnemann, who made this dud as you smoke a Lucky Strike, carries his passion for cigarettes a little too far:

he even shows a chef smoking a cigarette while tasting the bouillabaisse! So does the Mafia chef in *Mean Streets*: his cooking tools are *gli spaghetti*, *il capello bianco* and *la sigaretta*. But this would be a standard fixture not only in soldierly *Beetle Bailey* but in urbane *Blondie* as well. Both funnies feature a cook with a perennial cigarette hanging from his lower lip. Over soup, salad and salami in *Blondie* and in *Beetle Bailey* above and beyond the call of duty. General Patton was wrong: ashes are for comic strip heroes too. Other cartoon-strip creations that smoke are Mr Jiggs, the old parvenu with a cigar in *Bringing Up Father*, Popeye and his pipe, Andy Capp with his cigarette glued to his lips – and Mammy Pansy Yokum and her corncob in *Li'l Abner*. All of them smoke in clouds and talk in balloons.

In *Rage in Heaven* Robert Montgomery is the owner of some steelworks in England, a large British concern near London. Nobody explains how Montgomery, as American as clam chowder, became heir to the British factory. Nobody cares really. Except me now. Be that as it may, on his first day in office Montgomery, a greenhorn, welcomes his shop stewards and offers them a treat worthy of a British steel baron. Scotch? Wrong. Tea? Wrong again. Sweets? Come on, give up – you'll never guess what. Cigars! One of his men refuses. 'Thank you sir. As you know, indulging in nicotine is against my principles.' A long-winded principle, if I ever heard one. Undaunted Montgomery opens his posh, polished cigar-case – to reveal it empty. Obviously those were the Invisible Man's own cigars. If you remember, he too was a trickster. By the way, this is the movie where the young Ingrid Bergman achieved a linguistic feat, unparalleled even by the Great Garbo. Bergman passionately informs gaoled George Sanders (sentenced to death for killing Robert Montgomery: he hates practical jokers) of what could only save him now: 'A miracle!' she intones, only that she pronounces it 'Amerika!' At the end, Sanders saved from a death not really worse than his fate (here called *smorgasbord* with everything) they are both seen on board a boat – sailing to America. That's how I like my Swedish stars, prescient.

In *Lifeboat*, another wartime movie, multi-millionaire Henry Hull is doing some cigar saving of his own. 'Light?' asks fellow traveller Hume Cronyn at seeing Hull with an unlit cigar in his mouth. But the old werewolf shakes his head and says: 'No thank you. I think I'll do some hoarding for the time being.' They are in an open boat in the middle of nowhere, castaways all. (*See Idiot's Delight.*)

In *Suspicion* Cary Grant's first words are to complain to Joan Fontaine that there is a man in the next compartment (from which he had to move as the train went into a tunnel) who was smoking 'the most vile cigah'. That man could be Hitchcock, you know. To make sure that he won't have Hitch in drag in the present compartment he, Grant, asks his present company, the very feminine and frail looking Miss Fontaine, 'You don't smoke, do you?' – and that's the beginning of a ruinous romance.

The gesture was repeated by the evil valet at the beginning of Hitchcock's *Secret Agent*, albeit defiantly. Here Hitchcock plays a lot with smoking contraptions. Robert Young, the villain, asks a Swiss for something to smoke in mock German: 'Cigarroozen,' he says and the man brings him two pipes: one for him and the other for Madeleine Carroll. R, the antecessor of M, is marinating himself, in a Turkish bath, partially clad in a towel, a fading cigar in his hand. The Havana becomes limp, flaccid and drooping like an impotent weapon as the Masterspy, fully in command, stands erect.

The State Security policeman ('The infamous State Security,' he jests, as if he didn't have to) welcomes physicist Paul Newman as a defector to East Germany: Germany must always be a police state, even if it is by half. The Security specialist's first grand gesture is to produce a cigar-case in black pigskin and tender it tenderly to Newman. 'Cigar?' whispers the German agent implying that the cheroots are in cahoots. 'They are Cuban.' He then adds, also in jest (he obviously belongs to the Jest Set), 'Your loss is our gain.' He means the cigar but also Cuba, the jester. Insipid Paul, like Cardinal Newman, does not smoke: 'I pass.' The joke is now on us in turn in *Torn Curtain*. Hitchcock, who directed this spy movie masterpiece, was a choice cigar-smoker and was delighted to be making the melodrama in Europe, so he could indulge in *le vice Cubain*.

In *Cuba*, misdirected by Richard Lester, they show the latest in cigar-rolling: a machine that makes all the cigars but it is operated only by women wearing rollers. This is 'Carmen' with a vengeance and Jones with a cigar. He is an American businessman played by Jack Weston in his usual *ipso fatso* from Philadelphia, who speaks now of loading military planes with cigars before the Batista regime collapses. It was not until 1984, with the famous auctions in New York where a single box of Havanas fetched $2,500, that anybody could realize what Weston was all about. Bring over the unlit cigars and build a Havana empire near the Empire State. Go Weston, young man!

In *The Strange Love of Martha Ivers* the bond between lissome Lizabeth Scott and rugged, Vangoghian Van Heflin is that cigarette constantly exchanged between them as smoky vows of love. Bond becomes bondage and both marry in the end, a happy end. It is however non-smoking Kirk Douglas, the only real Van Gogh in the room, he and his wife Barbara Stanwyck, who die in smoke – from a gun they fondled like a toy cigar – or an, er, ur-vibrator.

In *Intruder in the Dust*, both the novel and the movie, young Chick Stevens, to pay for Lucas Beauchamp's hospitality, buys him four black cigars – which he rejects of course. To try to buy his hospitality is to try to buy old Lucas off. But I simply cannot picture the haughty black man getting a pack of Camels as pay-off for his debt of gratitude.

John Ford, like most of his urban outlaws (in particular Ed Brophy and Jackie Gleason), seems to prefer five-cent cigars. At least that's how they look on the screen, even in *Stagecoach*, especially in *Stagecoach*. That's probably much more than the cigars are actually worth. Politicians smoke *tagarninas*, cops and robbers stogys, as to stoolies they favour cigarettes – except for George E. Stone in *Some Like It Hot*. He preferred a tooth-pick, to the extent that he died with a sliver stuck between his pursed lips (all informers are thin-lipped, at least in Hollywood), until Spats Colombo, daintily played by George Raft, neatly kicked the spill off his mouth, a finally and definitely shut trap.

As sullen, solemn Katy Jurado says to Lloyd Bridges, the only cigar-smoking cowboy in *High Noon*, 'It takes more than broad shoulders [and a cigar] to make a man!' The cigar is an interpolation of mine of course.

Ned Sparks was always seen mauling a cold cigar with his irascible foul mouth, while his eyes burnt with anger at the chorus girls as if they were trained albino seals: legless, armless and toddling around. He also used to snarl at chor-eographers in any musical of the early thirties: a vinegary character but an ever-faithful cigar-smoker. He just couldn't part from his dead stub stuck in his sourpuss like the traffic cop's clamp on an unlawfully parked car. Apparently there were more where he came from: Ned's true name was Spark-land and he was born in Canada.

Irascible Jesse White is a great one for chomping dead cigars while he keeps up with things in a lively, loud way. Elwood P. Dowd called him a dynamic personality. But White can scream, holler and shout with a cigar in his mouth. He and Wallace Ford, Wally to his fans, coincided only once, in *Harvey*. But Jesse did very little chomping in that one. Not even chomping at the Savoy Hotel. Wally, though he spoke little, was very eloquent as he carried the message of the movie: fools are only angels who never fear to tread.

But that's not of course why Victor McLaglen turned him over to the British Police in Dublin during the Sinn Fein rebellion in *The Informer*, John Ford's cry of the city and polity.

The heaviest cigar-smoker I ever encountered in fiction was enacted by Marvin Miller, a sourpuss. In *Deadline at Dawn* he is a blind pianist who can only play touch-key. He is also that fixture of the *film noir*, the pushover with a hangover who hangs for it. Now his addiction is the cigar. When his paramour Lola Lane needles him for it ('Still on your twenty cigars a day? Can your ticker take it?') all he does is to save his cigar for later with a whimper. He could have told her with a laugh 'Don't be cruel!' and scared her off, for Marvin has the tough mug of Ray Charles combined with the art of Art Tatum, blind pianists all. But Arty Fate, the resident writer in *films noirs*, forces the pianist whose name is Sleepy Parsons, to die of a too-sudden heart attack. Not before Joseph Calleia, the healthy heavy, roughs him up in his dressing room. 'He smoked too much,' is Calleia's sum-ming up, as if he belonged to the fire brigade. Even Captain Bender, from the nearest precinct, believed the mobster's verdict and goes away chomping his fiver for ever. Was he on a bender too?

Up In Smoke, needless to say, has nothing to do with cigars, pipes or cigarettes – though it is the story of a big roll-up.

In *House of Strangers* a cigar becomes a hatchet pipe. Luther Adler is brother to Richard Conte (yes, they *are* brothers: in Hollywood nobody is impossible and a German Jewish actor can have an Italian sibling) and offers him in sign of goodwill a big cigar early in the morning. Conte puffs at it once or twice but suddenly gets up from his comfortable armchair – to throw his cigar at Brother Luther. Bastard! *Basta*! No more fat cigars in the morning! Obviously this costly Havana was at first considered a peace pipe but later became the unburied hatchet of war. That's what the Cheyenne called a hatchet pipe.

In *The Pirate*, Gene Kelly is an itinerant *artiste* whose precious possessions are his illusionist's mirror and his last cigar. When he finally lights it, great magician that he is, makes his pauperized troupe believe that there are more cigars where this came from: a magic box indeed! They all contend for the container to find it empty: not even the smoky ghost of a cigar was left. In the street the magician's midget must accost Kelly to claim that last cigar as his own. Gene yields. 'I was only keeping it alight,' claims Kelly as if he meant to say alive – and so it is, so it is. Whenever there's light in a cigar, there's hope. Here, buy yourself a box of Pandoras.

This is how Louis Armstrong, part in rhyming slang, part in scat singing, introduces one of his jazz pals:

> Now here's Bud Scott
> and his old guitar,
> always smoking his big cigar.

Alas poor ole Bud Scott is seen smoking his fat cigar through a thick amber holder! Satchmo is the man who was jazz but he knew nothing about cigars. Neither did Bud Scott. He was no Charlie Christian either. His guitar playing was like his smoking: with a plastic plectrum. It happened in old *New Orleans*, that soulful silly symphony in which Arturo de Cordova, of all people, gave jazz its name.

The closest encounter ever between smoky music and burning cigars occurs in *The Best Things in Life Are Free*. There an all-male chorus is totally composed of fedora'd, pin-striped, pistol-packing gangsters who smoke Havanas as long as their jumps. The mobster's moll to beat them all is sweet Sheree North. The gunsel in distress is Jacques d'Amboisse, a dancer who could give you what the French call *angoisse*. Sartre is his sartor.

The most optimistic cigar-smoker ever is that rich traveller who arrives at the Last Chance eatery, in *The Petrified Forest*, and asks from Bette Davis: 'Have you got any good cigars?' Those *saguaro* cigars must be real tasty, for some time later none other than Humphrey Bogart, as Duke Mantee, says to Miss Davis: 'Gimme one of them cigars, sister.' They say the desert does things to you but I never heard of an *indoor* mirage before.

In *Mr Skeffington* good, weak Claud Rains offers Bette Davis, who is visiting his office, a cigar. It's not a joke, of course. Humourless Mr Skeffington only does business with men. He apologizes accordingly. The time and the place is USA 1914, just on the brink of the Great War. Skeffington has given up smoking anyway. There's always a lot of smoke in war.

In *The Conspirators* (1944), a sad sequel of *The Mask of Dimitrios* (or better still, as if Dimitrios had spent a night in *Casablanca*), every villain in Lisbon smokes a cigar. Even small Steven Geray, who was the doubly deceived civil servant in *Dimitrios*, wields an enormous cigar with evil authority enough to play the German ambassador. All the players from *Dimitrios* are here, plus Paul Henreid, who smoked two cigarettes at once in *Now Voyager*. He was outsmoked in *Casablanca* by a Humphrey Bogart who wore a cigarette to match with his white tuxedo. But the movie was a flop, a waste of talent which included photographer Arthur Edeson and director Jean Negulesco. It was a total loss. It couldn't be otherwise. In this madhouse movie the Nazis are hams who smoke cigars. The heroes, including the heroine (gorgeous Hedy Lamarr), smoke cigarettes. Straight, no filter. They must be all cancerous by now.

The only agreeable thing in the movie happened on the soundtrack, where they played 'Perfidia' one more time. This Mexican tune, a bolero, was once the private property of Warner Brothers. They played it in *Now Voyager* and played it again in *Casablanca*, where it vied for attention with 'As Time Goes By' (Needless to say, I prefer 'Perfidia'.) It was also heard, somewhat briefly, in *The Mask of Dimitrios*, in the seedy, smoky *boîte de minuit* owned by one of the most alluring women of Hollywood then, Faye Emerson, whose forehead alone was a true dome of pleasure. Now all the conspirators listen to the tune in Lisboa. At Estoril rather. By the by, the version I prefer is sung by Cliff Richard in Spanish. Here he turns 'Perfidia' into a perfidious tune. The way he pronounces the title when he sings 'Perfidia' what the listeners get is porphyria.

For Dickie Moore confessing his sins not to a priest but to sexy Signe Hasso in *Heaven Can Wait*, adulthood is one of the stages to hell. Always a handsome teenager, Moore closes the door to his room with Hasso (it rhymes with lasso) around his neck. He whispers something sweet in the ear of the fake French maid: 'I bet you can't guess in a million years what I have in my pocket.' Is it mirth for seeing Signe in private or just a gun? 'No, I don't know,' says Signe giggling with anticipation. 'But I'm sure eet ees somethink veree bad.' Dickie delves his hand in his coat pocket to produce – a cigar. 'You smoke beeg black ceegar?' 'Sure I'm going to smoke it. Any day now.' And Dickie puts it back in his pocket, probably for ever. Signe smiles, Dickie ducks the issue. That was coming of age in Manhattan circa 1900. Many ceremonies later – elopement, marriage and a lot of birthday parties – death comes to the reprobate in the nicest possible way. He is the puritan in Hell. Don Ameche, in another avatar of Dickie Wilson, goes to an interview with Mr Charon about the ferry fare. But he had the wrong number and goes to Paradise instead. It all happened in his deathbed though he didn't know it yet. He had a dream and that dream was Glory. 'There was this big luxury liner,' he recalls, 'floating on an ocean of whisky and soda and instead of funnels she had big black cigars. And on top of the boat, sitting in a life boat, was the most beautiful blonde!' That's Music Hell, my son.

The vindication of the cigar comes dandy in *Damn Yankees*, where the devil himself smokes cigarettes – which he lights with a mere flick of his wrist. 'Do you mind if I smoke?' he asks casually of Shoeless Joe from Hannibal, Mo – or Faust as a bush league baseball player who sells his soul (to the devil, naturally) in order to play with the Washington Senators against the Yankees. Joe is aghast at the common trick: 'Hey, how d'ya pull that off?' 'I'm handy with fire, Mac', answers Satan with the satin voice of Ray Walston *au gratin*. Naive Joe, a native son as played by Tab Hunter, tells the devil where *he* should go. But even the devil has a soul – or had one once. 'I have to do most things the hard way,' he explains. 'The only thing that comes easy is the cigarette trick,' and he lights a Camel to prove it, see? A whip of the hand and he is ready to smoke his cig – to cough terribly: 'Now I must break myself of the filthy habit!' But he doesn't and keeps puffing and coughing. We know, of course, that the devil is a sissy. However, he redeems himself later in this medieval movie. Now a winning Mephistopheles sports a cigar for us to meet our old menace, the self igniting cigar: quick, a flick and hey presto! – the devil is smoking a Havana! He has graduated from a poor devil into Lucifer himself. Folderol! Paradise is a cigar for men – hell is for the others.

In *The Natural* the villains smoke cigars, so do the heroes: all the baseball players smoke cigars as big as their bats. All except Robert Redford, that is. He has his personalized bat, called Wonderboy, which is a modern version of Arthur's Excalibur. When one has a flaming sword, who needs to light up a cigar to be somebody? Baseball as you can see has gone the way of all myths. Soon we'll have Don Juan in the bull-pen and Babe Ruth hitting Homers!

In *All That Money Can Buy* the devil appears for the first time enveloped in haze and mist – and smoking a cigar: a long panatella that seems to last an eternity. And indeed it does: it glows and glares in the devil's hand for ever. 'Call me Scratch,' announces Mephistopheles as an *introito ad altare Diaboli*. 'I go by that name in New England, you know' – and Walter Huston as the devil runs a crooked smile. Then to seal his compact Lucifer scratches a date on a tree with his cigar as a firebrand. Needless to mention that the devil is, as they say, the soul of the party. He is the smiler with a pact under his cloak. Never a sore loser he is even a good sport. Thanks to his cigar, no doubt. This entertaining exercise in theology couldn't have been made without the devil – or his cigar. All the devil's disciples in the movie smoke cigars. But so does Daniel Webster, witchfinder extraordinary. As everything happens in mid-nineteenth century all the cigars must be lit up with Lucifer matches. All except the devil's, that is.

Carnal Knowledge should be called *Wisdom and Smoke*, though Jack Nicholson, the fool, smokes *Winston* instead. He smokes cigarettes only, even when he smokes leaves of grass. First he smokes most of the time, later all the time – 'always quietly', as Jules Feiffer with two effs, the screenwriter, states. At the beginning Arty Garfunkel, his bosom pal, does not smoke and loves not too wisely or too well, while Nicholson finally marries Ann-Margret, again, his bosom gal, a busy body. He gets neurotic, hysterical, abusive, psychotic and mad. He shouts, rattles and rolls his eyes. As he is never seen eating or drinking anything stronger than beer, Nicholson's madness must come from his cigarettes: three packs a day, no filter, *tout* tar. Garfunkel in turn becomes more poised, more mature with the passing of time. This is not surprising since a quarter of a century elapsed from the college years, when he unwittingly shared his girl with Nicholson, to the time in which the latter proposes a teeny-weeny bit of wife-swapping – which the former accepts giggling and wiggling and wagging his circumcised tail. The poise and purpose may come when Art for Art's sake stopped being Simon Garfunkel to become Nicholson's chum. But in mid-movie he is seen smoking – a cigar! Ah! That's it! Cut! It's a take! Print it! New title for the movie: *Coronal Knowledge*.

In *Patton*, as they pin the four stars on the general's collar, he congratulates himself for the promotion by lighting a Havana as long as a tank gun. You have never seen a prouder soldier. Or a longer cigar.

In *Voyage of the Damned* Orson Welles leaves the little acting there is to do to his Havana. No wonder. In this movie made into a two-part television series (first the voyage, then the damned) Welles is a Cuban and lives in Havana. A likely story if I ever heard one. We all know that great Cubans always live abroad. In this masterpiece of documentary humbug a Cuban *presidente*, the aristocratic Federico Laredo Bru, becomes a concoction: he is always called President Brew. Obviously this is the story of Orson's life: always placed, on television at least, between the cigar and the beer. Strictly for lowbrows.

In *Confidential Report* Orson Welles, now the all-powerful

Mr Arkadin, gives his prospective son-in-law an enormous cigar, probably a Churchill. The man trying to cope or cop out is in charge of researching Arkadin's past. The meeting of crafty minds is over and the inlaw who is an outlaw is still struggling with his barbecue. To stress the importance of a Churchill cigar he is seen first smoking a stogy in a crummy joint in downtown Barcelona. But even there a waitress can complain: 'Would you put out that hideous stinko!' Orson Welles knows that in a movie you can tell the gentlemen from the errand boys by what they smoke.

In his next movie, *Touch of Evil*, which begins with a convertible being blown up by a stick of dynamite, Welles plays the rotten chief of police Hank Quinlan. He smokes only cigar-butts. A reformed wino, instead of drinking at bars he chews candy bars. A man with no time left, Quinlan finds cold comfort in a dead cigar and a dead man. Happiness for him is making an innocent man confess he is guilty. He is in fact the last stop for a Charles Foster Kane on his way out, to hell. To make a point of it Welles fosters a cane.

Mickey Rooney was not only a child prodigy, he was a man prodigy too. He could sing and smoke a cigar at the same time. He also could smoke a cigar and sing and compose a song too! Furthermore he could be Lorenz Hart, lyricist and mad about town and singer all rolled in one. And he loved Manhattan and Staten Island too. He did it all in *Words and Music* and it happened again in *That's Entertainment Part Two*!

When Iranoff, Bulkanoff and Kopalski, the three most lovable Soviet apparatchiks ever, defected to the free world (or at least to Paree when gay didn't mean Jean Cocteau and Co or Gay-Lussac but just Paris), and they took to Western ways, they chose as their symbols champagne, cigars and cigarette-girls. In that order. Every time we see *Ninotchka* we still can hear Iranoff, Bulkanoff and Kopalski utter, mutter and stutter in unison 'AH-AHH-AH!' That's Russian for delight.

God is always making us choose between two Jews: Cain or Abel, Jesus or Judas, Marx or Engels, Freud or Wilhelm Reich, Lou Andreas Salome or Alma Mahler, Gropius, Werfel, etc. etc. Now it's Mel Brooks or Woody Allen. Believe me, God sometimes behaves like a Dealer: when He is not playing dice with the universe he is forcing us to pick a card, any card. Or a bounder if you must. But between Mel and Woody, hell – so sorry, Sir! – my, they are not even really called Mel and Woody!

All right, give me Mel then. He cannot dance but at least he sings a little and shouts a lot. (No, not that Lot.) I prefer a loud comedian to a lousy one. Besides, between parody and paraphrase I'll choose parody any day. Any night too. As in slavery I'll always choose freedom. That applies to big stores also. Give me Liberty's or give me death! You can keep Herod's and Marx and Spengler too, I'll choose Brooks instead of Woods. Is that all right with you, God? I know, I know: Mel smokes cigars and Allen hates them. But believe You me, that had nothing to do with my choice. To choose is human, to make the right choice, divine – and I could never divine right. Not even at peas and nutshell.

In *Young Frankenstein* it is Gene Hackman as the Blind Hermit who once more offers a cigar to the Monster played by Peter Boyle. Unfortunately the Hermit is not only blind but terribly clumsy as well and while offering fire to the Monster inadvertently sets his thumb alight. Oops! So sorry. The Monster runs away screaming. End of a beautiful friendship.

In *The Producers* that archswindler Max Byalistov shows off his private machine to light up cigars. The lighter is a gas. She is in fact a blonde affair known as Lyuba, a hot Czech dish. She has a way with a panatella that nobody would have suspected in a girl from behind the Iron Curtain. She doesn't speak a word of English but she does to a cigar what Hitler did to Warsaw. She is what you can call an old flame.

That horrible, horrible Nurse Diesel in *High Anxiety* smokes the fattest, blackest cigars. She also wears black underwear under her Nazi uniform. She is deep into s&m, you see. I must add, I think, that she is not your typical woman cigar-smoker. But she certainly is the ugliest woman smoker ever.

The loveliest smoker ever in a picture is not on the screen but on a cover of *Playboy* and her name was Bo Constrictor. She appeared blowing at a cheroot to make it a heavenly smoke. No other weed, not even opium, could be smoked with such blonde savoir faire. In the photo Bo seems to be wearing a boa of smoke, the cigar her grasping, graceful garment: a brown kiss on pallid lips.

In Peter Brook's *Carmen* the wayward gypsy girl is first

seen smoking a cigar. But before lighting it up she kisses, licks and even blows the brown cylinder. A phallic symbol? Not so coy: the real McCoy this time Carmen holds her cigar like a true spear to ram it into Micaela's mouth. Poor Micaela doesn't smoke. She begs to pass and hands the panatella to a confused Don José. Bizet's bedazzled bedfellows begin their beguine as a *habanera*.

Alan Bates and James Mason vie for the love of Georgy, the fat and ungainly young lady so charmingly played by Lynn Redgrave in *Georgy Girl*. Both gentlemen callers wield black cigars: Mr Mason with Havanas, with a stinko Mr Bates. It is a joust: the rich versus the Cockney. May the best man win – and he does, he does!

Probably the smoker's last stand was gallantly adopted by John Wayne, the man who was once a slim panatella and like any old gun died smoking in *The Shootist*. Contrary to popular belief, Wayne died of cancer but not of the lungs. Contrary to myth Wayne never smoked cigars or cigarillos off the set, only cigarettes – three packs a day until stricken by what he called the Big C. Nobody, not even Clint Eastwood, has smoked a cigar in a western with the forceful grace John Wayne did. Then he could have played a character named John M. Gusto.

But in this movie Wayne trades his panatella for the bottle of tincture of opium. He ends up full of lead and laudanum in this grim reflection upon the death of a man of action. He shoots all his rivals but one misses his cigar. Like all gods, Big John is dead.

In the *Bowery* none other than George Raft gives an exploding cigar to a nonesuch like Wallace Beery. To add insult to injury Beery, a pub-owner, is the honorary head of the fire brigade in the Lower East Side of Manhattan way back in the 1900s. Beery is the butt of exploding cigars not only twice but *three* times. He never gives up, though. Neither does Raft, who seems to own a factory of exploding cigars. Ah, those were the good old days!

The best squashed cigars in showbusiness were made by the Three Stooges, Unlimited. But in one of their longest, zaniest comedies, *Uncivil Warriors*, they managed to work a miracle on their way to Catastrophe. They actually are spies for the Union now discussing plans to infiltrate the Confederate Army, seen in the background. Suddenly General Ulysses (us) Mayhem throws away but in foreground a perfectly safe and sound cigar. The truculent trio dart after it to retrieve – three cigars! That's a stogy for each Stooge.

After all those tedious, hedious jokes about boarding passes that smoke if you travel in the smoking section of the aircraft, I am glad nobody smoked an exploding cigar in *Airplane*! W. C. Fields was right. Never give a Zucker an even break.

In recent movies cigars have not been so hot. In *The China Syndrome* (which seems like a remake of *The Manchurian Candidate* but isn't) the villain or rather the heavy-water heavy Scott Brady is the only cigar-smoker in the atomic power plant. On top of that he visibly dyes his hair and audibly snarls at Jack Lemmon horribly. Lemmon is here some sweet softy involved in hard-core powernography based on nuclear energy. The rest of the clan is clean. Even Jane Fonda, who smoked a joint as the cutie in *Klute*, here is fond of claiming that she doesn't even know how to smoke when caught puffing at a Camel off camera. Aerobics next stop. Spot.

In *Magic* Burgess Meredith, a very small man, is a theatrical agent who wields the fattest cigars in Manhattan. Were they smoked upright they would be landmarks of the city: big brown chimneys of fragrant and useless smoke. Though his cigars come in glass tubes Burgess is very generous with them. None of that Sleeping Beauty complex for him: the coffin of glass can very well be a pleasure dome. Anthony Hopkins, a magician of fame, deserts him but Burgess traces him to the woods where he dwells. As a gesture of peace Burgess gives Hopkins, who actually is a crazed ventriloquist, one of his cigars. Hopkins accepts the present but doesn't even open the glass container or smoke the gift contained. Burgess should have known better. Five minutes later Hopkins kills him with blows of his dummy's head. Burgess never finished smoking his cigar: he never had a chance. Hopkins never lighted his up. *Warning to All Agents*: Non-smokers can be a hazard to your health.

Someone who called himself Count Kolowrat-Krokowsky claimed that he married the heiress to the Upmann cigar fortune. This could be the heiress to the Dutch cigars of the same name, not the Havana. I'm reminded of Bogus Beatty marrying Stockard Channing (but beautiful) by the *personne interposée* of Jack Nicholson treated as *personne*, in *The Fortune*. A marriage by proxy at the Roxy: love's hideous counterfeits are all the same. By the way, Beatty wore knickerbocker breeches and a Don Ameche moustache and smoked cigars which looked, under his patent-leather, sleek-black hair, like five-and-a-dime stogys. That's what cheap cheaters smoke in Beatty's banal beatitudes.

One from the Heart is a much maligned musical but it does for cigars what *The Godfather* did for guns and sons: *de la famiglia avant toute chose* or family comes first, graffito. But here you will find that Kinski girl looking like Marlene, like young Bergman, like luscious Lamarr and – why not? – like La Lolla, that vulgar Italian beauty, frigid Lollobrigid: this Nastassia is sometimes even the elfish Audrey Hepburn all over again. Delphic she delves now her hand in her bosom to fish out a long cigarette. Then she asks for a light from Frederic Forrest in the neon-lit night for day of Las Vegas. Is this the end of Rico? Not quite. This is a lurid,* lyrical comedy and Raul Julia comes to the rescue of all cigar-smokers in America with a song which reveals that though he sings to Teri Garr his lyrics are made of smoke:

> Kiss me tonight,
> It's raining
> Cuban cigars!

'Raining Cuban cigars?' asks in total disbelief Teri. She knows this is a miracle greater than pennies from heaven. Julia has a change of tune:

> Kiss me tonight
> and it will rain
> Chateaubriands!

That's his big mouth talking. His heart, though, belongs to Davidoff.

In *Blame it on Rio* Joe Bologna, an Italian Cary Grant,

*Says The Collins Dictionary of the English Language: lurid.[4] – glowing with an unnatural glare.

228

smokes his first cigar – a big Brazilian brute. Asks his sultry companion, a Carioca: 'How do you like it?' 'Mirvillous!' says Bologna. 'My husband,' confides that Rio woman, 'hated cigars, the big sod.' Inversions and diversions, obviously. But don't blame it on Rio, don't blame it on the moonlight. Blame it on director Donen, who makes gorgeous Michelle Johnson come next to kiss her father good night and react more repelled than rebelled: 'Ugh! Daddy, you reek of cigars.'

Bologna smelled of even bigger cigars in *My Favorite Year*, but there he was impersonating Sid Cesar, who smoked big, raged big and was himself a big man. He had to be aped big. A contemporary of Cesar, the late lamented Ernie Kovacs, was also a big cigar man. In *Our Man in Havana* he made the longest Lonsdales look like lipsticks. He was conceited, arrogant, a coxcomb in short. He was not short though: he was larger than life but in that wretched movie he was all the life there was – and a good match for Noel Coward, who was brief but brilliant. Coward with his umbrella, Kovacs with his cigar.

In *Moscow on the Hudson* well-dressed, tidy Alejandro Rey plays a Cuban lawyer in exile in New York. He is street-wise and has more than one ace in his sleeve. But when he lights up a cigar by actually burning its tip you know he is not only a shyster but an imposter too: he is no Cuban. Of course he is not, he is from Buenos Aires. Argentine, to your mate. Or from Mexico. Mexican to your *cuates. Tu tequila te delata.*

The most irreverent smoker ever was one Eddie Anderson, a.k.a. Rochester, who in *Green Pastures* became a version of Thomas Riley Marshall hit not by lightning but by sudden inflation. He addressed none other than God Himself with an immodest proposal: 'A ten-cent seegar, Lawd?'

Many welcomed the Philippines as if they were with the Philistines. But those who came to jeer stayed to cheer. 'Three cheers for a good cigar!', they shouted – and they gave each of the three a chair to sit on and smoke a good cigar in Peace. Filipino cigars are the best West of Los Angeles and East of Calcutta – except of course, Java, that old French tongue-twister loved by Flaubert, a man who hated the bourgeois as the Philistine amongst us. Out of them and for us he devised a dictionary in which cigars are *'tous infects!'* Here is how he proved his case: *Maintenant, mesdames et messieurs*! And now, ladies and gentlemen! *La pièce de résistance de notre soirée par Monsieur Flaubert lui meme*! Flaubert's last stunt! 'When I was young . . . whenever I went to a brothel with my friends I always picked the ugliest girl and insisted on making love to her in front of them without taking my cigar out of my mouth. It wasn't any fun for me: I just did it for the gallery.' (*The Goncourt Journal*, 1865)

The Philistines are no longer in the antipodes: they are on television. On television nothing can have value without being an object of futility. That's Marx *avant l'image*. From each performer according to his abilities, to each viewer never according to his needs. That's how the television commercial was born. Television is movies plus the electron. The commercials are mostly to watch how they wash their dirty linen in public. Cigarette commercials are forbidden in Britain but not commercials for cigars. Usually they are no cricket but, for some, a *cri de coeur* destined to the crematorium of a match, a puff here and there and finally an ashtray. Britishest and shortest is a slogan 'Happiness is a cigar called Hamlet'. This was obviously before Hamlet met Yorick in the cemetery, where he grew grave.

Castella, advertised as the Finest British Cigars, have a television commercial full of puns and panatellas. The puns are all right, the panatellas are pungent. In any case they are no Shamedpennies but more like Picayunes in fact. Picayune is a cheroot that is not as jejune as it sounds. Picayunes were smoked mainly by piccaninnies. We all know, however, that a piccaninny fire won't last long logs. The same can be safely said of a picayune cigar.

On the other hand, Panama sells cigars with sex. The slogan in their TV commercial is 'The only cigar with *six* appeal' – and to stress the pun further the six shine bright in the foggy London night. I forgot to mention that Panama is a brand name not a country in Central America, with several channels but only one canal.

A luxury liner in mid-ocean. Then – a loud report, followed by a louder report: the ship is sinking! At a bar, reclining on the mahogany counter and wearing a white suit and a Panama hat, a drink in hand, there is a man – or is there? Confusion now follows, the man follows suit, running. *Sauve qui peut!* But the man in white controls himself and comes back to the bar and counter to light a cigar from the pack he left behind. Insert: a Falstaff cigar. Smoking but cool, calm and collected, the man with the Falstaff cigar proceeds to abandon ship in a cowardly fashion: under his Panama hat he had hidden a blond wig. Now his white suit turns into a creamy silk gown and he drops his pants (he couldn't be wearing trousers, could he?) to board the last lifeboat, as crowd and crew cry out, 'Women and children first!' After the wreck, the reckoning.

Believe it or not, you have witnessed a British television commercial for a British product: Falstaff cigars. Evidently Falstaff is the cigar for bounders. It is either that or the Falstaff publicity men know no bounds. British private television shows commercials for pipe tobacco and cigars. There have been in the past very successful campaigns for pipe tobacco, like the Saint Bruno commercials, and for cigars and cigarillos, like the famous slogan for Hamlet, the mild cigar not the excessive play. Most commercials tell a story or run a gag to build a fire, but the commercial for Falstaff cigars backfired, at least with me. There are still human beings, albeit cigar-smokers, who, caught in the dilemma of saving their skin or their soul, will choose the latter – even if it means, instead of a hell of flames and smoke and showbusiness sinners, a heaven full of harps and no cigars.

How about the commercial of Smokes to Come? Here it is: A brand of cigars named Rosebud. A lithograph of a sled with a faded rosebud painted on it. The flames have started to make the rosebud turn gray, then charcoal, then ash blue and the name burns, frying crisply for a moment. Then it goes up in smoke, in smoke, in smoke.

There are the names of different cigars. Kanes (big, bald-headed and fat, like a Churchill), Lelands (long and elegant panatellas), Bernsteins (a cheroot pronounced 'Bernsteen'). Orson Welles should do the commercials. Not a very difficult man to secure for the job if you provide him with plenty of cigars. Another commercial could use Joseph Cotten as 'Jay Leland'. He is now a cigar smoker, a man of the world, a connoisseur. If he is our man for Havanas out of Havanas run the sequence from *Citizen Kane* (B&W) where he is seen as an old man, decrepitly sitting in a wheelchair on the old people's home roof. His voice sounds very, very old as he talks to 'Reporter'. He is saying, 'You don't happen to have a cigar, young man, do you? I've got a young physician who thinks I'm going to stop smoking.' (CUT to some time later.) 'You're absolutely sure you don't have a cigar?'

REPORTER: Mr Leland, what do you know about Rosebud?
LELAND: Rosebud? Oh! I'll tell you one thing you can do for me, young fellow.
REPORTER: Sure.
LELAND: On your way out you stop at a cigar store, will you, and send me up a couple of cigars.
(*Cut to present-day actor* JOSEPH COTTEN *in colour. He looks fit and vigorous as he talks to the camera*):
COTTEN: Then I told Mr Thompson, the reporter, the name of my favourite cigars – Rosebud Cigars, of course. I remember telling him – (*Cut to Citizen Kane scene again*) You won't forget, will you, about the cigars? (*Cut to present-day actor* COTTEN – *colour*) He didn't forget at all! (*Smiling*) Neither have I and it seems like ages since I first asked for a Rosebud, the best cigar for the present that brings back the best of the past. (*He produces a cigar, lights it and puffs at it.*) Rosebud, the cigar that goes up in smoke forever! (*He smiles again, puffs etc.*) Like a million dollars! I mean me not the cigar. It's Rosebud and it can afford to be the cheapest, without being a cheapo, of *all* cigars because it's also *the* best! (MR COTTEN *smiles and is finally enveloped in cigar smoke. Thick. Thick. Thickest!* COTTEN *begins to cough like a man choking badly.*)

Abrupt end of commercial.

In Low Tar television funnymen like Jackie Gleason, a heavy puffer, smoked cigars in front of the TV camera and cigarettes in movies. Contrary to George Burns those comedians only smoked Havanas. As a triple tautology Ernie Kovacs was in Havana to play the heavy in *Our Man in Havana*. Kovacs always had three enormous Lonsdales in his shirt pocket and another one already lit in his mouth, smiling and smoking. He smoked avidly, happy to have his Havana in Havana while it lasted. His next picture was *Wake Me When It's Over*. Danny Kaye as Gaylord Mitty, an avatar of Walter, puffed nonchalantly at a 'hand-made Havana'. There are, alas, machine-rolled Havanas too. On my desk I keep an empty box of Partagas that wears a notice specifying that the cigars are all machine-made, to maul Mitty's myth. Soon even the Monster will be made at the Frankenstein plant near Düsseldorf.

Warning – hand-made cigars are to machine-made ones what hard-cover books are to paperbacks. The smoke might be the same but they are better made and there is a distinct pleasure in having it in your hand. A hand-made cigar is something that if not actually made just for you, seems to be. It has in fact the quality and feel of a private press. The fastest (but not necessarily the best) cigar roller in the world can make, at the most, 300 cigars a day. An ordinary machine can manufacture 1000 cigars an *hour*. To borrow once more from Lord Thomas, a hand-made Havana is like a vintage wine, a machine-made cigar is *vin ordinaire*. Dracula never drinks wine. A wino never touches the stuff, meaning a vintage Château d'Yquem. Is this a vindication of Davidoff?

A storm-trooper's warning

Adolf Hitler said loudly (on the PA system in fact) in 1933: 'Those who *don't* smoke, follow me!' This man was one of the crudest inveighers against tobacco the world had ever known – and the world has known quite a few, believe me. Hitler was against men who smoke but had no qualms about sending millions of men (smoking and non-smoking Jews) and women and children to their deaths, their bodies reduced to columns of smoke coming out of obscene chimneys. Not all smoke-haters are like Hitler, of course. But they all share a fanatic streak, from King James to the usherette who comes fuming down the aisle to tell you that you are, sir, sitting on the *wrong* side of the house! A common sign reunites East and West Germany today. It is a notice that says *Rauchen Verboten*! You can see it the moment you deplane in Berlin and even before on the plane about to land. Somehow it has echoes of booted men marching down Unter den Linden in grey uniforms wearing red armbands with black swastikas. But it only means 'Don't Smoke' in German. A contradiction in smoke: cigars are never allowed on planes in flight but cigarettes are.

Everywhere people are trying to stop you from smoking, even strangers – especially strangers. Smoking is a very personal thing and only the totalitarian mind can conceive making you stop forcibly. Hitler used to advise his followers not to smoke, as if non-smokers were a chosen people or a master-race: Aryans never smoke – except Vikings on their slow boat to Valhalla. Jung tried to make Freud kick the habit under the couch, as if smoking cigars were like sniffing cocaine. (Freud smoked and sniffed by the way.) Jung argued that smoking cigars (he smoked a pipe) had caused Freud's cancer of the jaw. Freud used to joke that he had not cancer of the jaw, but cancer of the Jew. Freud never stopped smoking and lived thirty years with his cancer. It didn't kill him, Hitler did. A year after being expelled from his hated-but-beloved Vienna he died in smoggy London. England didn't kill him, exile did.

Nobody ever noticed that cigars smelled awfully until they banned smoking in places it was always allowed before. The current campaign against smoking (it is again, as in the sixteenth century, healthier not to smoke), the poor quality of most cigars and the exorbitant prices of Havanas (and even Jamaicas and Manilas), it all makes the famous slogan (altered) by Thomas Marshall more necessary than ever: 'What this country needs is a good non-smoking cigar.' The prohibition of smoking is always more religious than political or economical: it has for its butt a habit (*arch.*). It is ultimately a reactionary movement: let's go back to the times, as in Turkey and Russia, when tobacco was taboo. Or a little bit closer: when Victoria frowned upon it the way she disapproved of Bertie, the smoking son. Today's tobacco prohibitionists, like those of alcohol in the late 1920s, are creating new transgressors. Those are now, mostly, young girls. It is in fact a demonstration of irreverent independence from both father and preacher that young women smoke more than ever before. Moreover, they are doing it *en masse*, everywhere: at home and at work and above all in the streets. You can see now young delicate things smoking down the avenue, strolling in the park and in other public places all over the world – and they all smoke with a certain *hauteur*. They are defiant because most of them are, at least in England, white, young and single. Carmen, the smoker of *papaletes* though a promiscuous

234

dark gypsy, would have approved. Carmen Jones, her black American counterpart, would have sung in solidarity.

In *Carmen*, that opera full of fate and smoke, the curtain rises on a square in Seville, 'with a tobacco factory on one side', as the libretto precises. A chorus of fast girls come leisurely out of the factory smoking cigarettes. They all sashay about the square. The first-night audience was scandalized, as they were with Oscar Wilde later. Girls smoking on stage! Now really! But what would the Paris public have said if they saw not gypsy girls but secretaries, socialites, tourists and idle and ideal working girls going about everywhere as in a chorus – all-walking, all-smoking girls?

Girls, girls, girls, all smoking cigarettes, as we can see on a clear day in the streets of London, the former capital of the world now aping New York as sedulously as King Kong. Said the London *Evening Standard* quoting an American expert: 'Go to any shopping mall or rock concert and you'll see children smoking' – and they are not smoking marihuana joints but machine-made cigarettes. 'Among teenagers, many more girls than boys are smoking nowadays, a complete reversal of the Fifties and Sixties. One of the more unabashed appeals to the female smoker is a new cigarette called Satin.' It sounds in fact like Satan. Remember Lucifer, the match that promised sulfur and fire? Be a devil and strike one and light up a Satin. It is a vindication of E-330, that daring young thing, who once lived in the future.

The English newspaper claims that this is a twentieth-century habit, but women smoking cigars were an old Spanish custom spread all over Europe in the nineteenth century – not to mention Cuba and South America. George Sand was the most notorious (and nefarious) woman smoker of her day. But she didn't do it apparently as a provocation as blatant as her trousers and her frockcoat and necktie – not to mention lovers. Since the end of the nineteenth century (no more the *fin de siècle*) few women dared smoke cigars in public but they did in the privacy of their own homes, *zenanas* of sin. Why couldn't women be like smoking men? Marilyn Monroe, as always, had a theory about it. In *The Seven Year Itch* she confides to Tom Ewell, who is trying hard to kick his habit: 'At the club we had this girl: she smoked nothing but cigars.' Here is Marilyn's opinion of this oddity:

'Personally, I think she only did it to make herself look older.'
Deadlier too, as witness Bonnie Parker, who always had a
mean cheroot between her lipsticking lips but with her
lacquered finger on the trigger: first she smoked, then her
gun smoked too.

> Some women are born to smoke; others merely achieve
> the habit; and others have it thrust upon them. She knew
> the true pleasure of the cigarette; and she handled it with
> the more charm, perhaps, because its gracefulness was
> something akin to that of her, who was so small and
> dainty, slim yet round and beautifully moulded.

> *Confessions Unfinished*
> Anonymous

In *Confessions of Zeno* a man, Tom Ewell from Trieste, tries
to give up smoking cigarettes. In *Cold Turkey*, the movie, a
whole town does. I haven't yet seen a picture or a play or
read a book in which a character tries to give up smoking
cigars. On the contrary, the cigar-smoking gentleman, giving
the least fuss, doesn't even try. He is not in the claws of a
habit but enjoying himself. Somebody else, of course, will try
harder to make him stop the pleasure of the company a
panatella gives. These days you can suffer Mark Twain's
pangs not only once but twice. You go to your neighbourhood
cinema, where the familiar haunted house of lore has now
become four or five small, smart movie-houses or rather
shoe-boxes where they show you a mediocre movie on a wall
as the Biggest Production Since God Created the Cosmos.
(Gaseous ghosts were more fun, of course.) Or you go to your
friendly bookshop, suddenly transformed into a box-full of
shelves crammed with paperbacks, which no sooner are they
published than they are forgotten – even by the author – but
they never disappear completely from the shelves like rotten
fruits on a tree too tall to climb. Or you enter the well-known
exotic restaurant (Pakistani, Thai, even Italian from Ischia)
and they give you a shock of recognition of the new public
health ordinances: NO SMOKING. That's when you feel like Mark
Twain on board the steamboat in *The Innocents Abroad*. He
claimed to have 'picked up a good deal of information during

236

the afternoon'. All of it on his first stroll on deck. This is the information he gathered of an afternoon: 'At one time I was climbing up the quarter deck when the vessel's stern was in the sky; I was smoking a cigar and feeling passably comfortable. Somebody ejaculated: *'No smoking abaft the wheel!'*

Well (this is me back from my trip with Twain), I don't know if you can be abaft the wheel in a cinema or hitting the deck in a bookshop or with the stern up in the sky in a restaurant, but in all those places I've been shocked with an unfamiliar rite of passage where someone shouts 'with the Snark, so to speak, at the door' –

'NO SMOKING'

doing the police in different voices. Nobody called Mark Twain sir, for the voice shouting at him belonged to a certain Captain Duncan. But I can vouchsafe that I've been frozen with similar

'NO SMOKING'

shouts and signs delivered by vexed usherettes, angry booksellers and three-starred-crossed Italian waiters – and even by a busboy or two steaming out of fuming, malodorous kitchens. Since the days of Mark Twain smoking ain't what it used to be: a public pleasure. Now it has become the only sneaky vice. I've yet to see a sign saying 'NO SNIFFING ALOUD' and not meaning of course the brown stuff. The signs against smoking are everywhere: multilingual, visible, compulsory, lawful, awful. Some interdictions are in German and sound like Nazi propaganda from the Third Rauchen.

But Italians, as usual, are lackadaisacal: *'Fumare e Molto Pericoloso'*, which sounds more like instructions on how to play a pipe. The French sound gentle but full of passionate intensity: *'Ne Pas Fumer, S.V.P.'* The dichotomy (or hypocrisy if you want) is that in these three countries (as in Spain) the campaign against smoking is being carried out by the Government – which controls the monopoly on tobacco and sells cigarettes with costlier advertising than they employ to warn off the public from smoking!

HOLY SMOKELESS!
Try *Smokeless* and you'll be able to stop smoking!

SMOKELESS

If you are a smoking person you already know how difficult
it is to kick the habit. There's a reason for it. Tobacco
triggers in your system a craving for nicotine that is an
all-consuming passion.

SMOKELESS

diminishes it and then makes it disappear, for it works as an
astute substitute for nicotine. It also eliminates the toxic
effect that nicotine releases into your nervous system,
suppressing *all* desires. If you want to stop smoking

SMOKELESS

is the solution to your problem.

SMOKELESS

Just to Stop Smoking Forever!
(Sold in all drug-stores)

(Sign seen in Spain)

Now I know why Dr Pretorius, a brazen brigand, sounded so
apologetic when he confessed to the Monster that he smoked
cigars – his only vice. It was simply because Dr Pretorius *was*
apologetic. He had been reduced to smoke his cigar in an old,
sunken, decrepit crypt: *savoir vivre* is now possible among
corpses only. Nevertheless, when everything is said ('Cigarettes can burn a hole in your pocket') and done ('Ban
smoking now – and shoot the bastard when you see the grey
of his smoke!'), I'll still be able to go back to our dawn again
to try and regress and redress. There and then Chris Columbus,
that Jewish-Italian stand-up comedian, a *primo cartello* in the
New World, a top banana already, with his name above the
title (*America, America!*), actually addressed the Shaman after
the chamade, a showman finally accepting the fact that this
cham was a sham and no kin to the Khan. He firmly but
courteously rejected his offer of that second cigar in history –
de Xeres was here, remember? Columbus changing colours
like a chameleon with a gentle, sweet disposition, as a
discoverer should, the first declared non-smoker on record,
begging to be excused by genuflecting, said finally:
Do you mind if I don't smoke?

Ta Vague Littérature

From Sir Walter Raleigh, who according to some died smoking, to Evelyn Waugh, who smoked all his creative life, smoking is mentioned more in English writings than in any other literature in the West – even more so than in Spanish literature in any case. Spain, as we know, discovered tobacco to the world and a Spaniard was the first European who ever smoked. Nevertheless not much has been written concerning smoking and cigars in Spanish. One can safely say that it is in English where references to tobacco, snuff, cigars, cigarettes and pipe-smoking and chewing tobacco abound the most – even more so than in all the languages of the West put together. English is undoubtedly the language of smoking. Where else can one find a word to designate a garment made just for the purpose of being comfortable at home, the Englishman's castle, and for smoking? Still today in France and Spain an evening jacket or tuxedo is called a *smoking*, usually pronounced smokeen. A smoke-room is a typically British place and the Big Smoke is the name London has among Cockneys. A pipe is what we call a pipe in most European languages. An Englishman, John Florio, coined the word. Apart from aboriginal tobacco, cigar is the major contribution of the Spanish language to the art of smoking: *vitola, breva, panetela, corona, regalia* attest it. But what about a cigarette? Ah that! That, as the wag put it to differentiate fact from fiction, is a fag.

To quote from writers on their smoke might make a smoking-room anthology. You may point out that you can equally collect copy on wine. But wine has been with man (or rather, man has been with wine) for thousands of years. One of the first tasks Noah accomplished after the Flood was to plant a vineyard – the next was to drink his wine and get drunk. Like most drunks he immediately got rid of his clothes: Ham saw him naked. Later 'Noah awoke from his

241

wine'. This, in Genesis 9:24, is probably the first hangover ever registered. But Homer can be quoted on wine too. Not only did he call the sea wine-dark everywhere but he has in *The Odyssey* an ode to wine: 'The wine urges me on, the bewitching wine, which sets even a wise man to singing and to laughing gently and rouses him up to dance.' Though it 'brings forth words which were better unspoken'. That's wine too. But tobacco was discovered to Europe less than five centuries ago. What about coffee then? Or tea? Or chocolate? I take coffee but tea is not universal enough, thank you. Chocolate is a very rare drink. Mostly it takes the form of Hershey bars or Belgian bonbons. Not many writers will concede that they drink chocolate while they work. Or that tea makes you dream like legal opium. Besides, it's I who is writing this book and between tea and tobacco I'll always choose tobacco – though I'll never chew.

For those who prefer, like Mallarmé, the smoke of their cigars written in ink and not turned into images, moving or otherwise, here is an anthology that began in the eighteenth century but has not yet ended: only my book does. No elegy can be the cigar's swansong. The last word, though, like a good smoke is almost woman. But it truly belongs to the poor poet who played in earnest with words and blanks and verse and the erasures that make my writing, our writing, all writing: a vague literature, a vain glory, a varied cause – which some pronounce varicose. Those are the jesters who, reeking with body odour, dare call a cigar a stinker!

I must confess though that I'm convinced that smoking is not at all like writing. Cigars in particular are like movies: an art that is an industry, an industry to make art. Like movies cigars are the stuff dreams are made of. My idea of happiness is to sit alone in the lobby of any old hotel after a late dinner, when the lights go out at the entrance and only the desk and the doorman are visible from my comfortable armchair. I then smoke my long black cigar in peace, in the dark: once a primeval bonfire in a clear of the forest, now a civilized ember glowing in the night like a beacon to the soul. An elegy is my choice smoke and I, the worst Tibullus, become thus a vestibule.

GCI

FOLKLORE FIRST:

There was a young girl from Havana
who thought that she lived in Nirvana.
(This is not, I repeat, *not* a piece of Americana.)
But she met a new car
driven by a clean-cut young man
who belonged to an old Cuban clan
and wielded an enormous cigar!
Of course, they married *mañana*.
And that's why that about-to-be-married Cubana
still thinks that she lives in Nirvana.

TO AN HONEST TOBACCONIST

This is my friend, Abel, an honest fellow;
He lets me have good tobacco, and he does not
Sophisticate it with sack-lees or oil,
Nor washes it in muscadel and grains,
Nor buries it in gravel, under ground,
Wrapp'd up in greasy leather, or piss'd clouts;
But keeps it in fine lilly pots that, open'd,
Smell like conserve of roses, or French beans.
He has his maple block, his silver tongs,
Winchester pipes, and fire of Juniper:
A neat, spruce, honest fellow. . .

Ben Jonson
The Alchemist (1612)

BEFORE THE BEGINNING

Samuel Rowlands in his *Knave of Clubs* (1609) already mentioned all the possibilities of the weed:

> The leaf green, dry, steept, burned, dust:
> Have each their special praise.

He even suggests snuff! Later he composes the part we smokers know by heart:

> But he's a frugal man indeed,
> That with a leaf can dine,
> And needs no napkin for his hands,
> His fingers' ends to wipe,
> But keeps his kitchen in a box,
> And roast-meat in a pipe.

Another poet of the seventeenth century, George Wither, 'a man given to sudden and opposite loyalties', had attacked tobacco in his *Abuses Stript and Whipt* of 1613, but given time in 1661 wrote this:

> Here, all alone, I by myself have took,
> An Emblem of my Self, a Pipe of Smoke.
> For, I am but a little piece of Clay
> Filled with Smoke that quickly fumes away.

Whether Wither wrote this because he was in gaol or not is beside the point. He was, like many men before and after, enjoying a consolation devoutly to be whiffed. Whither Wither?

How do you attain the stage of the Perfect Smoker? As Charles Lamb said, 'I toiled after it, as some men t-t-toil after virtue.' Lamb was a determined stutterer. That's why it took him so long to say goodbye in his

A FAREWELL TO TOBACCO

May the Babylonish curse
Straight confound my stammering verse.
If I can a passage see
In this world-perplexity

Or a fit expression find,
Or a language to my mind
(Still the phrase is wide or scant),
To take leave of thee, Great Plant.

One hundred and thirty-five lines later Lamb at last says goodbye to tobacco – but not to smoking. Very soon he was back at it, at smoking and at writing verse. That is called in Australia to do a Melba.

May the Babylonish curse
Strait confound my stammering verse,
If I can a passage see
In this word-perplexity,
Or a fit expression find,
Or a language to my mind,
(Still the phrase is wide or scant)
To take leave of thee, GREAT PLANT!

Lamb was crazy about tobacco – or just plain crazy. In any case his sister truly was, crazy enough to kill her mother (and Lamb's too) in a fit of insanity. (To malicious gossip I can add that she never ever smoked.) Lamb later adopted her.

Or in any term relate
Half my love or half my hate.

Lamb adored tobacco too:

And the passion to proceed
More from a mistress than a weed.

Which makes Byron look like a wolf in Lamb's clothing.

Lamb's beautiful stroke of the smoking pen is actually a parting shot – from a boomerang.

Here he is at it again. Lamb loved his sister but apparently he loved tobacco more.

> Sooty retainer to the vine
> Bacchus' servant, negro fine.

Was it Othello he now versified about?

> Sorcerer that mak'st us dote upon
> Thy begrimed complexion

Does it scan – or is it cant?

> And, for thy pernicious sake,
> More and greater oaths to break
> Than reclaimed lovers take
> 'Gainst women: thou thy siege dost lay
> Much too in the female way.

He called tobacco, in a *contaminatio*, 'Brother of Bacchus, later born' – but the poem is much too long. Near the end he shows himself closer to Marlowe than Shakespeare:

> 'mongst the joys
> Of the blest Tobacco Boys.

But in the true end he scantly recant:

> For I must (nor let it grieve thee,
> Friendliest of plants that I must) leave thee.
> For thy sake, TOBACCO, I
> Would do anything but die,
> And but seek to extend my day
> Long enough to sing thy praise.

Is this the end of the poem? Could be. In any case it isn't the end of tobacco this Farewell of Lamb.

THE OVERTURE

I was yesterday in a coffee-house not far from the Royal Exchange, where I observed three persons in close conference over a pipe of tobacco; upon which, having filled one for my own use, I lighted it at the little wax candle that stood before them; and, after having thrown in two or three whiffs amongst them, sat down and made one of the company. I need not tell my reader, that lighting a man's pipe at the same candle is looked upon among brothersmoakers as an overture to conversation and friendship. As we here laid our heads together in a very amicable manner, being intrenched under a cloud of our own raising, I took up the last *Spectator*, and casting my eye over it, 'The *Spectator*,' says I, 'is very witty to-day': upon which a lusty lethargic old gentleman, who sat at the upper end of the table, having gradually blown out of his mouth a great deal of smoke, which he had been collecting for some time before, 'Ay,' says he, 'more witty than wise, I am afraid.' His neighbour, who sat at his right hand, immediately coloured, and, being an angry politician, laid down his pipe with so much wrath that he broke it in the middle, and by that means furnished me with a tobacco-stopper.

Joseph Addison:
The Spectator, No. 568 (1714)

This is the man who said that a pun is the lowest form of wit. Here he is, a chimney-sweeper come to dust, neither witty nor wise.

THE PLAGUE MEETS ROBINSON CRUSOE

Daniel Defoe in his masterpiece *Journal of the Plague Year* (plaguearized two centuries later by Albert Camus in *The Plague*) has something to say about the years of the plague: 'a very ill time to be sick in.' Then 'the minds of the people were agitated . . . and a kind of sadness and horror . . . sat upon the countenance even of the common people.' Soon there are common and uncommon remedies against the malady: 'sovereign cordials against the corruption of the air', 'anti-pestilentials pills', 'incomparable drinks against the plague', 'an universal remedy' and 'the true plague water'. Defoe's character finds that 'if the plague was not the hand of God, but a kind of a possession of an evil spirit, and that it was to be kept off with crossings, signs of the zodiac, papers tied up with so many knots, and certain words of figures written on them, as particularly the word Abracadabra, formed in triangle or pyramid.' But science knows best. A certain Dr John Hancocke to fight the malignant fever lists in his 'Febrifugium Magnum' that great febrifuge, powerfuel *Nicotiana Tabacum* and one John Hayward ('who was at that time under-sexton of the parish of St Stephen. By under-sexton was understood at that time gravedigger and bearer of the dead') put in practice medical theory: 'He never used any preservatives against the infection, other than holding garlic and rue in his mouth, and smoking tobacco. This I had from his own mouth,' says Defoe, who is once more sharing adventures and misadventures with his characters.

A better-known character by Defoe, Robinson Crusoe, added a new property to tobacco: he drank it, just as if it were green laudanum. A poison too early? No, a medicinal compound, half-medicine, half-narcotic. On the historical date of 28 June 1660, on that very day, on that night rather, the sailor disowned by his ship (Admiral Nelson would no doubt cast a critical eye upon this last remark) fell violently ill. '. . . As the apprehension of the return of my distemper terrified me very much, it occurred to my thought that the Brazilians take no physic but their tobacco for almost all distempers; and I had a piece of a roll of tobacco in one of the chests, which was quite cured, and some also that was green and not quite cured' – he knew he was cured.

I went, directed by Heaven, no doubt; for in this chest I found a cure both for the soul and body.' Please, let's have an instant rewrite: 'I found a cure for both soul and body.' May I have the last word? 'Body.' And the one before last, please. 'And.' No, not that one, the next word. 'Soul.' That's enough. Thank you. 'I opened the chest, and found what I looked for, viz., the tobacco; and as the few books I had saved lay there too, I took out one of the Bibles which I mentioned before, and which, to this time, I had not found leisure or so much as inclination to look into; I say, I took it out, and brought both that and the tobacco with me to the table.

What use to make of the tobacco, I knew not, as to my dispenser, or whether it was good for it or not. [Obviously Robinson by now knew only that tobacco was good for the soul.] But I tried several experiments with it, as if I was resolved it should hit one way or the other. [What you would call the hit-and-miss system or Crusoe subject to random.] I first took a piece of a leaf, and chewed it in my mouth, which, indeed, at first almost stupified my brain, the tobacco being greene and strong, and I had not been much used to it; then I took some and steeped it an hour or two in some rum, and resolved to take a dose of it when I lay down; and lastly, I burn some upon a pan [it's almost a pun upon a pan] of coals, and held my nose close over the smoke of it as long as I could bear it, as well for the heat as the virtue of it, and I held out almost to suffocation.

In the interval of this operation, I took up the Bible and began to read; but my head was too much disturbed with the tobacco to bear reading, at least at that time; only, having opened the book casually. [At random is better.]

The words were very apt to my case, and made some impression upon my thoughts at the time of reading them, though not so much as they did afterwards; for, as for being delivered, the word had no sound, as I may say, to me . . .

It grew now late, and the tobacco had, as I said, dozed my head so much that I inclined to sleep. So I left my lamp burning in the cave, lest I should want anything in the night, and went to bed. But before I lay down, I did what I had never done in my life – I kneeled down and prayed to

God to fulfil the promise to me, that if I called upon him in the day of trouble, he would deliver me. After my broken and imperfect prayer was over, I drunk the rum in which I had steeped the tobacco, which was so strong and rank of the tobacco that, indeed, I could scarcely get it down. Immediately upon this I went to bed, and I found presently it flew up into my head violently – but I fell into a sound sleep and waked no more till, by the sun, it must necessary be near three o'clock in the afternoon the next day; nay, to this hour, I am partly of the opinion that I slept all the next day and night, and till almost three the day after; for, otherwise, I know not how I should lose a day out of my reckoning in the days of the week, as it appeared, some years later, I had done; for if I had lost by crossing and recrossing the Line, I should have lost more than a day; but in my account it was lost, and I never knew which way.

'A potent brew!' said President Bru.

SILENCE

Tobacco-smoke is the one element in which, by our European manners, men can sit silent together without embarrassment, and where no man is bound to speak one word more than he has actually and veritably got to say. Nay, rather every man is admonished and enjoined by the laws of honour, and even of personal ease, to stop short of that point; at all events, to hold his peace and take to his pipe again the instant he *has* spoken his meaning, if he chance to have any. The results of which salutary practice, if introduced into Constitutional Parliaments, might evidently be incalculable.

Thomas Carlyle
Frederick the Great (1858–65)

EDGARPO

Poe, who drank almost everything drinkable (except water) from wine and whisky to morphine (he probably meant laudanum) and was a sherry expert (see 'The Cask of Amontillado') didn't smoke much, but his characters in the tales 'of Mystery and Raciocination' did. There is even a French tobacconist in 'The Murders in the Rue Morgue'. By the way, there's no street of that name in Paris but there's a tobacco shop on the corner owned by one Pierre Moreau, who calls it his *bureau de tabac*. One of the victims of the murderer in the rue Morgue, Madam l'Espanaye, visited this *tabac* frequently and bought not only 'small quantities of tobacco' but also some snuff. Obviously the old lady rolled her own and smoked and snorted at her ease 'for nearly four years'. That's only the time she bought it from M. Moreau, who declared to 'have been in the habit of selling the old lady what she asked for' before she suffered her sudden and brutal *passage au tabac*.

It is Marie Bonaparte in her *Psycho-Analitic Interpretation* who claims that Edgar Allan Poe invented the smoking detective: 'Even Sherlock Holmes's famous pipe is first smoked by Dupin in *The Purloined Letter.*' Dupin is the *chevalier* C. Auguste Dupin and he not only created the deductive method as applied to the detection of crimes, but invented a whole mode of smoking. Here is what the chronicler of his adventures has to say about the Dupin Whiff:

> At Paris, just after dark one gusty evening in the autumn of 18—, I was enjoying the twofold luxury of meditation and a meerschaum, in company of my friend . . . For one hour at least we had maintained a profound silence; while each, to any casual observer, might have seemed intently and exclusively occupied with the curling eddies of smoke that oppressed the atmosphere of the chamber . . . the door of our apartment was thrown open and admitted our acquaintance, M.G., the Prefect of the Parisian police.

Shades of Holmes: Not only his life with Watson but the antecedent of Inspector Lestrade. But wait! There is even more to meet the reading eye:

> We had been sitting in the dark, and Dupin now arose for the purpose of lighting a lamp, but sat down again, without doing so, upon G.'s saying that he called to consult us, or rather to ask the opinion of my friend, about some official business which had occasioned a great deal of trouble.
>
> 'If it is any point requiring reflection,' observed Dupin, as he forbore to enkindle the wick. [I like that phrase, 'he forbore to enkindle the wick': it is a smoker's sentence] 'We shall examine it to better purpose in the dark.' 'That is another of your odd notions,' said the Prefect.
>
> 'Very true,' said Dupin, as he supplied his visitor with a pipe and rolled towards him a comfortable chair.

All Holmes is there, except the American chair on castors. All Conan Doyle is also there: his fortune, his fame, even his knighthood. But all Poe ever got was penury, alcohol and drugs and madness. Some people love to say, 'Poor Poe!' I prefer to salute him as in a toast *funèbre*: 'Pour Poe!'

THE SINKING SHIP

'Sir,' said the first lieutenant, bursting into the Captain's cabin, 'the ship is going down'.

'Very well, Mr Spoker,' said the Captain; 'but that is no reason for going about half-shaved. Exercise your mind a moment, Mr Spoker, and you will see that to the philosophic eye there is nothing new in our position: the ship (if she is to go down at all) may be said to have been going down since she was first launched.'

'She is settling fast,' said the first lieutenant, as he returned from shaving.

'Fast, Mr Spoker?' asked the Captain. 'The expression is a strange one, for time (if you will think of it) is only relative.'

'Sir,' said the lieutenant, 'I think it is scarcely worth while to embark in such a discussion when we shall all be in Davy Jones' Locker in ten minutes.'

'By parity of reasoning,' returned the Captain gently, 'it would never be worth while to begin any inquiry of importance; the odds are always overwhelming that we must die before we shall have brought it to an end. You have not considered, Mr Spoker, the situation of man,' said the Captain, smiling, and shaking his head.

'I am much more engaged in considering the position of the ship,' said Mr Spoker.

'Spoken like a good officer,' replied the Captain, laying his hand on the lieutenant's shoulder.

On deck they found the men had broken into the spirit-room, and were fast getting drunk.

'My men,' said the Captain, 'there is no sense in this. The ship is going down, you will tell me, in ten minutes: well, and what then? To the philosophic eye, there is nothing new in our position. All our lives long, we may have been about to break a blood-vessel or to be struck by lightning, not merely in ten minutes, but in ten seconds; and that has not prevented us from eating dinner, no, nor from putting money in the Savings Bank. I assure you, with my hand upon my heart, I fail to comprehend your attitude.'

The men were already too far gone to pay much heed.

'This is a very painful sight, Mr Spoker,' said the Captain.

'And yet to the philosophic eye, or whatever that is,' replied the first lieutenant, 'they may have been getting drunk since they came aboard.'

'I do not know if you always follow my thought, Mr Spoker,' returned the Captain gently. 'But let us proceed.'

In the powder magazine they found an old salt smoking his pipe.

'Good God,' cried the Captain, 'what are you about?'

'Well, sir,' said the old salt, apologetically, 'they told me as she were going down.'

'And suppose she were?' said the Captain. 'To the philosophic eye, there would be nothing new in our position. Life, my old shipmate, life, at any moment and in any view, is as dangerous as a sinking ship; and yet it is man's handsome fashion to carry umbrellas, to wear india-rubber overshoes, to begin vast works, and to conduct himself in every way as if he might hope to be eternal. And for my own poor part I should despise the man who, even on board a sinking ship, should omit to take a pill or to wind up his watch. That, my friend, would not be the human attitude.'

'I beg pardon, sir,' said Mr Spoker, 'But what is precisely the difference between shaving in a sinking ship and smoking in a powder magazine?'

'Or doing anything at all in any conceivable circumstances?' cried the Captain. 'Perfectly conclusive; give me a cigar!'

Two minutes afterwards the ship blew up with a glorious detonation.

Robert Louis Stevenson
Fables

DICKENS AND THACKERAY

Thackeray always began writing with a cigar in his mouth. Every morning found him up and ready to begin work, though he sometimes was in doubt and difficulty as to whether he should commence operations sitting or standing, or walking about or lying down. Often he would light a cigar, and after pacing the room for a few minutes, would put the unsmoked remnant on the mantelpiece, and resume his work with increased cheerfulness, as if he had gathered fresh inspiration from the gentle odours of tobacco.

Tobacco Talk, 1897

Dickens was not an avid smoker as Thackeray, but he indulged in the weed. Once at Lausanne he met at an institution for the deaf and dumb a young man who was deaf and dumb and blind but partial to cigars. Dickens gave the boy all the cigars he had with him and on revisiting the place (Dickens was partial to asylums, reformatories and jails and visited them as often as he could) he left with the head of the institution some money, 'to be expended in cigars for the smoking patient'. The director tried to revive a recollection of Dickens in the invalid but with no sight or hearing it proved impossible. 'Ah,' said Dickens, 'if I had only brought a cigar with me! This could have established my identity.' This belies Casanova who thinks that smoking without seeing the smoke is not smoking. But perhaps Dickens was right after all.

At Boulogne Dickens smoked a farewell cigar with Thackeray, whom he met at the railroad station. He recalled a certain Lady A, 'a character on whose arsenal she had a cigar-box with some cigars made of negrohead'. These black cigars, according to Dickens, were powerful enough 'to quell an elephant in six whiffs'. But Thackeray always expressed his repugnance in seeing a lady 'with a cigar in her face'. What did he actually answer to Dickens's lady with a negrohead?

Thackeray was in fact a great cigar smoker. In *Vanity Fair* he gives the reader ample proof of it – plus that immortal line: 'You don't mind my cigar, do you, Miss Sharp?' Miss Sharp loved the smell of a cigar out of doors beyond everything in the world – and she just tasted one too in the prettiest way possible, gave a little puff, and a little scream and a little giggle, and restored the delicacy to the Captain, who twirled his moustache, and straightway puffed it into a blaze that glowed quite red in the dark plantation, and swore – "Jove – aw – Gad – aw – it's the finest seegaw I ever smoked in the world – aw", for his intellect and conversation were alike brilliant and becoming to a heavy young dragoon.'

A dragoon who puffs into a blaze that glows red in the dark – must be – By Jove! – aw – Gad – why yes – a *dragon*!

Cigars were essential to *Vanity Fair*, where you find men smoking in all occasions – even when they are leaving for Waterloo. The battle not the station. And they go to a debtor's prison in similar fashion: 'Rawdon put his wife into the carriage, which drove off. Mr Wenham had proposed to him to walk home, and offered the Colonel the refreshment of a cigar . . . They lighted their cigars by the lamp of one of the many link-boys outside and Rawdon walked on with his friend.' Crawley was then and there attacked by two men. 'That gallant officer at once knew what had befallen him. He was in the hands of bailiffs . . . "Lend me a hundred, Wenham, for God's sake," poor Rawdon said – "I've got seventy at home." "I've not got ten pound in the world," said poor Mr Wenham. "Good night, my dear fellow." "Good night," said Rawdon ruefully. And Wenham walked away.' But Rawdon Crawley had a consolation (and a consummation) devoutly to be wished: 'and Rawdon Crawley finished his cigar as the cab drove under Temple Bar.'

Becky Sharp even 'brought his cigar and lighted it for him.' I trust she didn't do a Gigi on him. Remember how Little Leslie caroned, *caromed* and caressed Louis Jourdan's cigar in *Gigi*? Rawdon Crawley, he with the crashingly boring name, fell for this trick in the past. Not for nothing is Becky called Sharp. Now George Osborne, whom Becky calls Cupid, exclaims: 'Gad, what a fine night and how bright the moon!' Obviously an after-effect of his cigar, which he puffed and saw it go 'soaring and up skywards'. Then he makes a remark that is a second habit with Thackeray's characters: 'How delicious they smell in the open air!' As every smoker worth his ashes knows cigars smell better, feel better, taste better, *are* better indoors. What Holmes once said of thoughts is also true about cigars: closed rooms tend to concentrate the smoky and foggy atmosphere.

Dickens didn't hate cigar-smoking women, only men who chew tobacco. In his *American Notes* he has much to say on the subject. He should have called his article 'A Spate of Spittoons'. This is how it begins:

> In the court of law the judge has his spittoon, the crier his, the warder his, and the prisoner his; while the jury-men and spectators are provided for as so many men who, in the course of nature, must desire to spit incessantly. In the hospitals the students of medicine are requested by notices upon the wall to eject their tobacco-juice into the boxes provided for that purpose and not to discolour the stairs. In public buildings visitors are implored through the same agency to squirt the essence of their quids, or 'plugs', as I have heard them called by gentlemen learned in this kind of sweet-meat, into the national spittoons, and not about the bases of the marble columns. In some parts this custom is inseparably mixed up with every meal and morning call, and with all the transactions of social life.

Dickens was right about the spit-boxes, as he sometimes calls the spittoons. This is a dreadful habit. But what happened in the USA then, when you didn't have enough spittoons? After travelling on a canal-boat on his way to the *tobacco* plantations of Richmond with not sufficient spit-boxes on board, Dickens writes: 'I was obliged this morning to lay my fur coat on the deck, and wipe the half-dried flakes of spittle from it with my handkerchief; and the only surprise seemed to be that I should consider necessary to do so! When I turned in last night, I put it on a stool beside me and there it lay, under a cross fire from five men – three opposite, one above, and one below.' As if in one of his nightmares, Dickens's fur coat was transformed during sleep into a black spittoon! (This is of course an early version of the 'Furry Tea-cup' now in a storm of spittle. Or quids pro quos. Or is it our spittality?)

But Thackeray was a much milder man and he had the stand-up comedian's conception of a cigar, which he called 'that great unbosomer of secrets'. Here is his revealing gag:

'Honest men with cigars in their mouths, have great physical advantages in conversation. You may stop talking if you like, but the breaks of silence never seem disagreeable, being filled up by the puffing of the smoke; hence there is no awkwardness in resuming the conversation, no straining for effect . . .' (See somewhere else in this book what Grouch Marx has to say on the subject.) Meanwhile, back to Thack: 'Sentiments are delivered in a grave, easy manner. The cigar harmonizes the society . . . I have no doubt that it is from the habit of smoking that American-Indians are such monstrous well-bred men.' Is he talking of the Patagons, the mythic inhabitants of Tierra del Fuego? To make peace with Thackeray I must leave him on a sweet and sour note: a cigar is 'the fragrant companion of solitude', he wrote. That is probably why his daughter, on being asked about her childhood, said: 'I can remember on one occasion, through a cloud of smoke –' Say no more, that was Father after dinner.

Both men were honoured, after a fashion. Thackeray has a street named after him and Dickens a cigar. According to *Tobacco Talk*, 'The London tobacco manufacturers elected to pay Charles Dickens a Cuban compliment. A neat little cigar costing only a penny, was devised and christened the "Pickwick", which still retains its popularity.' A 'Pickwick' penny-each? Humbug! But that was in 1897. Ah those were the times!

One final phrase from *Vanity Fair*, a book which truly cannot exist without cigars, sums up Thackeray's philosophy: 'I am done – pay the bills and get me a cigar.'

FAR INTO THE NIGHT

Next, let us proceed to the inchoative-contingent, which presupposes the habitude of smoking, and has reference to the hours of the day or night at which it is most pleasant to smoke. And as to this answer – at all hours – with certain necessary and obvious exceptions. Firstly, it is good to smoke one pipe, and one only, before breakfast, at which time the body being empty of food is most amenable to the nicotinic energy. Secondly, fail not to smoke three pipes at the least immediately after breakfast. And these should be performed in the open air, and if it is possible, while sauntering about a fair garden or pleasaunce, off which the dew has not yet gone, and odorous with the scents of flowers. Thirdly, in the afternoon smoke not less than three pipes, but not immediately after eating lest they breed heaviness and black choler. Fourthly, and lastly, in the evening, and far into the night, when hanging over your books, smoke as many pipes as possible, at the least not less than four. This I propound not as a maximum but a minimum, and necessary to be discharged by all. For any one who smokes less than eleven pipes per diem is not so much to be accounted a smoker as one who smoketh. And if at any time the student should feel his mouth to be, as it were, cloyed and brackish with much smoking, let him by all means pause for awhile, and drink a strong decoction of tea without either sugar or milk. For nothing is more recuperative and invigorant than this same black tea, and altogether a drink mightily to be commended. And thus in constant smoking and meditation passeth the life of the Pipe Philosopher. To him no place and no time are good save they give him liberty to smoke, and none ill save they take this liberty away. Although, by misfortune, he be compelled to battle with the world and earn his livelihood, yet it is but the body of the man that is so engaged, and his mind not at all. Wealth he only cares for as relieving him of this necessity, and enabling him to be more choice and curious in his fumificables. Opiparous fare and gentle living are held by him of no account, but rather as hindrances and stumbling-blocks to the spirit. Outward show, rich dress, and a fine appearance he dreams not of for himself, but delights to see them in others that he may on them vent his scorn. But most of all he despises that which men call love, and is wont, as we have seen, to look under a fair outside, and see the ruddy skin grow yellow and wrinkled, and at last, bursting asunder, disclose the grinning jaws, and holes for eyes, and layers of bone, about which, when they are covered over, there is such a pitiful to-do and exclamation. Thus, with much tobacco, many books, and a few friends, his life goes on, till at last the inchoative-contingent draws to an end, and the ultimate begins.

Arthur Machen
The Anatomy of Tobacco (1884).

SNUFF AND SNOW

Gogol has a character who lived in a house whose only furniture is a pipe. He might be a small character to you but for me he is a hero, the Great Jevakin. Gogol has smokers strewn all over his pages. Lieutenant Piragov, for instance, 'had a special art of getting smoke rings out of his pipe (sometimes he could even make ten of those, one ring inside the other), and could tell with much fun the story of the big cannon and the rhinoceros' – whatever that was. For Chichikov, the infamous hero of *Dead Souls*, pipes can be catching: 'Chichikov sat down. "Allow me to offer you a pipe." "Please don't. I don't smoke" . . . "Why not?" asked Manilov . . . "I haven't formed the habit yet; I'm afraid of it in fact. They say that the pipe slims." "Let me tell you that this is a prejudice. I believe it's even healthier than sniffing snuff. In our regiment there was a first lieutenant . . . who never let his pipe rest . . . He is now in his forties and, thank God, he enjoys the best of health."' Gogol has a phrase that many smokers would endorse: 'It seems that the devil dislikes tobacco.'

Chichikov refuses to learn how to smoke because he has his box. Of snuff. Of course. *Dead Souls*, Gogol's masterpiece, is *Vanity Fair* with snuff. The box of snuff is queen here and the book wouldn't be what it is if we forbade its character to sniff and sneeze. Says Vladimir Nabokov in his essay *Nikolai Gogol*: 'There is an orgy of snuff-taking,' in *Dead Souls*. Snuff is the snow: sooty snow, black as a winter night in Petersburg. 'Chichikov in *Dead Souls*,' writes Nabokov, 'is introduced to the remarkable trumpet blast he emits when using a hand-kerchief.' Result: 'Noses drip, noses twitch, noses are lovingly or roughly handled. The inhabitants of the moon (so a madman discovers) are Noses.' No wonder Gogol wrote a short story called 'The Nose' which has a roving nose for its main character. In Russia 'a man with the longest nose sees further.' This is a snuffist's proverb, naturally.

There is no snuff (or snuffist for that matter) without a snuff-box. 'Chichikov's aura is continued and symbolized by his snuff-box,' claims Nabokov. 'By that "silver and enamel snuff-box which he offered generously to everybody".' Going ever further another Russian writer, Andrey Biely, 'noted that this box was the wife of Chichikov'. Who was, by the way, impotent, fat and an arseful dodger: a *castrato*, unnaturally. *Dead Souls* is, by the same token, Gogol's snuff-box to play with snuff-balls and noses and snowses all over Russia where snow is the snuff of God. One wonders if Brummell ever read *Dead Souls*. Not in England but in the heaven of dandies. Would the snuff Beau love or even like his snuff Soul?

TOBACCO'S HARM AND EGOS

There are several photographs that show Anton Chekhov as a keen and elegant smoker. He is in fact the most photographed of Russian authors in the last century and he smoked avidly, cigars mostly. There he is with a very slim panatella in his hand or in his mouth, Chekhov looking at the camera (and at us) with intelligent eyes behind a cool pince-nez and yet somehow with much warmth in his gaze: the writer like his writing. He is still living mostly in the nineteenth century but there is also a modern aura about him. Chekhov was tubercular most of his life but being a doctor he didn't prescribe for himself abstinence of tobacco or of oral gratification. Just before dying he asked his wife for a tall glass of champagne. He died in Badenweiler, a German last resort for him.

A biographer says that while in Yalta, where he spent some time also vainly trying to recover from his tuberculosis, Chekhov 'came under and shortly fell out from under, the influence of Tolstoy'. Some of this philosophy of reneging had to do with smoking. Tolstoy, a renegade writer as well, said things about tobacco that were sheer nonsense. 'Nicotine drogues conscience . . . to smoke has for a goal to swamp reason . . . The need of smoking grows as a man is in need of gagging his remorse.' Things like that. Chekhov's creed was somewhat simpler: 'My business is only to be talented.' That, of course, he was. Very. Perhaps too much for his own good. Chekhov was in fact Gogol's direct and perhaps sole heir in Russian literature. He couldn't seek refuge in madness, as Gogol did, instead he found a palliative in tuberculosis. Contrary to Tolstoy he never gave up smoking – or living for that matter.

Chekhov wrote, à propos, a very funny playlet called 'On the Harm Done by Tobacco'. It is in the form of a lecture, given by one of those Chekhovian characters, ill with life, loafers, neurotics all. The lecturer, Ivan Niujin, has given many lectures before. One was on the harm done by insects – especially bedbugs. The lecturer is a smoker but his lecture against tobacco is a command performance – – commanded by his wife. The prime example he gives on how harmful

264

tobacco can be is to imprison a fly in a tobacco jar: it will die instantly! As a clue he tells his audience that tobacco is actually a plant. He then confesses many intimate secrets. His wife is a music teacher and it is she who has money. The lecturer hasn't got a kopek and he must do all the domestic chores at home. The lecture strays into music, ballet lessons and the site of the school, on 13 Piatisobachi.

The lecturer considers this address particularly unlucky. 'Above all,' he confesses, 'that number 13.' He let it be known that he is such a poor drinker that he gets stinkingly drunk on just one glass. In a paroxysm of sincerity, a moral strip without any tease, he finally takes off his cutaway coat 'in which I married thirty years ago'. Suddenly he looks at his watch and exclaims, 'The time allotted to this lecture is over.' But trying to leave the stage he glances at the wings and sees his wife. Quickly he collects himself and his papers: 'Once admitted that tobacco contains this terrible poison I've been telling you about,' he postscripts, 'I absolutely won't advise you to smoke.' And as a coda: 'I hope that this lecture of mine, titled "On the Harm Done by Tobacco", will be beneficial to you all.' *Dixi et animam levavi.*

TOLSTOYS IN THE ATTIC

I still keep some Tolstoy to play with. In Tolstoy's *Tales of Sevastopol*, published in 1946 by the Foreign Languages Publishing House (with no visible translator's name anywhere: probably the wretched soul was shot by Stalin – no name on the bullet and mum is the word) there is one Batrischev that undergoes a Black Sea change.

'Is it not so long ago,' muses one character, 'that this same Batrischev caroused with us, wore a dark cotton shirt for weeks on end', and that *before* deodorants were in use, 'and gorged himself with those eternal chops and dumplings without inviting anyone to share them?' Ah, *that* Batrischev! 'And now! A Holland shirt peeps out of his wide-sleeved cloth jacket, a 10–ruble cigar between his fingers and a 6–ruble bottle of Lafitte on the table –' I don't know a thing about Laffite, except to bet 100 dollars against a dead cigar that the bottle was not full of *eau du cologne*. But I approve wholeheartedly of Batrischev spending ten rubles on a cigar.

CRANE CAME

In the eastern sky there was a yellow patch like a rug laid for the feet of the coming sun; and against it, black and pattern-like, loomed the gigantic figure of the colonel on a gigantic horse. The regiment stood at rest for what seemed a long time. The youth grew impatient . . . He turned toward the colonel and saw him lift his gigantic arm and calmly stroke his moustache . . . As the horseman wheeled his animal and galloped away he turned to shout over his shoulder, 'Don't forget that box of cigars!' The colonel mumbled a reply. The youth wondered what a box of cigars had to do with war.

That's of course what the youth must find out for the next two hundred and fifty pages of *The Red Badge of Courage*. In peace as in war a cigar can help you tell the boys from the men. The colonel was right. A cigar is a soldier's best friend. Stephen Crane knew of men and smoke. Don't shoot until you see the band on their cigars.

ALLAIS SI

Alphonse Allais (1854–1905) was born in Honfleur, where his father had a chemist shop dispensing pills for the great and near great: amongst his clients were Courbet, Manet, Dr Flaubert (Gustave's brother) and even Charles Baudelaire, *malade imaginaire*. Baudelaire was to haunt Allais all his life and he died in the rue Amsterdam in Paris – not far from the house in which Baudelaire also died. Allais had only two loves in his entire life: chemistry and literature. He was a lousy chemist who burnt holes in his trousers and an amateur inventor who invented only acid rain or what already had a patent or was perfectly useless, like his electric fan with no blades that needed no power. But he became a professional humorist praised by almost everybody who was somebody in France then, from Alfred Jarry (who proposed this poor pun as a toast *fun-èbre*: '*Allais celui qui ira*') to André Breton, who proclaimed him a surrealist *avant la lettre* – and even *avant le mot*. Breton claimed that Allais was the originator of black humour in French, *l'humour noir*. But Allais, *allez-y*, was only a *bon vivant* and *bon buveur* just like Jarry – and like him a pipe smoker, as this short story proves:

THE FORGOTTEN PIPE
(A DIGEST)

In a London street (I'll give you its name in a minute, upon request) there were two telegraph offices, one for the cable London-Paris (via Douvres and Calais), the other for the cable London-Brussels (via Ostende). These two *offices* [italics by the author] were sited one in front of the other and their employees were on the best of terms. They visited each other frequently, exchanged witticisms and puns and argued about the *esthetism* or the *professionalism* of their job, according to daily events or their whim. Once an employee at the Belgian bureau forgot his pipe on the desk of his colleague across the street.

Politely he begged a young clerk to bring back his smoking utensil. The clerk, an opinionated young man, refused. He argued that he was there only to serve his office and not to retrieve forgotten pipes. (For the *resaerch* [sic] *of the forgotten pipes.*)

Coldly, the employee did not insist. He went over to his contact lever to ask Douvres, in Morse Code, to get in touch *telegraphiquement* with Calais. When this was done he begged Calais to put him in contact with Paris and then for Paris to communicate with Brussels and later Brussels to communicate with Ostende, and for Ostende to communicate with London.

It was his colleague with whom he had just had a chat who was at the telegraphic end.

'I forgot my pipe on your desk. Could you please return it to me with one of your *boys*. The only available clerk here refuses to do so.'

Thirty seconds later and the pipe, requested all over Europe, was returned to its owner.

DÉBRIS-À-BRAC

After Alphonse Allais

At the Cirque d'Hiver there was a troupe of Dutch aerialists whose superb act followed the Human Cannonball's splendidly: a roaring and smoky performance. The aerialists were called The Flying De Vries and they used to wait next to the cannon to make their entrance right after the Human Cannonball hit his distant target. But the best of the aerialists was an avid cigar-smoker and while he waited for their act to start, he used to smoke his butt not far from the cannon. One night he flicked his cigar to free it from the long ash-tip, but both ashes and the cigar's live tip fell into the open powder keg sitting by the cannon. Suddenly there was a huge explosion and all the de Vries flew every which way and loose – and high – higher than ever in fact. The delighted audience thought the Dutch flight was part of the act and perhaps even a new feat. All applauded heartily. Since then the troupe of scattered aerialists have been known in the Cirque as The Flying Débris Act.

Anon.

CATERING TO WHIFFS

The first dope smoker in children's books was the Caterpillar in *Alice in Wonderland*. This is a worm's view as Alice saw it: 'She stretched herself up on tiptoe, and peeped over the edge of the mushroom, and her eyes immediately met those of a large caterpillar that was sitting on the top, with its arms folded, quietly smoking a long hookah, and taking not the smallest notice of her or of anything else.'

According to my sources (and those of Lewis Carroll too: *The Encyclopaedia Britannica*), 'the actual smoking of an opium pipe takes about a minute' – just the time Alice spent on watching the caterpillar before making her mind up to address him. The caterpillar of the mushroom community was an opinionated opiumite if ever there was one. There are two: Alice is reeking with opinions too, some of them pretty strong. But Alice will cater to the caterpillar's smallest whims on top of the pillar. (It was in fact a vegetable column, a hallucinogenic, whew!, mushroom.) 'The caterpillar and Alice,' says Carroll, 'looked at each other for some time in silence: at last,' more than a minute, I believe, 'the caterpillar took the hookah out of its mouth, and addressed her in a languid, sleepy voice.' *Papaver somniferum* was working: 'The effects produced are immediate since the lungs present a large surface for absorption' – E.B. In other words, the vermin was barmy.

Walt Disney, a popular prude, understood perfectly well what a dose of drowse can do and his caterpillar is drawn to perfection (and perdition) when it smokes in rings that become letters and words and phrases and a soulful sentence or two before disappearing for good – or bad. Everybody could see the creature was a goner: 'Out of the mushroom,' said Christmas Carroll, 'and in another moment it was out of sight.' Outa site!

PASTEL

The light of our cigarettes
Went and came in the gloom:
It was dark in the little room.

Dark, and then, in the dark
Sudden a flash, a glow,
And a hand and a ring I know.

And then through the dark, a flush
Ruddy and vague, the grace –
A rose – of her lyric face.

Arthur Symons
Silhouettes (1892)

HOLMES SWEET HOLMES, SAID WATSON

The two most famous smokers in English literature are pipe men. They are both men of genius and intemperate of character. One is, elementary, Sherlock Holmes. As any good pipe-smoker, Holmes smoked several different pipes but never a *meerschaum* as shown in the illustrations from the *Strand* magazine and in the movies. Watson writes of the 'old black pipe' or the 'old and oily' one and once he shows Holmes smoking a briar, more fitting in a fable by La Bruyère. Holmes shares a filthy habit with many smokers, including my great-grandfather. In the morning he cooks for himself a heady mixture made of 'all the plugs and dottles left from smokes of the day before, all carefully dried and collected on the corner of the mantelpiece'. Holmes smokes it all *before* breakfast.

Sherlock and not by sheer luck (he is not a pipe reader) can tell the past of a man from his pipe: 'Nothing has more individuality, save perhaps watches and bootlaces.' I must confess that I have seen people take a watch to their ear, but I have never seen anybody put their bootlaces in their mouths – not even with their booted foot.

The other great English pipe-smoker was Uncle Toby. Says J. B. Priestley, himself a pipe-smoker, talking of *Tristram Shandy*: '. . . the pipe of Uncle Toby – a pipe that has not been allowed to go out for a century and a half!' I can only add: for *two* centuries already.

'I have my eye on a suite in Baker Street,' he said, 'which would suit us down to the ground. You don't mind the smell of strong tobacco, I hope?' (A. Conan Doyle, 'A Study in Scarlet?)

Holmes said to Watson in 'The Crooked Man', 'Hum! You still smoke the Arcadia mixture of your bachelor days, then!'

> 'They are the footprints of a giant hound!'
> 'I know.'
> 'Holmes, something's aloof!'
> 'Don't worry, Watson. It's me.'

That's exactly the matter with pipe smokers, that they are all aloof. It is the Holmes syndrome: you are as big as your pipe. Holmes smoked a calabash, the baritone saxophone of pipes. Pipes can be telling.

'Come along, doctor,' he said; 'we shall go and look him up. I'll tell you one thing which may help you in the case,' he continued, turning to the two detectives. 'There has been murder done, and the murderer was a man. He was more than six feet high, was in the prime of life, had small feet for his height, wore coarse, square-toed boots and smoked a Trichinopoly cigar . . .'
Lestrade and Gregson glanced at each other with an incredulous smile.

Surely they had never heard of the Trichinopoly, Lestrade and Gregson? It was a cigar made from dark tobacco grown near Trichinopoly in the Madras district of India. The Trichinopoly was usually a pierced cigar, open at both ends and was often sold with a straw inserted through the opening to keep it clear until smoking – all this information according to William S. Baring-Gould. On that occasion, 'A Study in Scarlet', Dr Watson said, 'I always smoke "ship's" myself.' 'Ship's' is a 'naval tobacco', also called 'naval choice' or just 'naval'. Players continue the 'ship's' tradition with their widely advertised 'navy cut'. In *After Many A Summer* the black chauffeur stuns the visiting English scholar he had just welcomed at the Los Angeles airport by pointing at some Okies and saying that they are transients 'who come to pick our navels'. But that's another story, as the driver was talking of navel oranges, also called navels. The navel orange, by the way, gave birth to the notion that the 'fruit of the tree of knowledge' was not an apple but an orange. But that too is another story.

THE STOLEN CIGAR CASE

I arose and embraced him warmly, yet he was already so engrossed in thought that at the same moment he mechanically placed his hand upon his watch as if to consult the time. 'Sit down,' he said. 'Have a cigar?'
'I had given up smoking,' I said.

'Why?' he asked.

I hesitated and perhaps I coloured. I had really given it up because, with my diminished practice, it was too expensive. I could afford only a pipe. 'I prefer a pipe,' I said laughingly. 'But tell me of this robbery. What have you lost?'

That much we guessed from the title. The two gentlemen we know already. They are of course Holmes and Watson. But this particular story was not written by Sir Arthur Conan Doyle but by an American upstart called Bret Harte. This is in fact a parody. I call your attention to it because Sherlock Holmes was never a great cigar-smoker. The pipe was his thing. As parodies go this is not even a good one but Bret Harte was a friend of Mark Twain's and he knew that after a horse a cigar is a man's best friend. He also knew that a stolen cigar case could be of more value to its owner than a necklace. After all pearls can be false, diamonds made of cut glass and tiaras just flashy paste – but a cigar, a cigar is a burning passion!

THIS OLD MAN WAS RIGHT

Jack London's short story 'To Build a Fire' teaches you not only how to build a fire but the convenience of carrying it with you if you are in the Arctic regions. In this grim, gripping tale of life and death in the Yukon a young prospector, whose main 'trouble was that he was without imagination', is indeed in dire straits. He was a stubborn man, like most men without imagination. Brave too. Like most people partial to the weed then but with no imagination. The young man was a chewer of tobacco. This young man of a morning left camp unescorted. Abroad it was more (or rather less) than fifty-five below zero Fahrenheit. He 'was chewing tobacco' when he decamped alone – or rather followed by his husky, who was trotting at his heels. This is how this tobacco-chewer looked like when last seen: 'The muzzle of ice held his lips so rigidly that he was unable to clear his chin when he expelled the juice. The result was a crystal beard of the color and solidity of amber.' Hell below zero no less. London, who knew this people well, remarks: 'It was the penalty all tobacco-chewers paid in this country.' He paid a stiffer penalty than the hideous sight he offered next day when they discovered his corpse, a frozen carcass. The young man died stubbornly trying to build a fire to warm himself before the livid winter sun went down. Had he been a smoker he would have carried all along that promising fire he futilely tried to build. The last dream this foolhardly chewer had was 'a vision of the old-timer'. (This was the name he gave the seasoned prospector who warned him about the killing cold in the Arctic.) In this dream 'he could see him quite clearly, warm and comfortable and smoking a pipe.' There's a ritual refrain running along the short story. It says 'The old man was right'.

THE MAN WHO WOULD BE SMOKE

Chesterton, who was a smoker and a gentleman, asks in *The Man Who Was Thursday*, precisely, politely:

> 'May I smoke?'
> 'Certainly!', said Gregory, producing a cigar-case. 'Try one of mine.'
> Syme took the cigar, clipped the end off with a cigar-cutter out of his waistcoat pocket, put it in his mouth, lit it slowly, and let out a long cloud of smoke. It is not little to his credit that he performed these rites with so much composure . . .

(It is all indeed to the cigar's credit: a magic flute.)

> . . . for almost before he had begun the table at which he sat had begun to revolve, first slowly, and then rapidly, as if at an insane seance.

(Gregarious Gregory's gracious gravity?)

> 'You must not mind it,' said Gregory, 'it's a kind of screw.'

(It is not 'a kind of screw', of course, but the effect of the panatella or corona or whatever.)

> The next moment the smoke of his cigar, which had been wavering across the room in snaky twists, went straight up as if from a factory chimney, and the two, with their chairs and table, shot down through the floor as if the earth had swallowed them. They went rattling down a kind of roaring chimney . . . Syme was still smoking, with one leg thrown over the other, and had not turned a yellow hair.

(What a smoke! What a smoker! What a single cigar can do to you! But wait. Please note the De Xeres Effect. There's more in store in the cigar.)

They passed through several such passages, and came out at last into a queer steel chamber, with curved walls, almost spherical in shape . . .

They were no doubt inside a hollow cigar – or rather in the heart of the *vitola*.

> . . . round the walls of it were hung more dubious and dreadful shapes, things that looked like the bulbs of iron plants or the eggs of iron birds. They were bombs, and the very room itself seemed like the inside of a bomb.

(Why, that's an exploding cigar, no doubt! No wonder that Syme, cautiously 'knocked his cigar ash off against the wall' before entering. This is the smoker's dream turned nightmare. Or was it all the effect of the cigar Syme, 'the poet who had become a detective', was smoking? For he usually smoked 'a long, lean, black, cigar, bought in Soho for twopence'. Twopence? My God, that's worse than Riley's raillery! Two pence! No wonder Syme 'paced the Thames Embankment, bitterly biting' his cigar! 'and brooding on the advance of Anarchy. There was no anarchist with a bomb in his pocket so savage or so solitary as he.' That's what cheap cigars foment: mere anarchy loosed upon the world. The Second Coming is a five-cent cigar slouching towards a cigar-store in Bethlehem.)

A CLERIHEW BY BENTLEY

Edmund Clerihew Bentley, who didn't manufacture the car that bears his name but gave his middle name to the clerihew, once concocted this sample:

> 'Dear me!', exclaimed Homer,
> 'What a delicious aroma!
> It smells as if a town
> Was being burnt down.'

But with your Havana you're burning a whole city. In slang a burn is tobacco or cigarette but never a cigar. To burn is human, to combust, divine!

MY FIRST CIGAR

It was not in my chambers, but three hundred miles further north that I learned to smoke. I think I may say with confidence that a first cigar was never smoked in such circumstances before.

At that time I was a schoolboy, living with my brother who was a man. People mistook our relations, and thought I was his son. They would ask me how my father was, and when he heard of this he scowled at me. Even to this day I look so young that people who remember me as a boy, now think I must be that boy's younger brother. I shall tell presently of a strange mistake of this kind, but at present I am thinking of the evening when my brother's eldest daughter was born – perhaps the most trying evening he and I ever passed together. So far as I knew the affair was very sudden, and I felt sorry for my brother as well as for myself . . .

He was laughing and joking in what seemed to me a flippant kind of way, considering the circumstances. When his hand touched the door I snatched at my book and read as hard as I could. He was swaggering a little as he entered, but the swagger went out of him as soon as his eye fell on me. I fancy he had come down to tell me, and now he did not know how to begin. He walked up and down the room restlessly, looking at me as he walked the one way while I looked at him as he walked the other way. At length he sat down again and took up his book. He did not try to smoke. The silence was something terrible; nothing was to be heard but an occasional cinder falling from the grate. This lasted I should say for twenty minutes, and then he closed his book and flung it on the table. I saw that the game was up, and closed *Anne Judge, Spinster*. Then he said, with affected jocularity, 'Well, young man, do you know that you are an uncle?' There was silence again, for I was still trying to think out some appropriate remark. After a time I said, in a weak voice, 'Boy or girl?' 'Girl,' he answered. Then I thought hard again, and all at once remembered something. 'Both, doing well?' I whispered. 'Yes,' he said, sternly. I felt that something great was expected of me, but I could not jump up and wring his hand. I was an uncle. I stretched out my arm toward the cigar-box, and firmly lit my first cigar.

J. M. Barrie
My Lady Nicotine

THE BETROTHED

'You must choose between me and your cigar.'

Open the old cigar-box, get me a Cuba stout,
For things are running crossways, and Maggie and
I are out.

We quarrelled about Havanas – we fought o'er a
good cheroot,
And I know she is exacting, and she says I am a
brute.

Open the old cigar-box – let me consider a space;
In the soft blue veil of the vapour musing on
Maggie's face.

Maggie is pretty to look at – Maggie's a loving lass,
But the prettiest cheeks must wrinkle, the truest of
loves must pass.

There's peace in a Laranaga, there's calm in a
Henry Clay,
But the best cigar in an hour is finished and
thrown away –

Thrown away for another as perfect and ripe and
brown –
But I could not throw away Maggie for fear o' the
talk o' the town!

Maggie, my wife at fifty – grey and dour and old –
With never another Maggie to purchase for love or
gold!

And the light of Days that have Been the dark of
the Days that Are,
And Love's torch stinking and stale, like the butt
of a dead cigar –

The butt of a dead cigar you are bound to keep in
your pocket –
With never a new one to light tho' it's charred and
black to the socket.

Open the old cigar-box – let me consider a while –
Here is a mild Manilla – there is a wifely smile.

Which is the better portion – bondage bought
    with a ring,
Or a harem of dusky beauties fifty tied in a string?

Counsellors cunning and silent – comforters true
    and tried,
And never a one of the fifty to sneer at a rival
    bride.

Thought in the early morning, solace in time of
    woes,
Peace in the hush of the twilight, balm ere my
    eyelids close,

This will the fifty give me, asking nought in
    return,
With only a *Suttee*'s passion – to do their duty and
    burn.

This will the fifty give me. When they are spent
    and dead,
Five times other fifties shall be my servants
    instead.

The furrows of far-off Java, the isles of the Spanish
    Main,
When they hear that my harem is empty will send
    me my brides again.

I will take no heed to their raiment, nor food for
    their mouths withal,
So long as the gulls are nesting, so long as the
    showers fall.

I will scent 'em with best Vanilla, with tea will I
    temper their hides,
And the Moor and the Mormon shall envy who
    read of the tale of my brides.

For Maggie has written a letter to give me my
    choice between

The wee little whimpering Love and the great god
    Nick o' Teen.

And I have been servant of Love for barely a
    twelve-month clear,
But I have been Priest of Partagas a matter of seven
    year;

And the gloom of my bachelor days is flecked with
    the cheery light
Of stumps that I burned to Friendship and
    Pleasure and Work and Fight.

And I turn my eyes to the future that Maggie and I
    must prove,
But the only light on the marshes is the Will-o'-
    the-Wisp of Love.

Will it see me safe through my journey or leave me
    bogged in the mire?
Since a puff of tobacco can cloud it, shall I follow
    the fitful fire?

Open the old cigar-box – let me consider anew –
Old friends, and who is Maggie that I should
    abandon *you*?

A million surplus Maggies are willing to bear the
    yoke;
And a woman is only a woman, but a good cigar is
    a Smoke.

Light me another Cuba – I hold to my first-sworn
    vows,
If Maggie will have no rival, I'll have no Maggie
    for Spouse!

Rudyard Kipling
Departmental Ditties (1890)

THE SMALL RED GLOW

And later on, many times, in distant parts of the world, Marlow showed himself willing to remember Jim, to remember him at length, in detail and audibly.

Perhaps it would be after dinner, on a verandah draped in motionless foliage and crowned with flowers, in the deep dusk speckled by fiery cigar-ends. The elongated bulk of each cane-chair harboured a silent listener. Now and then a small red glow would move abruptly, and expanding light up the fingers of a languid hand, part of a face in profound repose, or flash a crimson gleam into a pair of pensive eyes overshadowed by a fragment of an unruffled forehead: and with the very first word uttered Marlow's body, extended at rest in the seat, would become very still, as though his spirit had winged its way back into the lapse of time and were speaking through his lips from the past.

Joseph Conrad
Lord Jim (1900)

THE WAY OF ALL HEMINGWAYS

Hemingway starts the day with a smoke in *The Sun Also Rises.*

'In the morning I walked down the Boulevard to the Rue Soufflot for coffee and brioche.' There 'I read the papers with the coffee and then smoked a cigarette.' He goes to work as Jake Barnes: 'Upstairs in the office I read the French morning papers smoked and then', and only then, 'sat at the typewriter', for 'in the newspaper business . . . is such an important part of the ethics that you should never seem to be working.' Later, at night, he meets his lover and his lover's lover, a Greek count. The Count was looking at Brett across the table under the gaslight. She was smoking a cigarette and flicking ashes on the rug. Lady Brett, a true lady, saw her former lover taking notice of it. He was a tidy man, also impotent. "Can't you give a chap an ashtray?" She said to him.' Meanwhile, the Count 'took out a heavy pigskin cigar-case and offered it to me. "Like to try a real American cigar?"' What could *that* be? Not a good five-cent cigar I hope. 'Thanks,' I said 'I'll finish the cigarette.' Then the Count proceeds to 'cut off the end of his cigar with a gold cutter he wore on one end of his watch-chain.' Cigar-cutters used to be very good to tell the time at the time. 'I like a cigar to really draw,' said the Count. Me too.

As a matter of fact, my youngest cigar draws beautifully. His name is Count Lautrec. 'Half the cigars you smoke don't draw.' The other half are better chess players and prefer to lose. That was Lautrec again. 'I'm not joking you.' The Count blew a cloud of smoke . . . '"I'd tell you,' said the Count. "I'm not joking you, I never joke people. Joke people and you make enemies."' Is he telling *me*? 'The Count was beaming. He was very happy . . . He was smoking his cigar again.' The rest of the book is all bulls and horns: in the bullring, in the streets, even in bed. One of the bulls is called Dilemma. Poor old Jake does not know where to grab him but Brett does: by the balls.

In his last book, which is probably his second best bet on Posterity, *A Moveable Feast*, he, E.H., never mentions smoking, not even steam coming out of a mouth in the European winter he said he loved so much that he lived the rest of his life in the tropics. Here's Hem (he was not yet Papa but just Ernest to his friends and Tatie to his first wife) on Gertrude Stein, one of the writer's magnified obsessions: 'She got to look like a Roman emperor, and that was fine if you liked women to look like Roman emperors.' He also says of her household, writing from Finca Vigia, in Havana, Cuba that 'it was sad to see new worthless pictures hung in with great pictures' in Miss Stein's big studio. As a matter of fact he had in La Vigia, in the dining room 'The Farm' probably Miro's finest masterpiece, hung with the trite and the trivia of painting – plus many stuffed heads of kudu and gazelles and water buffalos. It was indeed sad.

In passing, in *A Moveable Feast*, Hemingway says of Gertrude Stein, that her head was covered with 'immigrant hair'. I couldn't help seeing Miss Stein's frizzy hair-do stand on her 'Roman Emperor head' to become a Moveable Fleet and sail from one side of her head to the next, from forehead to the Roman temples, always on the move, immigrant hair, endlessly trying to evade Immigration. It's hairy scary! Some writing can do that to you, you know.

THE PRISONER OF ZELDA

Scott Fitzgerald, a drunk writer for dumb waiters, never knew enough of cigars to write about them. Not even when he wrote about the very rich who were, so different from you and me, meaning Hemingway and him. Hem, so shallow, said that he had said, yes, they have more money, when that was not the point at all. The truth came from Yeats, Irish like Fitzgerald but older therefore wised up: 'the rich/Are driven by wealth as beggars by itch . . . /And cannot have a humorous speech.'

In *The Last Tycoon* the characters sit mostly morosely: 'Even when he lit a cigarette on Stahr's invitation, one felt that the match was held to it by exterior forces he disdained to control.' In a conference office with Hollywood producers spreading wall to wall all he has to say about Havanas, or whatever, is that 'there was smoke in the room'. The Marx Brothers trying to smoke Monroe Stahr out of his office

Gatsby on the other hand is the novel where law and order become lawn and ordure. When Fitzgerald speaks of smoke is to announce the reader, like a well-trained butler, that 'there were no cigarettes' – sir. The narrator goes 'out to buy some at the drugstore on the corner'. When he comes back everybody had disappeared. That's a neat vanishing act if I ever saw one. There are, as usual with Fitzgerald, roomfuls of smoke but no smoking or smokers to speak of. Only a 'little dog was sitting on the table looking with blind eyes through the smoke' – that could come from roasting chestnuts for all I know. The lapdog is like so many Hollywood producers in *The Last Tycoon*: they wag their tales at Big Boss, who's looking at your movie as if he were watching you. Or bark at the family tree: it is the rise of the son-in-law. Then the narrator posts a sign saying succinctly 'Gatsby's career as Trimalchio is over'. Was the dog barking at the wrong Trimalchio then? But all is not over yet, really. As a matter of fact it never started. Thus trite Trimalchio's guests were only boors and bores. That's why five pages before the end a minor character, who commits the sin of pronouncing Oxford Oggsford with ogg all over his face, offers the U-person a cigar. However the narrowtar never lights it up. Probably he considers himself somebody from the upper riches.

BEING BORES TOGETHER

According to Kay Boyle, in *Being Geniuses Together*, Gertrude Stein, who had an obnoxious brother too, met Raymond Duncan in the palace of the Dayang Muda of Sarawak. Raymond, Isadora Duncan's brother, was there on a visit. Gertrude was being a genius alone when suddenly Raymond came along. 'As for Gertrude Stein', says Boyle, 'she was a transformed woman.' A Lady Macbeth in waiting. Instantly she began needling Duncan, who was now some sort of Greek à la mode, wearing sandals and a robe all over Paris. 'You were such a fop, such a dandy, Raymond! Gertrude Stein chortled,' said Kay Boyle. 'Then she almost choked with laughter.' I don't now see the source of the mirth, but soon enough Miss Stein was into revelations: Raymond Duncan, 'before he was Greek, used to wear carnations in his buttonhole and smoke long cigars.' There you are! 'You have an excellent memory, Gertrude,' said Raymond, 'probably due to the fact that you keep repeating things over and over.' Here Alice B. Toklas intervened, like the Dark Rabbit emerging from a hole, and looked at her watch. Time to say goodnight, Gertie. Good night Gertie!

Raymond Duncan was one of the few Americans who gave Gertrude Stein her comeuppance in her lifetime. Hemingway did something of the sort but in *The Moveable Feast*, twenty years after Miss Stein was buried in Père Lachaise, an unmoveable feat. Then the subject was not Greeks smoking cigars but Jews being lesbians together.

The next entry is called 'Joyce and cigars' and is told by Robert McAlmon in his own *Being Geniuses Together*. Half of the book suffers from Kay Boyle but this is the part where McAlmon is a young man and Joyce is a piss artist: 'Joyce and I lingered until five in the morning, when the *patron* told us to get out. Out we got, and ensconced ourselves in a small bistro on the Boulevard St Germain. We bought cigars, and we drank. As we had decided to drink through the list of French drinks, Joyce began dropping his cigars.' This sounds as if your regular Irishman dropped his Gs, but earlier in the evening McAlmon places Joyce in an Irish situation. Djuna Barnes and Mina Loy (not *Mirna* Loy the actress, *Mina* Loy the literary groupie) were adoring Joyce together. 'Joyce then enjoyed a thoroughly Irish period of despair . . . The women tried to comfort him, but he preferred to drink.' Very Irish this. Djuna and Mina went away in a Huff. That year Huffs didn't have a hardtop and were very convertible.

Now McAlmon, co-author, does a good turn, some kind of McAlmony: 'At first I leaned to pick them up and return them to him.' (Obviously, it was Joyce who bought the cigars!) 'When I could no longer lean without falling on my face I took to lighting the cigars and handing them to him. He almost immediately dropped them, and I lighted cigar after cigar until they were all gone, and then we took to cigarettes.' (Pallid placebo.) 'At ten in the morning we sat alone in the small bistro, the floor covered with some twenty cigars, innumerable cigarettes' (*pauvres* placebos) 'and the table with the forty glasses . . .' The end came, of course, with Joyce (Dewlysses to her) returning to Nora (Penny to him) with the help of McAlmon. But he didn't want to leave the Joyces with his unmoveable feet. Then a discreet screen Irish in on them.

ORTIZ OR LEZAMA

Ortiz once said: 'Tobacco is a quest for art,' and Lezama Lima, a baroque poet in the twentieth century, seems to agree in reverse: his art is looking for a good cigar. He begins with cigar boxes: 'The allegories on the cigar boxes had the imagination of the Maria Cristina period: a grand Homeric wheel was leaning on a throne, where the King merely hinted that he was about to stand up to draw the curtains. The crown wobbled.' This is from his monumental book *Paradiso*, the only novel written by the poet. Here is some legerdemain with a cigar as a magic wand: 'The sentry in his box, when he lit a new cigar, seemed to be in touch with the fish out of the water, establishing a momentary voltaic arc . . . On the coils of the arc built between the cigar of the sentry and the fragmented tail of fish, the masks of the ectoplasmic bodies showed strange depressions, scars, swollen bumps: an immense skin without eyes but with as many tits as stars there are in heaven.'

Lezama the poet transformed into the novelist Lezama is talking of course (of course!) of the sea and cigars. He even speaks of the sentry 'measureless *vitola*'. Later he writes of 'two cigar-boxes with engravings allusive to the smoker's delights.' He dares describe extensively the contents of its *cromo*: 'One of the engravings showed on its upper section a staff and a legend: *The Farm*. On the lower section of the engraving there was another inscription. It said: *Superior leaf from Vuelta Abajo*. Underneath there was an address: *Amargura Street No. 6, Havana*'. *Paradiso* is a hell of a book – full of smoke and sounds. Before a character (a heavy cigar smoker) dies after leaving in a taxi with a guitar-playing friend, the latter sings to him this dolorous ditty:

> Playing cards on the sand
> Still in the entire night
> Eternity – and a smoke.

IF I HAD A HAMMETT

Dashiell Hammett was a misogynist and a cigar hater, perhaps in that order. In one of his first short stories performing the Continental Op (with not much Continental zest, I must say,) titled 'The Farewell Murder', 'Kavalov and Ringgo (sic) were smoking cigars, Mrs Ringgo and I cigarettes over a *creme de menthe*'. Later there is the smell of something burning, but it isn't Mrs Ringgo's cigarette or her liqueur. It is Kavalov 'who crunched his cigar between his teeth and looked pointedly at me.' Cigars, for the non-smoker, can smell like arson. Or like arsenic. But it's not only the man's cigar. 'When Kavalov sat down I saw the shape of an automatic pistol in his hip pocket.' That man is lethal! As a matter of fact, in the murder in the title he provides the corpse – his own.

In one of Hammett's best short stories told by the nameless narrator there are more murders and more killer cigars. The Op cop has been invited into a modest house in San Francisco by a charming, lovable old lady. Inside the sleuth snooping shamelessly meets her elderly husband, a man with a cup of kindness in every wrinkle of his face. The old lady offers First Person a cup of tea yet.

> I had to drink a cup of tea with them and eat some little spiced cookies before I could get them to listen to a question. Then Mrs Quarre made little sympathetic clicking sounds with her tongue and teeth, while I told them about the elderly lady who had fallen off a street car. The old man rumbled in his beard that it was 'a damn shame' and gave me a fat cigar . . . Darkness settled. The old man turned on a light in a tall lamp that threw a soft yellow circle upon us and left the rest of the room dim . . . I didn't expect to get any good information here: but I was comfortable and the cigar was a good one. Time enough to go out into the drizzle when I had finished my smoke. Something cold touched the nape of my neck.
> 'Stand up!'
> I didn't stand up: I couldn't. I was paralyzed.

That's what a bad cigar can do to you. But according to Hammett you suffer the same sinister symptoms from a good cigar too. 'Mrs Quarre still sat primly upright against the cushions her husband had adjusted to her back; her eyes still twinkled with friendliness behind her glasses. The old man still stroked his white beard, and let cigar smoke drift unhurriedly from his nostrils.'

A cigar smoker who inhales? Fishy. But wait. The best smoke is yet to come: 'From somewhere among his whiskers, his coat and his stiff vest the old man brought out a big black' – another cigar? – 'revolver, which he handled with no signs of unfamiliarity . . . Mrs Quarre smiled up at me. "Do sit down, Mr Tracy," she said. I sat.' But the joke is on the Oppity cop. He had given the name of the great Dick Tracy as an *alias inter pares* and now the old lady shows him she reads the comic strip too. What about Mr Quarre: 'The old man carefully laid his cigar, came to me and ran his hand over my body.' Then the old couple is gone, out of the house but not of the story. They come back later with a gun and a cigar like a recurrent nightmare: 'Through the other door . . . popped Mrs Quarre, an enormous cocked revolver in her thin hand.' Her husband was not far behind. Cigar in hand? Surprise, surprise! He is packing another gun, twin to his wife's. But he to 'all appearances was still the same mild old man who had given me an excellent cigar.'

Hammett hated cigars not only in his short stories. Since the masterpiece of larceny and old lace he proved that the detective story is actually some sort of play. 'The House in Turk Street' is composed of only two rooms and lots of lethal conversation – plus guns and cigars.

Hammett hated cigars not only in his sort stories. Since the very beginning of his first novel, *Red Harvest*, his Continental Op sees cigar smoking as the sign of a dereliction of duty. On his arrival at Personville (code name Poisonville) 'in the centre of the city's main intersection . . .' a third wayward policeman, 'with a cigar in a corner of his mouth' – was directing traffic!

Not only cops do it. Corrupted politicians smoke cigars. Cheap crooks too do it. Even stoolies do it – and all fall down in smoke. That embodiment of evil in *The Maltese Falcon*, Casper Gutman, is fat and flabby and flatulent. To top it all he is a cigar-smoker. But he is also a disappointment. He has, central on a centre table, beside 'a bottle of Johnnie Walker whisky on a tray, a box of cigars'. So far so Gutman. But the box, mind you, is of Coronas del Ritz. (A fake name for fake Havanas if ever I heard one!) Spade is not so hot either. As a cigar-smoker, that is. Here is what Hammett has to say about it. The Fat Man 'set his glass on the table and held the box of Coronas del Ritz to Spade. "A cigar, sir?"' Spade took a cigar, trimmed the end of it – and lighted it! Ready to be somebody, Spade allowed himself some fancy smoking: 'Spade blew smoke above the fat man's head in a long slanting plume.' Not only that: 'He frowned thoughtfully at the ash-tipped end of his cigar.'

I wouldn't be surprised if Spade, after blowing those baroque plumes above the fat man's head (good name for a pub that), to show off his smoker's mettle would have frowned at the moist end of his cigar and stuck in his mouth the lighted tip, ashes and all. A few lines later Spade points his cigar at his own chest and says, more cryptically than critically: 'That's me.' Next, says Hammett, 'Spade's face became pale and hard.' (We recognize the symptoms, don't we?) Then he turns and more in anger than in jest tosses his glass at the table. The Fat Man ('tolerantly', says Hammett: yes, it is the tolerance of cigar-smokers), said: 'Well sir, I must say you have a most violent temper.' It must be the cigar. Coronas del Ritz! My God, what they'll think of next, those counterfeiters? Panatellas del Savoy, perhaps?

MARLOWE AND SMOKE

After cigarette-smoking, cigar-hating Spade, Chandler's Marlowe is a mellow Camel-and-brier man. In *The Big Sleep*, Chandler's first novel, he manages to charm old General Sternwood, once upon a time hard as flint, by literally blowing smoke in his wooden, stern face. When Colonel Sternwood sees Marlowe hesitate between a cigarette and boredom he approves heartily, though he is closer to a cardiac arrest than Marlowe is to a citizen's arrestation. 'You may smoke, sir,' concedes Colonel Sternwood. 'I like the smell of tobacco.' I suppose he also loved the smell of tar and paper burning. Anyway Marlowe complies. 'I lit the cigarette and blew a lungful at him . . .' Did he kill the cold old man with a single blow of a Camel? Far from it: '. . . he sniffed at it like a terrier at a rathole.' Eventually smoke got in the eyes and nostrils of the invalid and a 'faint smile pulled at the shadowed corners of his mouth.' Which opened not to curse or dismiss the visitor, as it would have been the case today, but for Sternwood to praise Marlowe while despising himself: 'A nice state of affairs when a man has to indulge his vice by proxy.' That was the first cigarette Marlowe ever smoked in public. The private detective's last name seemed even to have been chosen because of his ancestor, the poet who smoked in bed and blew smoke in his by now strange bedfellow's face. It is apparently the beginning of the decadence of the hard-boiled school of cigarette smoking and some say that Marlowe was named in fact after Philip Morris, the cigarette brand.

The last cigarettes Marlowe smokes are all gathered in a pack in Chandler's near posthumous novel, *Playback*. At the very beginning Marlowe puts his best pussyfoot forward to climb aboard a train coach 'already full of the drifting cigarette smoke that is so kind to your throat and nearly leaves you with one good lung.' General Sternwood would have indeed envied him! But he would have been envying another man, the old hard-boiled Marlowe. The present Marlowe scornfully 'filled and lit a pipe and added to the general frowst.' Not, mind you, to smog, so Angeleno a word. In the intervening years Marlowe had become anglicized. General

294

Frowst sounds like a British military man about to become Marshall. Nobody, not even Marlowe, would dare blow smoke in his face.

The most beautiful cigarette-smoker in the hard-boiled *corpus* appears in *Playback* though. It is one Miss Vermilyea, who 'wore night-sheer stockings'. Marlowe, the hetero Phil, 'stared at them rather intently, especially when she crossed her legs and held out a cigarette to be lighted'. She added to the general lust. But Marlowe is no longer so nimble with cigarettes and a lighter: 'I shook a cigarette out of a packet and tried to push up the top of my Zippo', Zippo, mind you, not zipper, 'with my thumb and rotate the wheel. You should be able to do it one-handed.' Perhaps Harpo but not Zippo: 'It's an awkward process. I made it at last and got the cigarette going, yawned, and blew smoke out through my nose. "What do you do for an encore?", she asked.' She is just another gorgeous girl who can crack well but not too wisely. But let's see. Let's see. Marlowe is about to do what he always does for an anchor man.

'I crossed my legs and leaned back and lifted the green glass ashtray from the table beside the chair and balanced it on my knee and held the cigarette I was smoking between the first and second fingers of my right hand.'

He then announces: 'I wouldn't get any of the way across the room.' Indeed he wouldn't! 'I'd be sitting here like this, quite comfortable and relaxed.'

Marlowe is, as usual, a gay dissembler – old usage, naturally. And I don't mean dissembler, a cruel *mot*. Marlowe's other country is a territory full of smokers. A taxi driver 'stuck a pill in his kisser and lit it with a Ronson.' It is also a country of slang and brands in the morning.

No wonder that when Marlowe sits and lights a cigarette he has to feel: 'the always mechanical reaction that gets so boring when someone else does it.' Later, things get worse and even his clients won't smoke. They are the opposite of Colonel Sternwood though they might be even mightier: 'I lit a cigarette, first offering one to Mr Henry Clarendon IV. He refused with a vague nod.' It's either that – or worse. One Captain Alessandro 'made a smooth gesture with his hand and fished a cigarette out of a drawer. He stuck it in his big mouth but didn't light it.' Colonel Sternwood would have demoted Captain Alessandro to corporal on the double. When Big Brandon (another heavy) is ready for a smoke, Marlowe becomes sarcastic: 'He flicked a gold lighter at a gold-tipped cigarette. Big deal.' Or rather small deal. Small is also the talk we get throughout the novel, the saddest because the poorest of Chandler's books. *Playback* was Raymond Chandler's feedback. Unlike Christopher, Philip Marlowe died with his boots on.

'I kicked open the bottom drawer of her desk, let two inches of rye trickle down my craw, kissed Birdie square on her lush, red mouth and set fire to a cigarette.' That was S. J. Perelman giving Philip Marlowe his comeuppance or the desserts he deserved: 'I let a cigarette burn down between my fingers until it made a small red mark.' The real Mars-mellow? It looks like a bit of Philip Morris.

MY, MY, MENCKEN

H. L. Mencken had a grandfather and like most grand-fathers of great men he looked like a great-grandfather. But he was a great man himself. He, Mencken, our man Mencken, became aware of his great grandfather when he (his grand-father) was approaching sixty. He 'wore a Gladstonian collar and a stock-like cravat of archaic design'. Mencken's grand-father was more outstanding for what he grew than for what he wore. 'In his backyard . . . he carried on extensive horti-cultural experiments, virtually all of which . . . failed. What I chiefly remember of them is his recurrent reports that . . . some act of God had wrecked his effort to produce a strain of tobacco resistant to worms, high winds – and the irrational fluctuations of the market.' Just like the planters in Cuba at the time: just like old man Sosa and his father. With a good propellant I'll even be able to travel back to Pela and Panduca.

Mencken's grandfather was a born trader: he bought from German planters in Pennsylvania and 'sold their tobacco all over. For some of it he actually went to Key West, which was then assumed by most Americans to be foreign', that is Cuban, 'territory, using only Havana leaf in its celebrated cigars.' Celebrated in fact because all the cigar-rollers in Cayo Hueso were Cuban or of Cuban descent. Then Mencken relates some act of fraud very often committed with the Cuban leaf: 'In deference to the visitors who sometimes dropped in at the factories, the Pennsylvania leaf sent to them was repacked in empty Havana tobacco bales.'

('Heave a Havana! Pull that stunt! Lift that bale! From the Pinar vale!', to be sung by a *basso profondo* voice.)

'My grandfather, as a moral theologian, admitted that there was something irregular about the transaction, but he con-soled himself saying that Key West was full of swindlers escaped from Cuba . . .' Fidel Castro, today, would vouch to that. Chicanery is for Chicanos.

But men like Mencken, like Conrad, are worth their salt. Even if in the case of Mencken it's salt and pepper too. Here's listening to him talking of his father, his grandfather's own son: 'To my brother Charlie and me our father seemed to be a most tremendous traveller – indeed, almost a Marco Polo. His trips to buy tobacco ranged from . . . Connecticut in the North to Cuba in the South.' (Please notice the slight note of imperialism.) Father brought back souvenirs 'from his tobacco buying trips, so that the house was always well supplied. I recall especially some ornate fans from Havana, some jars of guava jelly from the same place' – and then a tall story or two: 'My father's traveller's tales were full of thrills . . . especially those that had to do with bullfighting in Cuba.' This must be taken with a lot of salt, of course. There were no bullfights in Cuba you could call *corridas*. Surely the old man, like a character in Sherwood Anderson, was a fibber for his sons. Either that or Mencken senior travelled down Mexico way – perhaps even to Venezuela or Colombia, looking for frills and thrills. However some note or other rings a bell with 'a black crêpe on the handle of the doorbell'. From Dublin, Ireland, from Joyce, from *Dubliners*: 'Old Cotter was sitting at the fire, smoking . . . He began to puff at his pipe, no doubt arranging his opinion in his mind. Tiresome old fool! When we knew him first he used to be rather interesting . . . but I soon grew tired of him and his endless stories . . .' All old men are fibbers at heart.

You have probably heard of or seen people who smoke while they eat, spoiling both the smoke and the eat. They do it mostly at lunch, don't ask me why. The first time I saw this perverted habit being performed in public was in New York, the summer of 1955, watching two dainty damsels (gloved hands, hatted heads, all in white) eating on a terrace, at a health restaurant, from big plates of fruit salad and solid yoghurt. I've seen this performance many times after in Paris and London (and now even in Madrid), but instead of health food it was English cookery or, later, *la nouvelle cuisine*, which one could call *la cuisine bête*. The crime, as in any *film noir*, was always committed by women. As one can see everywhere these days there are more women smokers of cigarettes than men smoking cigars – am I entitled to infer that cigarettes are the culprits? Both men and women always eat thus smoked food other than salmon.

Mme Genot, cook extraordinaire, did not welcome but a few gourmets to her restaurant in the rue de la Banque. She was particularly impatient with her American clients guilty of lighting up their cigarettes the moment they had had a delicious odorous soup. Coolly Mme Genot served them coffee. If the smoking client complained, Mme Genot glared to say 'I thought Monsieur had finished eating.'

Le Livre blanc du tabac

This is bad but what Mencken mentions is ridiculous! Captain Asmus Leonhardt was 'marine superintendent of the Munson Line', whatever that was. When Mencken 'finally made Havana and passed the Morro, a smart young mulatto in Captain Leonhardt's launch put out from shore, took me aboard his craft and whisked me through the customs. The captain himself was waiting in front of the Pasaje Hotel in the Prado, eating a plate of bean-soup and simultaneously smoking a Romeo y Julieta cigar.' My God! Either smoke gets in your soup or Romeo y Julieta are about to be drowned in a ceremony of innocence like Ophelia. The cigar must have a taste of olive oil. The captain spills his beans to Mencken about the Cuban little war between dyspeptic General Menocal, now the President, and General Gómez, a cigar-smoking soldier, formerly the President now a renegade. Without even stopping to enquire about his baggage, Mencken departs to interview President Menocal. Obviously Mencken was as full of beans as the Captain.

BLIXEN'S BLISS

Karen Blixen has a marvellous beginning for her master-piece *Out of Africa*: 'I had a farm in Africa, at the foot of the Ngong Hills.' No nostalgia and no self-pity for the woman who took the name of a man as a pen-name, Isaak Dinesen, whom the natives called Lioness Blixen. In this book she gives what could be an explanation to the mysterious pleasure of tobacco smoking. She talks of smoking's earliest ancestor: 'Charcoal-burning is a pleasant job. There is undoubtedly something intoxicating about it, and it is known that charcoal-burners see things in a different light from other people.' No doubt due to light always filtering through smoke, an effect not unlike a cigar weaving smoke shawls in the air. 'They are,' assures us Baroness Blixen, 'given to poetry and tara-diddle.' The poetry, I believe, belongs to a master, Isaak Dinesen. The taradiddle, I'm afraid, to your humble servant. She claims that 'Charcoal is a beautiful thing to turn out.' So is a well-lit cigar.

SET WODEHOUSE ON FIRE

Rappeeists can be snuffers but smoker-haters are sniffers.
In *Piccadilly Jim* Old P.G. attests to it:

> Mr Pett was sniffing suspiciously.
> 'You've been smoking.'
> 'Me!'
> 'Smoking cigarettes.'
> 'No, sir!'
> 'There are two butts in the ash-tray.'
> 'I didn't put them there.'
> 'One of them is warm.'
> 'It's a warm day.'

Mr Wodehouse goes on, but we don't. Not because of the
law of copyright but because we know a masterful thing
when we see even the tip of one. Though, truly, there's no
way anybody can spoil a masterpiece – not even it's author.
Especially not its author.

WHAT MAKES SCHULBERG WRITE?

Budd Schulberg's father, B.P., the Big Boss at Paramount in the late 1920s and early 1930s used to smoke enormous, costly cigars. But his son wrote not about him but about Sammy. 'I hadn't been on exactly chummy terms with Sammy for quite a time now but one afternoon he came up to me at Bleek's and, without taking his ten-cent cigar out of his mouth' (this was a new addition to the evolving personality of Sammy Glick) 'he said, "Hello, Al, can I buy you a drink?"'

(That's what made Sammy run, a ten-cent cigar! Inflation had begun to set in on cigars already, but Sammy was undaunted:)

. . . you should have seen Sammy go to work. He offered Opdyke a cigar.

(It couldn't have been your regular ten-cent cigar, I tell you, for Opdyke was a three-time winner of the Pulitzer Prize. Later, with better cigars, he spelt his name Updike. Yet sometime later:)

The band broke into a rhumba. Sammy rose and reached out his hand for Kit. 'I feel like dancing', he said with a cigar in his mouth.

(There you have it! Sammy's cigar must be an Upmann. He is not having any problems now with his Havana but with his Cuban heels:)

'You don't know how to rhumba', she said . . . 'I hate a bad rhumba. There's something about a bad rhumba that's indecent.'

(Must be the spelling.)

'What do you think the rhumba is,' Sammy said, 'a spring dance?'

(Sammy had a point. A rude point but a point.)

'Now look,' she said, 'either dance with me – or the cigar.'

(Guess what Sammy did?)

Sammy rose, thrusting his cigar through his lips, and there was something pugnacious about the way he clenched it between his teeth in the corner of his mouth. It stuck out in front of him like a cannon levelled at the world.

(Or a smoker about to explode, like a cigar. But Sammy's cigar has just the opposite effect:)

Sammy jerked the cigar from his mouth as if it were a stopper checking his flow of words.

(Sic transit Sammy.)

Budd Schulberg
What Makes Sammy Run

THE O'HORRORS

In John O'Hara's *Appointment in Samarra* priests smoke again after five hundred years. 'It was Father Creedon. "Oh Father. Good evening. Cigarette?" "No thanks. Cigar for me." The priest took a cigar from a worn, black leather case. He amputated the end of the cigar with a silver cutter.'

As George Burns used to say when his wife was still alive, 'I hate Grace before meals.' I suppose he could love her again after dessert and coffee. But for me what is hateful is not Grace but a cigar before meals. And then again, a cigar after coffee could be Gloria. (As a matter of fact I once knew a cigar by the name Glorias del Pino). But I can also feel heartburns – or is it Burns' heart? After Grace a consommé is devoutly to be wished. Though in Andalusia I'd rather have gazpacho by gaslight. And then drink the wine of summertime, that vapourous distillment Hemingway once called grapes under pressure.

COCTEAU

Jean Cocteau is so opinionated in *Opium* that his book should better be called *Opinions*. He writes, badly, of old saws and he makes them sound like seesaws: 'A smoker who smoked twelve pipes a day all his life would be protected not only from the flu, colds and anginas but also in less danger than a man who drank a glass of cognac and four Havanas.' Cocteau even has some dope not on dope but on cigars: 'Tobacco is almost harmless. After combustion nicotine disappears. Usually one takes for nicotine (a white salt) that sort of yellow paste produced by modifying by fire all combustible matters. You'll need four or five fat Havanas a day to provoke in you *angina pectoris*. Most of what is said on the harm produced by tobacco are spasms with no real danger.' A white Cococteau projected on a smoke screen.

LORCA MEETS CUTE WITH FONSECA

Lorca, who was not a cigar smoker, had everybody guessing who was Fonseca, his companion on his famous trip to Santiago. Writes Lorca in his poem 'A *Son*, the Song of blacks in Cuba'

> I'll go to Santiago
> with Fonseca's blond thick of hair.
> I'll go there!

Fonseca, as every Cuban smoker knew, was the cigar manufacturer who pictured himself on every box made by him above his name Fonseca y Cia. Why did Lorca choose Fonseca as his fellow-traveller? Another non-smoker, Borges, had the answer. 'Lorca was actually a silly man. He used to tell everybody in Buenos Aires that the most profound character, the greatest invention of mankind was – Mickey Mouse! Now really!'

A splendid Spanish poet heir to Lorca, Jaime Gil de Biedma, goes to Manila three times a year not with the head of Fonseca or Bock's beard but wearing in his business suit lapel the flower of Isabella, the best Filipinos since Amy Lowell ordered ten thousand 'of those'.

MACKENZIE GALORE

Compton Mackenzie did for the weed in *Sublime Tobacco* what in his *Whiskey Galore* he had earlier done for spirits. Nobody would dare say that Mackenzie was a great writer, not even a good one. But his *Sublime Tobacco* (dedicated to his wife: 'This is the story of a golden leaf to commemorate a golden wedding') is one of the best books on smoking ever. His title is not the graceful find *My Lady Nicotine* was but it contains more leaves on the leaf than Barrie's masterpiece. It is also a more contemporary book, though considerably less English. (Mackenzie was a Scot.) But then again, you couldn't find a more English writer than Barrie.

This is how Compton Mackenzie begins his book:

> If a grave-eyed doctor after feeling my pulse and tapping my chest and testing my blood pressure should declare at the end of this examination that I must either give up smoking or give up drinking alcohol in any form for the rest of my life, I should reply without a moment's hesitation and with the austerity of a stoic: 'Then I renounce wine and spirits and will drink nothing but water for the rest of my life; but I will never renounce my pipe and whenever anybody offers me a cigar I shall accept that cigar with gratitude and smoke it with pleasure.'

Those are the words of a true smoker and, I'd dare say, of a cigar smoker, who is true-blue to the blue smoke.

Mackenzie's mother 'disliked equally the fumes of pipes or cigarettes but much liked those of cigars' and his father smoked cigars only. It was therefore a question of genes more than fate that Mackenzie should become a cigar smoker, a cigar-lover, a cigar-historian and a poet. Here is the case of a minor writer who had problems with his commas but who became a very interesting chronicler when he wrote of cigars. It must be the Scot in him. Mackenzie begins with the revelation that his mother, 'after maintaining aversion from cigarettes for most of her life, took to smoking them when she died in her eighty-eighth year.' Mackenzie is nothing if not honest. He could have said that his mother in her old age took to cigars or the pipe, and he would have made a nice, neat story. But he tells the truth and we are the more grateful to him for it.

Trivia laughs, always. 'There was a legend current at this date that Egyptian cigarettes derived their potent fumes by blending the tobacco with camel's dung.' That's the last straw for Camels!

Surely Oscar Wilde, after hearing the following, would exclaim that Bosie was outliving him beyond his means:

> One evening in the company of some people I knew I met Lord Alfred Douglas at the Exhibition. He was in his usual condition of feverish excitement at this period, and suddenly announced that everybody must dine with him . . . I remember being staggered by his ordering a dozen Murias cigars for about a half dozen people at eighteenpence a piece – long slim cigars which we smoked in a box at the Pavilion Music-hall.

Obviously the balcony became a box of cigars.

Or: 'We have a relic of the Victorian attitudes towards tobacco in waiting to light a cigar or cigarette until the Loyal Toast has been drunk.' That's in England but what about the good old USA? 'As we crossed the frontier with Indiana in a train the conductors came along to warn passengers that until the train had passed out of the Hoosier State no cigarettes must be smoked.'

Customs and Excise

'There is a growing tendency to pass round cigarettes about five minutes before the cigars arrive. The true cigar-smoker does not want a cigarette as a preliminary to a Punch or a Partagas or a Henry Clay.'

'. . . the whiff, that is, the very small cigar or cheroot.'

'The first woman I ever saw smoking a cigar was the late Mrs Bernard Berenson. That was fifty years ago.' I hope the cigar didn't hasten her early departure.

Compton Mackenzie found a brand of cigars called Moonriders: the perfect name for a cigar. 'If I could only find them again', he lamented when he lost the cigars named after its metaphor.

Prohibitions and Addictions

'A sadder loss than the Havanas of once upon a time was the disappearance of the Old Manilla cheroot after the Philippines were taken away from Spain by the United States. The old Manilla cheroot was almost twice as large as the skimpy product of today, and the flavour was at least three times as good. I remember my doctor at Oxford telling me that Manilla cheroots contained a very small amount of opium.' *Ah, voila!* Those were the days when the popular Mariani wine from Italy had a base of cocaine and the Coca-Cola could be called Coke without alluding to its trade mark. Freud was young then. So was the century and nobody dared call the famous tenant of 221B Baker Street by the name of Schlock Holmes.

Those were the days when 'it was permissible to smoke a cigarette in any London street, but it was not considered good form to smoke a pipe in the West End.' Strange!

A Skit

'You're not going to smoke a pipe in Bond Street?'
'Why not?'
'Look here, if I buy you a cigar will you smoke that instead?'

I agreed with alacrity and we turned into Morris's shop for me to acquire a more becoming smoke for Bond Street than a pipe.

Other Prohibitions

'Women were not allowed to smoke in public, except between 5 pm and 7 pm at a *thé dansant* held daily in the Plaza Hotel on Central Park and at Rector's Restaurant down-town.'

COLETTE & CO

For Colette a lifetime of depravity always begins where it ends for Cocteau: in an opium den – even if you are well past forty. 'One of the guests came to life,' she writes in *The Pure and the Impure*, 'rose from his couch to offer me a pipe of opium, a pinch of cocaine or a cocktail. At each refusal he raised his hand limply in a gesture of disappointment. He finally handed me a box of cigarettes and with an English smile said: "Really, can't I do anything for you?"' The English smile is a trick on the part of Mme Colette. Probably the complaisant gentleman offered her a pack of Benson & Hedges and from it she extracted the smile and the simile. Later, much later, she runs the gauntlet of lesbians' embraces – and what does she find? 'At the home of the best-known woman among them – the best known and the most misunderstood – fine wines and long cigars . . . bespoke the sensual and rakish life of a bachelor.' This cigar-smoking lesbian kept, like a butterfly collector, 'one or two portraits of very pretty women.' She is called, by the way, *La Chevalière*.

Colette has a reflection on smoking and sex hidden here somewhere: 'I fear there is not much difference between the habit of obtaining sexual satisfaction and, for instance, the cigarette habit. Smokers, male and female, inject and excuse idleness in their lives every time they light a cigarette.' As a goodbye note she has this Parisian shot: 'The habit of obtaining sexual satisfaction is less tyrannical than the tobacco habit, but it gains on one.' Besides, it is not forbidden in cinemas, theatres and railway coaches.

Colette, a cigarette-smoking writer, had ideas of her own on how to smoke or not to smoke: 'A really idle person never lets a cigarette go out.' That's even truer of a cigar-smoker, where idleness is much more important that in cigarette-smoking. To be idle is the ideal state for the cigar-smoker, be he a gentleman or the total toiler. Or a teething teetotaller for that matter. To a tee. Ta ta!

ORTIZ'S ART OF THE FUGUE

Fernando Ortiz is how I like my writers: excessive, rhe-torical, baroque – and broke. The quote below is from his vegetable garden of a book, or greenhouse rather, *Counter-point Between Sugar and Tobacco*. (Also called *A Cuban Counterpoint*.) 'There is in smoking the survival of both religion and magic: the beliefs of the *behiques* or Cuban sorcerers. The slow fire that burns a cigar is a rite of atone-ment. The smoke that goes up to the heavens seems like a spiritual evocation. Its fragrance, more alluring than incense, is like a purifying form of frankincense. The dirty but tenuous final ashes is the funeral suggestion of a late penance.'

WAUGH, WAUGH!

'Worked quite well. Drank good wine and smoked good cigars.'

The Diaries of Evelyn Waugh

Evelyn Waugh came back to his hotel to be interviewed – to be *what*? interviewed: so he was the, excuse me, interview*ee*? – by the *Paris Review* carrying a parcel. Waugh was carrying the parcel, the *Paris Review* was carrying a tape recorder. In his parcel Waugh had hidden a box of cigars. He said to his interviewer who was now smoking a cigarette, 'I think cigarettes are rather squalid in a bedroom.' Then he lit a cigar and got into bed. Waugh was the writer who declared that he would consider himself happy if only he could have, in that order, a decent meal a day with a bottle of wine and a Havana cigar. Waugh hated Maugham, whom he called in cold scorn a pederast in his *Diaries*. But the mystic band of a cigar made of the two men, one.

ISHAVOOD IS A VOID

At the beginning of Christopher Isherwood's *Prater Violet* his hero, called not by chance Isherwood, is seen in London after breakfast: 'I stood just inside the doorway and lit a cigarette . . . I blew out a lot of smoke, frowning at the mantelpiece clock.' Dr Bergmann, a film director no kin to Ingmar, who will be his employer and his friend later on, also smokes cigarettes, of 'the Continental kind'. It's all right that Isherwood's Ishavood smokes cigarettes but it is somehow incongruous that the imperious Dr Bergmann smoke them too.

Some time later 'coffee was served and Chatsworth produced a formidable red morocco leather case of beautiful workmanship, as big as a pocket Testament, which contained his cigars. They cost five-and-sixpence each, he informed us. I refused but Bergmann took one . . . "Once you've got a taste for them you'll never smoke anything else", Chatsworth warned him and added graciously: "I'll send you a box tomorrow . . ." The cigar somehow completed Chatsworth. As he puffed it, he seemed to grow larger than life-size. His pale eyes shone with a prophetic light . . . Bergmann turned and gave a rapid, enigmatic glance. Then he exhaled, with such force that Chatsworth's cigar-smoke was blown back around his head. Chatsworth looked pleased. Evidently this was the right kind of reaction.'

The subject, however, was not Havanas but Garbo, Greta Garbo. You see, Chatsworth was a generous producer and thought big. Small time producers smoke cigarillos and constantly complain about constipation and piles.

WAITING FOR PUNCH

Samuel Beckett's writings are redolent of two opposite maladies: constipation and polyuria. This can create not only foul smells but tension too. As seen in his most famous play, *Waiting for Godot*, tramps, bums and beggars are lice in waiting for some pointless miracle. They do the waiting with the help of the most waitful of instruments, the pipe. Here it is shown in the characters' lines and even in the author's stage directions.

Pozzo, after finishing eating, hollers: 'Basket!' strikes a match and begins to light his pipe . . . Then 'he strikes another match and lights his pipe'. Later, 'he pulls at his pipe . . .' Then again 'He knocks out his pipe and reflects: "Unless I smoke another pipe before I go . . ."' He explains himself thus: 'Oh I'm only a smoker, a very small smoker. I'm not in the habit of smoking two pipes one on top of the other, it makes *(hand to heart, sighing)* my heart go pit-a-pat . . . It's the nicotine one absorbs in spite of one's precautions.' *(Sighs)* That sighing Pozzo (his name means well in Italian) shows he is not a true smoker – or perhaps his pipe is not real enough. Cough. He fills his pipe again and having lit it he exclaims: 'The second is never so sweet . . . as the first, I mean.' He puts his pipe back in his mouth. Put out the pipe and then put out the pipe. He takes the pipe out of his mouth again and examines it to explain 'I'm out!' That's exactly the problem with pipes: as soon as they're on, they're out. They are difficult to light up and very easy to lose: 'What have I done with my pipe?' asks Pozzo – and all is pozzo that ends pozzo. Let's not wait for Godot any longer and drop Pozzo's pipe into the well of forgetfulness. I'm sure, however, that *Waiting for Godot* would have been a totally different – and better – play if Pozzo smoked cigars. Even the name would have changed. With a cigar-smoking Pozzo the play could have been titled *Waiting for Fonseca*. Then Beckett would have profited from Lorca's charm and Fonseca's expertise. Or could have been called, with more expectations than Pip's, *Waiting for Montecristo*. There's a treasure hidden here somewhere, lads!

IRISH TWILIGHT

Every day begins in Ireland in mourning since Myles na gCopaleen died. As in any respectable Irish wake sadness does not come with death but with oblivion. Sir Myles is on his way to be forgotten because he was in the remembering business. But, Lo and Behold (the Dublin Duo!), my Myles forgot, or rather he didn't remember his cigars. Give my regards to Upmann, remember me to Partagas.

Myles away now I must tell the truth. He never, *ever* even deigned to speak of Havanas or the tiniest Schimmelpenninck (any one for Ms and Ns?), he who lived in a humidor. He didn't write of pipes but he wrote about, of all things, Irish cigarettes: 'I sit at home every night,' he avers, 'thinking about it' (probably a sin) 'and smoking endless cigarettes.' Yes, he has, yes, finally, yes, oh yes!, a confession to make: 'My endless cigarettes are made specially for me by Carrols of Dundalk.' Why not Carroll on the Isis? That's who he got the habit from, Don Lewis Carlos. But he will show you one of them, saying: 'I will show you one of them.' Then the truth, the awful Irish truth, thick as Irish coffee and as heady: Myles's (and miles of them) cigarettes are 'Quite circular, like a hoop.' End of tale. Myles na gCopaleen or Flann O'Brien or Brian O'Nolan or even Brian O Nuallain, all those names, all those men died of throat cancer. Give me a straight a cigarette or give me death! What about both? Be Gorrah!

Every day begins in Ireland, the land of Ire, in morning since Myles na gCopaleen died.

And yet, and yet Yeats never mentioned cigars though he sang to towers and sails. For we smokers know that a cigar is a tower with sails.

THIS THURBER

If the Termagant hadn't made her debut in a morality play some time ago, Thurber would have been compelled to invent her. Had he not been born in high Ohio, ill in Illinois, he would have rhymed Chicago with virago, as Porter did some time before. What Thurber couldn't do to women – ignore them – he did to cigars. Of tea he sings and coffee and milk but he never sang to a Havana or promised you a *corona grande*. He wrote about pipes and cigarettes, though somewhat mischievously and mystifyingly.

In 'The Lady on 142' Thurber thunders thus: 'I was opening a pack of cigarettes when I heard the stationmaster talking on the phone again.' Before, he had seen a 'tanned man sucking dreamily on the stem of an unlighted pipe.' Some time later the expression on the face of 'the man with the pipe had not changed'. And somewhat later: 'The man with the pipe seemed oblivious.' Sucker! Then he, the narrator, Thurber no doubt, 'lighted a cigarette and sat thinking'. This double action (inner, outer) made everybody, waiting for a train that is late, Thurber-conscious: 'The only person who did not stare at me was the man with the pipe.' Never give a pipe-sucker an even break – not even to stare at you while you light a cigarette.

But things grow worse: 'When the train came clanking in' (those were the days when trains came clanking in) 'I said in Sylvia's car', I mean ear, 'in Sylvia's *ear*, "He'll sit near us. You watch." "Who will?" she said. "The stranger," I told her, "the man with the pipe."' As in *Seven Footprints to Satan* with the dreaded man with the crutches, the booming voice of doom warns us now, *Beware the man with the pipe*! In effect: 'The man with the pipe was sitting three seats in front of us, across the aisle, when we got settled.' Then the conductor comes down the aisle and truth hits Thurber to blind him: 'I'm going to tell the conductor,' he announces, 'that Reagan on 42 has got the woman.' Obviously she was the First Lady of the Trains. She must be. But Sylvia (who is this Sylvia? what is she?) ridicules further Thurber or Thurber further when she remarks that the conductor 'looks exactly as if he knew where the Maltese Falcon is hidden'.

Things can always get worse and they do now – do they do now! After the cries of *Down Mata*! and *Down Pedro*! (two too-cocky spaniels maybe? Gundogs!) are heard as in 'leaned a thin, undersized young man, with his hand in the pocket of his coat and a cigarette hanging from his lower lip.' Then things get worser: 'Who got Sandra Gail?' 'Reagan, on 142.' Wait a minute, wait a minute! It should be Reagan *in 84* if we want to have the man whole. In 42 we could get only a piece of him. Remember the man himself was anxiously asking where was the *rest* of him then. Now comes the worst, now comes the worst! 'The squat, swarthy man jumped to his feet "Al da time Egypt say keel dees Reagan!" he shouted. "Al da time Egypt say bomp off dees Reagan!"' I know, I know! It should be Libya or Syria not Egypt – but don't you think somebody must alert the President?

Obviously Thurber was nuts or bananas but not Havanas. Finally, he 'lighted a cigarette. "The lady on 142," I said firmly, "was definitely not sick,"' he mused bemused. Evidently his cigarette was a disjointed or anointed joint. '"Oh Lord", said Sylvia', whoever she was, '"here we go again."' But we don't. For you see, this ur-Thurber ends just right there. Though this, I must admit, will be meat for myth – or Mitty.

L'EROTOMANE PAR EXCELLENCE

But surely you must know now, after Freud and friends, that a cigar is a phallic object – or is it perhaps a phallic subject? The word ithyphallic (in Greek a penis without the envy) applies to the unlit cigar, a penis erect, or the cigar held languidly in a male but limp hand, masturbation over, or even the already-lit Havana stuck between gross, greedy lips, *felix fellatio*. One can see the content and utter pleasure in the face of the holder, enveloped in a haze of costly smoke – the heathen's frankincense. But what about the cigar's burning end? It can also be a source of erotic delights, according to the *érotomane par excellence* in modern French literature, Alain Robbe-Grillet. 'A canopied bed, a cord,' is the startling start of the list of bric-à-bracs that Robbe-Grillet compiles at the beginning of *La Maison de rendez-vous*. He goes on thus: 'the white-hot tip of a cigar accompany me for hours on end.' Then follows a famous French phrase ready to come out of the closerie and jump into any dirty dictionary: 'In the gardens I organize parties.' Originally it had a flavour of *partouzes* (or *parties étrangées*), for an orgy is only one morass. Now it probably means much less than what Katherine Mansfield had in mind.

BURGESS NOT BORGES

It is exactly four years since Kingsley Amis last gave us a novel, and that has been a long time to wait. None of us is getting any younger, time is short and so on, and, despite what lady reviewers tell ageing male novelists about the necessity of taking time off to think things out thoroughly before blowing Schimmelpenninck smoke over the noisy keys, we ought to be pushing on with the job.

Anthony Burgess
(reviewing Kingsley Amis)
The Observer

But Burgess, himself a Schimmelpenninck man, has a sad lawman, Loewe, smoking by proxy in MF. 'I drew in the last of my cigarette and subdued it among the other stubs. Loewe snuffed the smoke like a beast.' This happened of course at the Algonquin, where everybody received Ross's dross by osmosis. Masochism or machism? Much miching malecho, for Loewe, or Leo the Lion, was looking for the grass harpy: tea, pot, or marihuana. What both Chano Pozo and Dizzy Gillespie knew as *manteca* – hence the bebop hit that made both famous: '*Manteca, Manteca*! What makes your big head so high?' Why, cannabis of course.

LITTLE BIG LIAR

The chief held a stone pipe which had a wooden shank a foot and a half in length and was decorated with a series of brass tacks that winked in the firelight. We just stood watching him, on account of having no place else to go. He filled his pipe bowl from a little leather pouch and then a stout woman put a stick in the fire until it caught and blew it into a burning coal, fetching it to him, who thereupon lighted up, sucking so hard his cheeks caved in like a skull's. Owing to the length of the stem, it was powerful hard to keep one of them pipes going, but he got it to where he was satisfied, then all at once shoved it towards Caroline . . . Caroline accepted the mouthpiece and went to puffing according to Old Lodge Skin's model. Of course, to her this, I believe, was a type of sexual ritual or the like. The chief, however, was muttering incantations against what he thought was her bad medicine directed at him, and the fact that she had taken the pipe encouraged him to believe that his charms would work, because an Indian holds by smoking above all things . . . The chief now loosened the ashes in the pipe bowl and poured them out on the toes of Caroline's boots, so as to give her bad luck, only we didn't know it at the time. Then he stoked up again from his beaded pouch with what was actually in small part tobacco, the rest being made up of red-willow bark, sumac leaves, the marrow from buffalo bones, and several other ingredients. Indians of course invented the habit of smoking and almost nothing else.

Thomas Berger
Little Big Man

OLD HAVANA, OLD HAVANAS

. . . All of this I saw reflected in the boy with peaked hair at the next table. He took a cigarette from a black silk case and I was immediately reminded of my cigar.

It had been chosen with immense care in the Inglaterra café for bonbons and souvenirs, liqueurs and cigars. How remarkable it was, I had thought, hovering above the case which contained a bewildering choice of shapes and colours, to be in a land where all the cigars were, in the sense I knew, imported. I hesitated for a minute or more between Larrañaga and a banquet Corona, and finally decided on the former. It was as long as the cigar called Fancy Tales, but slightly thicker and rolled to a point at either end; and the first breath of its smoke, drifting in a blue cloud away from the window, told me that until then I had known but little of tobacco. Coffee so black that it stained the white shell of its cup, a diminutive glass of Grand Marnier, the distilled last saturation of oranges and fin champagne, and the Larrañaga, the colour of oak-leaves freshly brown, combined in a transcended magic of contentment . . . The cigar continued to veil me in its reflective smoke for another half-hour . . . The tempered heat of the day lay over me like a spell, like an armour against the chill, the gaunt winds and rain of the North . . . All this, every aspect of Havana's being, was the gift – the dangerous gift – of its situation, its weather. The blinding day, the city veiled in sparkling night, like a vision in blanched satin with fireflies in her hair, were nothing more than meteorological.

Joseph Hergesheimer
San Cristóbal de
La Habana (1921)

SMOKE GETS IN YOUR I'S

For Faulkner (in *The Wild Palms*), 'cigarettes and pyjamas were for dudes and women.' The doctor who is so prejudiced 'smoked a pipe which he had never learned and knew that he would never learn to like, between the occasional cigar which clients gave him in the interval of Sundays on which he smoked the three cigars which he felt he could buy for himself . . .' Faulkner produces in the same novel the best lighting of a cigar this side of Edward G. Robinson: 'the tall convict . . .', ends *The Wild Palms*, with a cigar 'burning smoothly and richly in his clean steady hand, the smoke wreathing upward across his face saturnine, humourless, and calm.' The face of a cigar smoker, no doubt.

SMOKESCREAMS

2 May 1983

Dear Guillermo,

I regret not having been able to stop back to see you in London for I would have told you of my own entry into the ranks of the paranoiac. You see, the evening Nestor Almendros introduced us I returned to my hotel to find my room rank with the odour of cigar smoke. Neither of the chambermaids being the cigar-smoking type I snapped back ten years and found myself once again staring at the butt of a Kent cigarette laying on the floor of my room in Leningrad's Astor Hotel. Russian chambermaids smoking American cigarettes? Not likely. Whoever the careless smoker was he (or she) had obviously been distracted by my innocuous luggage. From the moment I opened the windows to let the cigar smoke out of my room and through the next morning's English breakfast I fantasized about having been followed from your apartment, through my afternoon's errands, back to the hotel, then being observed leaving the hotel thus permitting the cigarsmoker to surreptitiously enter my room. Ah, but after breakfast cigarsmoking painters were on the ladders I had seen in the hall the previous day leaving their smoke to be bottled up in my unventilated room. Out the window went the smoke and the drama.

William B. Stern

MEN WOE WOMEN

The author can only add: Women are now a public domain. Women must have the last word.

The man in the knee-length Burberry raincoat wrinkles the wrapper from a slim cigar, flicks the lid of his pigskin lighter, bends forward, inhales, then exhales on a gust. Irritation exposes the blades of his regular, neat, white teeth. How is a person supposed to enjoy one of life's more sensual pleasures in such unsavoury surroundings? What point to the milky-thick coil of his smoke, when the air into which he expels it is choked with the dank, brown, bitter staleness of hundreds of cheap cigarettes?

Worse, when there is no one to see, to appreciate it but himself?

The man's mouth puckers at the thought of his wife, of his new, young wife, who herself does not smoke: after dinner, when he lights his cigar, how she'll slide round the table to climb on his lap and how, dark eyes closed, she will flare her hard nostrils and whisper, Ah, let me . . . you know how I love it.

It's Harriett Gilbert
in *The Riding Mistress*

LE HAVANE POUR UN INSTANT PARFUM

Toute l'âme résumée
Quand lente nous l'aspirons
Dans plusieurs ronds de fumée
Abolis en d'autres ronds

Atteste quelque cigare
Brûlant savammant pour peu
Que la cendre se sépare
De son clair baiser de feu

Ainsi le choeur des romances
A la lèvre vole-t-il
Exclues-en si tu commence
Le réel parce que vil

Le sens trop précis rature
Ta vague littérature

Stéphane Mallarmé

Acknowledgements

For permission to reprint poems and prose extracts from copyright material the publishers gratefully acknowledge the following:

J. M. Barrie: 'My First Cigar' from *My Lady Nicotine*, reprinted by permission of Hodder and Stoughton Ltd; Samuel Beckett: *Waiting for Godot*, reprinted by permission of Faber and Faber Ltd; E. Clerihew Bentley: 'Homer', reprinted from *The Complete Clerihews of E. Clerihew Bentley* (1981) by permission of Oxford University Press; Thomas Berger: *Little Big Man* (1965), reprinted by permission of Eyre and Spottiswoode; Karen Blixen: (Isak Dinesen) *Out of Africa* (1938), Random House Inc.; Vincent Brome: *Freud and his Disciples* (1984), Caliban; Anthony Burgess reviewing Kingsley Amis in the *Observer*; Anthony Burgess: MF (1971), copyright, Liana Burgess; Charlotte Chandler: *Hello, I Must Be Going* (1978), Sphere Books Ltd; Raymond Chandler: *The Big Sleep* and *Playback*, copyright, Mrs Helga Greene; G. K. Chesterton: *The Man Who Was Thursday* (1908); Sydney Clark: *All The Best in Cuba* (1956), reprinted by permission of Dodd, Mead & Company Inc.; Jean Cocteau: *Opium* (1930), reprinted by permission of Editions Stock, Paris; Hubert Cole: *Beau Brummell* (1977), reprinted by permission of Granada Publishing Ltd; Colette: *The Pure and the Impure* (Le Pur et L'Impur), reprinted by permission of Farrar, Straus & Giroux Inc.; Cyril Connolly: *The Unquiet Grave* (1944), reprinted by permission of Deborah Rogers Ltd; Encyclopaedia Britannica, Inc.; *Evening Standard*: 'Ban on Smoking "unfair"'; William Faulkner: *The Wild Palms*, copyright © 1934, renewed 1966 by Jill F. Summers and Estelle Faulkner; Hubert Fiche: 'A Jean Genet Interview' (1977), Gay Sunshine Press, San Francisco; William E. Geist: 'Humidor-Room Closing Ends Cigar Era' from the *International Herald Tribune*; Harriet Gilbert: *The Riding Mistress* (1983), reprinted by permission of Constable & Company Ltd; *The Goncourt Journal* (trans. Robert Baldick), 1962, copyright © 1865 Ernest Flammarion, Paris; Jacques Grancheur (ed.) *Le Livre Blanc du Tabac*, Confrerie Jean Nicot; Alain Robbe-Grillet: *The House of Assignation* ('La Maison de Rendezvous'), translated by A. M. Sheridan Smith, reprinted by permission of John Calder (Publishers) Ltd; Dashiell Hammett: *The Farewell Murder* © 1974, *Red Harvest* © 1962, both reprinted by permission of Alfred A. Knopf, Inc.; Ernest Hemingway: *Fiesta* ('The Sun Also Rises'), reprinted by permission of the Executors of the Ernest Hemingway Estate and Jonathan Cape Ltd; Christopher Isherwood: *Prater Violet*, reprinted by permission of Methuen (London) Ltd; Raymond Jahn:

Trust and the Hutchinson Group Ltd; Yevgeny Zamyatin: *We* (translated by Bernard Guilbert Guerney), reprinted by permission of Jonathan Cape Ltd.

Faber and Faber apologize for any errors or omissions in the above list and would be grateful to be notified of any corrections that should be incorporated in the next edition of this volume.